STUDENT
ATLAS

First published 1996, reprinted 1997
Revised 1998, reprinted 1998, 1999(twice), 2000

© Collins-Longman Atlases 1996, 1998

The maps in this atlas are licensed to Collins-Longman Atlases
and are derived from databases © Bartholomew Ltd.

HarperCollins Publishers, Westerhill Road, Bishopbriggs, Glasgow G64 2QT

Pearson Education Ltd., Edinburgh Gate, Harlow, Essex CM20 2JE

Printed in Italy

NL10713

SYMBOLS

Maps use special signs or symbols to represent location and to give information of interest.

Map symbols can be points, lines or areas and vary in size, shape and colour. This allows a great range of different symbols to be created. These have to be carefully selected to make maps easy to understand. Usually the same symbols are used to represent features on maps of the same type and scale within an atlas.

An important part of any map is the key which explains what the symbols represent. Each map in this atlas has its own key. Shown below are typical examples of the keys found on each reference map in the atlas. The first is found on all of the British Isles 1:1 200 000 series of maps. The second is found on the smaller scale maps of the rest of the world.

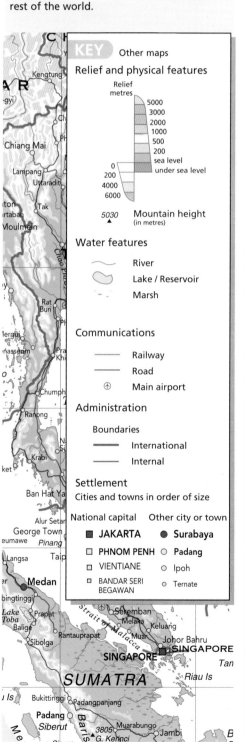

KEY British Isles maps

Relief and physical features

Relief metres
1000
500
200
100
0 sea level
50 under sea level
200

977 ▲ Mountain height (in metres)

Water features

～～ River
～～ Canal
▨ Lake / Reservoir

Communications

── Railway
═══ Motorway
── Road
⋯⋯ Car ferry
⊕ Main airport
✈ Local airport

Administration

Boundaries

── International
── Internal

Settlement

🏙 Urban area

Cities and towns in order of size

National capital   Other city or town

□ DUBLIN   ○ Liverpool
                          ○ Belfast
                          ○ Carlisle
                          ○ Keswick

KEY Other maps

Relief and physical features

Relief metres
5000
3000
2000
1000
500
200
0 sea level
200 under sea level
4000
6000

5030 ▲ Mountain height (in metres)

Water features

～～ River
▨ Lake / Reservoir
Marsh

Communications

── Railway
── Road
⊕ Main airport

Administration

Boundaries

── International
── Internal

Settlement

Cities and towns in order of size

National capital   Other city or town

■ JAKARTA   ● Surabaya
□ PHNOM PENH   ○ Padang
□ VIENTIANE   ○ Ipoh
□ BANDAR SERI   ○ Ternate
    BEGAWAN

TYPE STYLES

Various type styles are used to show the difference between features on the maps in this atlas. Physical features are shown in italic and a distinction is made between land and water features.

· Mountain Peaks are shown in small italics.
eg. *Ben Nevis   Mt Kenya   Fuji-san*

Large mountain ranges are shown in bold italic capitals.
eg. ***HIMALAYA   ALPS***
ROCKY MOUNTAINS

Rivers are also shown in small italics but in a different typeface from mountain peaks.
eg. *Thames   Euphrates   Rhine   Amazon*

Oceans are shown in large bold italic capitals.
eg. ***ATLANTIC OCEAN***
PACIFIC OCEAN
INDIAN OCEAN

When a feature covers a large area the type is letterspaced and sometimes curved to follow the shape of the feature.
eg. *S A H A R A*
B E A U F O R T   S E A

Settlements are shown in upright type. Country capitals are shown in capitals.
eg. **LONDON**
PARIS
TOKYO
MOSCOW

The size and weight of the type increases with the population of a settlement.
eg. Westbury
Chippenham
Bristol
Birmingham

Administrative names are shown in capitals.
eg. EAST SUSSEX
RONDONIA
KERELA
CALIFORNIA

Country names are shown in large bold capitals.
eg. **CHINA**
KENYA
MEXICO

An atlas map of the world shows the whole world on a flat surface of the page. yet in reality the earth is actually a sphere. This means that a system has to be used to turn the round surface of the earth into a flat map of the world, or part of the world. This cannot be done without some distortion - on a map some parts of the world have been stretched, other parts have been compressed.

A system for turning the globe into a flat map is called a **projection**.

There are many different projections, each of which distort different things to achieve a flat map. Correct area, correct shape, correct distances or correct directions can be achieved by a projection; but by achieving any one of these things the others have to be distorted. When choosing the projection to use for a particular map it is important to think which of these things is the most important to have correct.

The projections below illustrate the main types of projections, and include some of those used in this atlas.

Cylindrical projection

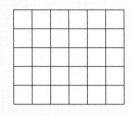

Cylindrical projections are constructed by projecting the surface of the globe on to a cylinder just touching the globe.

Conic projection

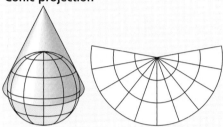

Conic projections are constructed by projecting part of the globe on to a cone which just touches a circle on the globe.

Azimuthal projection

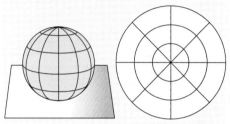

Azimuthal projections are constructed by projecting part of a globe on to a plane which touches the globe only at one point

Examples of projections

Mercator
Southeast Asia pp104-105

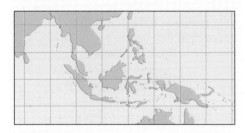

Mercator is a cylindrical projection. It is a useful projection for areas 15° N or S of the equator where distortion of shape is minimal. The projection is useful for navigation as directions can be plotted as straight lines.

Albers Equal Area Conic
Europe pp 34-35

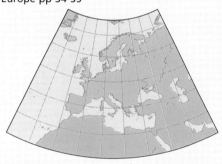

Conic projections are best suited for areas between 30° and 60° N and S with longer east-west extent than north-south. Such an area would be Europe. Meridians are straight and equally spaced.

Lambert Azimuthal Equal Area
Australia p 110

Lambert's projection is uselful for areas which have similar east-west, north-south dimensions such as Australia.

Eckert IV
World pp 114-115

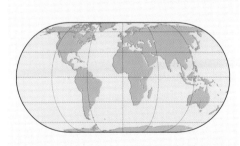

Eckert IV is an equal area projection. Equal area projections are useful for world thematic maps where it is important to show the correct relative sizes of continental areas. Ecker IV has a straight central meridian but all others are curved which help suggest the spherical nature of the earth.

Chamberlin Trimetric
Canada pp 62-63

Chamberlin trimetric is an equidistant projection. It shows correct distances from approximately three points. It is used for areas with a greater north-south than east-west extent, such as North America.

Polar stereographic
Antarctica p 112

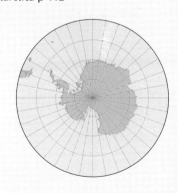

This projection shows no angular or shape distortion over small areas. All points on the map are in constant relative position and distance from the centre.

LATITUDE

Lines of latitude are imaginary lines which run in an east-west direction around the world. They are also called **parallels** of latitude because they run parallel to each other. Latitude is measured in **degrees** (°).

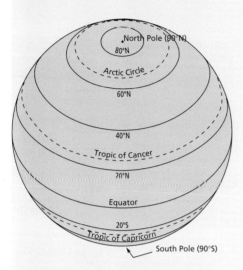

The most important line of latitude is the **Equator** (0°). The North Pole is 90° North (90°N) and the South Pole is 90° South (90°S). All other lines of latitude are given a number between 0° and 90°, either North (N) or South (S) of the Equator. Some other important lines of latitude are the Tropic of Cancer (23½°N), Tropic of Capricorn (23½°S), Arctic Circle (66½°N) and Antarctic Circle (66½°S).

The Equator can also be used as a line to divide the Earth into two halves. The northern half, north of the Equator, is the **Northern Hemisphere**. The southern half, south of the Equator, is the **Southern Hemisphere**.

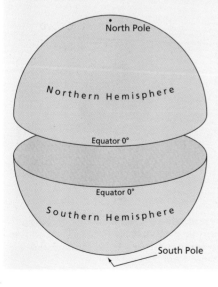

LONGITUDE

Lines of longitude are imaginary lines which run in a north-south direction, from the North Pole to the South Pole. These lines are also called **meridians** of longitude. They are also measured in **degrees** (°).

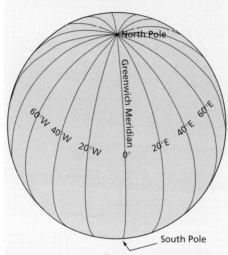

The most important line of longitude is the prime meridian (0°). This line runs through the Greenwich Observatory in London and is therefore known as the Greenwich Meridian. Exactly opposite the Greenwich Meridian on the other side of the world is the 180° line of longitude known as the International Date Line. All the other lines of longitude are given a number between 0° and 180°, either East (E) or West (W) of the Greenwich Meridian.

The Greenwich Meridian (0°) and the International Date Line (180°) can also be used to divide the world into two halves. The half to the west of the Greenwich Meridian is the Western Hemisphere. The half to the east of the Greenwich Meridian is the Eastern Hemisphere.

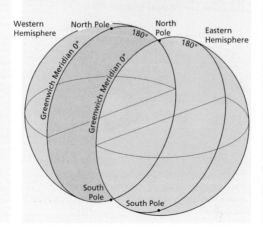

FINDING PLACES USING LATITUDE AND LONGITUDE

When lines of latitude and longitude are drawn on a map they form a grid pattern, very much like a pattern of squares.

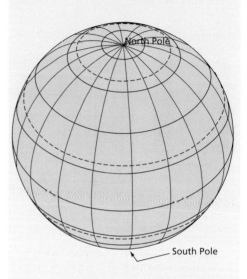

By stating the **latitude** and then the **longitude** of a place, it becomes much easier to find. On the map (below) Point A is very easy to find because it is exactly latitude 58° North of the Equator and longitude 4° West of the Greenwich Meridian (58°N,4°W).

To be even more accurate in locating a place, each degree of latitude and longitude can also be divided into smaller units called **minutes** ('). There are 60 minutes in each degree. On the map (below) Halkirk is one half (or 30/60ths) of the way past latitude 3°N, and two-thirds (or 40/60ths) of the way past longitude 3°W. Its latitude is therefore 58 degrees 30 minutes North and its longitude is 3 degrees 30 minutes West. This can be shortened to 58°30'N, 3°30'W.

SCALE

To draw a map of any part of the world, the area must be reduced in size, or scaled down so that it will fit on to a page. The scale of a map tells us by how much the area has been reduced in size.

The scale of a map can also be used to work out distance and area. The scale of a map will show the relationship between distances on the map and distances on the ground.

Scale can be shown on a map in a number of ways:

(a) **in words**
e.g. 'one cm. to one km.' (one cm. on the map represents one km. on the ground). 'one cm. to one m.' (one cm. on the map represents one m. on the ground).

(b) **in numbers**
e.g. '1 : 100 000' or '1/100 000' (one cm. on the map represents 100 000 cm., or one km., on the ground). '1 : 25 000' or '1/25 000' (one cm. on the map represents 25 000 cm, or 250 m., on the ground). '1 : 100' or '1/100' (one cm. on the map represents 100 cm, or one m., on the ground).

(c) **as a line scale**
e.g.

MEASURING DISTANCE ON A MAP

When a map does not have distances printed on it, we can use the scale of the map to work out how far it is from one place to another. The easiest scale to use is a line scale. You must find out how far the places are apart on the map and then see what this distance represents on the line scale. To measure the straight line distance between two points:

a) Place a piece of paper between the two points on the map,
(b) Mark off the distance between the two points along the edge of the paper,
(c) Place the paper along the line scale,
(d) Read off the distance on the scale.

Step 1

Line up the paper and mark off the distance from A to B.

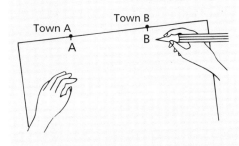

Step 2

Compare this distance with the line scale at the bottom of the map. The distance between A and B is 1.5 km on the line scale.

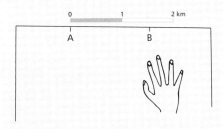

To measure the distance between two points where there are bends or curves:
(a) Place a sheet of paper on the map and mark off the start point on the edge of the paper,
(b) Now move the paper so that its edge follows the bends and curves on the map (Hint: Use the tip of your pencil to pin the edge of the paper to the curve as you pivot the paper around the curve),
(c) Mark off the end point on your sheet of paper,
(d) Place the paper along the line scale,
(e) Read off the distance on the scale.

Using a sheet of paper around a curve : Mark off the start point then twist the paper to follow the curve.

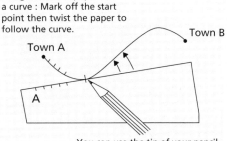

You can use the tip of your pencil to pin the paper to the curve. This stops the paper jumping off course.

MAP SCALE AND MAP INFORMATION

The scale of a map also determines how much information can be shown on it. As the area shown on a map becomes larger and larger, the amount of detail and the accuracy of the map becomes less and less.

The scale of this map is 1:5 000 000

The scale of this map is 1:10 000 000

The scale of this map is 1:20 000 000

UNITED KINGDOM

SCOTLAND

ENGLAND

WALES

NORTHERN
IRELAND

REPUBLIC
OF
IRELAND

Edinburgh

London

Cardiff

Belfast

WEST CENTRAL SCOTLAND

1. WEST DUNBARTONSHIRE
2. EAST DUNBARTONSHIRE
3. EAST RENFREWSHIRE

NORTH
LANARKSHIRE

GLASGOW
CITY

Motherwell

Kirkintilloch

Dumbarton

RENFREW-
SHIRE

Paisley

Giffnock

INVER-
CLYDE

Greenock

EAST CENTRAL SCOTLAND

EAST
LOTHIAN

Haddington

Dalkeith

CITY OF
EDINBURGH

MIDLOTHIAN

CLACKMANNAN-
SHIRE

Alloa

WEST
LOTHIAN

Bathgate

FALKIRK

Falkirk

SHETLAND

Lerwick

ORKNEY

Kirkwall

HIGHLAND

Inverness

MORAY

Elgin

ABERDEEN-
SHIRE

Banff

Inverurie

ABERDEEN
CITY

Stonehaven

ANGUS

Forfar

DUNDEE CITY

PERTH
AND
KINROSS

Perth

FIFE

Glenrothes

SCOTLAND

STIRLING

Stirling

ARGYLL
AND
BUTE

Lochgilphead

Dumbarton

RENFREW-
SHIRE

GLASGOW
CITY

FALKIRK

EAST
LOTHIAN

Haddington

CITY OF
EDINBURGH

WEST
LOTHIAN

MID-
LOTHIAN

SCOTTISH
BORDERS

Newtown
St. Boswells

NORTHUMBERLAND

Morpeth

Hamilton

SOUTH
LANARK-
SHIRE

Kilmarnock

EAST
AYRSHIRE

NORTH
AYRSHIRE

Irvine

Ayr

SOUTH
AYRSHIRE

WESTERN
ISLES

Stornoway

Kirkintilloch

SCOTLAND

1. WEST DUNBARTONSHIRE
2. EAST DUNBARTONSHIRE
3. EAST RENFREWSHIRE
4. INVERCLYDE
5. NORTH LANARKSHIRE
6. CLACKMANNANSHIRE

International boundary
National boundary
Administrative boundary
National capital
Main city / town

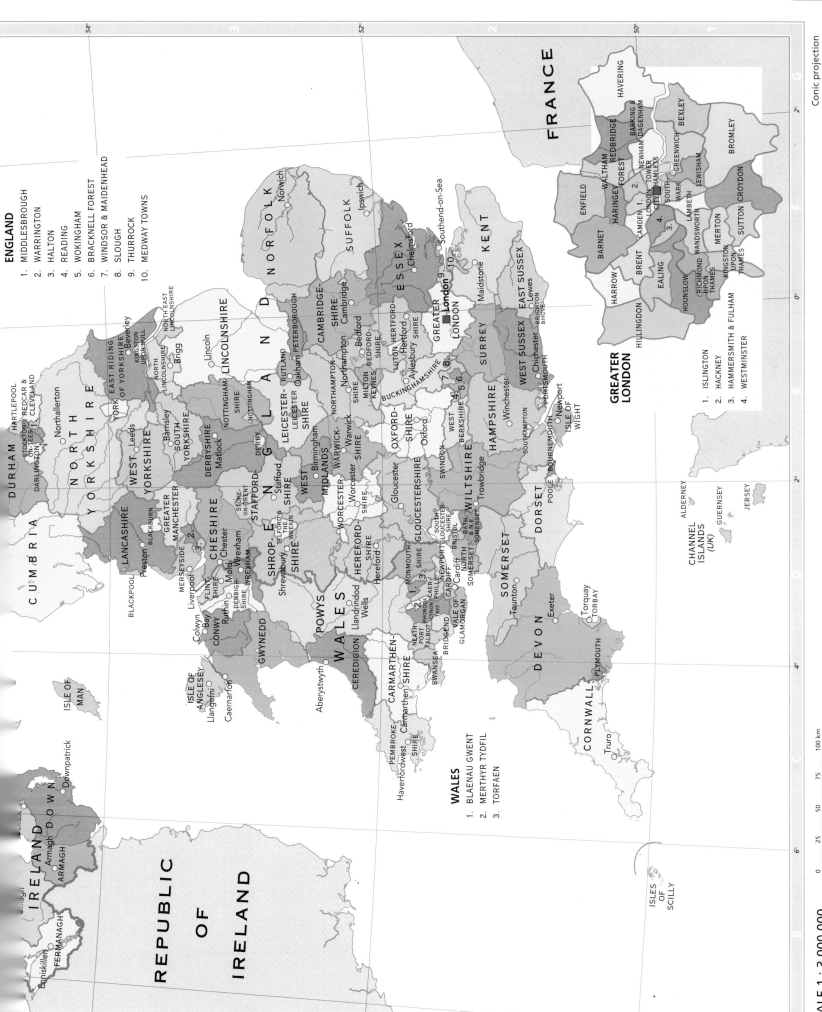

ENGLAND
1. MIDDLESBROUGH
2. WARRINGTON
3. HALTON
4. READING
5. WOKINGHAM
6. BRACKNELL FOREST
7. WINDSOR & MAIDENHEAD
8. SLOUGH
9. THURROCK
10. MEDWAY TOWNS

GREATER LONDON
1. ISLINGTON
2. HACKNEY
3. HAMMERSMITH & FULHAM
4. WESTMINSTER

WALES
1. BLAENAU GWENT
2. MERTHYR TYDFIL
3. TORFAEN

FRANCE

GREATER LONDON

HAVERING
BARKING & DAGENHAM
NEWHAM
BEXLEY
REDBRIDGE
WALTHAM FOREST
TOWER HAMLETS
GREENWICH
HARINGEY
BROMLEY
LEWISHAM
ENFIELD
CAMDEN
SOUTHWARK
LAMBETH
BRENT
WANDSWORTH
CROYDON
SUTTON
BARNET
MERTON
EALING
KINGSTON UPON THAMES
RICHMOND UPON THAMES
HARROW
HOUNSLOW
HILLINGDON
LONDON CITY

IRELAND
DOWN
Downpatrick
ARMAGH
Armagh
FERMANAGH
Enniskillen

REPUBLIC
OF
IRELAND

ISLE OF MAN

CUMBRIA

DURHAM
HARTLEPOOL
STOCKTON-ON-TEES
REDCAR & CLEVELAND
Darlington
Northallerton
NORTH YORKSHIRE

LANCASHIRE
Blackburn
Preston
BLACKPOOL

GREATER MANCHESTER
MERSEYSIDE
Liverpool

EAST RIDING OF YORKSHIRE
Beverley
KINGSTON UPON HULL
YORK
Leeds
WEST YORKSHIRE
Barnsley
SOUTH YORKSHIRE
NORTH LINCOLNSHIRE
NORTH EAST LINCOLNSHIRE
Brigg

ISLE OF ANGLESEY
Llangefni
Caernarfon
GWYNEDD
CONWY
Colwyn Bay
DENBIGHSHIRE
Ruthin
FLINTSHIRE
Mold
WREXHAM
Wrexham
CHESHIRE
Chester
STOKE-ON-TRENT
STAFFORDSHIRE
Stafford
SHROPSHIRE
Shrewsbury
TELFORD & THE WREKIN
DERBYSHIRE
Matlock
DERBY
NOTTINGHAMSHIRE
Nottingham
LINCOLNSHIRE
Lincoln
LEICESTERSHIRE
Leicester
RUTLAND
Oakham
NORFOLK
Norwich

CEREDIGION
Aberystwyth
POWYS
Llandrindod Wells
WALES
NEATH PORT TALBOT
RHONDDA CYNON TAFF
SWANSEA
BRIDGEND
VALE OF GLAMORGAN
CARDIFF
CAERPHILLY
NEWPORT
MONMOUTHSHIRE
PEMBROKESHIRE
Haverfordwest
CARMARTHENSHIRE
Carmarthen

WEST MIDLANDS
Birmingham
WARWICKSHIRE
Warwick
WORCESTERSHIRE
Worcester
HEREFORDSHIRE
Hereford
GLOUCESTERSHIRE
Gloucester
SOUTH GLOUCESTERSHIRE
BRISTOL
NORTH SOMERSET
BATH & N.E. SOMERSET
SOMERSET
Taunton

NORTHAMPTONSHIRE
Northampton
CAMBRIDGESHIRE
Cambridge
PETERBOROUGH
SUFFOLK
Ipswich
BEDFORDSHIRE
Bedford
LUTON
MILTON KEYNES
HERTFORDSHIRE
Hertford
ESSEX
Chelmsford
Southend-on-Sea
OXFORDSHIRE
Oxford
BUCKINGHAMSHIRE
Aylesbury
BERKSHIRE
SWINDON
WILTSHIRE
Trowbridge
GREATER LONDON
London
SURREY
KENT
Maidstone
WEST SUSSEX
Chichester
EAST SUSSEX
Lewes
BRIGHTON & HOVE
HAMPSHIRE
Winchester
SOUTHAMPTON
PORTSMOUTH
ISLE OF WIGHT
Newport
DORSET
BOURNEMOUTH
POOLE
DEVON
Exeter
Torquay
TORBAY
PLYMOUTH
CORNWALL
Truro

ISLES OF SCILLY

CHANNEL ISLANDS (UK)
ALDERNEY
GUERNSEY
JERSEY

SCALE 1 : 3 000 000

Conic projection

0   25   50   75   100 km

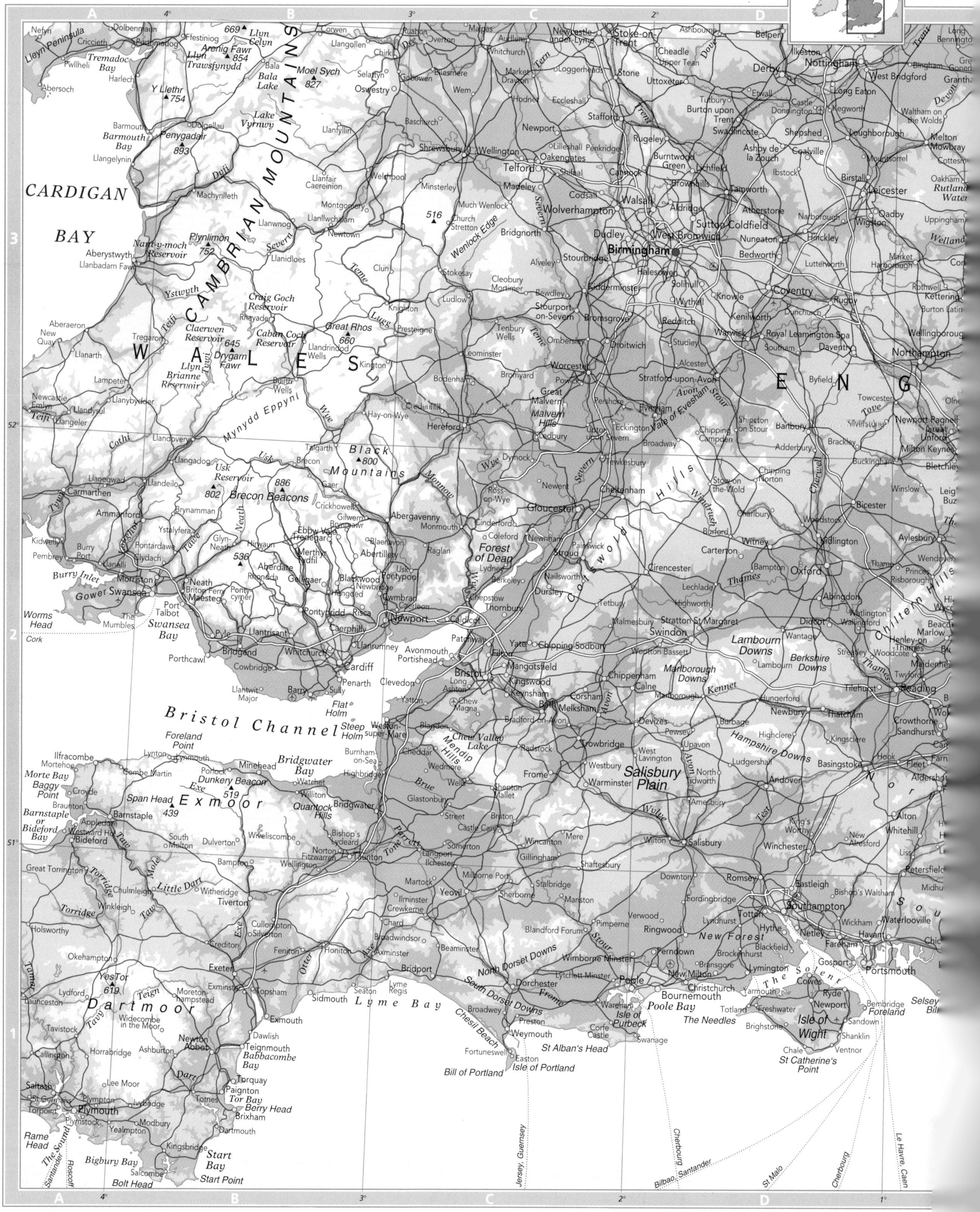

CARDIGAN BAY

WALES

CAMBRIAN MOUNTAINS

ENG

Bristol Channel

Dartmoor

Exmoor

Brecon Beacons

Black Mountains

Forest of Dean

Cotswold Hills

Chiltern Hills

Salisbury Plain

Lambourn Downs

Berkshire Downs

Marlborough Downs

Hampshire Downs

Mendip Hills

Quantock Hills

New Forest

Lyme Bay

Poole Bay

Isle of Wight

The Solent

The Needles

Bill of Portland

Isle of Portland

Chesil Beach

Bridgwater Bay

Swansea Bay

Gower

Worms Head

Burry Inlet

Morte Bay

Baggy Point

Barnstaple or Bideford Bay

Bala Lake

Lake Vyrnwy

SCALE 1 : 1 200 000

0   10   20   30   40 km

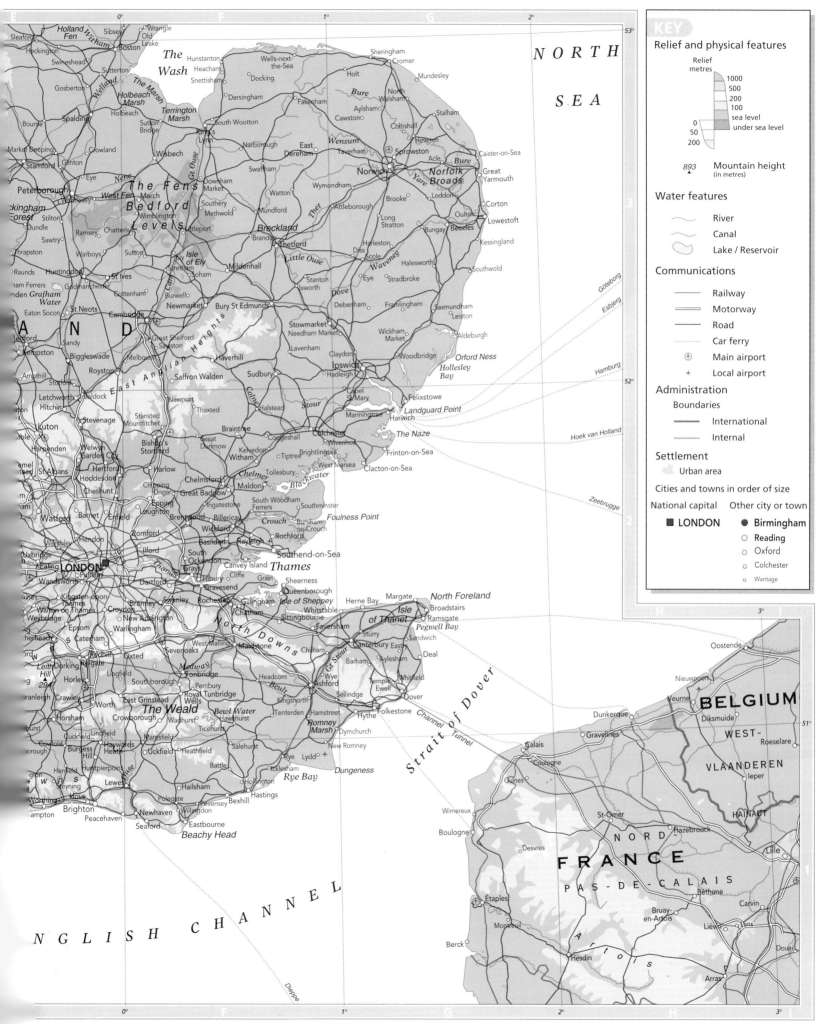

KEY

Relief and physical features

Relief
metres
1000
500
200
100
sea level
0
50
200 under sea level

▲ 893 Mountain height
(in metres)

Water features

～～ River

～～ Canal

⬭ Lake / Reservoir

Communications

Railway

Motorway

Road

Car ferry

⊕ Main airport

✦ Local airport

Administration

Boundaries

International

Internal

Settlement

Urban area

Cities and towns in order of size

National capital   Other city or town

■ LONDON   ● **Birmingham**

○ **Reading**

○ Oxford

○ Colchester

○ Wantage

Conic projection

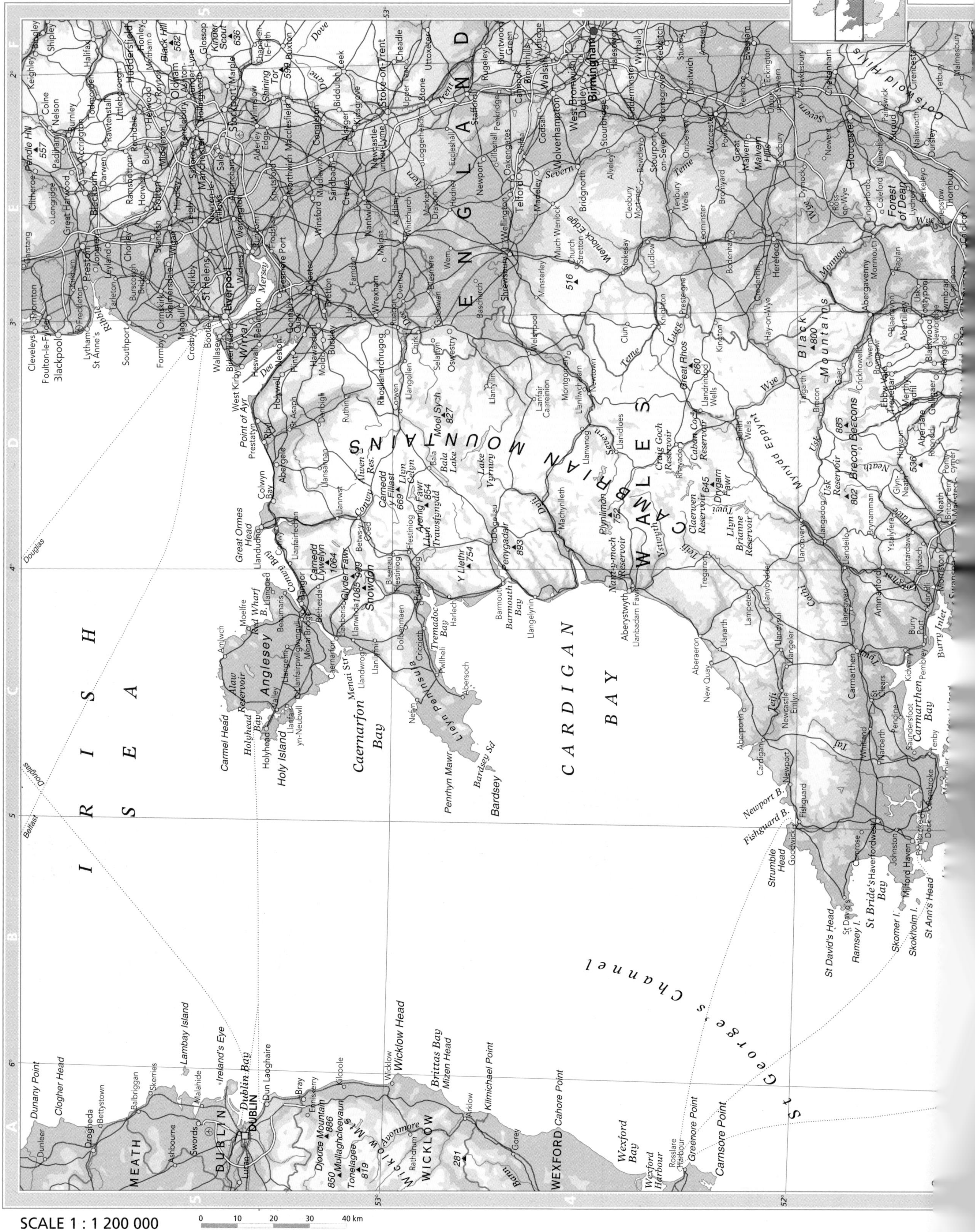

ENGLAND

WALES

CAMBRIAN MOUNTAINS

CARDIGAN BAY

IRISH SEA

St George's Channel

MEATH

DUBLIN

WICKLOW

WEXFORD

Anglesey

Holy Island

Llŷn Peninsula

Birmingham

Liverpool

SCALE 1 : 1 200 000

0   10   20   30   40 km

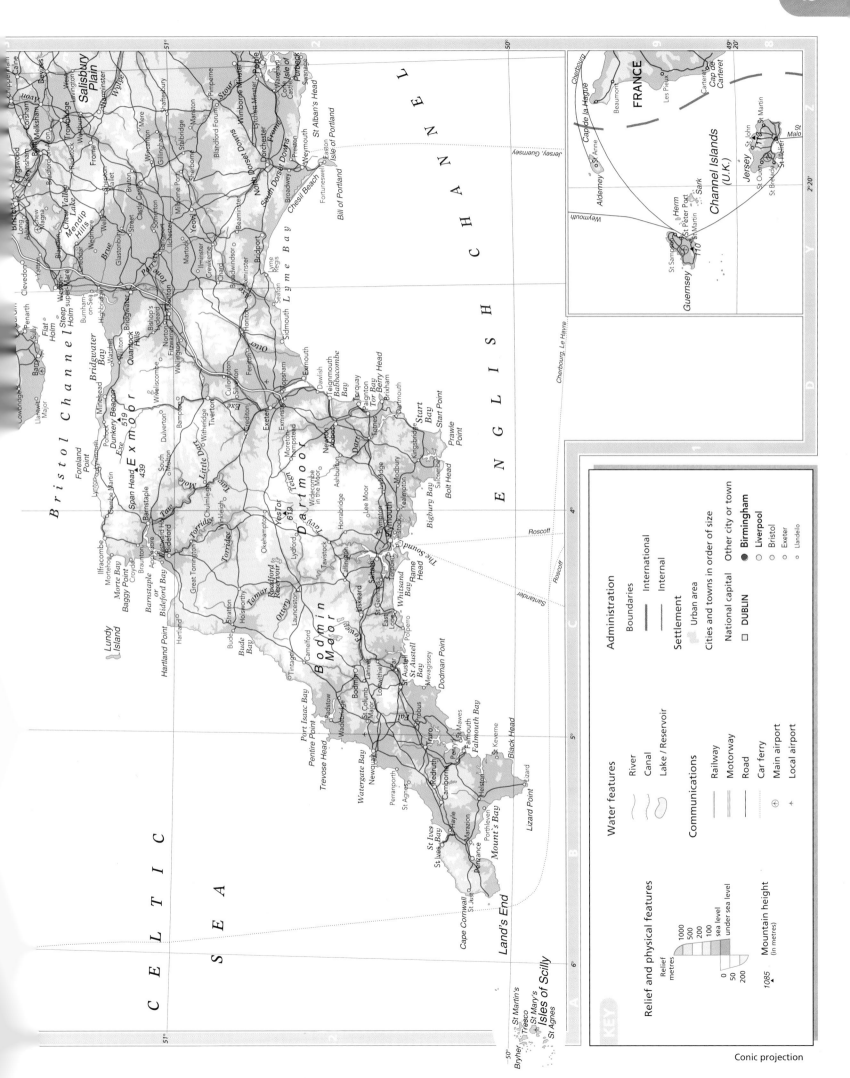

Key

Water features

- River
- Canal
- Lake / Reservoir

Communications

- Railway
- Motorway
- Road
- Car ferry
- ⊕ Main airport
- ✈ Local airport

Administration

Boundaries

- International
- Internal

Settlement

Urban area

Cities and towns in order of size

National capital
- ☐ DUBLIN

Other city or town in order of size
- ● Birmingham
- ◉ Liverpool
- ○ Bristol
- ○ Exeter
- ○ Llandeilo

Relief and physical features

Relief metres
1000
500
200
100
sea level
under sea level
0
50
200

Mountain height (in metres)
▲ 1085

Conic projection

FRANCE

Channel Islands (U.K.)

Guernsey

Jersey

C E L T I C   S E A

B r i s t o l   C h a n n e l

E N G L I S H   C H A N N E L

Land's End

Isles of Scilly

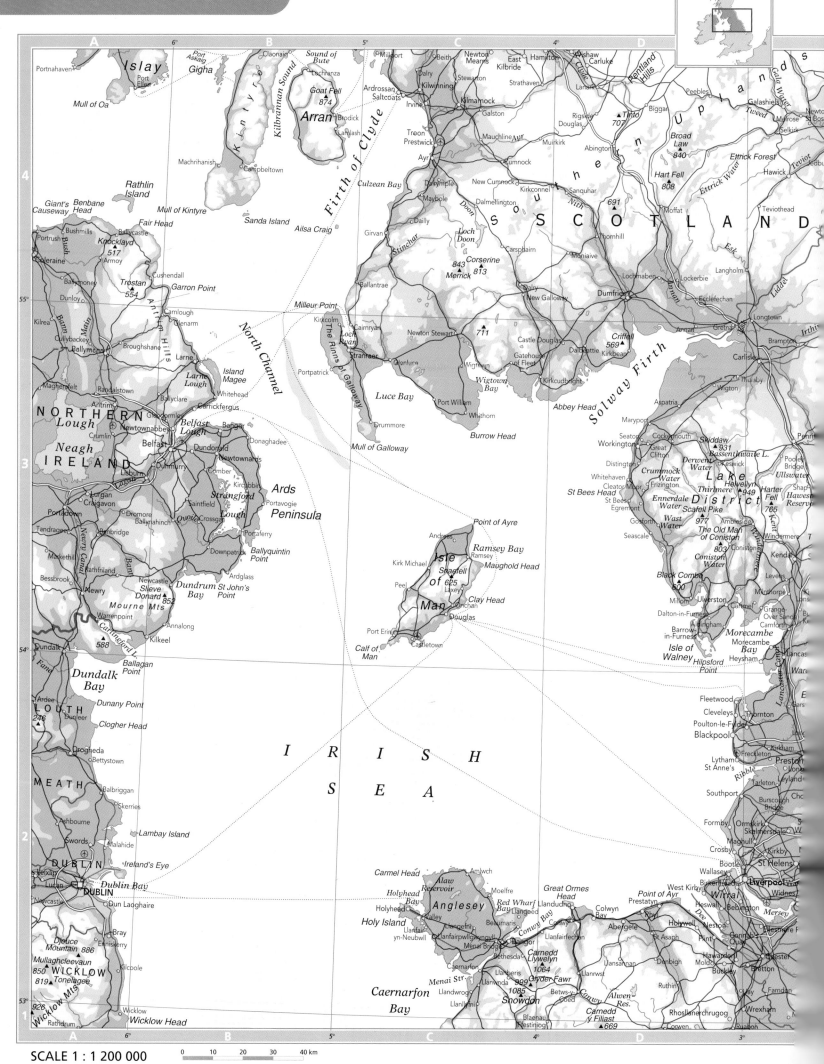

SCALE 1 : 1 200 000

0   10   20   30   40 km

SCALE 1 : 1 200 000

0   10   20   30   40 km

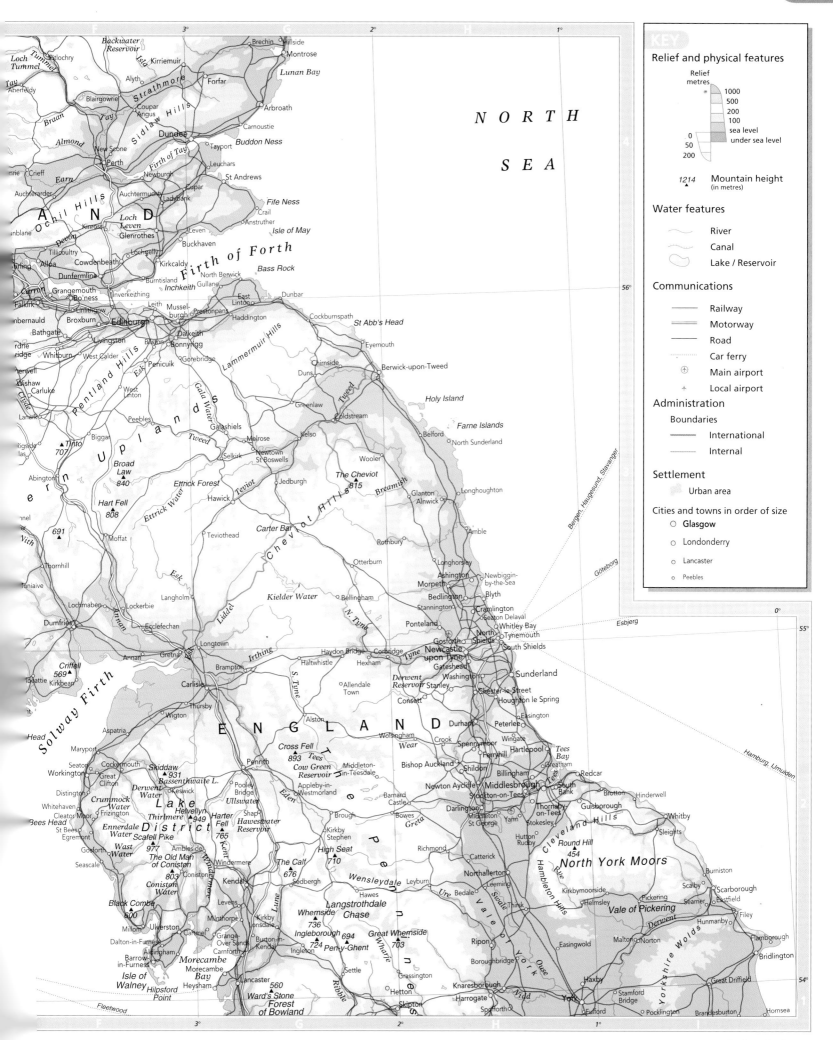

KEY

Relief and physical features

Relief
metres
1000
500
200
100
0
sea level
50
under sea level
200

1344 ▲ Mountain height
(in metres)

Water features

～～ River

～～ Canal

◯ Lake / Reservoir

Communications

──── Railway

──── Road

········ Car ferry

⊕ Main airport

✈ Local airport

Settlement

Cities and towns in order of size

◉ Aberdeen

◎ Inverness

◦ Kirkwall

ATLANTIC

OCEAN

Outer Hebrides

Flannan Isles

St Kilda

West
Loch Rodg
Great
Bernera
Callanish

LEWIS

Mealasta
Island

Scarp

Tirga Mor
679
Clisham
799

Loch
Langavat

Muirneag
248

Broad
Bay
Eye
Peninsula
Stornoway

Butt of
Lewis
Port of Ness

Tolsta Head

Kebock Head

Harris

Loch
Langavat
Rodel

Pabbay
Berneray
Boreray

Sound of Harris

Tarbert
E. L.
Tarbert
Scalpay

**North
Uist**

Lochmaddy

Sd of Monach

Monach Islands

Benbecula

Balivanich

Sd of Barra

**South
Uist**

Lochboisdale

Eriskay

Barra

Vatersay

Castlebay

Pabbay

Sandray

Mingulay

Berneray

Rubha Hunish

Skye

L. Dunvegan

L. Bracadale

Loch
Snizort
Uig

Portree

The Storr
719

Cuillin Hills
993
Sgurr
Alasdair
Blaven
928

Soay

Cuillin Sound

Canna

Rum

Muck

Point of
Ardnamurchan

Coll

Coll

Shiant Islands Rubha Reidh

Greenstone Point

The Minch

Little Minch

Cape
Wrath

Kinlochbervie
Loch Inchard
L. Laxford
Fulnaven
915

Handa
Island
Scourie

Point of
Stoer

Loch
Assynt
Canisp
846
Ben Mo
Assyn
998

Lochinver

Rubha
Coigeach

Summer
Isles

Cul Mor
849

Loch
Lurgainn

Ben
Assyn

Ullapool
Loch Broom

An Teallach
1062
Fionn Loch

Gair Loch

Gairloch
Loch Maree

Beinn Dear
1084

Sgurr Mor
1110

WESTER

ROSS

L. Ewe

L. Torridon

Torridon

Shieldaig

Inner Sound

Sound of Raasay

Rona

Raasay

Scalpay

Kyle of
Lochalsh

L. Eishort

Ardvasar

Sd of Sleat

Ladhar Bheinn

Mallaig

Arisaig

Eilean
Shona

Sgurr
Dhomhnuill
888

Sound of Arisaig

Loch Morar

Eigg

Loch Monar

Carn Eighe
1183

A'Chralaig
1120

Loch
Cluanie
L. Loy
Garry

Loch
Quoich

L. Hourn
1020

L. Nevis

Loch Arkaig

Loch Shiel

Sgurr

Loch
Leven

Fort William
1344

Ben Nevis

Bidean
nam Bian
1150

Loch Fannich

Glen

Glen Garr

Glen Co

Glen Co

SCALE 1 : 1 200 000

0   10   20   30   40 km

Conic projection

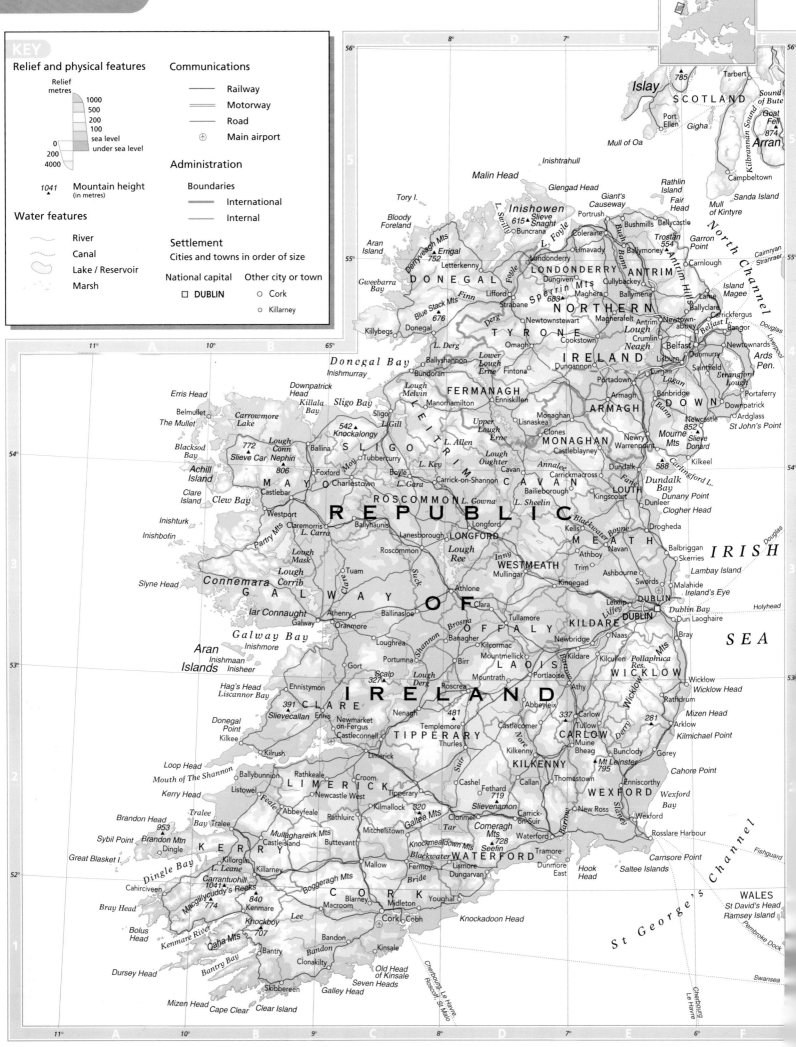

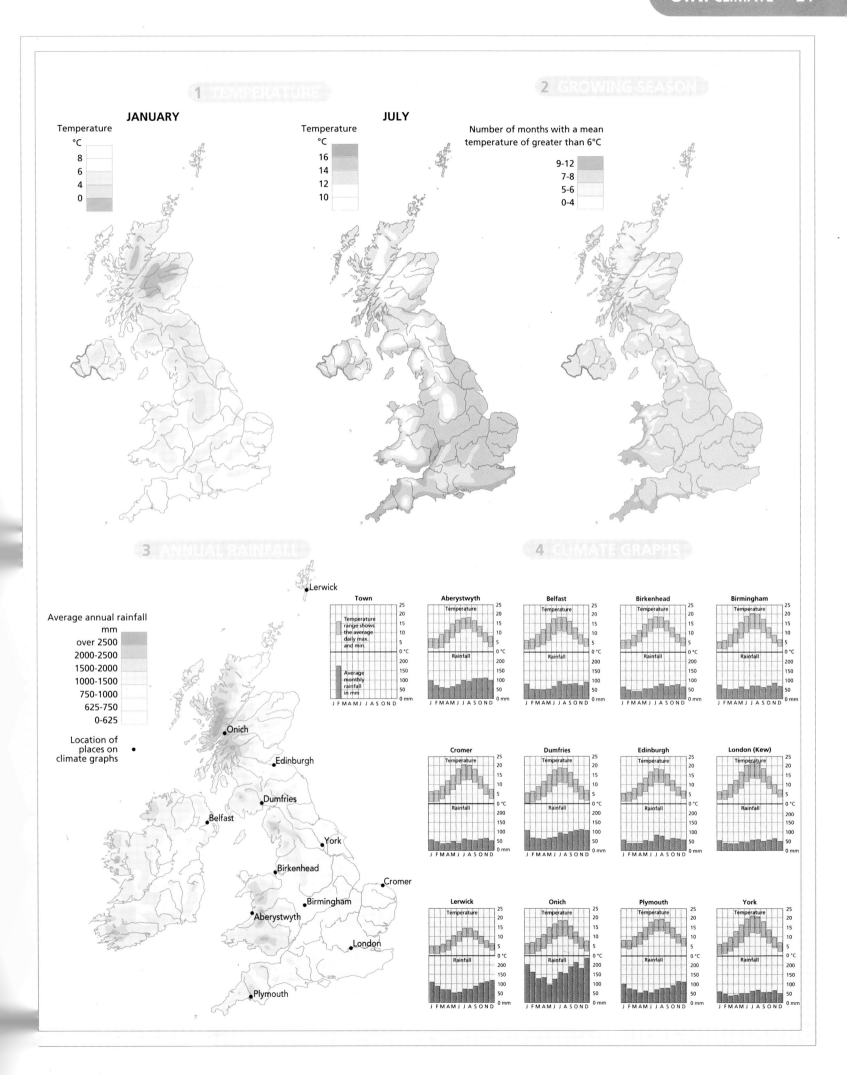

1 TEMPERATURE

JANUARY

Temperature
°C
8
6
4
0

JULY

Temperature
°C
16
14
12
10

2 GROWING SEASON

Number of months with a mean
temperature of greater than 6°C

9-12
7-8
5-6
0-4

3 ANNUAL RAINFALL

Lerwick

Average annual rainfall
mm
over 2500
2000-2500
1500-2000
1000-1500
750-1000
625-750
0-625

Location of
places on
climate graphs •

Onich
Edinburgh
Dumfries
Belfast
York
Birkenhead
Cromer
Birmingham
Aberystwyth
London
Plymouth

4 CLIMATE GRAPHS

Town

Temperature
range shows
the average
daily max.
and min.

Average
monthly
rainfall
in mm

Aberystwyth
Temperature
Rainfall

Belfast
Temperature
Rainfall

Birkenhead
Temperature
Rainfall

Birmingham
Temperature
Rainfall

Cromer
Temperature
Rainfall

Dumfries
Temperature
Rainfall

Edinburgh
Temperature
Rainfall

London (Kew)
Temperature
Rainfall

Lerwick
Temperature
Rainfall

Onich
Temperature
Rainfall

Plymouth
Temperature
Rainfall

York
Temperature
Rainfall

SCALE 1 : 4 000 000

0   50   100   150 km

Conic projection

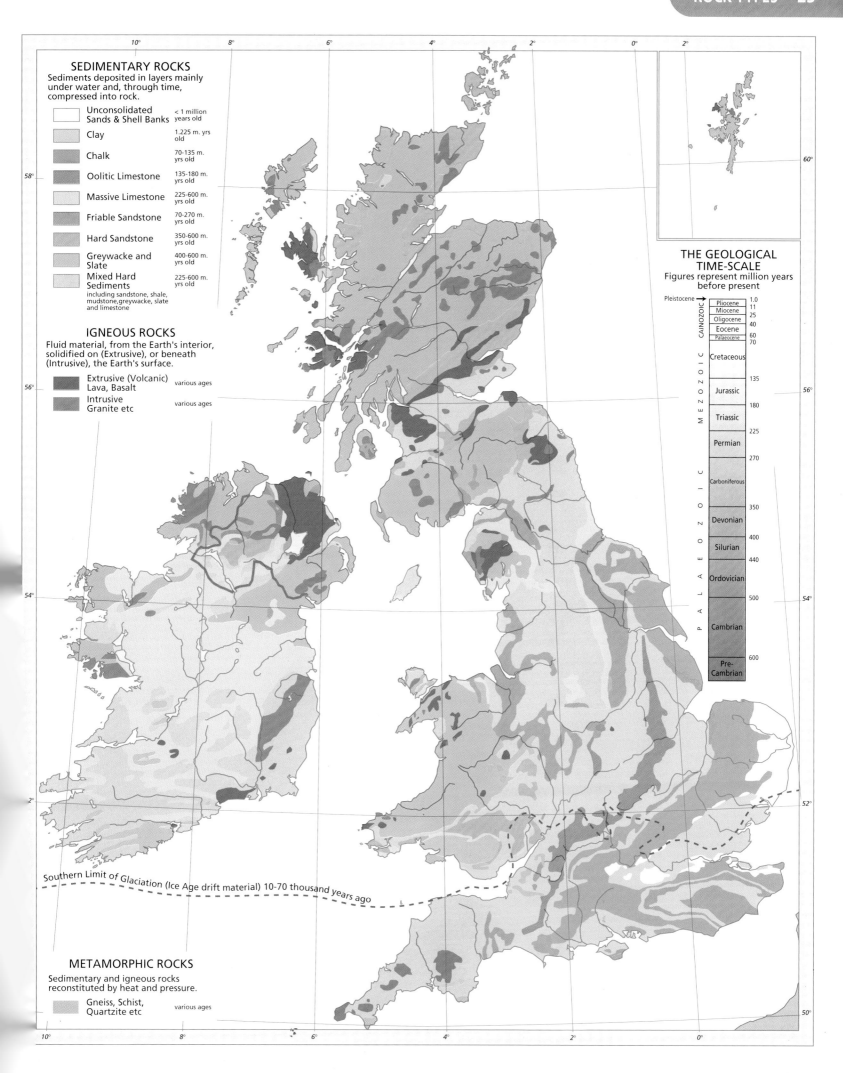

SEDIMENTARY ROCKS

Sediments deposited in layers mainly under water and, through time, compressed into rock.

	Unconsolidated Sands & Shell Banks	< 1 million years old
	Clay	1.225 m. yrs old
	Chalk	70-135 m. yrs old
	Oolitic Limestone	135-180 m. yrs old
	Massive Limestone	225-600 m. yrs old
	Friable Sandstone	70-270 m. yrs old
	Hard Sandstone	350-600 m. yrs old
	Greywacke and Slate	400-600 m. yrs old
	Mixed Hard Sediments	225-600 m. yrs old

including sandstone, shale, mudstone, greywacke, slate and limestone

IGNEOUS ROCKS

Fluid material, from the Earth's interior, solidified on (Extrusive), or beneath (Intrusive), the Earth's surface.

	Extrusive (Volcanic) Lava, Basalt	various ages
	Intrusive Granite etc	various ages

THE GEOLOGICAL TIME-SCALE

Figures represent million years before present

Pleistocene →

CAINOZOIC		
	Pliocene	1.0
	Miocene	11
	Oligocene	25
	Eocene	40
		60
	Palaeocene	70

MEZOZOIC		
	Cretaceous	
		135
	Jurassic	
		180
	Triassic	
		225
	Permian	
		270

PALAEOZOIC		
	Carboniferous	
		350
	Devonian	
		400
	Silurian	
		440
	Ordovician	
		500
	Cambrian	
		600
	Pre-Cambrian	

Southern Limit of Glaciation (Ice Age drift material) 10-70 thousand years ago

METAMORPHIC ROCKS

Sedimentary and igneous rocks reconstituted by heat and pressure.

	Gneiss, Schist, Quartzite etc	various ages

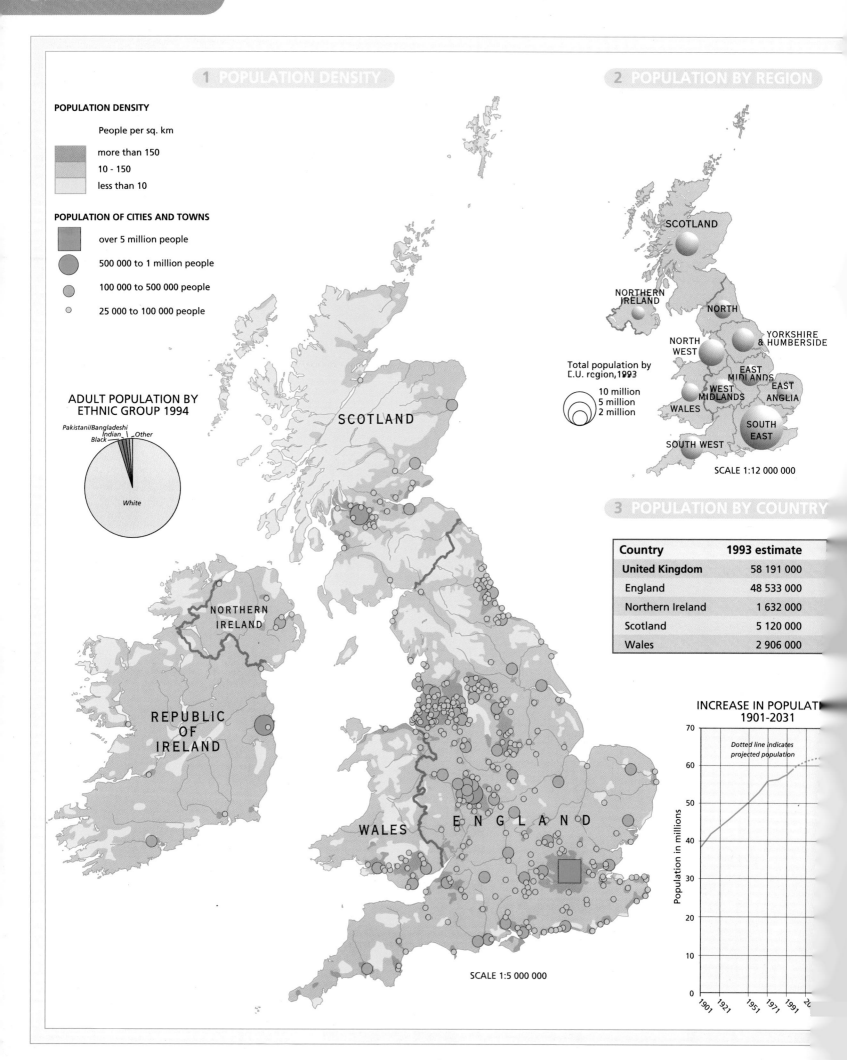

1 POPULATION DENSITY

POPULATION DENSITY

People per sq. km

- more than 150
- 10 - 150
- less than 10

POPULATION OF CITIES AND TOWNS

- over 5 million people
- 500 000 to 1 million people
- 100 000 to 500 000 people
- 25 000 to 100 000 people

ADULT POPULATION BY ETHNIC GROUP 1994

Pakistani/Bangladeshi
Indian
Black
Other
White

SCOTLAND

NORTHERN IRELAND

REPUBLIC OF IRELAND

WALES

ENGLAND

SCALE 1:5 000 000

2 POPULATION BY REGION

SCOTLAND

NORTHERN IRELAND

NORTH

YORKSHIRE & HUMBERSIDE

NORTH WEST

EAST MIDLANDS

WEST MIDLANDS

EAST ANGLIA

WALES

SOUTH EAST

SOUTH WEST

Total population by
E.U. region, 1993

10 million
5 million
2 million

SCALE 1:12 000 000

3 POPULATION BY COUNTRY

Country	1993 estimate
United Kingdom	58 191 000
England	48 533 000
Northern Ireland	1 632 000
Scotland	5 120 000
Wales	2 906 000

INCREASE IN POPULATION 1901-2031

Dotted line indicates projected population

Population in millions

1901 1921 1951 1971 1991

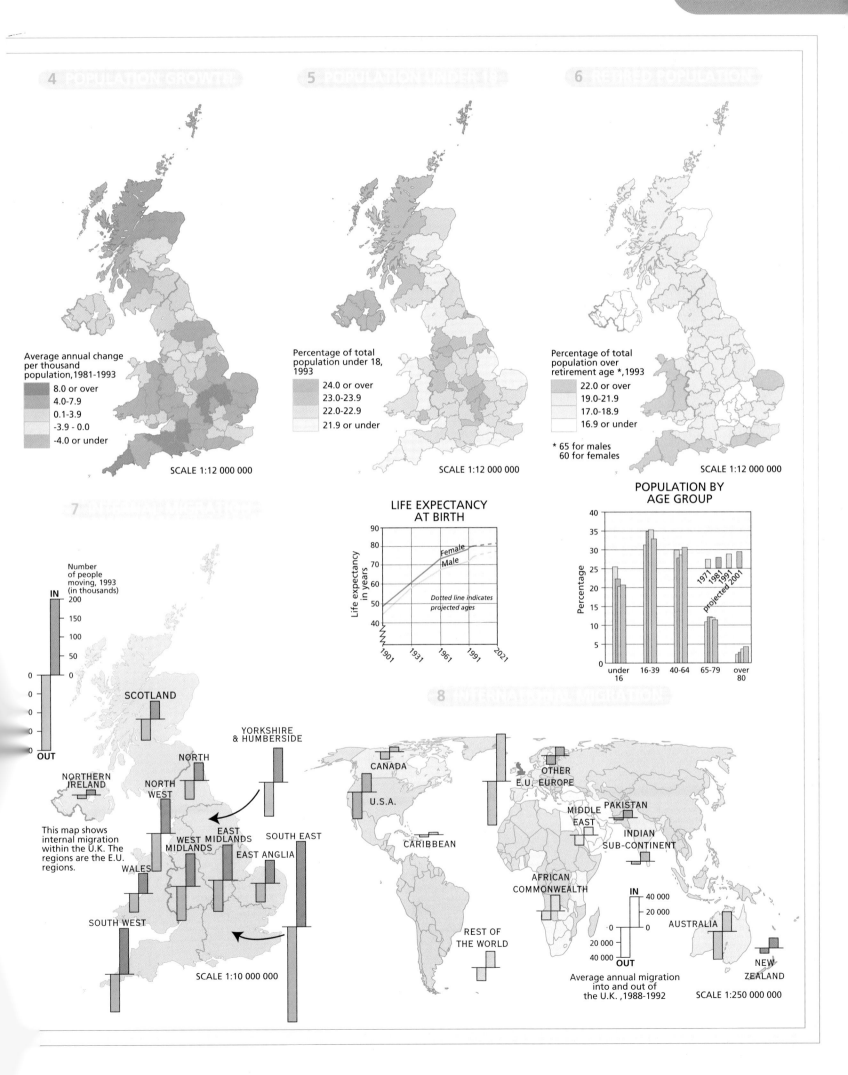

4 POPULATION GROWTH

Average annual change
per thousand
population,1981-1993

- 8.0 or over
- 4.0-7.9
- 0.1-3.9
- -3.9 - 0.0
- -4.0 or under

SCALE 1:12 000 000

5 POPULATION UNDER 18

Percentage of total
population under 18,
1993

- 24.0 or over
- 23.0-23.9
- 22.0-22.9
- 21.9 or under

SCALE 1:12 000 000

6 RETIRED POPULATION

Percentage of total
population over
retirement age *,1993

- 22.0 or over
- 19.0-21.9
- 17.0-18.9
- 16.9 or under

* 65 for males
  60 for females

SCALE 1:12 000 000

LIFE EXPECTANCY AT BIRTH

Life expectancy in years

Female
Male

Dotted line indicates
projected ages

1901 1931 1961 1991 2021

POPULATION BY AGE GROUP

Percentage

1971
1981
1991
projected 2001

under 16   16-39   40-64   65-79   over 80

7 INTERNAL MIGRATION

Number
of people
moving, 1993
(in thousands)

IN
200
150
100
50
0

0
0
0
0

OUT

SCOTLAND

YORKSHIRE
& HUMBERSIDE

NORTHERN
IRELAND

NORTH

NORTH
WEST

This map shows
internal migration
within the U.K. The
regions are the E.U.
regions.

WALES

EAST
WEST MIDLANDS
MIDLANDS

EAST ANGLIA

SOUTH EAST

SOUTH WEST

SCALE 1:10 000 000

8 INTERNATIONAL MIGRATION

CANADA

U.S.A.

CARIBBEAN

OTHER
E.U. EUROPE

MIDDLE
EAST

PAKISTAN

INDIAN
SUB-CONTINENT

AFRICAN
COMMONWEALTH

REST OF
THE WORLD

IN
40 000
20 000
0

0
20 000
40 000
OUT

AUSTRALIA

NEW
ZEALAND

Average annual migration
into and out of
the U.K. ,1988-1992

SCALE 1:250 000 000

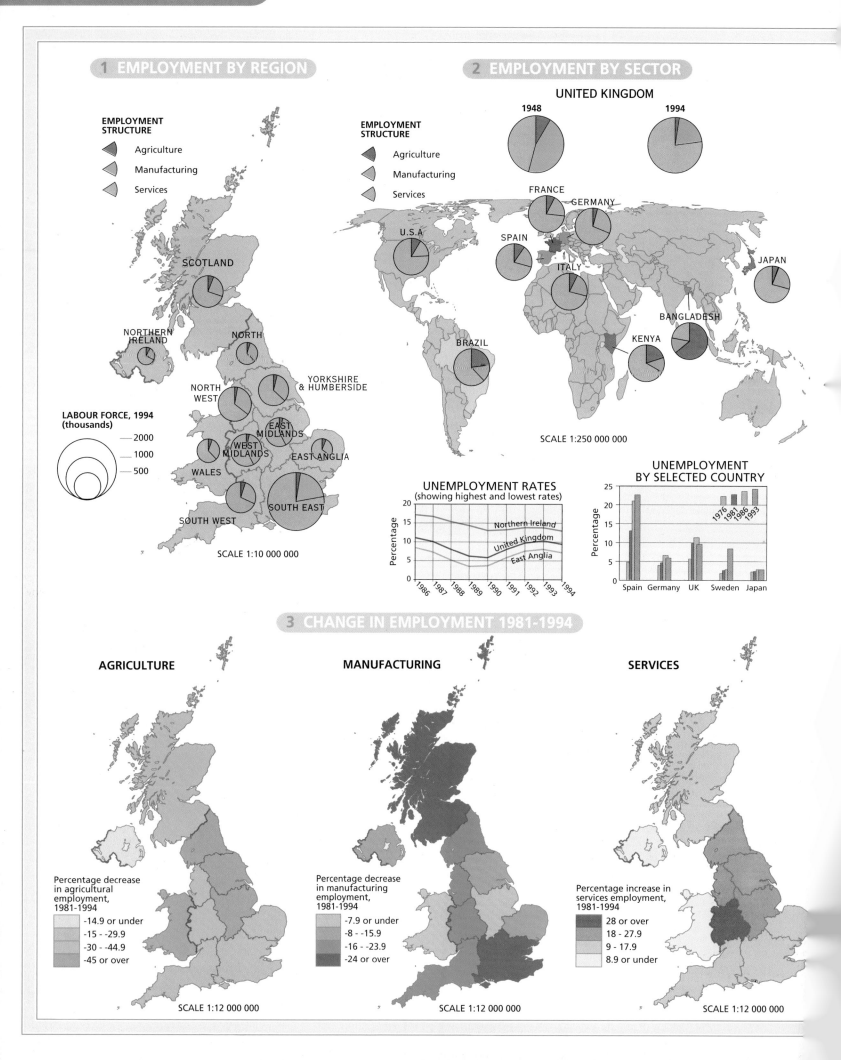

1 EMPLOYMENT BY REGION

EMPLOYMENT STRUCTURE
- Agriculture
- Manufacturing
- Services

LABOUR FORCE, 1994 (thousands)
— 2000
— 1000
— 500

SCOTLAND

NORTHERN IRELAND

NORTH

YORKSHIRE & HUMBERSIDE

NORTH WEST

EAST MIDLANDS

WEST MIDLANDS

EAST ANGLIA

WALES

SOUTH EAST

SOUTH WEST

SCALE 1:10 000 000

2 EMPLOYMENT BY SECTOR

EMPLOYMENT STRUCTURE
- Agriculture
- Manufacturing
- Services

UNITED KINGDOM

1948   1994

FRANCE

GERMANY

U.S.A

SPAIN

ITALY

JAPAN

BRAZIL

BANGLADESH

KENYA

SCALE 1:250 000 000

UNEMPLOYMENT RATES
(showing highest and lowest rates)

Percentage

Northern Ireland
United Kingdom
East Anglia

1986 1987 1988 1989 1990 1991 1992 1993 1994

UNEMPLOYMENT BY SELECTED COUNTRY

Percentage

1976 1981 1986 1993

Spain Germany UK Sweden Japan

3 CHANGE IN EMPLOYMENT 1981-1994

AGRICULTURE

Percentage decrease in agricultural employment, 1981-1994
- -14.9 or under
- -15 - -29.9
- -30 - -44.9
- -45 or over

SCALE 1:12 000 000

MANUFACTURING

Percentage decrease in manufacturing employment, 1981-1994
- -7.9 or under
- -8 - -15.9
- -16 - -23.9
- -24 or over

SCALE 1:12 000 000

SERVICES

Percentage increase in services employment, 1981-1994
- 28 or over
- 18 - 27.9
- 9 - 17.9
- 8.9 or under

SCALE 1:12 000 000

4 LAND USE

CHANGE IN AGRICULTURAL LAND USE 1961-1991

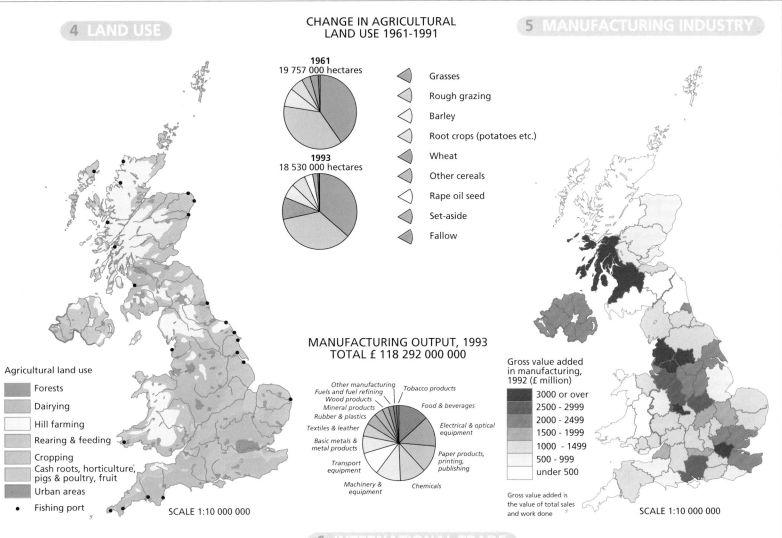

1961
19 757 000 hectares

1993
18 530 000 hectares

- Grasses
- Rough grazing
- Barley
- Root crops (potatoes etc.)
- Wheat
- Other cereals
- Rape oil seed
- Set-aside
- Fallow

Agricultural land use
- Forests
- Dairying
- Hill farming
- Rearing & feeding
- Cropping
- Cash roots, horticulture, pigs & poultry, fruit
- Urban areas
- • Fishing port

SCALE 1:10 000 000

MANUFACTURING OUTPUT, 1993
TOTAL £ 118 292 000 000

Other manufacturing
Fuels and fuel refining
Wood products
Mineral products
Rubber & plastics
Textiles & leather
Basic metals & metal products
Transport equipment
Machinery & equipment
Tobacco products
Food & beverages
Electrical & optical equipment
Paper products, printing, publishing
Chemicals

5 MANUFACTURING INDUSTRY

Gross value added in manufacturing, 1992 (£ million)
- 3000 or over
- 2500 - 2999
- 2000 - 2499
- 1500 - 1999
- 1000 - 1499
- 500 - 999
- under 500

Gross value added is the value of total sales and work done

SCALE 1:10 000 000

6 INTERNATIONAL TRADE

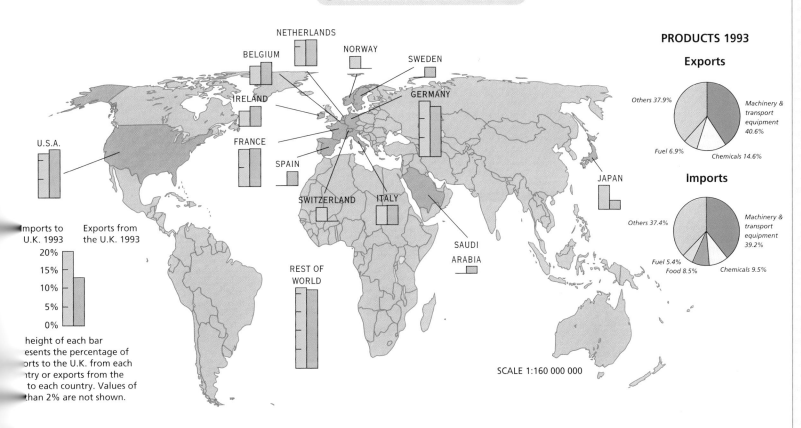

NETHERLANDS
BELGIUM
NORWAY
SWEDEN
IRELAND
GERMANY
FRANCE
U.S.A.
SPAIN
SWITZERLAND
ITALY
JAPAN
SAUDI ARABIA
REST OF WORLD

Imports to U.K. 1993   Exports from the U.K. 1993
- 20%
- 15%
- 10%
- 5%
- 0%

height of each bar ...esents the percentage of ...orts to the U.K. from each ...ntry or exports from the ... to each country. Values of ...han 2% are not shown.

SCALE 1:160 000 000

PRODUCTS 1993

Exports

Others 37.9%
Machinery & transport equipment 40.6%
Fuel 6.9%
Chemicals 14.6%

Imports

Others 37.4%
Machinery & transport equipment 39.2%
Fuel 5.4%
Food 8.5%
Chemicals 9.5%

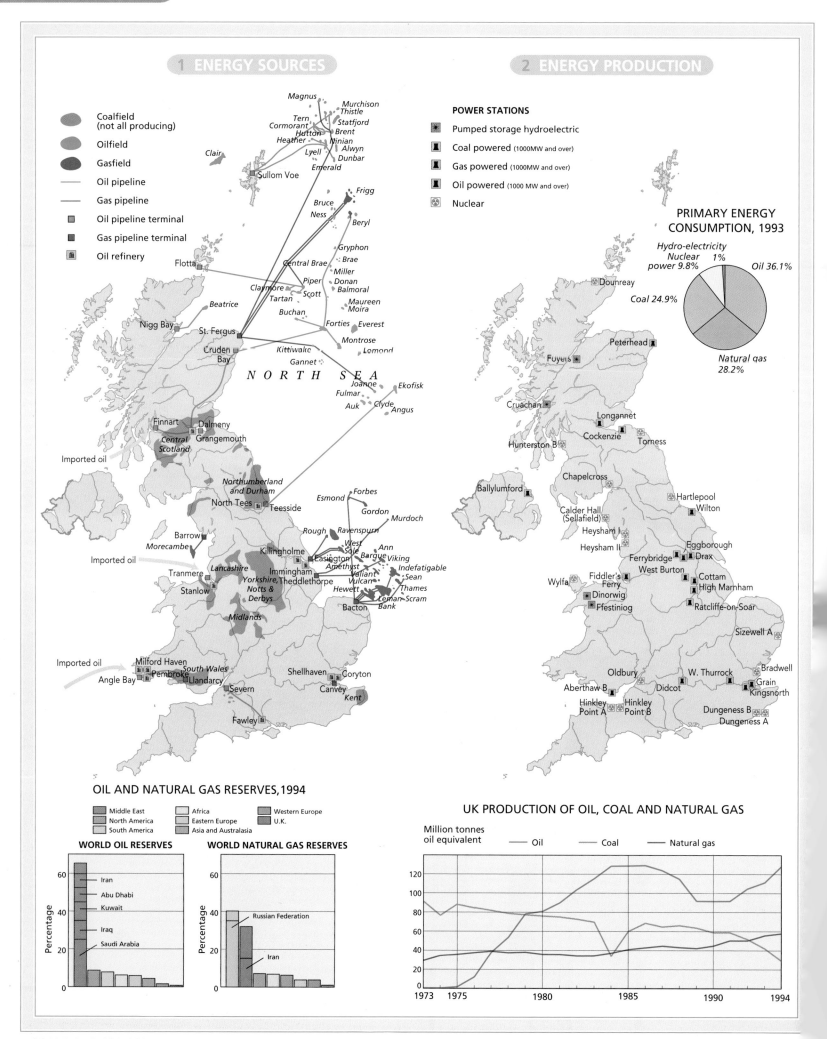

1 ENERGY SOURCES

Coalfield (not all producing)

Oilfield

Gasfield

Oil pipeline

Gas pipeline

Oil pipeline terminal

Gas pipeline terminal

Oil refinery

Magnus
Murchison
Thistle
Tern
Statfjord
Cormorant
Brent
Hutton
Ninian
Heather
Alwyn
Clair
Lyell
Dunbar
Emerald

Bruce
Frigg
Ness
Beryl

Gryphon
Brae
Central Brae
Miller
Piper
Donan
Claymore
Balmoral
Tartan
Scott
Beatrice
Maureen
Moira
Buchan
Forties
Everest
Montrose
Lomond
Kittiwake
Gannet

N O R T H   S E A

Joanne
Ekofisk
Fulmar
Auk
Clyde
Angus

Flotta
St. Fergus
Cruden Bay
Nigg Bay

Finnart
Dalmeny
Central Scotland
Grangemouth

Imported oil

Northumberland and Durham
North Tees
Teesside

Esmond
Forbes
Gordon
Murdoch
Rough
Ravenspurn
West Sole
Ann
Killingholme
Barque
Viking
Easington
Amethyst
Indefatigable
Immingham
Valiant
Sean
Yorkshire, Notts & Derbys
Theddlethorpe
Vulcan
Hewett
Thames
Leman Bank
Scram

Barrow
Morecambe

Imported oil
Tranmere
Lancashire
Stanlow

Midlands

Bacton

Imported oil
Milford Haven
South Wales
Pembroke
Shellhaven
Coryton
Angle Bay
Llandarcy
Severn
Canvey
Kent
Fawley

OIL AND NATURAL GAS RESERVES, 1994

Middle East
North America
South America
Africa
Eastern Europe
Asia and Australasia
Western Europe
U.K.

WORLD OIL RESERVES

Iran
Abu Dhabi
Kuwait
Iraq
Saudi Arabia

Percentage
60
40
20

WORLD NATURAL GAS RESERVES

Russian Federation
Iran

Percentage
60
40
20

2 ENERGY PRODUCTION

POWER STATIONS

Pumped storage hydroelectric

Coal powered (1000MW and over)

Gas powered (1000MW and over)

Oil powered (1000 MW and over)

Nuclear

PRIMARY ENERGY CONSUMPTION, 1993

Hydro-electricity 1%
Nuclear power 9.8%
Oil 36.1%
Coal 24.9%
Natural gas 28.2%

Dounreay
Peterhead
Fuyels
Cruachan
Longannet
Cockenzie
Torness
Hunterston B
Chapelcross
Ballylumford
Hartlepool
Wilton
Calder Hall (Sellafield)
Heysham I
Heysham II
Eggborough
Drax
Ferrybridge
West Burton
Wylfa
Fiddler's Ferry
Cottam
High Marnham
Dinorwig
Ffestiniog
Ratcliffe-on-Soar
Sizewell A
Oldbury
W. Thurrock
Bradwell
Aberthaw B
Didcot
Grain
Kingsnorth
Hinkley Point A
Hinkley Point B
Dungeness B
Dungeness A

UK PRODUCTION OF OIL, COAL AND NATURAL GAS

Million tonnes oil equivalent

Oil — Coal — Natural gas

120
100
80
60
40
20

1973 1975 1980 1985 1990 1994

Conic projection

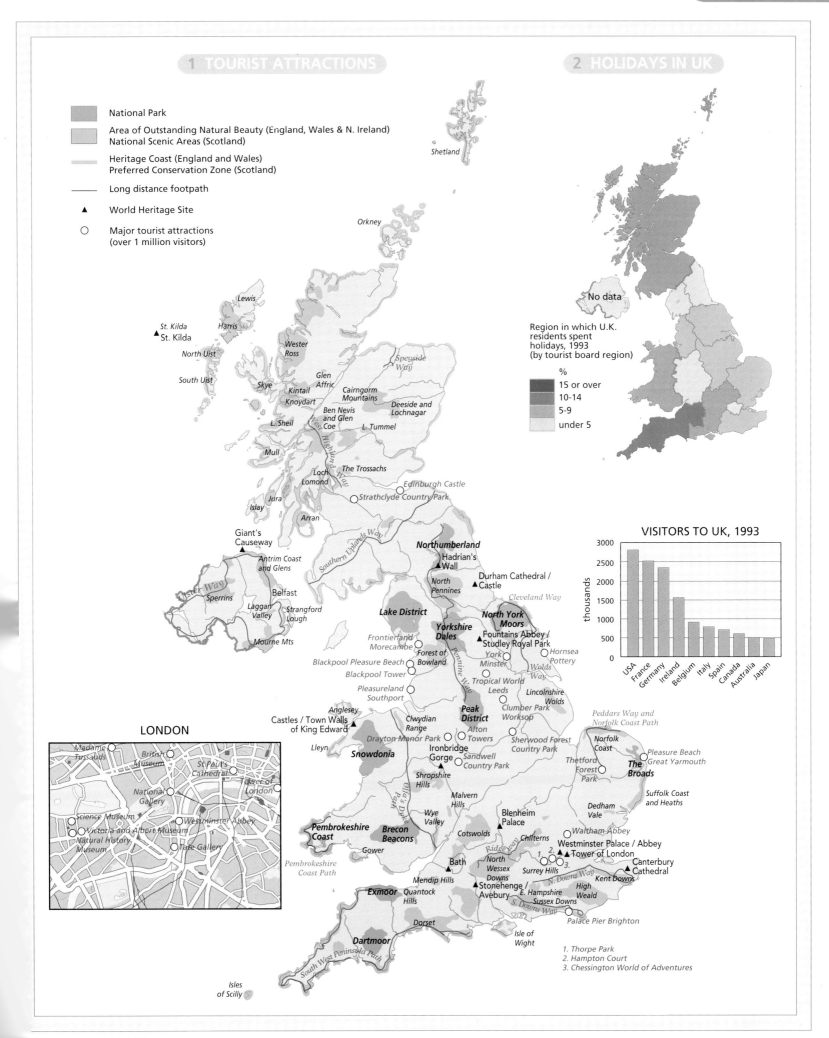

1 TOURIST ATTRACTIONS

2 HOLIDAYS IN UK

National Park

Area of Outstanding Natural Beauty (England, Wales & N. Ireland)
National Scenic Areas (Scotland)

Heritage Coast (England and Wales)
Preferred Conservation Zone (Scotland)

Long distance footpath

▲ World Heritage Site

○ Major tourist attractions (over 1 million visitors)

Shetland

Orkney

Region in which U.K. residents spent holidays, 1993 (by tourist board region)

%
15 or over
10-14
5-9
under 5

No data

Lewis

St. Kilda
▲ St. Kilda

Harris

North Uist

South Uist

Wester Ross

Speyside Way

Skye
Glen Affric
Kintail
Knoydart
Cairngorm Mountains
Deeside and Lochnagar
Ben Nevis and Glen Coe
L. Sheil
L. Tummel

Mull

Loch Lomond
The Trossachs

Jura
Islay

Arran

Giant's Causeway ▲
Antrim Coast and Glens

Ulster Way
Sperrins

Belfast
Laggan Valley
Strangford Lough

Mourne Mts

Northumberland
Hadrian's ▲ Wall

Edinburgh Castle ○
○ Strathclyde Country Park

Southern Uplands Way

Durham Cathedral / ▲ Castle

North Pennines

Cleveland Way

Lake District

Yorkshire Dales

North York Moors
▲ Fountains Abbey / Studley Royal Park

Frontierland Morecambe

Forest of Bowland

York
Minster ○

○ Hornsea Pottery

Blackpool Pleasure Beach
Blackpool Tower

Pennine Way

Wolds Way

○ Tropical World
Leeds
Lincolnshire Wolds

Pleasureland Southport

Anglesey

Peak District

Clumber Park Worksop ○

Castles / Town Walls of King Edward ▲
Clwydian Range
○ Alton Towers
Drayton Manor Park ○

Sherwood Forest Country Park

Norfolk Coast

Lleyn

Snowdonia

Ironbridge Gorge ▲
Sandwell ○ Country Park

Thetford Forest Park
The Broads

Peddars Way and Norfolk Coast Path

○ Pleasure Beach Great Yarmouth

Shropshire Hills

Offa's Dyke Path

Malvern Hills

Wye Valley

Dedham Vale

Suffolk Coast and Heaths

Blenheim Palace

Pembrokeshire Coast
Brecon Beacons

Cotswolds

Chilterns
○ Waltham Abbey

Westminster Palace / Abbey ▲
▲ Tower of London

Gower

Ridgeway
1. 2.
3.

Bath

North Wessex Downs
Surrey Hills

▲ Canterbury Cathedral

Pembrokeshire Coast Path

Mendip Hills

▲ Stonehenge / Avebury

N. Downs Way
Kent Downs

Exmoor
Quantock Hills

E. Hampshire
Sussex Downs
High Weald

Dorset

S. Downs Way
SU

○ Palace Pier Brighton

Dartmoor

Isle of Wight

South West Peninsula Path

Isles of Scilly

1. Thorpe Park
2. Hampton Court
3. Chessington World of Adventures

LONDON

Madame Tussauds ○
British Museum ○
St Paul's Cathedral ○
Tower of London ○
National Gallery ○
Science Museum ▲
Victoria and Albert Museum ○
Natural History Museum ○
Westminster Abbey ○
Tate Gallery ○

VISITORS TO UK, 1993

thousands

| 3000 |
| 2500 |
| 2000 |
| 1500 |
| 1000 |
| 500 |
| 0 |

USA France Germany Ireland Belgium Italy Spain Canada Australia Japan

SCALE 1 : 5 000 000

Conic projection

1 ROAD NETWORK

—— Motorway and number

—— Linking primary road and number

2 RAIL NETWORK

—— Inter-city and express routes

---- Channel Tunnel

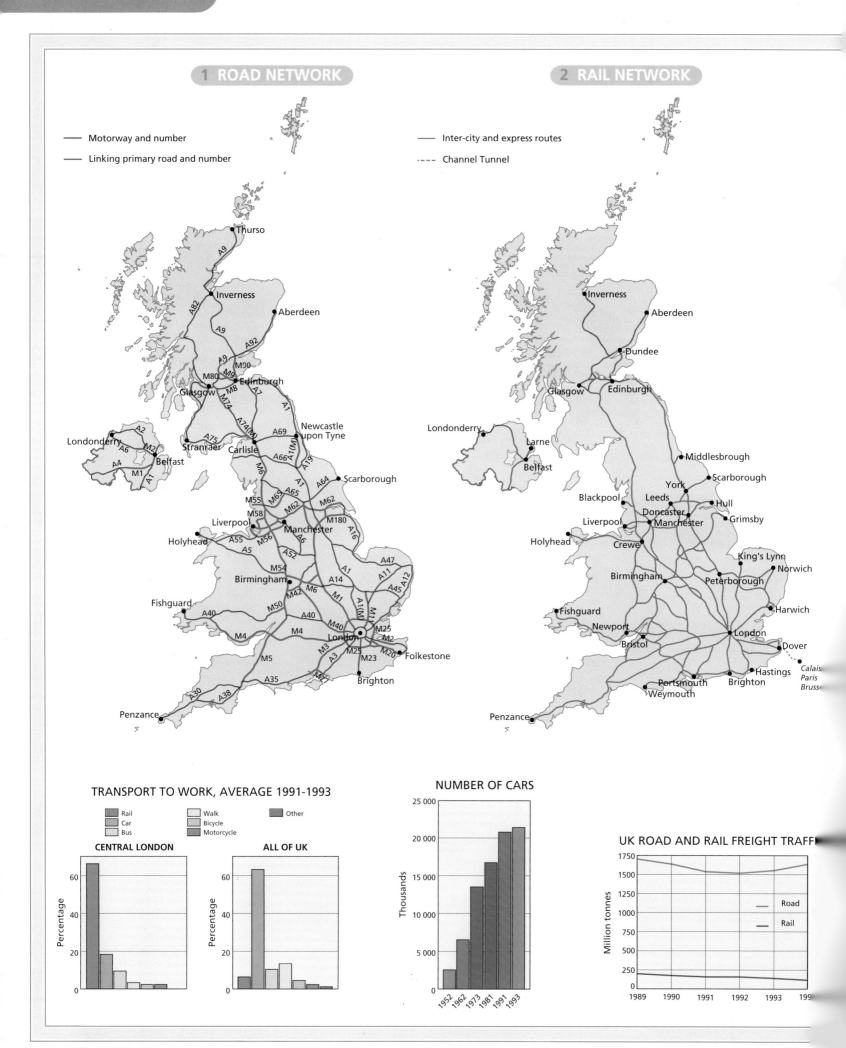

TRANSPORT TO WORK, AVERAGE 1991-1993

- Rail
- Car
- Bus
- Walk
- Bicycle
- Motorcycle
- Other

CENTRAL LONDON

ALL OF UK

NUMBER OF CARS

1952 1962 1973 1981 1991 1993

UK ROAD AND RAIL FREIGHT TRAFFIC

Road
Rail

1989 1990 1991 1992 1993 199

SCALE 1 : 8 000 000

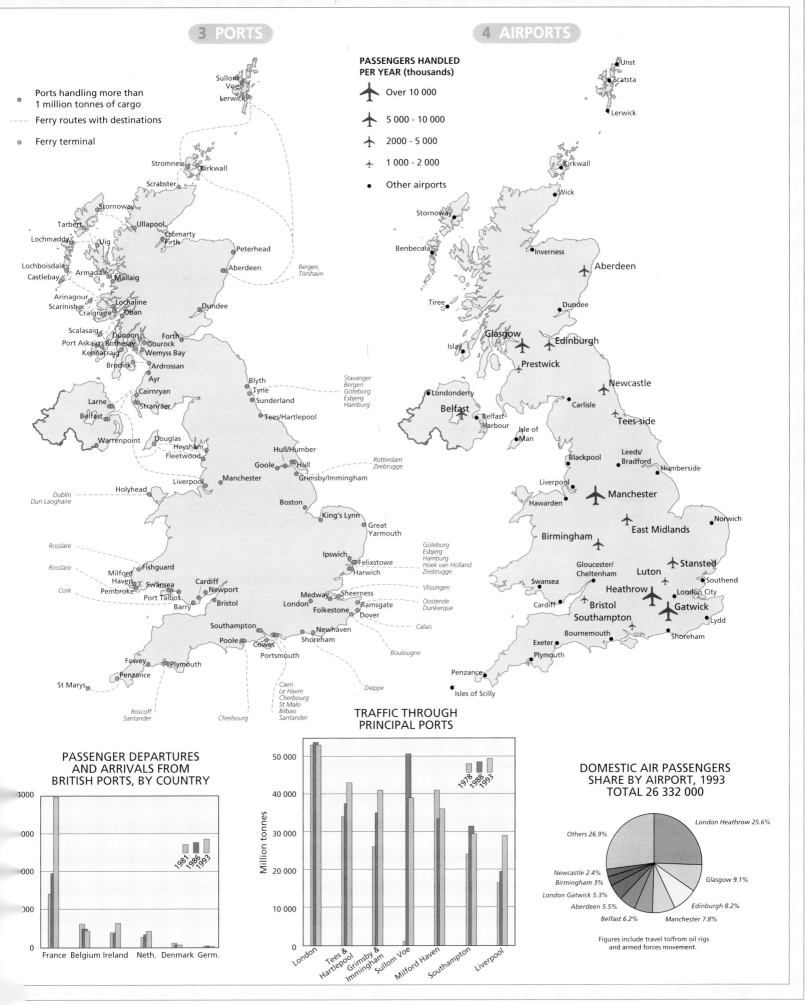

3 PORTS

4 AIRPORTS

PASSENGERS HANDLED PER YEAR (thousands)

✈ Over 10 000

✈ 5 000 - 10 000

✈ 2000 - 5 000

✈ 1 000 - 2 000

• Other airports

- • Ports handling more than 1 million tonnes of cargo
- - - Ferry routes with destinations
- • Ferry terminal

Ports labels: Sullom Voe, Lerwick, Stromness, Kirkwall, Scrabster, Stornoway, Tarbert, Ullapool, Lochmaddy, Uig, Cromarty Firth, Peterhead, Lochboisdale, Castlebay, Armadale, Mallaig, Aberdeen, Arinagour, Scarinish, Lochaline, Oban, Craignure, Dundee, Scalasaig, Dunoon, Forth, Port Askaig, Rothesay, Gourock, Kennacraig, Wemyss Bay, Brodick, Ardrossan, Ayr, Blyth, Cairnryan, Tyne, Larne, Stranraer, Sunderland, Belfast, Tees/Hartlepool, Warrenpoint, Douglas, Heysham, Fleetwood, Hull/Humber, Goole, Hull, Liverpool, Manchester, Grimsby/Immingham, Holyhead, Boston, King's Lynn, Great Yarmouth, Fishguard, Ipswich, Felixstowe, Milford Haven, Swansea, Harwich, Pembroke, Cardiff, Newport, Medway, Sheerness, Port Talbot, Barry, Bristol, London, Folkestone, Ramsgate, Southampton, Newhaven, Dover, Poole, Cowes, Shoreham, Fowey, Portsmouth, Plymouth, Penzance, St Marys

Ferry destinations: Bergen, Tórshavn; Stavanger Bergen Göteborg Esbjerg Hamburg; Rotterdam Zeebrugge; Dublin Dun Laoghaire; Göteborg Esbjerg Hamburg Hoek van Holland Zeebrugge; Rosslare; Cork; Vlissingen; Oostende Dunkerque; Calais; Boulogne; Caen Le Havre Cherbourg St Malo Bilbao Santander; Cherbourg; Dieppe; Roscoff Santander

Airports labels: Unst, Scatsta, Lerwick, Kirkwall, Wick, Stornoway, Benbecula, Inverness, Aberdeen, Tiree, Dundee, Glasgow, Edinburgh, Prestwick, Islay, Newcastle, Londonderry, Carlisle, Belfast, Belfast Harbour, Tees-side, Isle of Man, Leeds/Bradford, Blackpool, Humberside, Liverpool, Manchester, Hawarden, East Midlands, Norwich, Birmingham, Stansted, Gloucester/Cheltenham, Luton, Swansea, Southend, Heathrow, London City, Cardiff, Bristol, Gatwick, Southampton, Lydd, Bournemouth, Shoreham, Exeter, Plymouth, Penzance, Isles of Scilly

TRAFFIC THROUGH PRINCIPAL PORTS

PASSENGER DEPARTURES AND ARRIVALS FROM BRITISH PORTS, BY COUNTRY

1981 1986 1993

France, Belgium, Ireland, Neth., Denmark, Germ.

Million tonnes

50 000
40 000
30 000
20 000
10 000
0

1978 1988 1993

London, Tees & Hartlepool, Grimsby & Immingham, Sullom Voe, Milford Haven, Southampton, Liverpool

DOMESTIC AIR PASSENGERS SHARE BY AIRPORT, 1993 TOTAL 26 332 000

- London Heathrow 25.6%
- Others 26.9%
- Glasgow 9.1%
- Edinburgh 8.2%
- Manchester 7.8%
- Belfast 6.2%
- Aberdeen 5.5%
- London Gatwick 5.3%
- Birmingham 3%
- Newcastle 2.4%

Figures include travel to/from oil rigs and armed forces movement.

Conic projection

Highland

The blue/green colour corresponds to grassland over 300 metres above sea level on the map opposite. In the higher areas of the Pennines the colour becomes greener as grassland changes to moorland, for example around Shining Tor.

Lowland and arable land

The areas around Manchester appear as shades of orange and red. The cultivated areas near the river Mersey are redder.

Built up area

These areas are dark blue on the satellite image. The largest area is the Manchester urban sprawl. In the top left of the image the built up areas of Blackburn and Accrington stand out from the surrounding farmland.

Woodland

Some areas of woodland can be seen on the lower slopes of Shining Tor. is also a small area near Alderley Edge.

Reservoir

The small distinctive shape of these can be seen in the Pennines area. Ex are Watergrove Reservoir near Whitworth and Errwood Reservoir south Whaley Bridge.

Canal

The straight line of the Manchester Ship Canal can be seen running alo the winding course of the river Mersey.

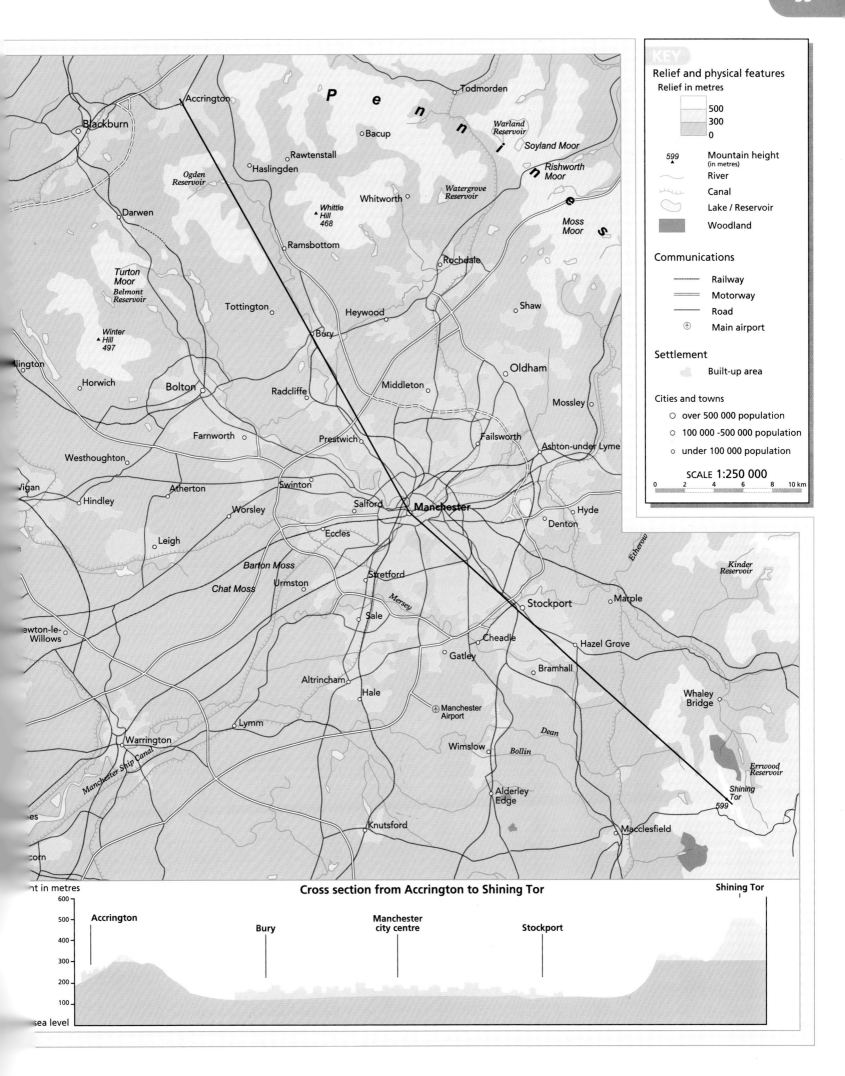

KEY

Relief and physical features
Relief in metres

	500
	300
	0

599 ▲   Mountain height (in metres)

~~~~~ River

Canal

Lake / Reservoir

Woodland

Communications

---- Railway

═══ Motorway

—— Road

⊕ Main airport

Settlement

Built-up area

Cities and towns

○ over 500 000 population

○ 100 000 - 500 000 population

○ under 100 000 population

SCALE 1:250 000

0   2   4   6   8   10 km

Pennines

Todmorden
Warland Reservoir
Soyland Moor
Bacup
Rishworth Moor
Rawtenstall
Haslingden
Watergrove Reservoir
Moss Moor
Ogden Reservoir
Whitworth
Accrington
Blackburn
Darwen
Whittle Hill 468
Ramsbottom
Rochdale
Turton Moor
Belmont Reservoir
Tottington
Heywood
Shaw
Winter Hill 497
Bury
Horwich
Bolton
Radcliffe
Middleton
Oldham
llington
Farnworth
Prestwich
Failsworth
Mossley
Westhoughton
Ashton-under Lyme
Wigan
Atherton
Swinton
Salford
Manchester
Hyde
Hindley
Worsley
Denton
Leigh
Eccles
Etherow
Barton Moss
Stretford
Kinder Reservoir
Chat Moss
Urmston
Mersey
Stockport
Marple
ewton-le-Willows
Sale
Cheadle
Hazel Grove
Gatley
Bramhall
Altrincham
Hale
Whaley Bridge
Lymm
Manchester Airport
Dean
Warrington
Wimslow
Bollin
Errwood Reservoir
Manchester Ship Canal
Alderley Edge
Shining Tor 599
orn
Knutsford
Macclesfield

Cross section from Accrington to Shining Tor

ht in metres

600	Shining Tor
500	Accrington Manchester city centre
400	Bury Stockport
300	
200	
100	
sea level	

Relief

Relief
metres
5000
3000
2000
1000
500
200
0
sea level
under sea level
200
4000
6000

Ice cap

Arctic Circle

Iceland

Faxaflói

Vestmannaeyjar

Snaefell 1833

Vatnajökull

Hünaflói

Fontur

Jan Mayen

North Cape

Søraya

Inarijärvi

Öz. Ima

Lofoten

Vesterålen

Vestfjorden

Scandinavia

Lappland

Lule

Kemi

Ume

Indals

A T L A N T I C   O C E A N

Norwegian Sea

Faeroes

Shetland

Orkney

Outer Hebrides

Ben Nevis 1344

Malin Head

Donegal Bay

Galway Bay

Shannon

Cape Clear

Ireland

Irish Sea

The Pennines

Great Britain

British Isles

N o r t h   S e a

Snowdon 1085

St George's Channel

Land's End

Isles of Scilly

English Channel

Channel Islands

Strait of Dover

The Wash

Thames

Gulf of Bothnia

Åland

Mälaren

Vänern

Vättern

Gotland

Öland

Skagerrak

Kattegat

Baltic Sea

Fyn

Sjaelland

Bornholm

Hiiumaa

Saaremaa

Gulf of Riga

Lake Peipus

Gulf Of Finland

NORTH EUROP

Pripet Marshes

Frisian Is

Ijsselmeer

Maas

Rhine

Weser

Elbe

Elbe

Oder

Warta

Vistula

Bug

Vistula

Seine

Marne

Ardennes

Moselle

Taunus

Ore Mts

Bohemian Forest

Sudeten Mts

Dniester

Carpathian Mts

B a y   o f   B i s c a y

Brittany

Loire

Vienne

Seine

Saône

Gironde

Massif Central

Mt Dore 1885

Allier

L. Geneva

Jura

Vosges

Rhine

Danube

Bodensee

Inn

Danube

Gross Glockner 3798

Balaton

Hungarian Plain

A L P S

Mont Blanc 4808

Matterhorn 4478

Po

Sava

Tisza

Mureş

Danub

Transylvanian Alps

Moravia

Gulf of Gascony

C. Finisterre

Cantabrian Mts

Douro

Duero

Ebro

Pyrenees

Pico de Aneto 3404

Gulf of Lions

Côte d'Azur

Gulf of Genoa

Ligurian Sea

Apennines

Dinaric Alps

Adriatic Sea

Balkan Mts

Danub

Tagus

C. St. Vicente

Sierra Morena

Guadalquivir

Sierra Nevada

Gulf of Valencia

Balearic Is

Menorca

Ibiza

Mallorca

Corsica

Strait of Bonifacio

Sardinia

Tyrrhenian Sea

Vesuvius 1281

G. of Taranto

Rhodope Mts

Morava

A e g e a n

Corfu

Pindus Mts

Evvia

Strombali

Strait of Gibraltar

M E D I T E R

Sicily

Mt Etna 3323

C. Passero

Zakynthos

I o n i a n   S e a

R

A

N

E

A

N

Crete

Naxi

High Atlas

Toubkal 4167

Hauts Plateaux

Saharan Atlas

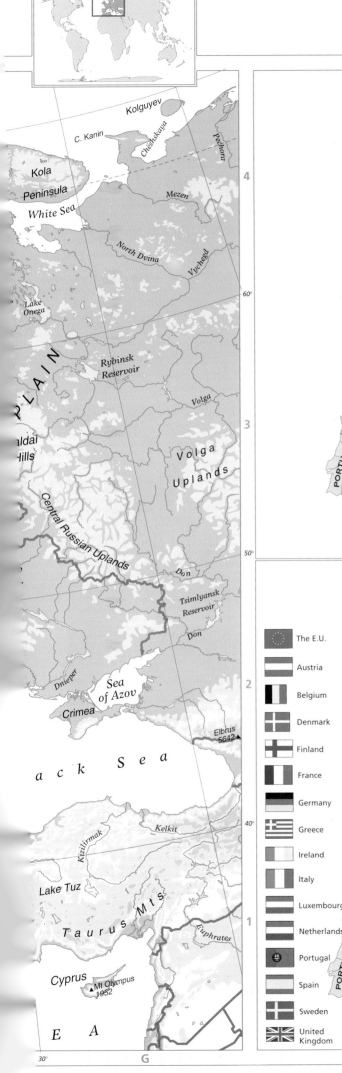

1 COUNTRIES

A. ANDORRA
AL. ALBANIA
B.-H. BOSNIA-HERZEGOVINA
BEL. BELGIUM
L. LIECHTENSTEIN
LUX. LUXEMBOURG
MAC. MACEDONIA
MOL. MOLDOVA
NETH. NETHERLANDS
R.F. RUSSIAN FEDERATION
SL. SLOVENIA
SW. SWITZERLAND

SCALE 1:30 000 000

2 EUROPEAN UNION

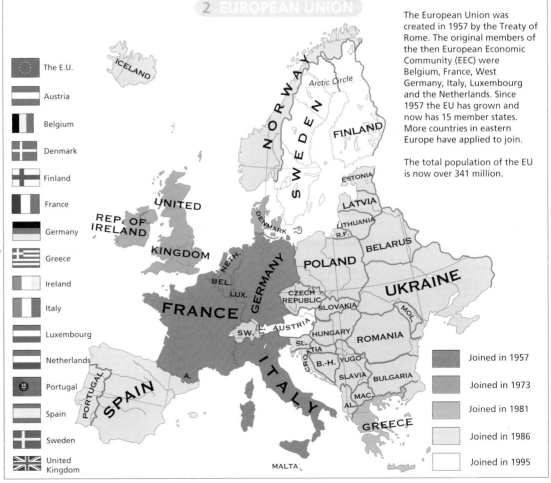

The European Union was created in 1957 by the Treaty of Rome. The original members of the then European Economic Community (EEC) were Belgium, France, West Germany, Italy, Luxembourg and the Netherlands. Since 1957 the EU has grown and now has 15 member states. More countries in eastern Europe have applied to join.

The total population of the EU is now over 341 million.

The E.U.
Austria
Belgium
Denmark
Finland
France
Germany
Greece
Ireland
Italy
Luxembourg
Netherlands
Portugal
Spain
Sweden
United Kingdom

Joined in 1957
Joined in 1973
Joined in 1981
Joined in 1986
Joined in 1995

Albers Equal Area Conic projection

Conic projection

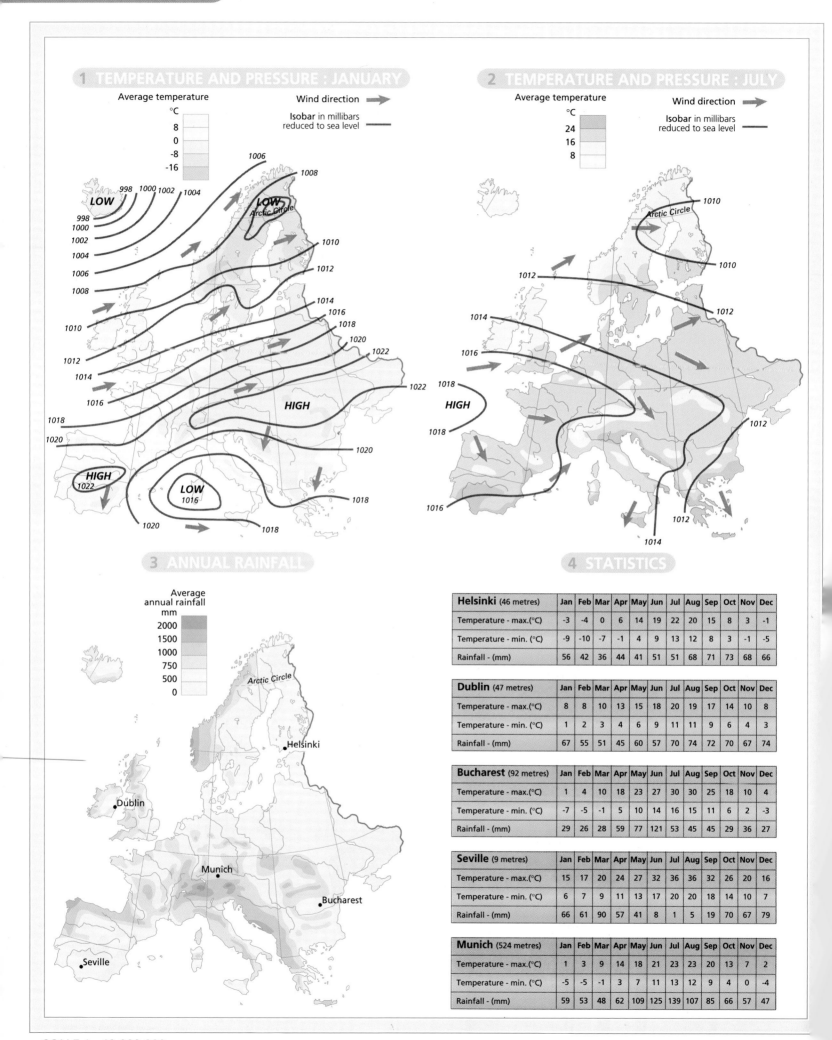

1 TEMPERATURE AND PRESSURE : JANUARY

Average temperature
°C
8
0
-8
-16

Wind direction →

Isobar in millibars reduced to sea level ——

2 TEMPERATURE AND PRESSURE : JULY

Average temperature
°C
24
16
8

Wind direction →

Isobar in millibars reduced to sea level ——

3 ANNUAL RAINFALL

Average annual rainfall
mm
2000
1500
1000
750
500
0

4 STATISTICS

Helsinki (46 metres)	Jan	Feb	Mar	Apr	May	Jun	Jul	Aug	Sep	Oct	Nov	Dec
Temperature - max.(°C)	-3	-4	0	6	14	19	22	20	15	8	3	-1
Temperature - min. (°C)	-9	-10	-7	-1	4	9	13	12	8	3	-1	-5
Rainfall - (mm)	56	42	36	44	41	51	51	68	71	73	68	66

Dublin (47 metres)	Jan	Feb	Mar	Apr	May	Jun	Jul	Aug	Sep	Oct	Nov	Dec
Temperature - max.(°C)	8	8	10	13	15	18	20	19	17	14	10	8
Temperature - min. (°C)	1	2	3	4	6	9	11	11	9	6	4	3
Rainfall - (mm)	67	55	51	45	60	57	70	74	72	70	67	74

Bucharest (92 metres)	Jan	Feb	Mar	Apr	May	Jun	Jul	Aug	Sep	Oct	Nov	Dec
Temperature - max.(°C)	1	4	10	18	23	27	30	30	25	18	10	4
Temperature - min. (°C)	-7	-5	-1	5	10	14	16	15	11	6	2	-3
Rainfall - (mm)	29	26	28	59	77	121	53	45	45	29	36	27

Seville (9 metres)	Jan	Feb	Mar	Apr	May	Jun	Jul	Aug	Sep	Oct	Nov	Dec
Temperature - max.(°C)	15	17	20	24	27	32	36	36	32	26	20	16
Temperature - min. (°C)	6	7	9	11	13	17	20	20	18	14	10	7
Rainfall - (mm)	66	61	90	57	41	8	1	5	19	70	67	79

Munich (524 metres)	Jan	Feb	Mar	Apr	May	Jun	Jul	Aug	Sep	Oct	Nov	Dec
Temperature - max.(°C)	1	3	9	14	18	21	23	23	20	13	7	2
Temperature - min. (°C)	-5	-5	-1	3	7	11	13	12	9	4	0	-4
Rainfall - (mm)	59	53	48	62	109	125	139	107	85	66	57	47

SCALE 1 : 40 000 000

Conic projection

1 POPULATION DENSITY

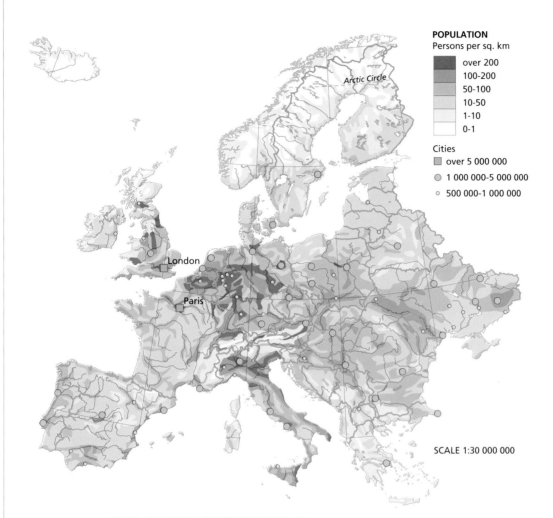

POPULATION
Persons per sq. km

- over 200
- 100-200
- 50-100
- 10-50
- 1-10
- 0-1

Cities

- ■ over 5 000 000
- ● 1 000 000-5 000 000
- ○ 500 000-1 000 000

Arctic Circle

London

Paris

SCALE 1:30 000 000

2 POPULATION TABLE

Country	% Change 1990-1995	Life expectancy (years) 1990-1995
Albania	0.9	72
Austria	0.67	76
Belarus	-0.14	70
Belgium	0.32	76
Bosnia-Herzegovina	-4.39	72
Bulgaria	-0.5	71
Croatia	-0.1	71
Czech Republic	-0.02	71
Denmark	0.16	75
Estonia	-0.58	69
Finland	0.48	76
France	0.44	77
Germany	0.55	76
Greece	0.41	78
Hungary	-0.49	69
Iceland	1.06	78
Italy	0.06	77
Latvia	-0.87	69
Lithuania	-0.06	70
Luxembourg	1.26	76
Macedonia	1.11	
Malta	0.67	76
Moldova	0.32	68
Netherlands	0.72	77
Norway	0.45	77
Poland	0.14	71
Portugal	0.09	75
Republic of Ireland	0.28	75
Romania	-0.32	70
Slovakia	0.36	71
Slovenia	0.29	73
Spain	0.18	78
Sweden	0.51	78
Switzerland	1.05	78
Ukraine	-0.1	69
United Kingdom	0.29	76
Yugoslavia	1.32	72

3 POPULATION UNDER 15

4 POPULATION OVER 60

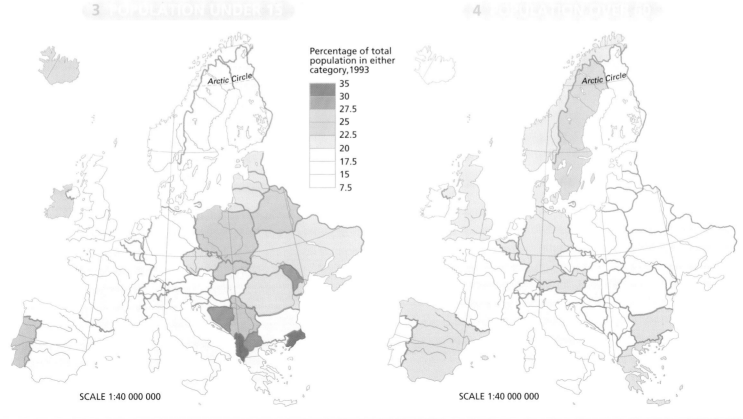

Percentage of total population in either category, 1993

- 35
- 30
- 27.5
- 25
- 22.5
- 20
- 17.5
- 15
- 7.5

Arctic Circle

Arctic Circle

SCALE 1:40 000 000

SCALE 1:40 000 000

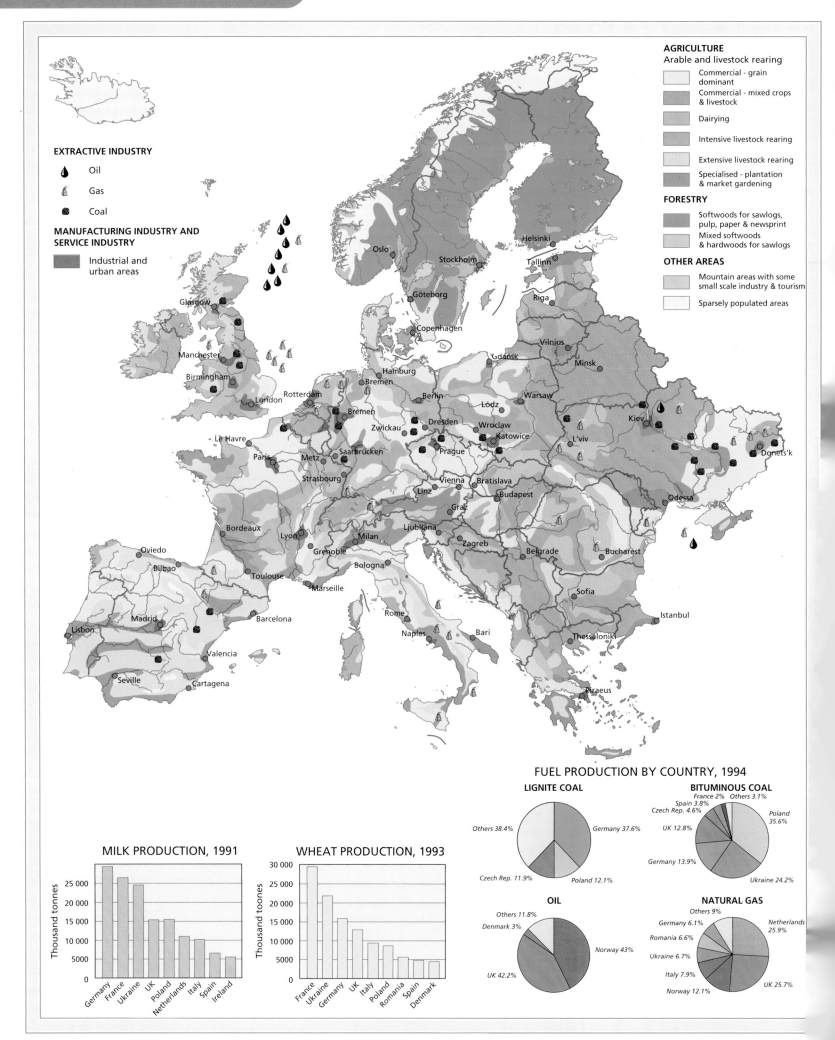

EXTRACTIVE INDUSTRY

- Oil
- Gas
- Coal

MANUFACTURING INDUSTRY AND SERVICE INDUSTRY

Industrial and urban areas

AGRICULTURE
Arable and livestock rearing

Commercial - grain dominant

Commercial - mixed crops & livestock

Dairying

Intensive livestock rearing

Extensive livestock rearing

Specialised - plantation & market gardening

FORESTRY

Softwoods for sawlogs, pulp, paper & newsprint

Mixed softwoods & hardwoods for sawlogs

OTHER AREAS

Mountain areas with some small scale industry & tourism

Sparsely populated areas

SCALE 1 : 20 000 000

Albers equal area conic projection

FUEL PRODUCTION BY COUNTRY, 1994

LIGNITE COAL

Others 38.4%
Germany 37.6%
Czech Rep. 11.9%
Poland 12.1%

BITUMINOUS COAL

France 2%   Others 3.1%
Spain 3.8%
Czech Rep. 4.6%
UK 12.8%
Poland 35.6%
Germany 13.9%
Ukraine 24.2%

OIL

Others 11.8%
Denmark 3%
Norway 43%
UK 42.2%

NATURAL GAS

Others 9%
Germany 6.1%
Romania 6.6%
Netherlands 25.9%
Ukraine 6.7%
Italy 7.9%
Norway 12.1%
UK 25.7%

MILK PRODUCTION, 1991

Thousand tonnes

Germany, France, Ukraine, UK, Poland, Netherlands, Italy, Spain, Ireland

WHEAT PRODUCTION, 1993

Thousand toones

France, Ukraine, Germany, UK, Italy, Poland, Romania, Spain, Denmark

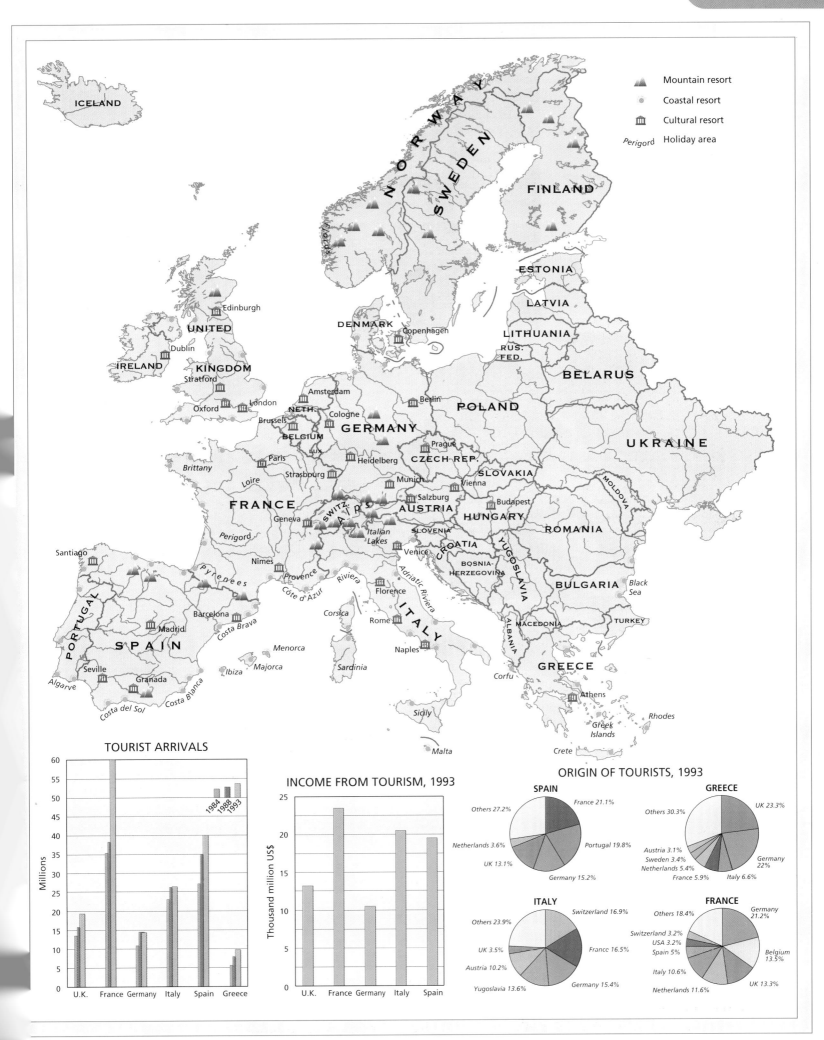

Mountain resort
Coastal resort
Cultural resort
Perigord Holiday area

ICELAND

NORWAY
SWEDEN
FINLAND
ESTONIA
LATVIA
LITHUANIA
RUS. FED.
BELARUS
POLAND
UKRAINE
DENMARK
Copenhagen
Edinburgh
UNITED KINGDOM
Stratford
Dublin
IRELAND
Oxford
London
Amsterdam
NETH.
Brussels
BELGIUM
LUX.
Berlin
Cologne
GERMANY
Heidelberg
Prague
CZECH REP.
SLOVAKIA
Paris
Strasbourg
Munich
Vienna
Salzburg
AUSTRIA
HUNGARY
Budapest
MOLDOVA
ROMANIA
Brittany
Loire
FRANCE
Geneva
SWITZ.
Alps
SLOVENIA
Italian Lakes
Venice
CROATIA
BOSNIA-HERZEGOVINA
YUGOSLAVIA
BULGARIA
Black Sea
Perigord
Nimes
Provence
Côte d'Azur
Riviera
Adriatic Riviera
Florence
Rome
ITALY
MACEDONIA
ALBANIA
TURKEY
Santiago
Pyrenees
Barcelona
Costa Brava
Corsica
Naples
GREECE
Madrid
SPAIN
PORTUGAL
Seville
Granada
Menorca
Ibiza
Majorca
Sardinia
Corfu
Algarve
Costa Blanca
Costa del Sol
Sicily
Malta
Greek Islands
Crete
Athens
Rhodes

TOURIST ARRIVALS

Millions

60
55
50
45
40
35
30
25
20
15
10
5
0

1984
1988
1993

U.K. France Germany Italy Spain Greece

INCOME FROM TOURISM, 1993

Thousand million US$

25
20
15
10
5
0

U.K. France Germany Italy Spain

ORIGIN OF TOURISTS, 1993

SPAIN
Others 27.2%
France 21.1%
Netherlands 3.6%
Portugal 19.8%
UK 13.1%
Germany 15.2%

GREECE
Others 30.3%
UK 23.3%
Austria 3.1%
Sweden 3.4%
Netherlands 5.4%
France 5.9%
Italy 6.6%
Germany 22%

ITALY
Others 23.9%
Switzerland 16.9%
UK 3.5%
France 16.5%
Austria 10.2%
Germany 15.4%
Yugoslavia 13.6%

FRANCE
Others 18.4%
Germany 21.2%
Switzerland 3.2%
USA 3.2%
Spain 5%
Belgium 13.5%
Italy 10.6%
Netherlands 11.6%
UK 13.3%

SCALE 1 : 20 000 000

Albers equal area conic projection

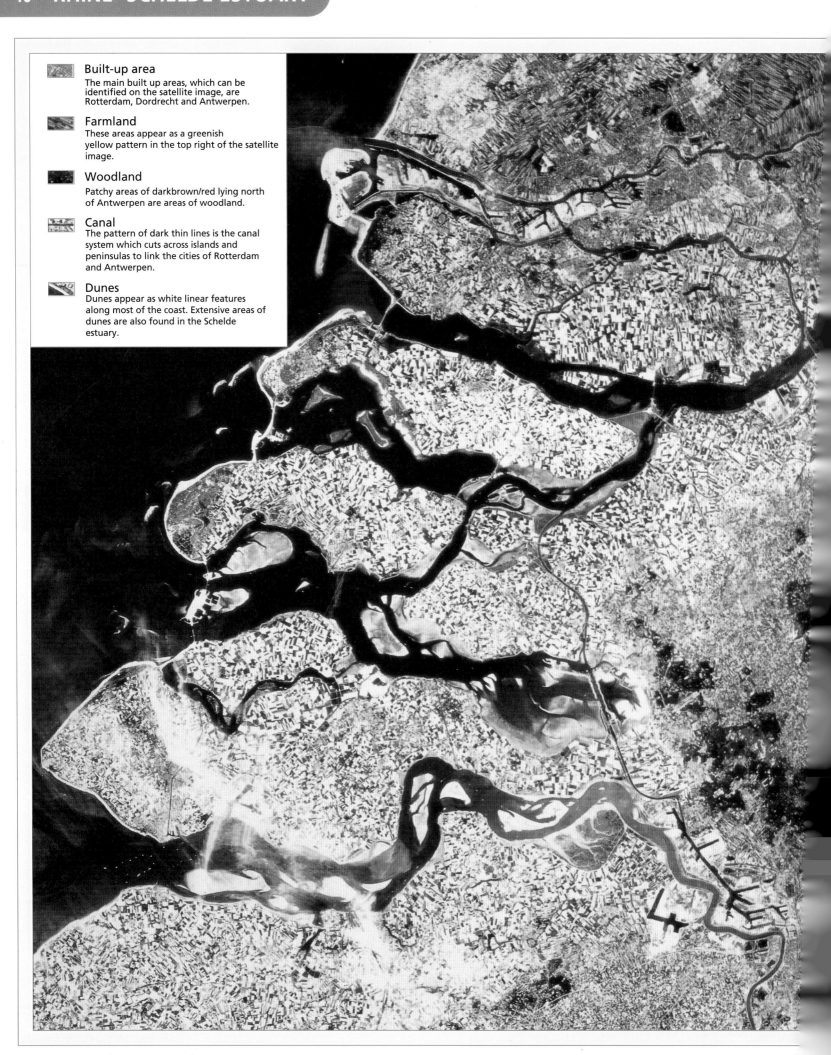

Built-up area
The main built up areas, which can be identified on the satellite image, are Rotterdam, Dordrecht and Antwerpen.

Farmland
These areas appear as a greenish yellow pattern in the top right of the satellite image.

Woodland
Patchy areas of darkbrown/red lying north of Antwerpen are areas of woodland.

Canal
The pattern of dark thin lines is the canal system which cuts across islands and peninsulas to link the cities of Rotterdam and Antwerpen.

Dunes
Dunes appear as white linear features along most of the coast. Extensive areas of dunes are also found in the Schelde estuary.

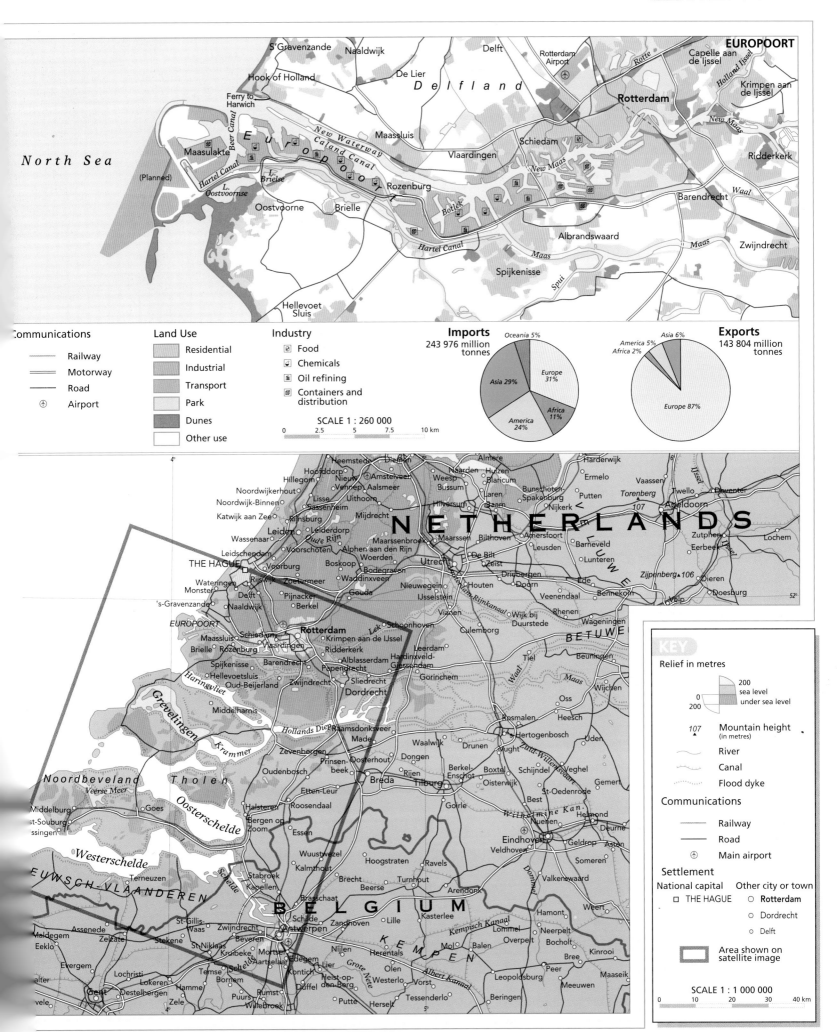

Lambert Azimuthal Equal Area projection

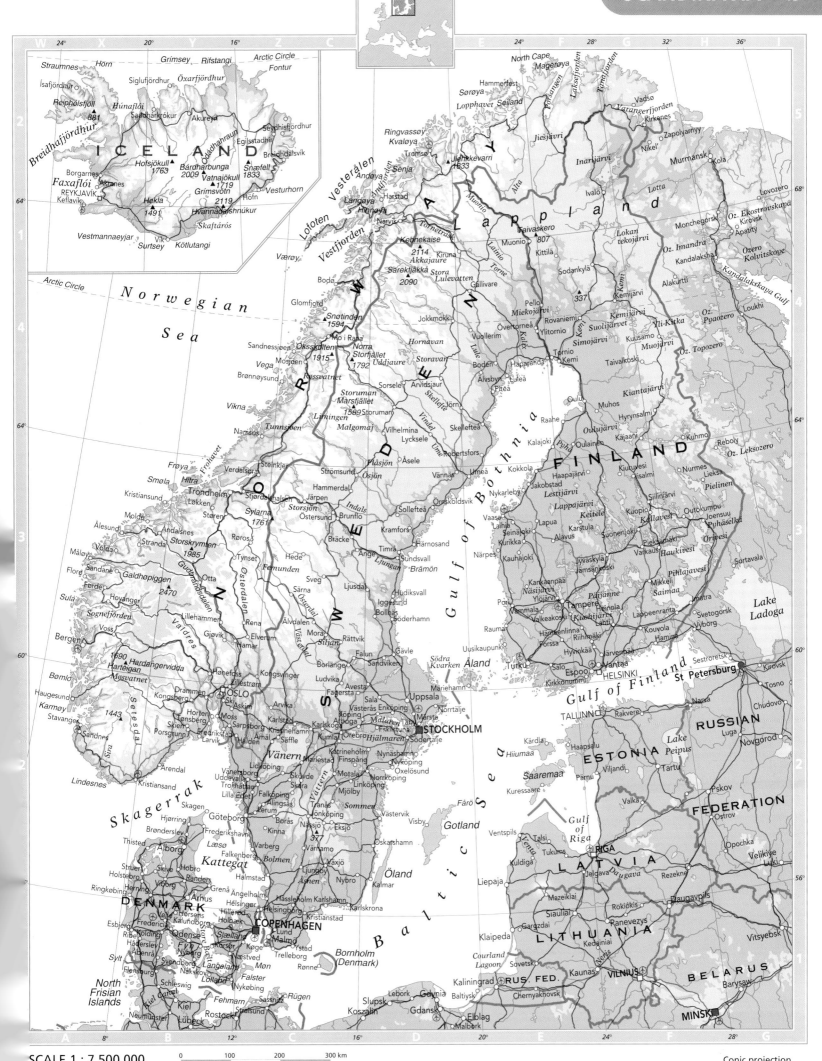

SCALE 1 : 7 500 000

0   100   200   300 km

Conic projection

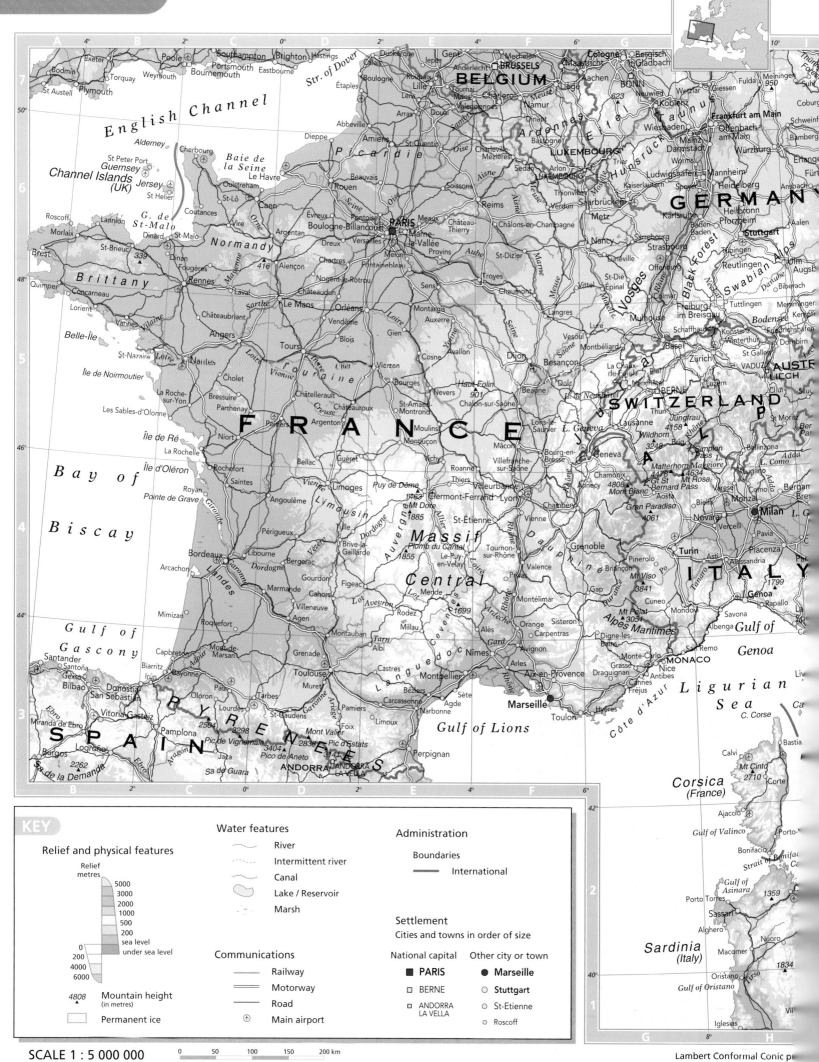

KEY

Relief and physical features

Relief
metres
5000
3000
2000
1000
500
200
sea level
0
200
under sea level
4000
6000

4808 ▲ Mountain height
(in metres)

Permanent ice

Water features

~ River
..... Intermittent river
~ Canal
Lake / Reservoir
Marsh

Communications

Railway
Motorway
Road
⊕ Main airport

Administration

Boundaries

International

Settlement

Cities and towns in order of size

National capital

■ PARIS

□ BERNE

□ ANDORRA
LA VELLA

Other city or town

● Marseille

◎ Stuttgart

○ St-Etienne

○ Roscoff

SCALE 1 : 5 000 000

0   50   100   150   200 km

Lambert Conformal Conic pr

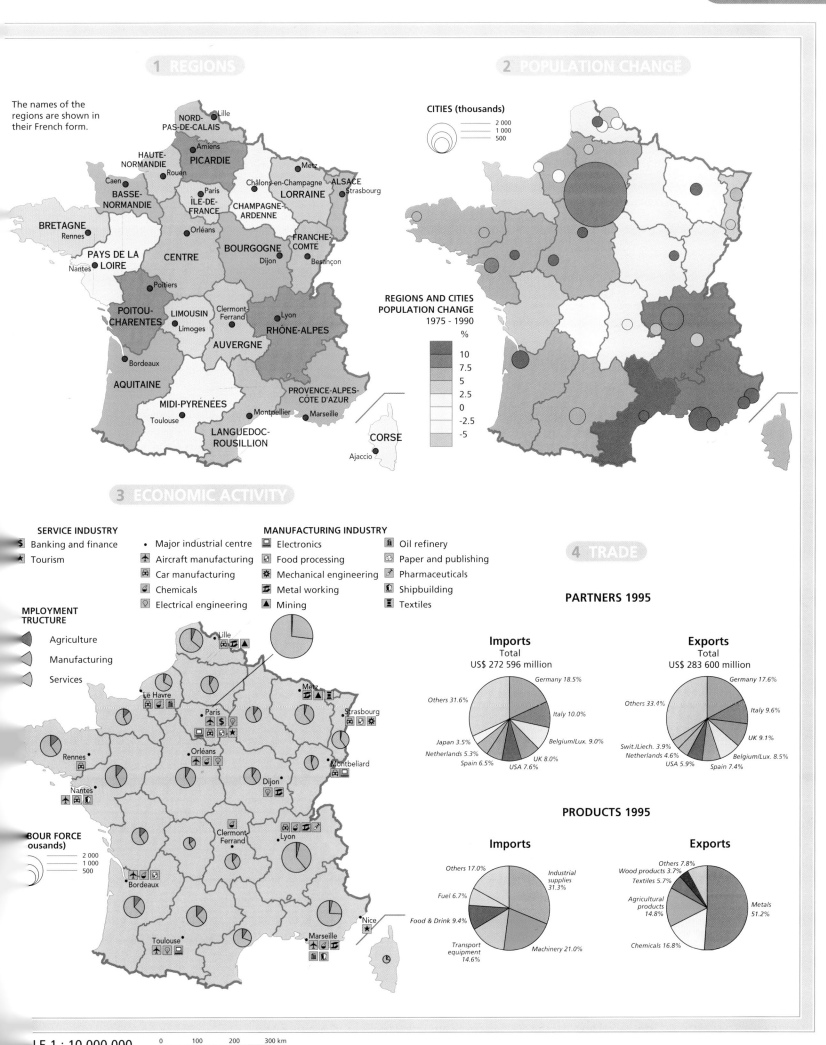

1 REGIONS

The names of the regions are shown in their French form.

NORD-PAS-DE-CALAIS
Lille
HAUTE-NORMANDIE
Amiens
PICARDIE
Metz
ALSACE
Caen
Rouen
Châlons-en-Champagne
Strasbourg
LORRAINE
BASSE-NORMANDIE
Paris
ÎLE-DE-FRANCE
CHAMPAGNE-ARDENNE
BRETAGNE
Rennes
Orléans
BOURGOGNE
FRANCHE-COMTÉ
PAYS DE LA LOIRE
CENTRE
Dijon
Besançon
Nantes
Poitiers
POITOU-CHARENTES
LIMOUSIN
Clermont-Ferrand
Lyon
Limoges
RHÔNE-ALPES
AUVERGNE
Bordeaux
AQUITAINE
PROVENCE-ALPES-CÔTE D'AZUR
MIDI-PYRÉNÉES
Montpellier
Marseille
Toulouse
LANGUEDOC-ROUSILLION
CORSE
Ajaccio

2 POPULATION CHANGE

CITIES (thousands)

2 000
1 000
500

REGIONS AND CITIES POPULATION CHANGE
1975 - 1990
%

10
7.5
5
2.5
0
-2.5
-5

3 ECONOMIC ACTIVITY

SERVICE INDUSTRY

$ Banking and finance
Tourism

MANUFACTURING INDUSTRY

• Major industrial centre
Aircraft manufacturing
Car manufacturing
Chemicals
Electrical engineering

Electronics
Food processing
Mechanical engineering
Metal working
Mining

Oil refinery
Paper and publishing
Pharmaceuticals
Shipbuilding
Textiles

EMPLOYMENT STRUCTURE

Agriculture
Manufacturing
Services

LABOUR FORCE (thousands)

2 000
1 000
500

Lille
Le Havre
Metz
Paris
Strasbourg
Orléans
Montbeliard
Rennes
Dijon
Nantes
Clermont-Ferrand
Lyon
Bordeaux
Nice
Toulouse
Marseille

4 TRADE

PARTNERS 1995

Imports
Total
US$ 272 596 million

Germany 18.5%
Others 31.6%
Italy 10.0%
Belgium/Lux. 9.0%
Japan 3.5%
Netherlands 5.3%
UK 8.0%
Spain 6.5%
USA 7.6%

Exports
Total
US$ 283 600 million

Germany 17.6%
Others 33.4%
Italy 9.6%
UK 9.1%
Swit./Liech. 3.9%
Netherlands 4.6%
Belgium/Lux. 8.5%
USA 5.9%
Spain 7.4%

PRODUCTS 1995

Imports

Others 17.0%
Industrial supplies 31.3%
Fuel 6.7%
Food & Drink 9.4%
Machinery 21.0%
Transport equipment 14.6%

Exports

Others 7.8%
Wood products 3.7%
Textiles 5.7%
Agricultural products 14.8%
Metals 51.2%
Chemicals 16.8%

SCALE 1 : 10 000 000

0   100   200   300 km

KEY

Relief and physical features

Relief
metres
5000
3000
2000
1000
500
200
sea level
0
under sea level
200
4000
6000

3482 ▲ Mountain height (in metres)

Water features

~ River
Intermittent river
Canal
Lake / Reservoir
Marsh

Communications

Railway
Motorway
Road
⊕ Main airport

Administration

Boundaries
International

Settlement

Cities and towns in order of size

National capital
■ MADRID
□ ANDORRA LA VELLA

Other city or town
● Barcelona
○ Malaga
○ Pamplona
○ Benidorm

Map labels

FRANCE
Limousin
Massif Central
Auvergne
Poitiers, Montluçon, Guéret, Vichy, Moulins, Bellac, Limoges, Puy de Dome 1463, Clermont-Ferrand, St-Étienne, Périgueux, Brive-la-Gaillarde, Tulle, Mt Dore 1885, Le-Puy-en-V., Bergerac, Gourdon, Figeac, Mende 1699, Villeneuve, Agen, Cahors, Rodez, Millau, Montauban, Albi, Tarn, Castres, Montpellier, Toulouse, Muret, St-Gaudens, Carcassonne, Limoux, Béziers, Agde, Sète, Narbonne, Perpignan, Gulf of Lion

PYRENEES
ANDORRA LA VELLA
Oloron 2504, Pau, Lourdes, Mont Valier 2838, Pic de Vignemale 3298, Pico de Aneto 3404, Pic d'Estats 3141, Figueres, Girona, Costa Brava

SPAIN
PORTUGAL

Gulf of Gascony
Cape Finisterre, A Coruña, Ferrol, Cervo, Luarca, Avilés, Gijón, Llanes, Santander, Santoña, Capbreton, Bayonne, Biarritz, San Sebastián, Donostia-San Sebastián, Irún, Bilbao, Gexto

CANTABRIAN MTS
Picos de Europa 2648, 2081, 2450, Espigüete, 2117, Aguilar de Campóo, Betanzos, Santiago, Vilagarcía, Pontevedra, Vigo, Tui, Ourense, Lugo, Sarria, Monforte, Ponferrada, Astorga, León, Benavente, Oviedo, Infiesto, Reinosa, Miranda de Ebro, Vitoria-Gasteiz, Logroño, Pamplona, Jaca, Sa de Guara, Huesca, Monzón, Barbastro, Aragón, Sa de la Demanda 2262, Soria, Tudela, Zaragoza, Cinca, Lleida, Manresa, Sabadell, Terrassa, Barcelona, Hospitalet de Llobregat, Mataró, Reus, Tarragona, Gulf of St Jordi, 1201

Ebro, Duero, Tormes
Aranda de Duero, Burgos, Palencia, Valladolid, Zamora, Tordesillas, Medina del Campo, Salamanca, Peñaranda de Bracamonte, Ávila, Segovia, Sierra de Guadarrama 2430, MADRID, Alcalá de Henares, Guadalajara, Arganda del Rey, Sigüenza, Henares, Serranía de Cuenca 1920, Calatayud, Jalón, Calamocha, Alcañiz, Tortosa, Guadalope

Oporto, Braga, Bragança, Macedo de Cavaleiros, Mirandela, Vila Real, Lamego, Viseu, Guarda, Aveiro, Viana do Castelo, 1415, Mino, 1205, Sa da Estrela 1993, Coimbra, Covilhã, Figueira da Foz, Mondego, Pombal, Caldas da Rainha, Torres Vedras, Santarém, Portalegre, Amadora, LISBON, Setúbal, Bay of Setúbal, Sines, C. da Roca

Ciudad-Rodrigo, Béjar, Plasencia, Navalmoral de la Mata, Almanzor 2592, Tiétar, Sierra de Gredos, Sierra de Guadalupe 1410, Montes de Toledo 1601, Talavera de la Reina, Toledo, Aranjuez, Tarancón, Cuenca 2020, Millárs, Castelló de la Plana, Sagunto, Valencia, Gulf of Valencia, Utiel, Cabriel, Júcar, Cáceres, Sa de San Pedro, Valencia de Alcántara, Elvas, Badajoz, Mérida, Don Benito, Guadiana, Zafra, Llerena, Zújar, Ardila, Beja, Évora, Setúbal, Grândola, Sado, Almodôvar, Portimão, Lagos, Cape St Vincent, Algarve, Faro, Tavira, Gulf of Cádiz

SIERRA MORENA
1104, 1300, Cijara L., Ciudad Real, Puertollano, Pozoblanco, Andújar, Linares, Úbeda, La Sagra 2382, Sierra de Segura 1897, La Mancha, Tomelloso, Villarrobledo, Manzanares, Valdepeñas, Albacete, Almansa, Gandía, Cullera, C. de la Nao, Alcoy, Villena, Elda, Benidorm, Alicante, Elche, Costa Blanca, Murcia, Torrevieja, C. de Palos, Cartagena, Águilas, Lorca, Caravaca de la Cruz, Baza, Huércal-Overa, Vera

Córdoba, Écija, Puente-Genil, Lucena, Alcalá la Real, Jaén, Guadix, Granada, Sierra Nevada, Mulhacén 3482, Almuñécar, Motril, Almería, C. de Gata

Seville, Las Marismas, Huelva, La Palma del Condado, Sanlúcar de Barrameda, Jeréz de la Frontera, Cádiz, Puerto de Santa Maria, San Fernando, C. Trafalgar, Morón de la Frontera, Utrera, Antequera, Vélez-Málaga, Ronda, Málaga, Torremolinos, Marbella, Costa del Sol, La Línea de la Concepción, Algeciras, Gibraltar (UK), Strait of Gibraltar, Pta Almina Ceuta (Sp.), Tangier, Tetouan, C. Negro, I. de Alboran (Sp.), Melilla (Sp.)

MOROCCO
Asilah, Larache, Chaouen, Al Hoceima

Guadalquivir, Guadalete, Genil

MEDITERRANEAN SEA

Menorca
Ciutadella de Menorca, Mahón

Balearic Islands
Mallorca 1445, Palma de Mallorca, Alcúdia, Ibiza, Eivissa, Formentera

Canary Islands
La Palma 2426, Sta Cruz de la Palma, Los Llanos de Aridane, San Cristóbal de la Laguna, Puerto de la Cruz, Pico del Teide 3718, Tenerife, Sta Cruz de Tenerife, Las Palmas de Gran Canaria, Gáldar, La Gomera 1487, San Sebastián de la Gomera, Frontera, Valverde, 1500, El Hierro, Pico de las Nieves 1949, Gran Canaria, Ingenio, Lanzarote, Arrecife, Corralejo, Fuerteventura 724, Tuineje 807

SCALE 1 : 5 000 000

0   50   100   150   200 km

Lambert Conformal Conic projection

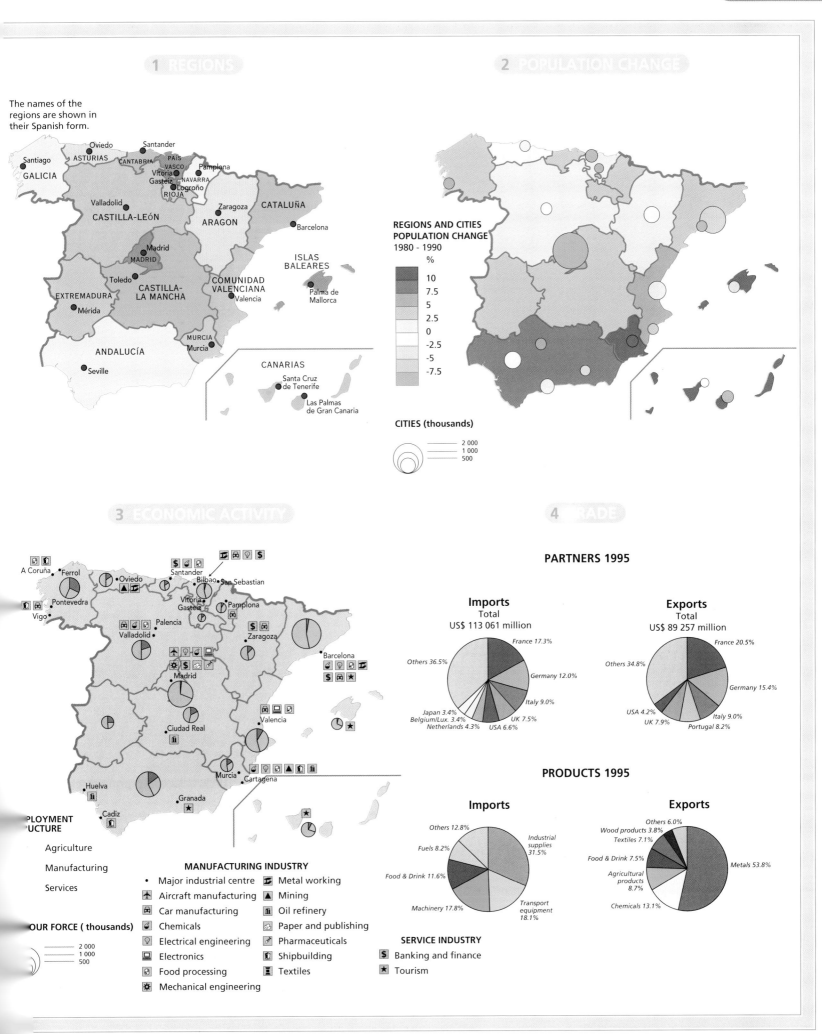

The names of the regions are shown in their Spanish form.

1 REGIONS

Santiago
GALICIA
Oviedo
ASTURIAS
CANTABRIA
Santander
PAÍS VASCO
Vitoria Gasteiz
Pamplona
NAVARRA
Logroño
RIOJA
Valladolid
CASTILLA-LEÓN
Zaragoza
ARAGON
CATALUÑA
Barcelona
Madrid
MADRID
Toledo
EXTREMADURA
Mérida
CASTILLA-LA MANCHA
COMUNIDAD VALENCIANA
Valencia
ISLAS BALEARES
Palma de Mallorca
MURCIA
Murcia
ANDALUCÍA
Seville
CANARIAS
Santa Cruz de Tenerife
Las Palmas de Gran Canaria

2 POPULATION CHANGE

REGIONS AND CITIES
POPULATION CHANGE
1980 - 1990
%
10
7.5
5
2.5
0
-2.5
-5
-7.5

CITIES (thousands)
2 000
1 000
500

3 ECONOMIC ACTIVITY

A Coruña
Ferrol
Oviedo
Santander
Bilbao
San Sebastian
Pontevedra
Vitoria Gasteiz
Pamplona
Vigo
Palencia
Valladolid
Zaragoza
Barcelona
Madrid
Ciudad Real
Valencia
Huelva
Murcia
Cartagena
Granada
Cádiz

EMPLOYMENT STRUCTURE

Agriculture

Manufacturing

Services

LABOUR FORCE (thousands)
2 000
1 000
500

MANUFACTURING INDUSTRY

- Major industrial centre
- Aircraft manufacturing
- Car manufacturing
- Chemicals
- Electrical engineering
- Electronics
- Food processing
- Mechanical engineering
- Metal working
- Mining
- Oil refinery
- Paper and publishing
- Pharmaceuticals
- Shipbuilding
- Textiles

SERVICE INDUSTRY

- Banking and finance
- Tourism

4 TRADE

PARTNERS 1995

Imports
Total
US$ 113 061 million

France 17.3%
Germany 12.0%
Italy 9.0%
UK 7.5%
USA 6.6%
Netherlands 4.3%
Belgium/Lux. 3.4%
Japan 3.4%
Others 36.5%

Exports
Total
US$ 89 257 million

France 20.5%
Germany 15.4%
Italy 9.0%
Portugal 8.2%
UK 7.9%
USA 4.2%
Others 34.8%

PRODUCTS 1995

Imports

Others 12.8%
Fuels 8.2%
Food & Drink 11.6%
Machinery 17.8%
Industrial supplies 31.5%
Transport equipment 18.1%

Exports

Others 6.0%
Wood products 3.8%
Textiles 7.1%
Food & Drink 7.5%
Agricultural products 8.7%
Chemicals 13.1%
Metals 53.8%

SCALE 1 : 12 000 000

0   100   200   300 km

North Frisian Is

NORTH

SEA

Heligoland Bay

West Frisian Islands

East Frisian Islands

Texel

Waddenzee

Den Helder

IJsselmeer

Zaandam

Haarlem

Leeuwarden

Groningen

Leer

Emden

Wilhelmshaven

Cuxhaven

Elbe

Itzehoe

Flensburg

Schleswig

Husum

Kiel Canal

Kiel

Neumünster

Kiel Bay

Fehmarn

Lübeck Bay

Lolland

Nakskov

Nykøbing

Falster

Stralsund

Rügen

Sassnitz

Greifswald

Baltic Sea

Słupsk

Łebork

Kołobrzeg

Koszalin

Szczecinek

Piła

Notec

Chojnice

NETHERLANDS

AMSTERDAM

THE HAGUE

Leiden

Utrecht

Hilversum

Apeldoorn

Arnhem

Enschede

Bremerhaven

Bremen

Oldenburg

Hamburg

Lüneburg

Schwerin

Wismar

Rostock

Neubrandenburg

Neustrelitz

L. Müritz

Schwedt

Eberswalde

Szczecin

Stargard

Gorzów Wielkopolski

Poznań

Gniezno

POLAND

Rotterdam

Dordrecht

Breda

Nijmegen

Bocholt

Münster

Hamm

Osnabrück

Celle

Aller

Hannover

Wolfsburg

Braunschweig

Hildesheim

Salzgitter

Magdeburg

Dessau

Brandenburg

Havel

BERLIN

Potsdam

Frankfurt

Eisenhüttenstadt

Oder

Zielona Góra

Głogów

Leszno

Rawicz

Zeebrugge

Oostende

Brugge

Antwerpen

Mechelen

Eindhoven

Tilburg

Krefeld

Duisburg

Essen

Dortmund

Wuppertal

Bielefeld

Paderborn

Kassel

Göttingen

Nordhausen

Elsleben

Halle

Leipzig

Cottbus

Spree

Hoyerswerda

Görlitz

Legnica

Wrocław

Wałbrzych

BELGIUM

BRUSSELS

Lille

Roubaix

Tournai

Mons

Charleroi

Namur

Liège

Maastricht

Aachen

Mönchengladbach

Düsseldorf

Leverkusen

Cologne

Bergisch Gladbach

Siegen

Marburg

Wetzlar

Giessen

Fulda

Meiningen

Suhl

Thüringian Forest

Erfurt

Jena

Gera

Zwickau

Chemnitz

Dresden

Freiberg

Děčín

Liberec

Jelenia Góra

Sudeten Mountains

Paczków

G E R M A N Y

1142

950

Ore Mts

CZECH

REPUBLIC

Anderlecht

Douai

Valenciennes

Sambre

Dinant

Ardennes

Eifel

BONN

Neuwied

Koblenz

Taunus

Wiesbaden

Mainz

Frankfurt am Main

Offenbach am Main

Darmstadt

Schweinfurt

Coburg

Bayreuth

Plauen

Hof

Cheb

Karlovy Vary

940

Kladno

PRAGUE

Plzeň

Pardubice

Svitavy

Brno

St-Quentin

Oise

Charleville-Mézières

Aisne

Sedan

Arlon

LUXEMBOURG

LUXEMBOURG

Trier

Mosel

Hunsrück

Worms

Ludwigshafen

Mannheim

Würzburg

Bamberg

Erlangen

Fürth

Nürnberg

Ansbach

Regensburg

Bohemian Forest

1453

Pisek

Tábor

Jihlava

České Budějovice

Znojmo

Brec

Reims

Soissons

Château-Thierry

Marne

Verdun

Metz

Nancy

Thionville

Saarbrücken

Kaiserslautern

Speyer

Heidelberg

Heilbronn

Karlsruhe

Pforzheim

Aalen

Ingolstadt

Straubing

Landshut

Passau

Linz

Gmünd

Hollabrunn

Provins

Aube

St-Dizier

Châlons-sur-Marne

Vittel

Épinal

St-Dié

Strasbourg

Offenburg

Baden-Baden

Tübingen

Reutlingen

Stuttgart

Alps

Ulm

Swabian Alps

Danube

Biberach

Augsburg

Memmingen

Kempten

Rosenheim

Steyr

Enns

St Pölten

VIENNA

BRATIS

Wiener Neustadt

Aspang-Markt

Troyes

Sens

Auxerre

Avallon

Provins

Langres

Lunéville

Nancy

Sarrebourg

Lure

Vesoul

Colmar

Mulhouse

Freiburg im Breisgau

Vosges

Black Forest

Rhine

Neckar

Tuttlingen

Schaffhausen

Konstanz

Friedrichshafen

Bodensee

Winterthur

St Gallen

Dornbirn

2962

Zugspitze

Innsbruck

Garmisch-Partenkirchen

Inn

Lech

Munich

Chiemsee

Salzburg

Kapfenberg

Leoben

Judenburg

Graz

Maribor

2140

F R A N C E

Besançon

Dole

Biel

Zurich

Basel

Rhine

Aar

SWITZERLAND

LIECH.

A U S T R I A

Villach

Klagenfurt

Drau

Udine

Gorizia

Trieste

Celje

SLOVENIA

LJUBLJANA

Sava

1796

Kupa

ZAGR

Dijon

Saône

Montbéliard

Mulhouse

Gulf of Venice

Istra

Krk

Rijeka

CROAT

Cres

Pula

Pag

Gospić

Karlovac

Sisak

Bihać

Osijek

Dinant

623

1 REGIONS

1. BERLIN
2. BREMEN
3. HAMBURG
4. SAARLAND

Kiel
SCHLESWIG-
HOLSTEIN
3. Hamburg
MECKLENBURG-
Schwerin
VORPOMMERN
2. Bremen
NIEDERSACHSEN
Hannover
Potsdam
1. Berlin
Magdeburg
BRANDENBURG
NORDRHEIN-
WESTFALEN
SACHSEN-
ANHALT
Düsseldorf
Erfurt
Dresden
THÜRINGEN
SACHSEN
HESSEN
RHEINLAND-
Wiesbaden
PFALZ
Mainz
4.
Saarbrücken
BAYERN
Stuttgart
BADEN-
WÜRTTEMBERG
Munich

The names of the
regions are shown
in their German form.

2 POPULATION CHANGE

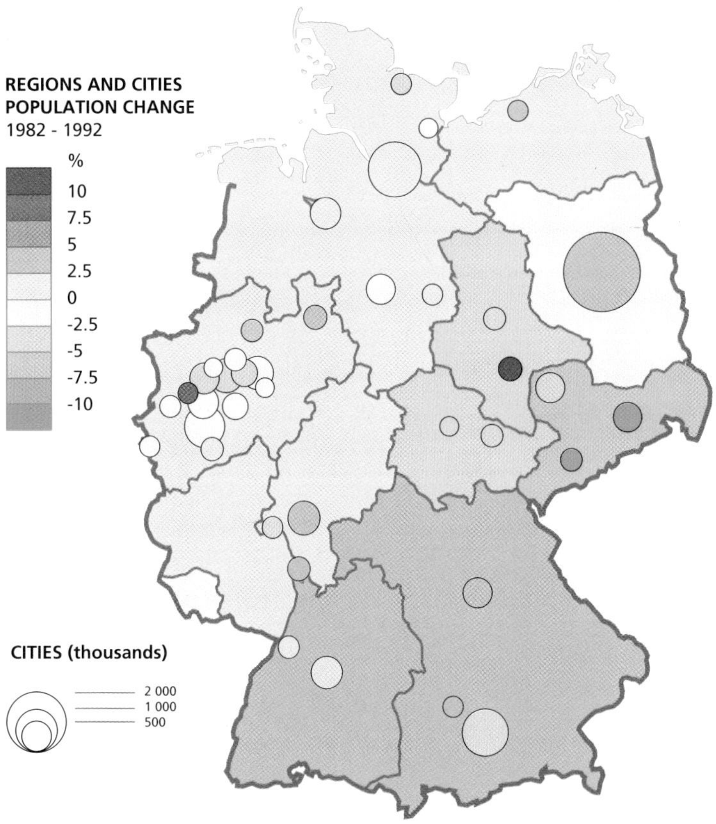

REGIONS AND CITIES
POPULATION CHANGE
1982 - 1992

%
10
7.5
5
2.5
0
-2.5
-5
-7.5
-10

CITIES (thousands)

2 000
1 000
500

3 ECONOMIC ACTIVITY

SERVICE INDUSTRY

Banking and finance
Tourism

MANUFACTURING INDUSTRY

Major industrial centre

Aircraft manufacturing
Car manufacturing
Chemicals
Electrical engineering
Electronics
Food processing
Mechanical engineering
Metal working
Mining
Oil refinery
Paper and publishing
Pharmaceuticals
Shipbuilding
Textiles

EMPLOYMENT
STRUCTURE

Agriculture

Manufacturing

Services

LABOUR FORCE
(thousands)

2 000
1 000
500

Hamburg
Bremen
Hannover
Braunschweig
Berlin
Düsseldorf
Kassel
Cologne
Dresden
Koblenz
Frankfurt
Saarbrücken
Nürnberg
Stuttgart
Munich

4 TRADE

PARTNERS 1995

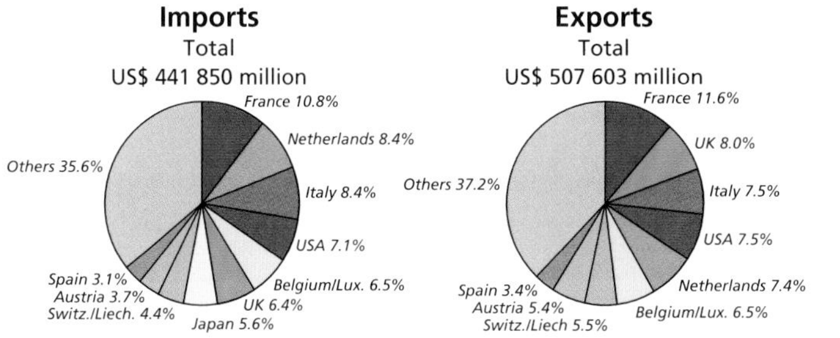

Imports
Total
US$ 441 850 million

Others 35.6%
France 10.8%
Netherlands 8.4%
Italy 8.4%
USA 7.1%
Belgium/Lux. 6.5%
UK 6.4%
Japan 5.6%
Switz./Liech. 4.4%
Austria 3.7%
Spain 3.1%

Exports
Total
US$ 507 603 million

Others 37.2%
France 11.6%
UK 8.0%
Italy 7.5%
USA 7.5%
Netherlands 7.4%
Belgium/Lux. 6.5%
Switz./Liech. 5.5%
Austria 5.4%
Spain 3.4%

PRODUCTS 1995

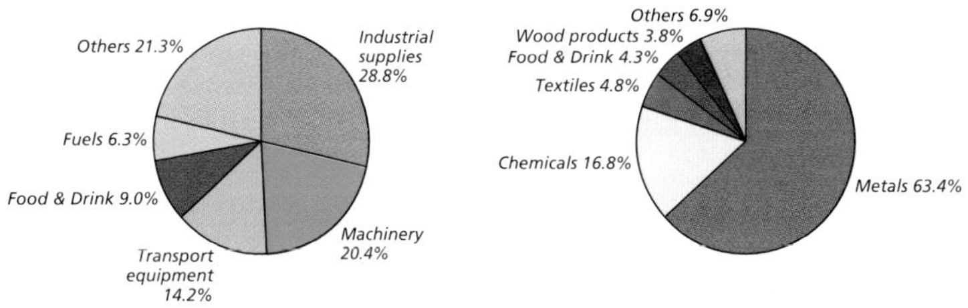

Imports

Others 21.3%
Industrial
supplies
28.8%
Fuels 6.3%
Food & Drink 9.0%
Transport
equipment
14.2%
Machinery
20.4%

Exports

Others 6.9%
Wood products 3.8%
Food & Drink 4.3%
Textiles 4.8%
Chemicals 16.8%
Metals 63.4%

SCALE 1 : 7 500 000

0   100   200   300 km

Administration

Boundaries

———— International

Settlement

Cities and towns in order of size

National capital   Other city or town

■ ROME   ● Milan

□ SARAJEVO   ○ Genoa

□ SAN MARINO   ○ Venice

                          ○ Ragusa

KEY

Relief and physical features

Relief
metres
5000
3000
2000
1000
500
200
sea level
under sea level
0
200
4000
6000

▲ 4634   Mountain height
          (in metres)

          Permanent ice

Water features

～～ River

～～ Canal

◯ Lake / Reservoir

Communications

——— Railway

═══ Motorway

——— Road

⊕ Main airport

SCALE 1 : 5 000 000

0   50   100   150   200 km

Lambert Conformal Conic pr

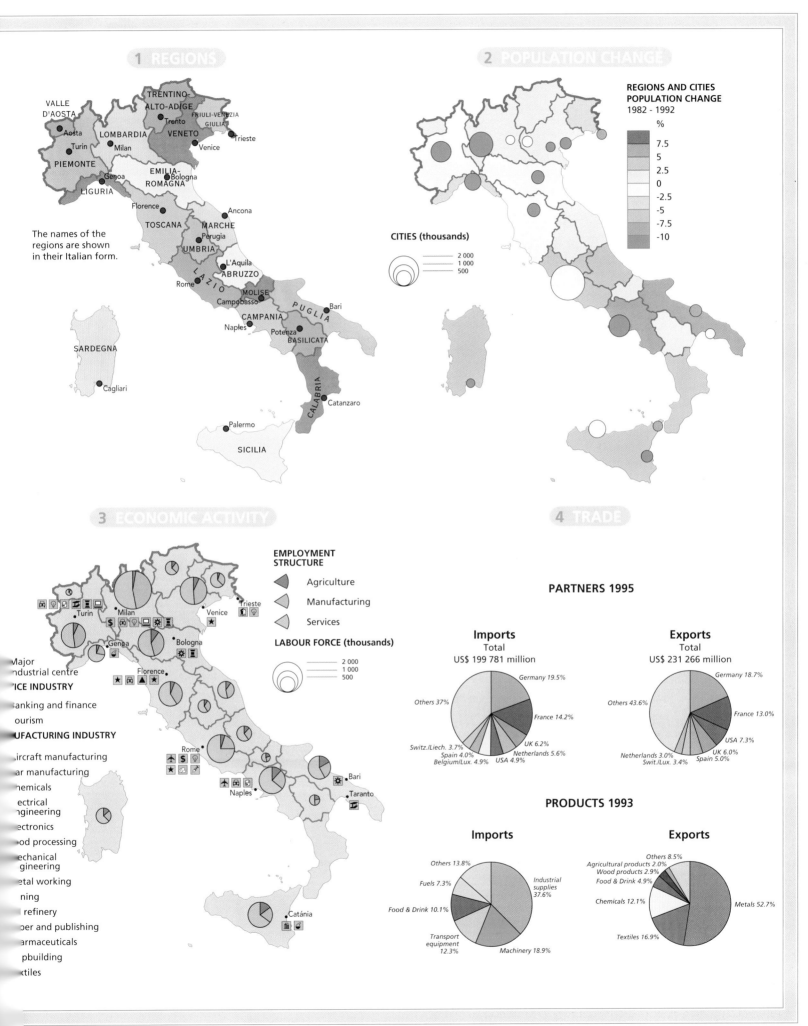

1 REGIONS

VALLE D'AOSTA
Aosta
Turin
PIEMONTE
LOMBARDIA
Milan
TRENTINO-ALTO-ADIGE
Trento
FRIULI-VENEZIA GIULIA
VENETO
Venice
Trieste
Genoa
LIGURIA
EMILIA-ROMAGNA
Bologna
Florence
TOSCANA
Ancona
MARCHE
Perugia
UMBRIA
L'Aquila
ABRUZZO
Rome
LAZIO
MOLISE
Campobasso
PUGLIA
Bari
CAMPANIA
Naples
Potenza
BASILICATA
CALABRIA
Catanzaro
Palermo
SICILIA
SARDEGNA
Cagliari

The names of the regions are shown in their Italian form.

2 POPULATION CHANGE

REGIONS AND CITIES POPULATION CHANGE
1982 - 1992

%
7.5
5
2.5
0
-2.5
-5
-7.5
-10

CITIES (thousands)
2 000
1 000
500

3 ECONOMIC ACTIVITY

Turin
Milan
Venice
Trieste
Genoa
Bologna
Florence
Rome
Naples
Bari
Taranto
Catánia

EMPLOYMENT STRUCTURE
Agriculture
Manufacturing
Services

LABOUR FORCE (thousands)
2 000
1 000
500

Major industrial centre

SERVICE INDUSTRY
Banking and finance
Tourism

MANUFACTURING INDUSTRY
Aircraft manufacturing
Car manufacturing
Chemicals
Electrical engineering
Electronics
Food processing
Mechanical engineering
Metal working
Mining
Oil refinery
Paper and publishing
Pharmaceuticals
Shipbuilding
Textiles

4 TRADE

PARTNERS 1995

Imports
Total
US$ 199 781 million

Germany 19.5%
France 14.2%
UK 6.2%
Netherlands 5.6%
USA 4.9%
Belgium/Lux. 4.9%
Spain 4.0%
Switz./Liech. 3.7%
Others 37%

Exports
Total
US$ 231 266 million

Germany 18.7%
France 13.0%
USA 7.3%
UK 6.0%
Spain 5.0%
Swit./Lux. 3.4%
Netherlands 3.0%
Others 43.6%

PRODUCTS 1993

Imports
Industrial supplies 37.6%
Machinery 18.9%
Transport equipment 12.3%
Food & Drink 10.1%
Fuels 7.3%
Others 13.8%

Exports
Metals 52.7%
Textiles 16.9%
Chemicals 12.1%
Food & Drink 4.9%
Wood products 2.9%
Agricultural products 2.0%
Others 8.5%

E 1 : 10 500 000

0   100   200   300 km

Bay of Biscay

GERMANY

FRANCE

Massif Central

Pyrenees

PORTUGAL

SPAIN

MOROCCO

ALGERIA

TUNISIA

HIGH ATLAS

Hauts Plateaux

Saharan Atlas

MEDITERRANEAN

KEY

Relief and physical features

Relief
metres

	5000
	3000
	2000
	1000
	500
	200
	sea level
	under sea level
	200
	4000
	6000

▲ 4808   Mountain height
(in metres)

Water features

〜 River
⋯ Intermittent river
〜 Canal
⬭ Lake / Reservoir
⬭ Intermittent lake
⬭ Marsh

Communications

—— Railway
—— Road
⊕ Main airport

Administration

Boundaries

—— International
--- Disputed

Settlement

Cities and towns in order of size

National capital   Other city or town

■ ALGIERS   ● Naples
□ ATHENS   ○ Valencia
□ TIRANA   ○ Nice
▫ VALLETTA   ○ Faro

SCALE 1 : 10 000 000   0 100 200 300 400 km

Conic projection

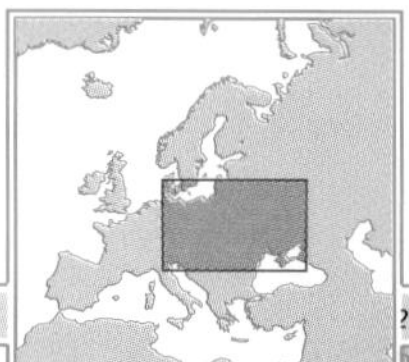

KEY

Relief and physical features

Relief metres

5000
3000
2000
1000
500
200
0 sea level
under sea level
200
4000
6000

▲ 3798 Mountain height (in metres)

Permanent ice

Water features

River
Canal
Lake / Reservoir
Marsh

Communications

Railway
Motorway
Road
⊕ Main airport

Administration

Boundaries
International

Settlement

Cities and towns in order of size

National capital | Other city or town
■ WARSAW | ● Kharkhiv
□ CHIŞINĂU | ◉ Krakow
□ BRATISLAVA | ○ Brno
□ VADUZ | ○ Chelm

SCALE 1 : 5 000 000

0   50   100   150   200 km

DENMARK

SWEDEN

COPENHAGEN

Kiel Bay

Baltic Sea

Bornholm

Gulf of Gdańsk

RUSSIAN FED

Klaipėda

Kaliningrad

GERMANY

BERLIN

Potsdam

Magdeburg

Leipzig

POLAND

WARSAW

Poznań

Wrocław

Łódź

Kraków

Silesian Plateau

Sudeten Mts

Ore Mts

CZECH REPUBLIC

PRAGUE

Bohemian Forest

Carpathian Mts

SLOVAKIA

Košice

VIENNA

BRATISLAVA

AUSTRIA

Munich

SWITZERLAND

VADUZ

ALPS

Dolomites

ITALY

Milan

SLOVENIA

LJUBLJANA

ZAGREB

CROATIA

BOSNIA-HERZEGOVINA

YUGOSLAVIA

HUNGARY

BUDAPEST

Gr. Glockner ▲ 3798

Zugspitze 2962

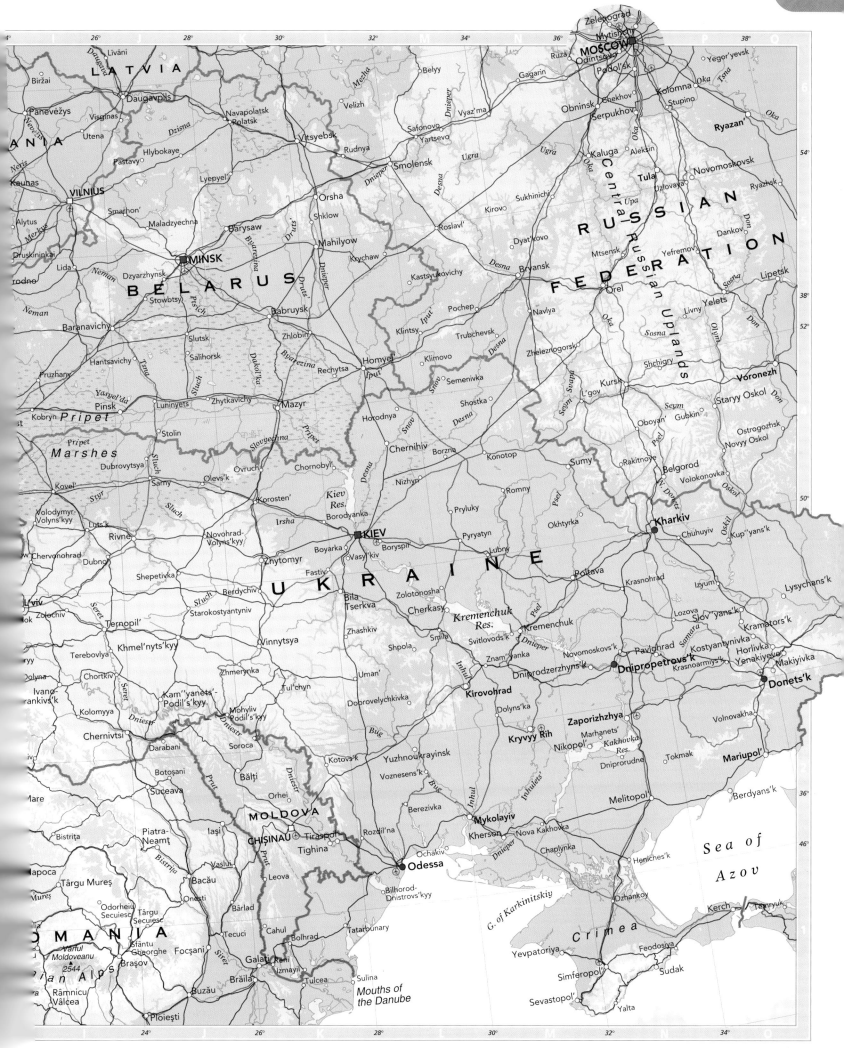

KEY

Relief and physical features

Relief
metres
5000
3000
2000
1000
500
200
sea level
0
under sea level
200
4000
6000

3971 ▲ Mountain height
(in metres)

Water features

~~~ River
···· Intermittent river
Canal
Lake / Reservoir
Intermittent lake
Marsh

Communications

Railway
Motorway
Road
⊕ Main airport

Administration

Boundaries
International
Internal

Settlement

Cities and towns in order of size

National capital | Other city or town
■ ATHENS | ● İstanbul
□ SKOPJE | ○ Konya
□ NICOSIA | ○ Thessaloniki
| ○ Dubrovnik

SCALE 1 : 5 000 000

0   50   100   150   200 km

ADRIATIC SEA
ITALY
IONIAN SEA
MEDITERRAN
Sea of Crete

CROATIA
BOSNIA-HERZEGOVINA
YUGOSLAVIA
ROMANIA
BULGARIA
MACEDONIA
ALBANIA
GREECE

ZAGREB
SARAJEVO
BELGRADE
BUCHAREST
SOFIA
SKOPJE
TIRANË
ATHENS

Dinaric Alps
Dalmatia
Transylvanian Alps
Balkan Mts
Rhodope Mts
Pindus Mountains
Cyclades
Ionian Islands
Strait of Otranto
Gulf of Taranto

Istra, Pula, Cres, Krk, Rijeka, Ogulin, Karlovac, Metlika, Varaždin, Drava, Sisak, Subotica, Sombor, Kikinda, Arad, Lipova, Brad, Alba Iulia, Onesti, Sfântu Gheorghe, Braşov, Focşani

Pag, Dugi Otok, Zadar, Knin, Bosanska Dubica, Banja Luka, Bihać, Novi Sad, Zrenjanin, Vršac, Reşiţa, Timişoara, Lugoj, Deva, Sibiu, Vârful Moldoveanu 2544, Mt Mindra 2519, Târgu Jiu, Râmnica Vâlcea, Buzău

Gospić 1758, Šibenik, Split, Brač, Vis, Hvar, Korcula, Mljet, Dobor, Tuzla, Zenica, Travnik, Srebrenica, Sava, Ruma, Šabac, Loznica, Valjevo, Požarevac, Kragujevac, Orşova, Drobeta-Turnu Severin, Negotin, Vidin, Craiova, Slatina, Pitești, Drăgăşani, Ploiești, Ialomiţa

Pescara, Termoli, Campobasso, San Severo, Manfredonia, Dubrovnik, Kotor, Podgorica, Nikšić, Pljevlja, 2522 Tara, Novi Pazar, Ibar, Kraljevo, Kruševac, Niš, Pirot, Zaječar, Lom, Pleven, Vratsa, Lovech, Osŭm, Veliko Tŭrnovo, Razgrad, Ruse

Bar, L. Shkodër, Shkodër, Peshkopi, Durrës, Debar, 2650, 2656 Daravica, Peć, Đakovica, Prizren, Kosovska Mitrovica, Priština, Kuršumlija, Leskovac, Vranje, Kumanovo, Kočani, Veles, Vardar, Kyustendil, Pernik, Botevgrad, Blagoevgrad, Pazardzhik, Plovdiv, Stara Zagora, Sliven, Karnobat, Elkhovo

Brindisi, Lecce, Otranto, C. Sta Maria di Leuca, Gallipoli, Vlorë, Berat, Seman, Elbasan, Tiranë, Ohrid, Lake Ohrid, L. Prespa, Bitola, Strumica, Gevgelija, Petrich, Kilkis, Serres, Drama, Xanthi, Komotini, Kavala, Smolyan, Kŭrdzhali, Kırklareli, Edirne

Korçë, Florina, Kastoria, Kozani, Edessa, Thessaloniki, Kalamaria, C. Platí, Thasos, Samothraki, Alexandroupoli, Keşan, G. of Saros, Gökçeada, Gallip

Sarandë, Corfu, Ioannina, Igoumenitsa, Preveza, Arta, Trikala, Pineios, Larisa, Ossa 1978, Volos, Northern Sporades, Limnos, Dardanelles, Ezine, Edremit, Ayva, Smolikas 2637, Grammos, Mt Athos 2033, Agios Efstratios, Lesvos, Mytilini

Lefkada, Kefallonia, Mesolóngi, G. of Patras, Patras, Oiti 2152, Parnassos 2457, Chalkida, Evvoia, Skyros, 1343, Psara, Chios, G. of Izmir, Karaburun

Zakynthos, Pyrgos, Kyparissia, Kyllini 2376, Corinth, G. of Corinth, Megara, ATHENS, Piraeus, Marathonas C., Kafireas, Andros, Tinos, Ikaria, Samos, Nafplio, Aigina, Kea, Kythnos, Paros, Naxos, Amorgos

Sparti, Kalamata, G. of Messinia, G. of Lakonia, C. Matapan, C. Maléa, Kythira, Milos, Ios, Thira, Tripoli

Antikythira, C. Spátha, Chania, Rethymno, Idi 2456, Crete, Iraklion, Siteia, Karpath, Kasos

Achelöos, Acheloos, Kalamata

MOLDOVA

UKRAINE

Sea of Azov

RUSSIAN FEDERATION

Crimea

Kerch

Krasnodar

Korenovsk

Kuban'

GEORGIA

BLACK SEA

Pontine Mountains

Sinop

Samsun

Trabzon

Rize

ANKARA

TURKEY

Anatolia

Taurus Mountains

Konya

Adana

Aleppo

Euphrates

CYPRUS

NICOSIA

SYRIA

LEBANON

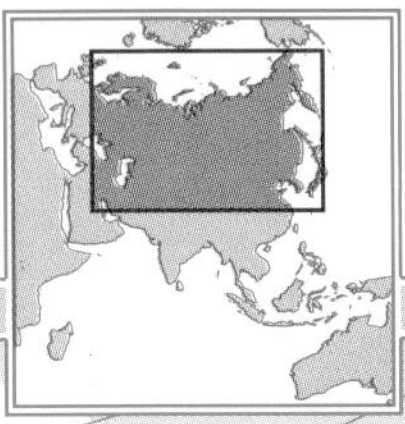

KEY

Relief and physical features

Relief
metres
5000
3000
2000
1000
500
200
sea level
0
under sea level
200
4000
6000

▲ 4750 Mountain height (in metres)

Permanent ice

Water features

~ River

Intermittent river

Lake / Reservoir

Intermittent lake

Marsh

Communications

Railway

Road

⊕ Main airport

Administration

Boundaries

International

Internal

Settlement

Cities and towns in order of size

National capital | Other city or town
■ MOSCOW | ● Ufa
□ RIGA | ○ Penza
□ TALLINN | ○ Archangel
▫ ULAN BATOR | ○ Kotlas

SCALE 1 : 20 000 000

0   200   400   600   800 km

Map labels (selected):

ICELAND, Torshavn, Faeroes (Den.), NORWEGIAN SEA, Jan Mayen (Nor.), Arctic Circle, Svalbard (Norway), Spitsbergen, Nordaustlandet, Bear Island, BARENTS SEA, Franz Josef Land, Novaya Zemlya, Kara Sea, NORWAY, SWEDEN, Bergen, Trondheim, Oslo, Luleå, Tornio, North Cape, Murmansk, C. Kanin, Kolguyev, Vaygach, Yamal Pen., Gydan Peninsula, Gulf of Ob, Novyy Port, Salekhard, Vorkuta, Narodnaya 1894, STOCKHOLM, Uppsala, Turku, FINLAND, HELSINKI, Tampere, Baltic Sea, Gulf of Bothnia, G. of Finland, Kola Pen., Kem', White Sea, Archangel, Pinega, Mezen, Pechora, Naryan Mar, Ukhta, Pechorsk, Troitsko-Pechorsk

RIGA, LATVIA, ESTONIA, TALLINN, Tartu, Pskov, LITHUANIA, VILNIUS, Liepāja, Klaipeda, Šiauliai, Daugavpils, St Petersburg, Ladoga, L. Onega, Petrozavodsk, Novgorod, Cherepovets, Rybinsk Reservoir, Vel'sk, Kotlas, Syktyvkar, Solikamsk, Berezniki

BELARUS, MINSK, Homyel', Mahilyow, Vitsyebsk, Smolensk, Velikiye Luki, Tver', Yaroslavl', Vologda, Rybinsk, Kostroma, Ivanovo, MOSCOW, Dzerzhinsk, Nizhniy Novgorod, Vladimir, Murom, Ryazan', Vyatka, Kama, Izhevsk, Perm, Serov, Nizhniy Tagil, Khanty-Mansiysk, Surgut, Nizhnevartovsk

RUSSIAN FEDERATION, West Siberian Plain, Ob, Irtysh, Tobol, Tyumen, Yekaterinburg, Ural'skiy, Kamensk-Ural'skiy, Chelyabinsk, Kurgan, Petropavlovsk, Omsk, Novosibirsk

UKRAINE, Kyiv, Kharkiv, Dnipropetrovsk, Donets'k, Luhans'k, Zaporizhzhya, Mykolayiv, Odessa, Kherson, Kremenchuk, Kirovohrad, Cherkasy, Bryansk, Orel, Kursk, Belgorod, Voronezh, Lipetsk, Tambov, Penza, Saransk, Simbirsk, Syzran, Samara, To'lyatti, Saratov, Engels, Kazan, Naberezhnye Chelny, Ufa, Sterlitamak, Salavat, Magnitogorsk, Orenburg, Orsk, Aktyubinsk, Kustanay, Rudnyy, Kokshetau, AKMOLA

ROMANIA, BUCHAREST, MOLDOVA, BULGARIA, Istanbul, BLACK SEA, Sevastopol, Crimea, Sea of Azov, Mariupol', Rostov-na-Donu, Krasnodar, Novorossiysk, Sochi, Stavropol Highlands, CAUCASUS, Mt Elbrus 5642, Grozny, Makhachkala, Astrakhan', Caspian Depression, Volgograd, Volzhskiy, Kamyshin, Ural'sk, Ural, Atyrau, Fort Shevchenko, Aktau, CASPIAN SEA, Ust Urt Plateau, Aral Sea, UZBEKISTAN, Nukus, TURKMENISTAN, KAZAKHSTAN, Karaganda, Temirtau, Zhezkazgan, L. Balkhash, Kzyl-Orda, Syrdar'ya

TURKEY, ANKARA, GEORGIA, TBILISI, ARMENIA, YEREVAN, AZERBAIJAN, BAKU, Sumqayit, Gäncä, Tabriz, IRAN, Lake Urmia, Mt Ararat 5165, SYRIA, IRAQ, Mosul, Euphrates, Tigris

Conic Equidistant projection

Relief

Relief metres
5000
3000
2000
1000
500
200
sea level
0
200 under sea level
4000
6000

Ice cap

BERING SEA

Wrangel I.

Nunivak I.

St Lawrence I.

Bering Strait

Pt Barrow

BEAUFORT SEA

Brooks Range

Yukon

Bristol Bay

Alaska Range
▲Mt McKinley
6194

Alaska Pen.

Kodiak I.

GULF OF ALASKA

Alexander Archipelago

Queen Charlotte Islands

Mt Logan
6050

Mackenzie Mts

Coast Mountains

Vancouver Island

Fraser

Columbia

Cascade Ra.

Snake

Sierra Nevada

Mt Whitney
4418

Great Basin

Colorado

Grand Canyon

Colorado Plateau

Lower California

Gulf of California

Guadalupe

C. San Lucas

Sierra Madre Occidental

Altiplano Mexicano

Sierra Madre Oriental

Rio Grande

ROCKY MOUNTAINS

Great Salt L.

Yellowstone

Gannett Pk 4202

GREAT PLAINS

Missouri

Arkansas

Red

Edwards Plateau

Ozark Plateau

Mississippi

Ohio

Banks Island

Victoria Island

Parry Islands

Great Bear L.

Great Slave L.

Peace

Mackenzie

Lake Athabasca

Churchill

Nelson

Severn

Lake Winnipeg

HUDSON BAY

Southampton I.

Foxe Basin

Belcher Is

Queen Elizabeth Islands

Ellesmere Island

BAFFIN BAY

Baffin Island

Hudson Strait

CANADIAN SHIELD

Lake Superior

L. Huron

Lake Michigan

L. Erie

L. Ontario

St Lawrence

Gulf of St Lawrence

Newfoundland

Cape Breton I.

C. Sable

C. Cod

Chesapeake B.

C. Hatteras

C. Fear

C. Canaveral

Appalachian Mts

Greenland

Denmark Strait

Arctic Circle

Iceland

Faeroes

Davis Strait

Cape Farewell

Labrador Sea

Labrador

ATLANTIC OCEAN

Bermuda

Tropic of Cancer

Bahamas

GULF OF MEXICO

Str. of Florida

Cuba

Yucatán Channel

Campeche Bay

Yucatán

Popocatépetl
5452

Sierra Madre del Sur

G. of Honduras

Sierra Madre

L. Nicaragua

Greater Antilles

Hispaniola

Jamaica

CARIBBEAN SEA

Puerto Rico

Lesser Antilles

Curaçao

G. of Darién

Isthmus of Panama

Clipperton I.

I. de Coco

I. de Malpelo

Galapagos Islands

G. de Guayaquil

Cordillera Occidental

Cordillera Central

Cotopaxi
5896

Chimborazo
6310

Orinoco

Equator

Inset map

GREENLAND

U.S.A.

CANADA

UNITED STATES OF AMERICA

MEXICO

BAHAMAS

CUBA

H. D.R.

J.

B.
G. HO.
E.S. N.
C.R. P.

B. BELIZE
C.R. COSTA RICA
D.R. DOMINICAN REPUBLIC
E.S. EL SALVADOR
G. GUATEMALA
H. HAITI
HO. HONDURAS
J. JAMAICA
N. NICARAGUA
P. PANAMA

SCALE 1 : 90 000 000

Chamberlin Trimetric projection

1 TEMPERATURE AND PRESSURE : JANUARY

Average temperature °C
24
16
8
0
-8
-16
-24
-32

Wind direction

Isobar in millibars reduced to sea level

2 TEMPERATURE AND PRESSURE : JULY

Average temperature °C
32
24
16
8
0
-8

Wind direction

Isobar in millibars reduced to sea level

3 ANNUAL RAINFALL

Average annual rainfall mm
3000
2000
1000
500
250
0

4 STATISTICS

Saskatoon (515 metres)	Jan	Feb	Mar	Apr	May	Jun	Jul	Aug	Sep	Oct	Nov	Dec
Temperature - max.(°C)	-13	-11	-3	9	18	22	25	24	17	11	-1	-9
Temperature - min. (°C)	-24	-22	-14	-3	3	9	11	9	3	-3	-11	-19
Rainfall - (mm)	23	13	18	18	36	66	61	48	38	23	13	15

Vancouver (14 metres)	Jan	Feb	Mar	Apr	May	Jun	Jul	Aug	Sep	Oct	Nov	Dec
Temperature - max.(°C)	5	7	10	14	18	21	23	23	18	14	9	6
Temperature - min. (°C)	0	1	3	4	8	11	12	12	9	7	4	2
Rainfall - (mm)	218	147	127	84	71	64	31	43	91	147	211	224

Charleston (3 metres)	Jan	Feb	Mar	Apr	May	Jun	Jul	Aug	Sep	Oct	Nov	Dec
Temperature - max.(°C)	14	15	19	23	27	30	31	31	28	24	19	15
Temperature - min. (°C)	6	7	10	14	19	23	24	24	22	16	11	7
Rainfall - (mm)	74	84	86	71	81	119	185	168	130	81	58	71

Acapulco (3 metres)	Jan	Feb	Mar	Apr	May	Jun	Jul	Aug	Sep	Oct	Nov	Dec
Temperature - max.(°C)	31	31	31	32	32	33	32	33	32	32	32	31
Temperature - min. (°C)	22	22	22	23	25	25	25	25	24	24	23	22
Rainfall - (mm)	6	1	0	1	36	281	256	252	349	159	28	8

Detroit (189 metres)	Jan	Feb	Mar	Apr	May	Jun	Jul	Aug	Sep	Oct	Nov	Dec
Temperature - max.(°C)	-1	0	6	13	19	25	28	27	23	16	8	2
Temperature - min. (°C)	-7	-8	-3	3	9	14	17	17	13	7	1	-4
Rainfall - (mm)	53	53	64	64	84	91	84	69	71	61	61	58

SCALE 1 : 75 000 000

Bonne projection

In April 1999 NUNAVUT will be established as a new Canadian territory.

KEY

Relief and physical features

Relief
metres

5000
3000
2000
1000
500
200
0 sea level
under sea level
200
4000
6000

0194 ▲ Mountain height
(in metres)

☐ Permanent ice

Water features

~ River

~ Lake / Reservoir

~ Intermittent lake

~ Marsh

Communications

—— Railway

—— Road

⊕ Main airport

Administration

Boundaries

—— International

----- Internal

Settlement

Cities and towns in order of size

National capital   Other city or town

☐ OTTAWA   ● Montréal

☐ REYKJAVÍK   ◉ Winnipeg

                    ○ Québec

                    ○ Churchill

SCALE 1 : 17 000 000

0   200   400   600   800 km

Chamberlin trimetric projection

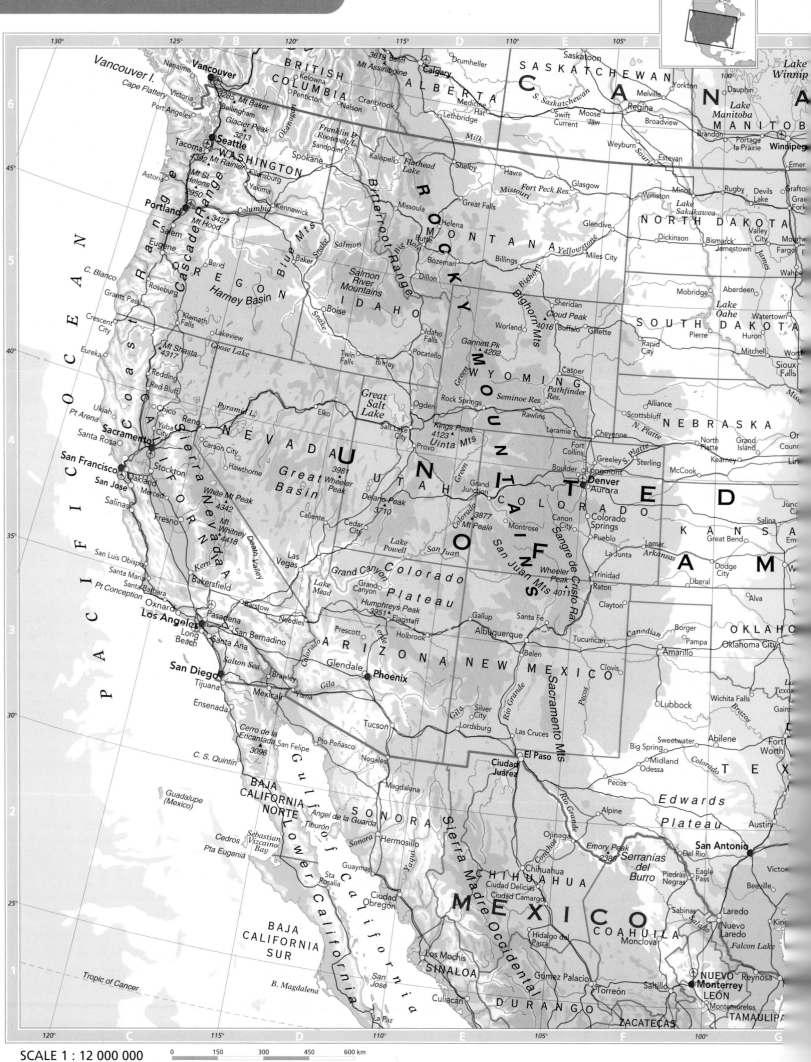

0   150   300   450   600 km

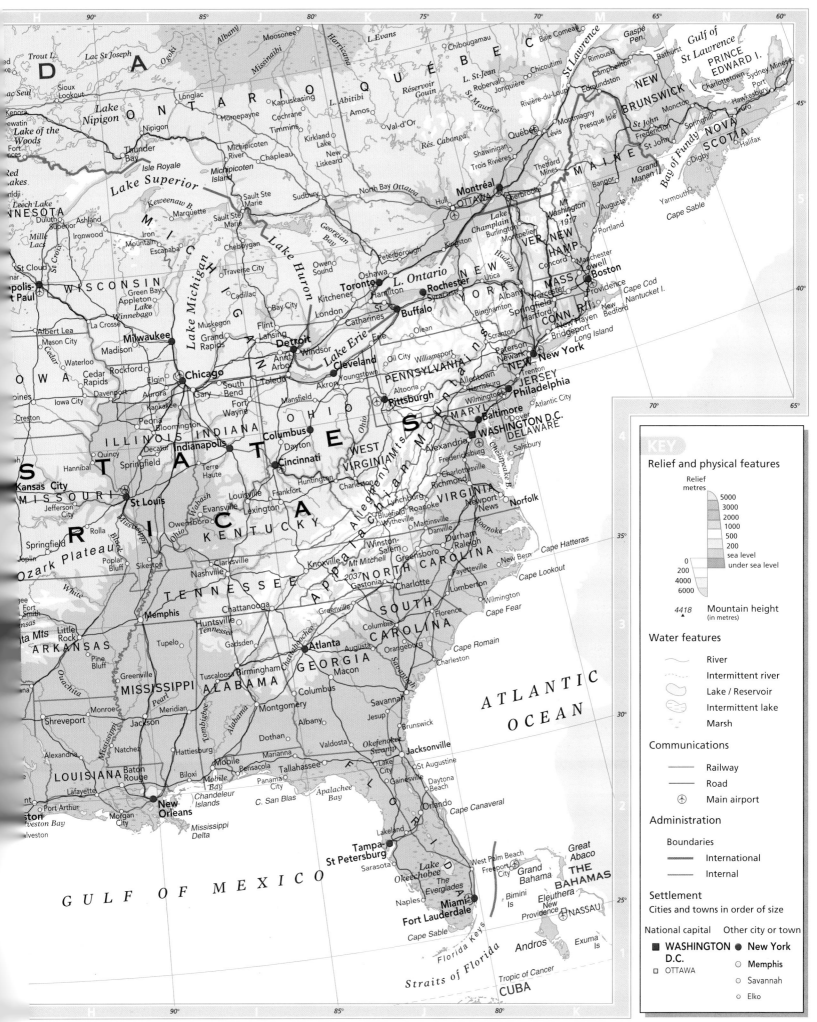

Lambert conformal conic projection

KEY

Relief and physical features

Relief
metres

5000
3000
2000
1000
500
200
sea level
0
under sea level
200
4000
6000

▲ 4418 Mountain height
(in metres)

Water features

～ River

Intermittent river

Lake / Reservoir

Intermittent lake

Marsh

Communications

— Railway

— Road

⊕ Main airport

Administration

Boundaries

━━━ International

━━ Internal

Settlement

Cities and towns in order of size

National capital | Other city or town

■ WASHINGTON D.C. | ● New York

□ OTTAWA | ○ Memphis

○ Savannah

∘ Elko

1 POPULATION DENSITY

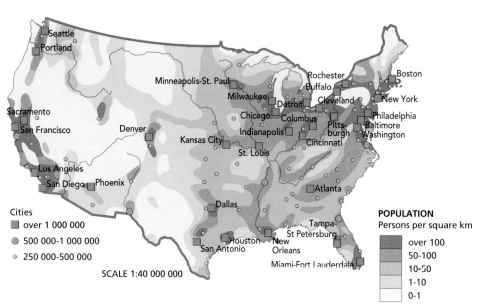

Cities
- ■ over 1 000 000
- ● 500 000-1 000 000
- ○ 250 000-500 000

SCALE 1:40 000 000

POPULATION
Persons per square km

- over 100
- 50-100
- 10-50
- 1-10
- 0-1

2 MAIN CITIES

City	1970 census	1990 census	% change
New York	7 771 730	7 322 564	-6
Los Angeles	2 782 400	3 485 398	25
Chicago	3 325 263	2 783 726	-16
Houston	1 213 064	1 630 553	34
Philadelphia	1 926 529	1 585 570	-18
San Diego	675 688	1 110 549	64
Detroit	1 492 914	1 027 974	-31
Dallas	836 121	1 006 877	20
Phoenix	580 275	983 403	69
San Antonio	650 188	935 933	44

3 POPULATION CHANGE

SCALE 1:40 000 000

POPULATION CHANGE
1970 - 1990

%
- over 50
- 31-50
- 16-30
- 0-15
- -1 - -5

CO.	CONNECTICUT	PENN.	PENNSYLVANIA
DEL.	DELAWARE	R.I.	RHODE ISLAND
MASS.	MASSACHUSETTS	S.C.	SOUTH CAROLINA
N.H.	NEW HAMPSHIRE	V.	VERMONT
N.J.	NEW JERSEY	W.V.	WEST VIRGINIA

4 STATE COMPARISONS

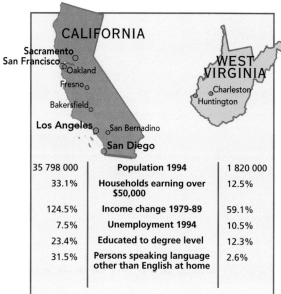

35 798 000	**Population 1994**	1 820 000
33.1%	**Households earning over $50,000**	12.5%
124.5%	**Income change 1979-89**	59.1%
7.5%	**Unemployment 1994**	10.5%
23.4%	**Educated to degree level**	12.3%
31.5%	**Persons speaking language other than English at home**	2.6%

5 POPULATION GROWTH

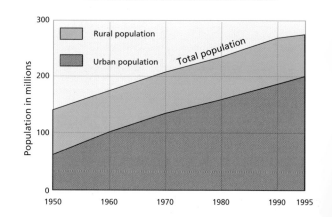

6 IMMIGRATION

IMMIGRATION INTO U.S.A
BY COUNTRY 1992
Total 974 000

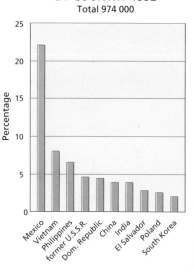

7 ECONOMIC ACTIVITY

- Major industrial centre

SERVICE INDUSTRY

- $ Banking and finance
- ★ Tourism

MANUFACTURING INDUSTRY

- ✈ Aircraft manufacturing
- 🚗 Car manufacturing
- 🧪 Chemicals
- 💡 Electrical engineering
- 🍴 Food processing
- ⚙ Mechanical engineering
- ⬜ Metal working
- 🛢 Oil refinery
- 📄 Paper and publishing
- ⚓ Shipbuilding
- 🧵 Textiles

SCALE 1:40 000 000

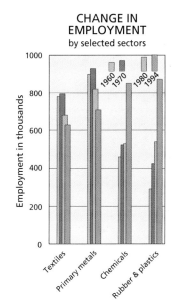

CHANGE IN EMPLOYMENT
by selected sectors

Employment in thousands

1960 1970 1980 1994

Textiles · Primary metals · Chemicals · Rubber & plastics

8 TRADE

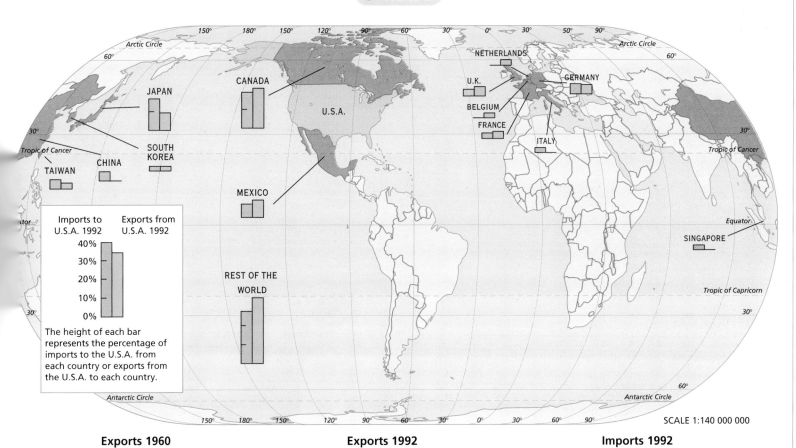

SCALE 1:140 000 000

Imports to U.S.A. 1992 / Exports from U.S.A. 1992

40% 30% 20% 10% 0%

The height of each bar represents the percentage of imports to the U.S.A. from each country or exports from the U.S.A. to each country.

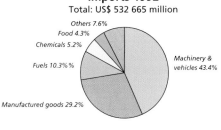

Exports 1960
Total: US$ 20 717 million

- Others 9.4%
- Textiles 10.8%
- Chemicals 11.7%
- Food 12.9%
- Metals & manufactures 13.1%
- Machinery & vehicles 42.1%

Exports 1992
Total: US$ 448 164 million

- Others 13.6%
- Crude materials 5.7%
- Food 7.3%
- Chemicals 9.8%
- Manufactured goods 18.8%
- Machinery & vehicles 44.8%

Imports 1992
Total: US$ 532 665 million

- Others 7.6%
- Food 4.3%
- Chemicals 5.2%
- Fuels 10.3%
- Manufactured goods 29.2%
- Machinery & vehicles 43.4%

Built-up area

The built up area shown as blue/green on the satellite image surrounds San Francisco Bay and extends south to San Jose. Three bridges link the main built up areas across San Francisco Bay.

Woodland

Areas of dense woodland cover much of the Santa Cruz Mountains to the west of the San Andreas Fault Zone. Other areas of woodland are found on the ridges to the east of San Francisco Bay.

Marsh / Salt Marsh

Areas of dark green on the satellite image represent marshland in the Coyote Creek area and salt marshes between the San Mateo and Dumbarton Bridges.

Reservoir / lake

Lakes and reservoirs stand out from the surrounding land. Good examples are the Upper San Leandro Reservoir east of Piedmont and the San Andreas Lake which lies along the fault line.

Airport

A grey blue colour shows San Francisco International Airport as a flat rectangular strip of land jutting out into the bay.

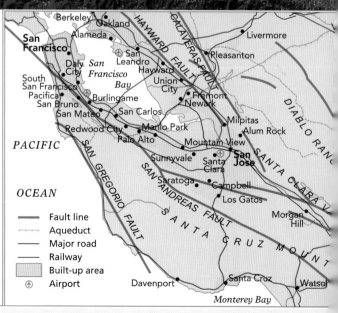

Fault line
Aqueduct
Major road
Railway
Built-up area
Airport

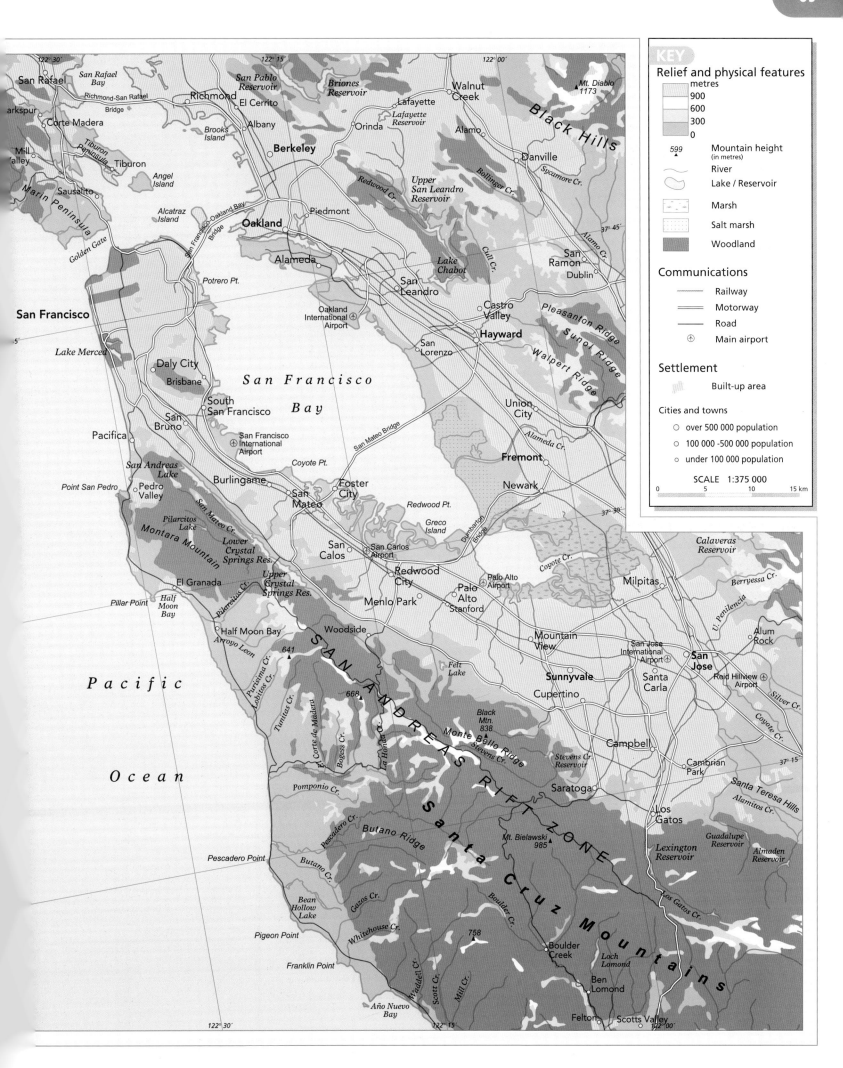

San Rafael
San Rafael Bay
Richmond-San Rafael Bridge
Larkspur
Corte Madera
Tiburon Peninsula
Tiburon
Mill Valley
Sausalito
Marin Peninsula
Angel Island
Golden Gate
San Francisco
Lake Merced
Daly City
Brisbane
San Bruno
Pacifica
Point San Pedro
Pedro Valley
San Andreas Lake
Pilarcitos Lake
Montara Mountain
Lower Crystal Springs Res.
Upper Crystal Springs Res.
El Granada
Pillar Point
Half Moon Bay
Arroyo Leon
Half Moon Bay
Woodside
641
Purisima Cr.
Lobitos Cr.
El Corte de Madera
Bogess Cr.
Tunitas Cr.
668
La Honda Cr.
Pomponio Cr.
Pescadero Cr.
Butano Ridge
Butano Cr.
Bean Hollow Lake
Gazos Cr.
Pescadero Point
Pigeon Point
Franklin Point
Año Nuevo Bay
Waddell Cr.
Scott Cr.
Mill Cr.
Whitehouse Cr.

Richmond
El Cerrito
Albany
Brooks Island
Berkeley
Alcatraz Island
San Francisco-Oakland Bay Bridge
Oakland
Piedmont
Alameda
Potrero Pt.
Oakland International Airport
San Francisco Bay
San Leandro
San Lorenzo
Coyote Pt.
Burlingame
San Mateo
San Francisco International Airport
Foster City
San Mateo Bridge
Redwood Pt.
Greco Island
San Calos
San Carlos Airport
Redwood City
Menlo Park
Woodside
Felt Lake
Black Mtn. 838
Monte Bello Ridge
Stevens Cr.
Stevens Cr. Reservoir
Mt. Bielawski 985
758
Boulder Cr.
Boulder Creek
Loch Lomond
Ben Lomond
Felton
Scotts Valley

San Pablo Reservoir
Briones Reservoir
Lafayette
Lafayette Reservoir
Orinda
Redwood Cr.
Upper San Leandro Reservoir
Lake Chabot
Cull Cr.
Castro Valley
Hayward
Union City
Alameda Cr.
Fremont
Newark
Dumbarton Bridge
Coyote Cr.
Palo Alto Airport
Palo Alto
Stanford
Mountain View
Sunnyvale
Cupertino
Campbell
Saratoga
Los Gatos
Lexington Reservoir
Los Gatos Cr.

Walnut Creek
Mt. Diablo 1173
Black Hills
Alamo
Danville
Bollinger Cr.
Sycamore Cr.
San Ramon
Dublin
Alamo Cr.
Pleasanton Ridge
Sunol Ridge
Walpert Ridge
Calaveras Reservoir
Milpitas
Berryessa Cr.
U. Penitencia
Alum Rock
San Jose International Airport
San Jose
Santa Carla
Reid Hillview Airport
Silver Cr.
Coyote Cr.
Cambrian Park
Santa Teresa Hills
Alamitos Cr.
Guadalupe Reservoir
Almaden Reservoir

SAN ANDREAS RIFT ZONE
Santa Cruz Mountains

Pacific
Ocean

Pescadero Point

37° 45'
37° 30'
37° 15'

122° 30'
122° 15'
122° 00'

Mexican States numbered on map
1. AGUASCALIENTES
2. DISTRITO FEDERAL
3. TLAXCALA

KEY

Relief and physical features

Relief metres
5000
3000
2000
1000
500
200
sea level
0
200 under sea level
4000
6000

5775 ▲ Mountain height (in metres)

Water features

~ River
Intermittent river
Lake / Reservoir
Intermittent lake
Marsh

Communications

Railway
Road
⊕ Main airport

Administration

Boundaries
International
Internal

Settlement
Cities and towns in order of size

National capital
■ MEXICO CITY
□ MANAGUA
□ SAN JOSÉ
▫ CASTRIES

Other city or town
● Puebla
○ Leon
○ Acapulco
▫ Guanajuato

SCALE 1 : 13 000 000

0   200   400   600   800 km

Lambert Azimuthal Equal Area projection

SCALE 1 : 80 000 000

SCALE 1 : 37 000 000

Lambert Azimuthal Equal Area projection

1 TEMPERATURE AND PRESSURE : JANUARY

Average temperature °C
24
16
8

Wind direction

Isobar in millibars reduced to sea level

2 TEMPERATURE AND PRESSURE : JULY

Average temperature °C
24
16
8
0

Wind direction

Isobar in millibars reduced to sea level

3 ANNUAL RAINFALL

Average annual rainfall mm
3000
2000
1000
500
250
0

4 STATISTICS

Quito (2879 metres)	Jan	Feb	Mar	Apr	May	Jun	Jul	Aug	Sep	Oct	Nov	Dec
Temperature - max.(°C)	22	22	22	21	21	22	22	23	23	22	22	22
Temperature - min. (°C)	8	8	8	8	8	7	7	7	7	8	7	8
Rainfall - (mm)	99	112	142	175	137	43	20	31	69	112	97	79

Belem (13 metres)	Jan	Feb	Mar	Apr	May	Jun	Jul	Aug	Sep	Oct	Nov	Dec
Temperature - max.(°C)	31	30	31	31	31	31	31	31	32	32	32	32
Temperature - min. (°C)	22	22	23	23	23	22	22	22	22	22	22	22
Rainfall - (mm)	318	358	358	320	259	170	150	112	89	84	66	155

Iguatu (209 metres)	Jan	Feb	Mar	Apr	May	Jun	Jul	Aug	Sep	Oct	Nov	Dec
Temperature - max.(°C)	34	33	32	31	31	31	32	32	35	36	36	36
Temperature - min. (°C)	23	23	23	23	22	22	21	21	22	23	23	23
Rainfall - (mm)	89	173	185	160	61	61	36	5	18	18	10	33

Santiago (520 metres)	Jan	Feb	Mar	Apr	May	Jun	Jul	Aug	Sep	Oct	Nov	Dec
Temperature - max.(°C)	29	29	27	23	18	14	15	17	19	22	26	28
Temperature - min. (°C)	12	11	9	7	5	3	3	4	6	7	9	11
Rainfall - (mm)	3	3	5	13	64	84	76	56	31	15	8	5

Punta Arenas (8 metres)	Jan	Feb	Mar	Apr	May	Jun	Jul	Aug	Sep	Oct	Nov	Dec
Temperature - max.(°C)	14	14	12	10	7	5	4	6	8	11	12	14
Temperature - min. (°C)	7	7	5	4	2	1	-1	1	2	3	4	6
Rainfall - (mm)	38	23	33	36	33	41	28	31	23	28	18	36

SCALE 1 : 72 000 000

Lambert Azimuthal Equal Area projection

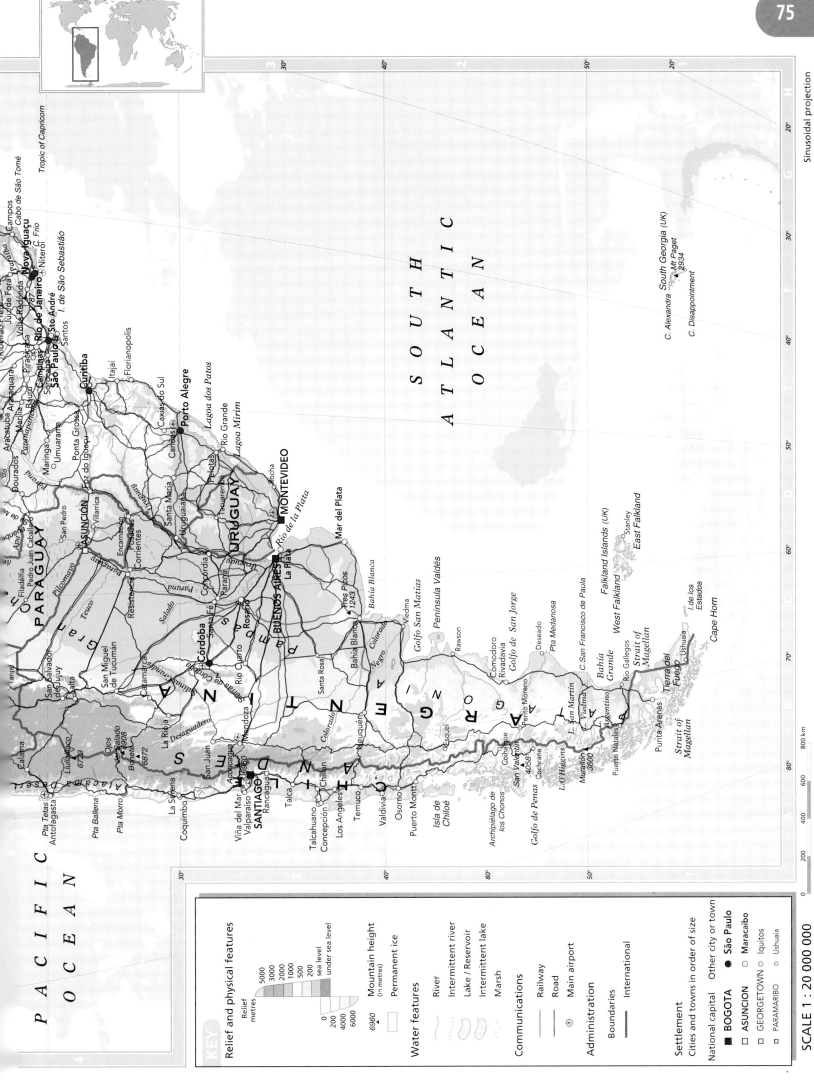

PACIFIC
OCEAN

SOUTH
ATLANTIC
OCEAN

Tropic of Capricorn

Cabo de São Tomé
Campos
Nova Iguaçu
C. Frio
Niterói
Rio de Janeiro
Sto André
São Paulo
2787
Campinas
Volta Redonda
Piraçicaba
Santos
I. de São Sebastião
Sorocaba
Juiz de Fora
Barra
Piraçununga
Juíz de Fora
Ribeirão Preto
Araçatuba
Araraquara
Marília
Bauru
Dourados
Maringá
Umuarama
Ponta Grossa
Curitiba
Itajaí
Florianópolis
Caxias do Sul
Canoas
Porto Alegre
Lagoa dos Patos
Rio Grande
Lagoa Mirim
Rocha
MONTEVIDEO
Mar del Plata

PARAGUAY
ASUNCIÓN
Villarrica
San Pedro
Pedro Juan Caballero
Filadélfia
Fuerte Olimpo
Pilcomayo
Teuco
GRAN
CHACO
Tarija
San Salvador de Jujuy
Salta
San Miguel de Tucumán
Santiago del Estero
Calama
Antofagasta
Pta Tetas
Pta Ballena
Pta Morro
Atacama Desert
Calama
Llullaillaco
6723
Ojos del Salado
6908
Bonete
6872
La Serena
Coquimbo
Viña del Mar
Valparaíso
SANTIAGO
Aconcagua
6960
San Juan
Mendoza
Rancagua
Talca
Chillán
Concepción
Talcahuano
Los Ángeles
Temuco
Valdivia
Osorno
Puerto Montt
Isla de Chiloé
Archipiélago de los Chonos
Golfo de Penas
San Valentín
4058
Cochrane
Coihaique
Esquel
L. O'Higgins
Murallón
3600
Puerto Natales
Punta Arenas
Strait of Magellan
Tierra del Fuego
Ushuaia
Cape Horn
I. de los Estados

Encarnación
Posadas
Corrientes
Resistencia
Formosa
Salado
Santa Fé
Paraná
Concordia
Uruguaiana
Santa María
Santa Rosa
Rosario
BUENOS AIRES
La Plata
Tres Picos
1243
Bahía Blanca
Bahía Blanca
Negro
Colorado
Viedma
Golfo San Matías
Península Valdés
Golfo San Jorge
Rawson
Comodoro Rivadavia
Deseado
Pta Medanosa
C. San Francisco de Paula
Bahía Grande
Río Gallegos
San Martín
L. Viedma
L. Argentino

URUGUAY
Rio de la Plata
Tacuarembó
Mercedes

PARAGUAY
Paraná
Córdoba
Sierras de Córdoba
Río Cuarto
La Rioja
Catamarca
Desaguadero

ANDES
PAMPA
PATAGONIA

South Georgia (UK)
C. Alexandra
Mt Paget
2934
C. Disappointment

Falkland Islands (UK)
West Falkland
East Falkland
Stanley

800 km

KEY

Relief and physical features

Relief
metres
5000
3000
2000
1000
500
200
sea level
under sea level

0
200
4000
6000

Mountain height
(in metres)
6960 ▲

Permanent ice

Water features

River

Intermittent river

Lake / Reservoir

Intermittent lake

Marsh

Communications

Railway

Road

⊕ Main airport

Administration

Boundaries

International

Settlement

Cities and towns in order of size

National capital   Other city or town

■ BOGOTA   ● São Paulo
□ ASUNCIÓN   ● Maracaibo
▫ GEORGETOWN   ○ Iquitos
▫ PARAMARIBO   ○ Ushuaia

SÃO PAULO

Relief and physical features

Relief
metres

5000
3000
2000
1000
500
200
sea level
under sea level
200
4000
6000

6908 ▲ Mountain height
(in metres)

Water features

River
Intermittent river
Lake / Reservoir
Intermittent lake
Marsh

Communications

Railway
Road
⊕ Main airport

Administration

Boundaries
International
Internal

Settlement
Cities and towns in order of size

National capital
■ BRASÍLIA
□ ASUNCIÓN

Other city or town
● Recife
○ Teresina
○ Vitória
○ Salto

KEY

Residential
Industrial
Commercial
Commercial/
Residential

Government
Recreation
Parks
Other use

Road
Railway

SCALE 1:750 000
0   5   10   15 km

SCALE 1 : 15 000 000
0   150   300   450   600 km

Galapagos Is

Equator

I. Isabela
I. Santa Cruz
I. San Cristóbal
Baquerizo Moreno

COLOMBIA
Popayán Huila 5750 Neiva
Pasto Florencia
Tumaco Cumbal 4764 Ibarra
Esmeraldas
C. de San Francisco
C. Pasado
QUITO Cotopaxi 5896
Manta Latacunga Tena
Portoviejo Chimborazo 6310 Ambato Riobamba
B. de Sta Elena Napo
ECUADOR Macas
Guayaquil Alausí
G. of Guayaquil Cuenca Azogues
Machala
Tumbes Loja
Talara Zamora
Pta Pariñas Sullana
Piura
Bahía de Sechura
Pta Negra
Chiclayo

Orinoco
3014 ▲ Pico da Neblina
Uaupés
Barce

AMAZ
Iquitos
Marañón
Cruzeiro do Sul
Feijó
ACRE
Pôrto Velho
Rio Branco
Cobija
Abunã
Arique

PERU
6768 ▲
Cerro de Pasco
Huacho
Callao
LIMA Huancayo
Pisco Ayacucho
Ica Abancay Cuzco
Nazca
Coropuna 6425
Arequipa Lake Titicaca
6402 ■ LA PAZ BOL
Cochabamba
Tacna Sajama 6542
Arica
Oruro
Iquique Salar de Coipasa
Salar de Uyuni
Tocopilla
Pta Tetas
Antofagasta
Pta Ballena
Chañaral
Pta Morro
Copiapó
La Serena
Coquimbo

Puerto Maldonado
Riberalta
Lago Rogaguado
Lago de San Luis
Trinic
Llanos de Mojos
Juliaca
Yunga
Potosí
Sucre
Tarija
Salta
San Salvador de Jujuy
6723 ▲ Salar de Arizaro 6720 ▲
Llullaillaco ARG
San Miguel de Tucumán
Ojos del Salado 6908
Bonete 6872
Mejicana 6250
Catamarca
C. de Oliva 6332
La Rioja
San Juan

Res. Juqueri
Juqueri
Caieiras
Res. Pirapora
Guarulhos
Tietê
Osasco
Tietê
SÃO PAULO
Suzano
Pinheiros
São Caetano do Sul
Cotia
Tamanduateí
Santo André
Res. Guarapiranga
Res. Billings
Res. Pedro Beicht
Res. Rio das Pedras

ATLANTIC

OCEAN

Equator

Lambert Azimuthal Equal Area projection

1 POPULATION DENSITY

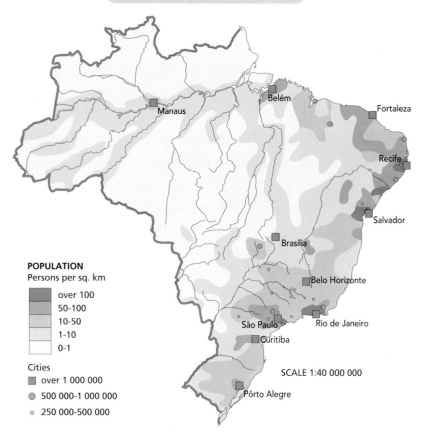

POPULATION
Persons per sq. km

- over 100
- 50-100
- 10-50
- 1-10
- 0-1

Cities
- ◼ over 1 000 000
- ⬤ 500 000-1 000 000
- ○ 250 000-500 000

SCALE 1:40 000 000

3 MAIN CITIES

City	1970 census	1991 census	% change
São Paulo	5 924 615	15 199 423	157
Rio de Janeiro	4 251 918	9 600 528	126
Belo Horizonte	1 235 030	3 461 905	180
Pôrto Alegre	885 545	3 015 960	240
Recife	1 060 701	2 859 469	169
Salvador	1 007 195	2 472 131	145
Fortaleza	857 980	2 294 524	167
Curitiba	609 026	1 975 624	224
Brasília	537 492	1 596 274	197
Belém	633 374	1 334 460	110

4 POPULATION GROWTH

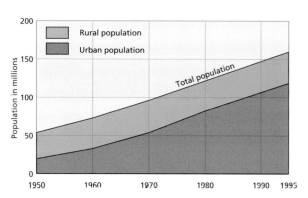

- Rural population
- Urban population

Total population

Population in millions

2 POPULATION CHANGE

POPULATION CHANGE
1970 - 1991

%
- over 1000
- 500-1000
- 250-500
- 200-250
- 150-200
- 100-150

SCALE 1:40 000 000

5 MIGRATION

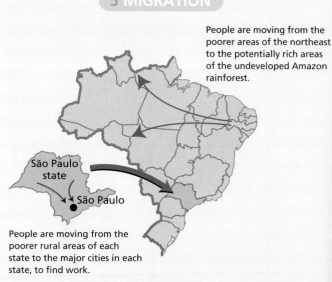

People are moving from the poorer areas of the northeast to the potentially rich areas of the undeveloped Amazon rainforest.

São Paulo state → São Paulo

People are moving from the poorer rural areas of each state to the major cities in each state, to find work.

6 URBAN AND RURAL CONTRASTS

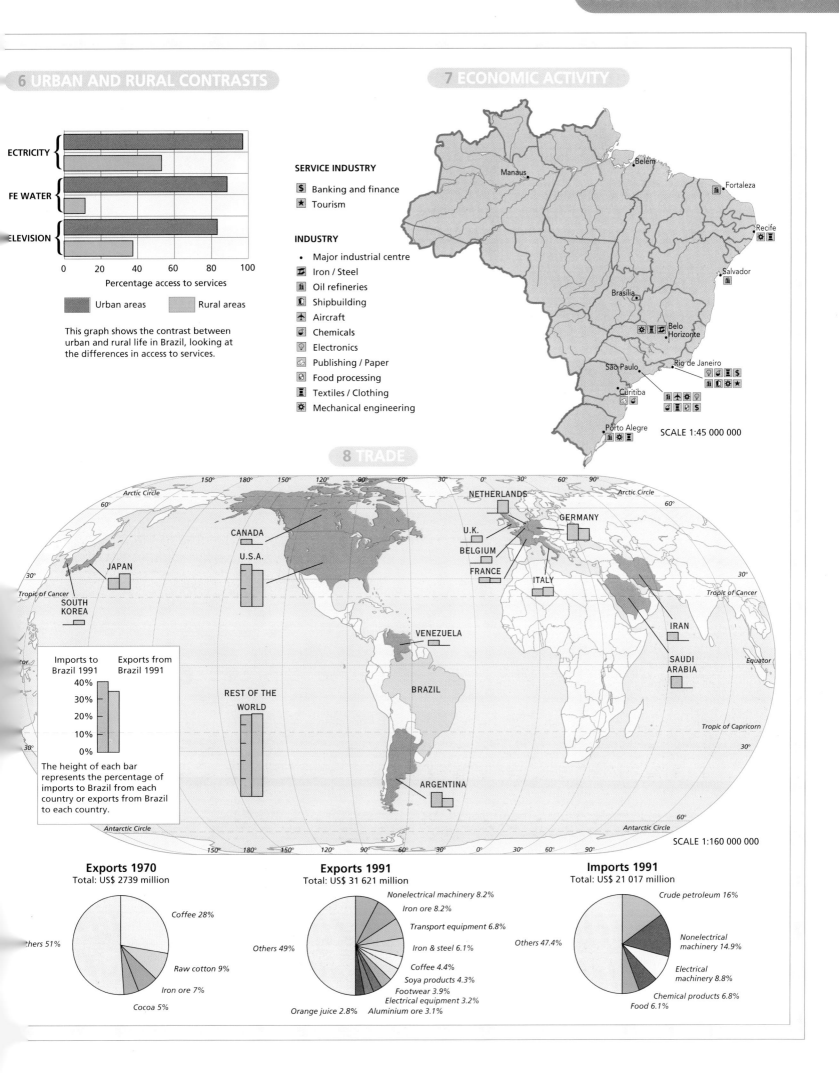

ECTRICITY

FE WATER

ELEVISION

Percentage access to services

0   20   40   60   80   100

■ Urban areas   ▢ Rural areas

This graph shows the contrast between urban and rural life in Brazil, looking at the differences in access to services.

7 ECONOMIC ACTIVITY

SERVICE INDUSTRY

$ Banking and finance
★ Tourism

INDUSTRY

• Major industrial centre
Iron / Steel
Oil refineries
Shipbuilding
Aircraft
Chemicals
Electronics
Publishing / Paper
Food processing
Textiles / Clothing
Mechanical engineering

Manaus

Belém

Fortaleza

Recife

Salvador

Brasília

Belo Horizonte

Rio de Janeiro

São Paulo

Curitiba

Porto Alegre

SCALE 1:45 000 000

8 TRADE

Arctic Circle

NETHERLANDS

GERMANY

CANADA

U.K.

BELGIUM

U.S.A.

FRANCE

ITALY

JAPAN

IRAN

SOUTH KOREA

VENEZUELA

SAUDI ARABIA

REST OF THE WORLD

BRAZIL

ARGENTINA

Tropic of Cancer

Equator

Tropic of Capricorn

Antarctic Circle

SCALE 1:160 000 000

Imports to Brazil 1991   Exports from Brazil 1991

40%
30%
20%
10%
0%

The height of each bar represents the percentage of imports to Brazil from each country or exports from Brazil to each country.

Exports 1970
Total: US$ 2739 million

Coffee 28%
thers 51%
Raw cotton 9%
Iron ore 7%
Cocoa 5%

Exports 1991
Total: US$ 31 621 million

Nonelectrical machinery 8.2%
Iron ore 8.2%
Transport equipment 6.8%
Iron & steel 6.1%
Coffee 4.4%
Soya products 4.3%
Footwear 3.9%
Electrical equipment 3.2%
Aluminium ore 3.1%
Orange juice 2.8%
Others 49%

Imports 1991
Total: US$ 21 017 million

Crude petroleum 16%
Nonelectrical machinery 14.9%
Electrical machinery 8.8%
Chemical products 6.8%
Food 6.1%
Others 47.4%

Forest
Dense forest covers much of this area and the courses of the many tributaries of the river Guaporé can be followed cutting through the forest areas.

Marshy Savanna
An area of marshy savanna lies between the forest and the river Guaporé. Similar areas can also be seen south of the river around Laguna Bella Vista.

Deforested Areas
Large rectangular areas of pale blue on the satellite image are areas of deforestation, probably from commercial logging. In the bottom right of the image the pale blue line patterns are systematic deforestation due to the practice of slash and burn farming.

Highland
The highland of the Serra dos Parecis can be seen at the top right of the image.

Lakes
Several small dark blue/black outlines of lakes can be seen along the course of the river Guaporé. Laguna Bella Vista stands out clearly as a much larger feature.

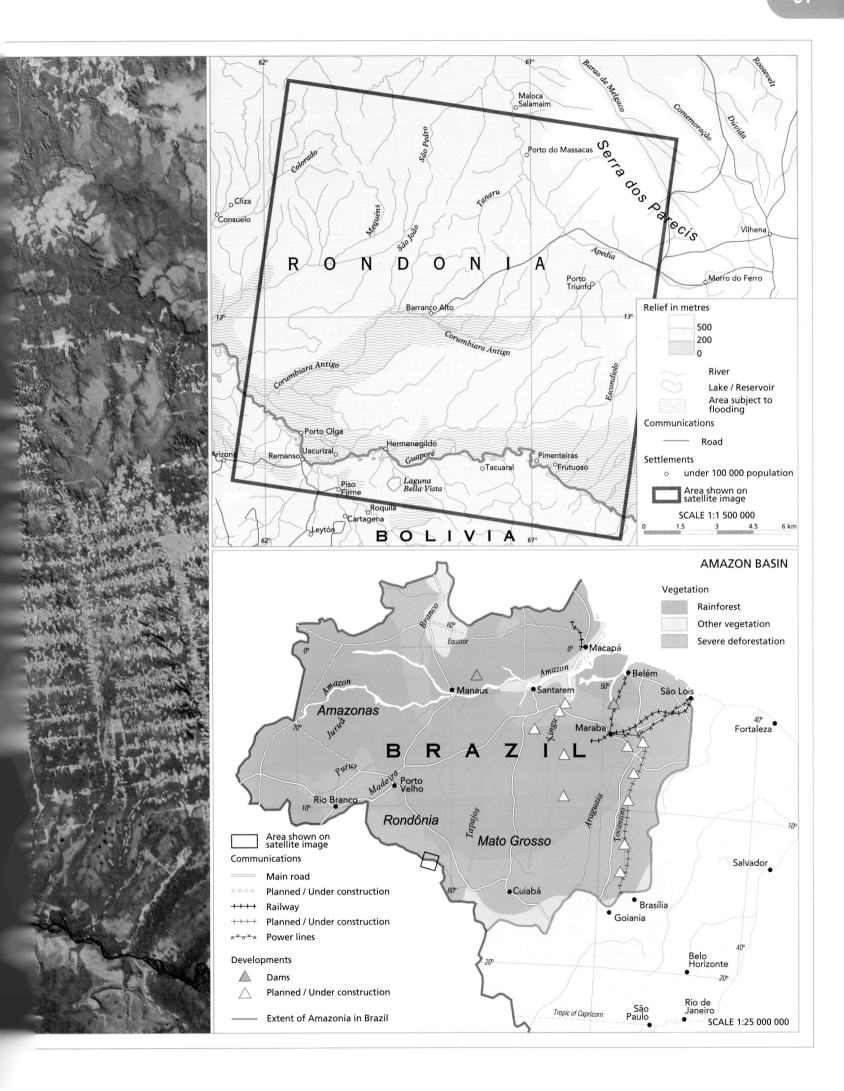

Serra dos Parecis

62°   61°

Maloca
Salamaim

Barao de Melgaço

Comemoração

Dúvida

Roosevelt

Porto do Massacas

Colorado

São Pedro

Vilhena

R O N D O N I A

Clíza
Consuelo

Meguéns

São João

Tanaru

Apedia

Morro do Ferro

Porto
Triunfo

Barranco Alto

13°   13°

Corumbiara Antigo

Escondiolo

Corumbiara Antigo

Porto Olga

Hermenegildo

Pimenteiras

Arizona
Remanso   Uacurizal
Guaporé
Tacuaral
Frutuoso

Laguna
Bella Vista

Piso
Firme

Roquila
Cartagena

Leytón

62°   61°
B O L I V I A

Relief in metres

500
200
0

River
Lake / Reservoir
Area subject to
flooding

Communications

Road

Settlements

o   under 100 000 population

Area shown on
satellite image

SCALE 1:1 500 000

0   1.5   3   4.5   6 km

AMAZON BASIN

Vegetation

Rainforest
Other vegetation
Severe deforestation

Branco

60°

Equator

0°   0°

Macapá

Amazon

Belém

Manaus

Santarem

São Lois

Amazonas

50°

40°

Maraba

Fortaleza

Juruá

B R A Z I L

Xingu

70°

Purus

Madeira
Porto
Velho

Amazon

Rio Branco

10°   10°

Rondônia

Tapajós

Mato Grosso

Araguaia

Tocantins

Salvador

Area shown on
satellite image

Cuiabá

Brasília

Communications

Goiania

Main road

Planned / Under construction

Railway

Belo
Horizonte

Planned / Under construction

20°

Power lines

20°

Developments

Dams

São
Paulo

Rio de
Janeiro

Planned / Under construction

Tropic of Capricorn

Extent of Amazonia in Brazil

SCALE 1:25 000 000

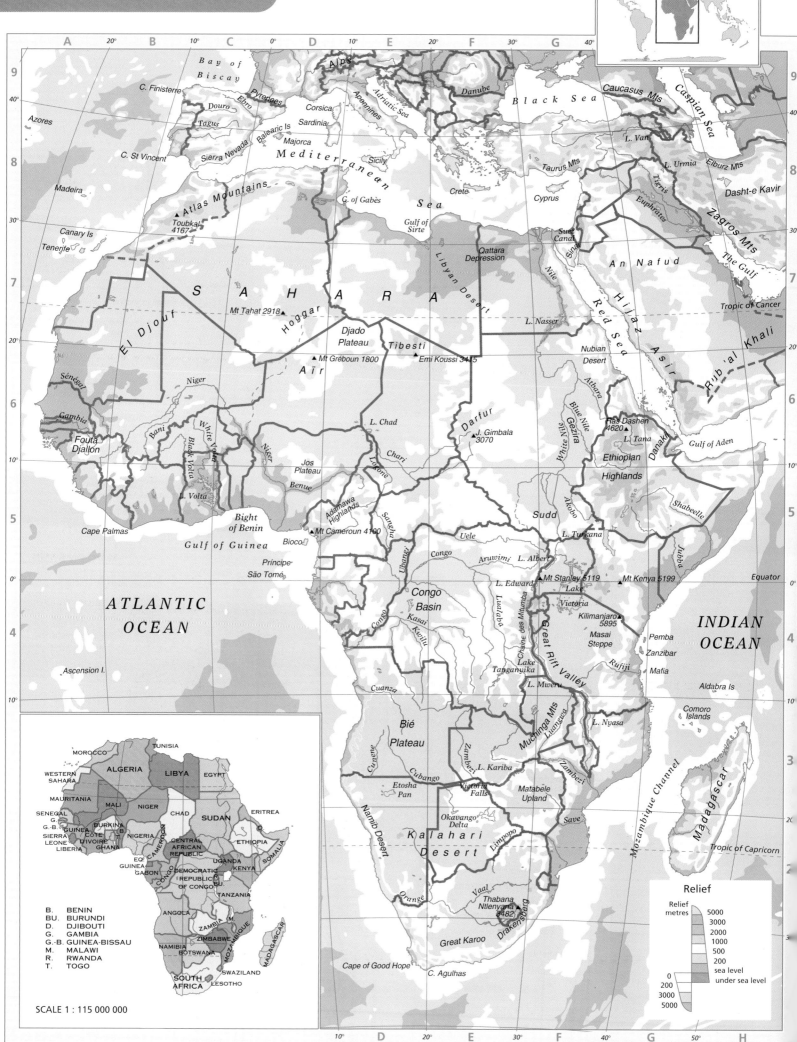

ATLANTIC OCEAN

INDIAN OCEAN

S A H A R A

El Djouf

Mt Tahat 2918▲ Hoggar

Djado Plateau

Tibesti

Aïr

▲Mt Gréboun 1800 Emi Koussi 3415

Libyan Desert

Qattara Depression

L. Nasser

Nubian Desert

Red Sea

An Nafud

Hijaz Asir

Rub' al Khali

Tropic of Cancer

Niger

Sénégal

Gambia

Fouta Djallon

Bani White Volta Black Volta

Niger

L. Chad

Chari

Jos Plateau

Benue

Darfur

J. Gimbala 3070

Blue Nile Gezira White Nile Atbara

Ras Dashen 4620▲ L. Tana

Ethiopian Highlands

Danakil

Gulf of Aden

Shabeelle

L. Volta

Cape Palmas

Bight of Benin

Gulf of Guinea

Bioco

Adamawa Highlands ▲Mt Cameroun 4100

Príncipe São Tomé

Ubangi Uele Congo

Sangha Aruwimi L. Albert

Congo Basin

Kasai Kwilu Lualaba

Sudd

Akobo

L. Turkana

L. Edward ▲Mt Stanley 5119 Lake Victoria

▲Mt Kenya 5199

Jubba

Equator

Kilimanjaro 5895

Masai Steppe

Pemba Zanzibar Mafia

Rufiji

Chaine des Mitumba Great Rift Valley

Lake Tanganyika

L. Mweru

Muchinga Mts Luangwa

L. Nyasa

Aldabra Is

Comoro Islands

Bié Plateau

Cuanza

Cunene

Cubango

Etosha Pan

Okavango Delta

Victoria Falls Zambezi

L. Kariba

Matabele Upland

Zambezi

Save

Limpopo

Mozambique Channel

Madagascar

Tropic of Capricorn

Namib Desert

K a l a h a r i D e s e r t

Orange

Vaal

Thabana Ntlenyana 3482▲ Drakensberg

Great Karoo

Cape of Good Hope

C. Agulhas

Relief

Relief metres

5000
3000
2000
1000
500
200
0
sea level
under sea level
200
3000
5000

Azores

C. Finisterre

Madeira

Bay of Biscay

Pyrenees

Ebro Douro Tagus

C. St Vincent

Sierra Nevada Balearic Is Majorca Majorca

▲Toubkal 4167

Canary Is Tenerife

Atlas Mountains

Corsica Sardinia

Alps

Apennines Adriatic Sea

Corsica

Sicily

Crete

Cyprus

Danube

Black Sea

Caucasus Mts

Caspian Sea

L. Van

L. Urmia Elburz Mts

Taurus Mts

Tigris Euphrates

Zagros Mts

Dasht-e Kavir

The Gulf

Mediterranean Sea

G. of Gabès

Gulf of Sirte

Suez Canal Sinai

Nile

Inset map (countries):

MOROCCO
WESTERN SAHARA
ALGERIA
TUNISIA
LIBYA
EGYPT
MAURITANIA
MALI
NIGER
CHAD
SUDAN
ERITREA
SENEGAL
G.
G.-B.
GUINEA
SIERRA LEONE
LIBERIA
BURKINA
CÔTE D'IVOIRE
GHANA
NIGERIA
CENTRAL AFRICAN REPUBLIC
ETHIOPIA
SOMALIA
CAMEROON
EQ. GUINEA
GABON
CONGO
DEMOCRATIC REPUBLIC OF CONGO
UGANDA
KENYA
TANZANIA
ANGOLA
ZAMBIA
ZIMBABWE
MOZAMBIQUE
NAMIBIA
BOTSWANA
SWAZILAND
SOUTH AFRICA
LESOTHO
MADAGASCAR

B. BENIN
BU. BURUNDI
D. DJIBOUTI
G. GAMBIA
G.-B. GUINEA-BISSAU
M. MALAWI
R. RWANDA
T. TOGO

SCALE 1 : 115 000 000

SCALE 1 : 37 000 000

Lambert Azimuthal Equal Area projection

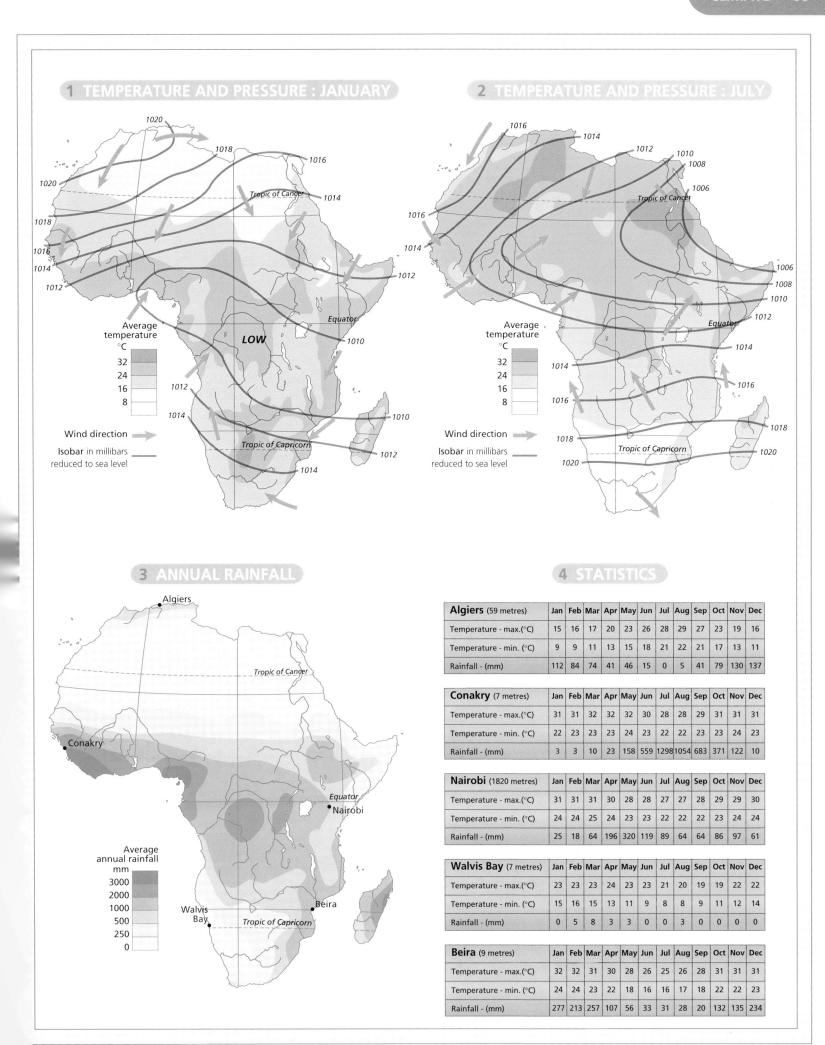

1 TEMPERATURE AND PRESSURE : JANUARY

1020
1018
1016
Tropic of Cancer
1014
1020
1018
1016
1014
1012
Equator
1010
LOW
1012
1014

Average
temperature
°C

32
24
16
8

Wind direction

Isobar in millibars
reduced to sea level

1012
1014
Tropic of Capricorn
1012
1010
1014

2 TEMPERATURE AND PRESSURE : JULY

1016
1014
1012
1010
1008
1006
Tropic of Cancer
1016
1014
1006
1008
1010
1012
Equator
1014
1014
1016
1016
1018
1018
1020
Tropic of Capricorn
1020

Average
temperature
°C

32
24
16
8

Wind direction

Isobar in millibars
reduced to sea level

3 ANNUAL RAINFALL

Algiers

Tropic of Cancer

Conakry

Equator
Nairobi

Average
annual rainfall
mm

3000
2000
1000
500
250
0

Walvis
Bay
Tropic of Capricorn
Beira

4 STATISTICS

Algiers (59 metres)	Jan	Feb	Mar	Apr	May	Jun	Jul	Aug	Sep	Oct	Nov	Dec
Temperature - max.(°C)	15	16	17	20	23	26	28	29	27	23	19	16
Temperature - min. (°C)	9	9	11	13	15	18	21	22	21	17	13	11
Rainfall - (mm)	112	84	74	41	46	15	0	5	41	79	130	137

Conakry (7 metres)	Jan	Feb	Mar	Apr	May	Jun	Jul	Aug	Sep	Oct	Nov	Dec
Temperature - max.(°C)	31	31	32	32	32	30	28	28	29	31	31	31
Temperature - min. (°C)	22	23	23	23	24	23	22	22	23	23	24	23
Rainfall - (mm)	3	3	10	23	158	559	1298	1054	683	371	122	10

Nairobi (1820 metres)	Jan	Feb	Mar	Apr	May	Jun	Jul	Aug	Sep	Oct	Nov	Dec
Temperature - max.(°C)	31	31	31	30	28	28	27	27	28	29	29	30
Temperature - min. (°C)	24	24	25	24	23	23	22	22	22	23	24	24
Rainfall - (mm)	25	18	64	196	320	119	89	64	64	86	97	61

Walvis Bay (7 metres)	Jan	Feb	Mar	Apr	May	Jun	Jul	Aug	Sep	Oct	Nov	Dec
Temperature - max.(°C)	23	23	23	24	23	23	21	20	19	19	22	22
Temperature - min. (°C)	15	16	15	13	11	9	8	8	9	11	12	14
Rainfall - (mm)	0	5	8	3	3	0	0	3	0	0	0	0

Beira (9 metres)	Jan	Feb	Mar	Apr	May	Jun	Jul	Aug	Sep	Oct	Nov	Dec
Temperature - max.(°C)	32	32	31	30	28	26	25	26	28	31	31	31
Temperature - min. (°C)	24	24	23	22	18	16	16	17	18	22	22	23
Rainfall - (mm)	277	213	257	107	56	33	31	28	20	132	135	234

SCALE 1 : 77 000 000

Lambert Azimuthal Equal Area projection

A   30°   B   20°   C   10°   D   0°   E   10°

PORTUGAL   Mérida   Valencia   Palma de
SPAIN   Mallorca   Mallorca (Italy)   Naples
Cape   Faro   Seville   Ibiza   Balearic Is   Cagliari   Sardinia (Italy)   Palermo
St Vincent   Málaga   Murcia   10°
Tangier   Gibraltar (UK)   Cartagena   ALGIERS   Béjaïa   Skikda   Bizerte   Annaba   TUNIS   Sicily
Tétouan   Ceuta (Sp.)   Oran   Ech Chélif   Blida   Sétif   Constantine   Sousse   VALLETTA   MALTA
RABAT   Melilla   Sidi Bel Abbès   Batna   Kairouan   TUNISIA   Sfax   G. of Gabès
Casablanca   Kenitra   Fez   Oujda   Tlemcen   Djelfa   Atlas   Gabès
El Jadida   Meknès   Biskra   Chott   Gafsa   Medenine   Chott el Jerid
Safi   Beni Mellal   Touggourt   Melrhir   TRIPC
Marrakesh   Bouârfa   Ghardaïa   Ouargla   Misratal
Agadir   Toubkal   Er Rachidia   Béchar   Hassi   Nalut
Tiznit   4167   Ouarzazate   Aïn Sefra   Abadla   Messaoud   Ghadamis

Madeira (Portugal)   Funchal

Canary Islands (Spain)   El Goléa
La Palma   Lanzarote   Tindouf   Reggane   In Salah   Illizi   Sabha
Santa Cruz   Fuerteventura   LAÂYOUNE   Bîr Mogrein   Murzuq
Tenerife   de Tenerife   ALGERIA   Ghat
Las Palmas   WESTERN   SAHARA   Hoggar
Gran   SAHARA   Fdérik   Zouérat   Mt Tahat   Djado
Canaria   Nouâdhibou   Atâr   2918   Tamanrasset   Plateau

Tropic of Cancer

Ponta   Sto. Antão
do Sol   Mindelo   Sal   MAURITANIA
CAPE   Boa Vista   NOUAKCHOTT   Tidjikja   Arlit   Aïr   Nguigmi
São Tiago   VERDE   Maio   St. Louis   Rosso   Tombouctou   Agadez   NIGER
Fogo   PRAIA   DAKAR   Senegal   Matam   Kayes   Gao   Zinder
C. Vert   Thiès   SENEGAL   Nioro   Tillabéri   NIAMEY   Sokoto   Maradi   Katsina   La
Kaolack   THE   Tambacounda   Mopti   Birnin   Kaura   Ch
GAMBIA   BANJUL   San   Konni   Namoda   Kano
GUINEA-   BISSAU   Fouta   Labé   Sikasso   BAMAKO   BURKINA   Tillabéri   Gusau   Zaria   NDJAMEN
BISSAU   Djallon   Fria   Kankan   Bobo-Dioulasso   OUAGADOUGOU   Gaya   Kaduna   Maidu
GUINEA   CONAKRY   Beyla   Ferkéssédougou   Wa   Volta   Dapaong   BENIN   Minna   Bauchi   Kumo
SIERRA   FREETOWN   Bo   CÔTE   Bouaké   Tamale   Parakou   NIGERIA   Jos   Garou
LEONE   LIBERIA   Daloa   D'IVOIRE   Lake   Kumasi   Ogbomoso   Ilorin   ABUJA   Benne   M
MONROVIA   YAMOUSSOUKRO   Volta   GHANA   Ibadan   Lokoja   Makurdi   Adamawa
Sassandra   Abidjan   ACCRA   Abeokuta   Iwo   Benin   Enugu   Highlands   Ngao
C. Palmas   Sekondi-   LOMÉ   Cotonou   Lagos   City   Onitsha   CAMEROON   Tibati
Takoradi   PORTO-   Bight   Warri   Calabar   Yaoundé
NOVO   of Benin   Port Harcourt   Mt Cameroon   Douala   YAOUNDÉ
EQUATORIAL   4100   Nkongsamba
GUINEA   MALABO   Bafoussam
Bioko   Sangmélima

ATLANTIC   OCEAN

Príncipe   Bata   EQUATORIAL
SÃO TOMÉ   GUINEA
& PRÍNCIPE
São Tomé   LIBREVILLE

Port-Gentil   Bifoun
GABON

Franceville

BRAZZAV
Pointe-Noire   KINSHA
ANGOLA
Cabinda   M'banza
Congo

KEY

Relief and physical features

Relief metres
5000
3000
2000
1000
500
200
sea level
0
under sea level
200
4000
6000

5895 ▲ Mountain height (in metres)

Water features

～～ River

⋯⋯ Intermittent river

Lake / Reservoir

Intermittent lake

Marsh

Communications

—— Railway

—— Road

⊕ Main airport

Administration

Boundaries

—— International

– – – Disputed

Settlement

Cities and towns in order of size

National capital
■ CAIRO
□ TUNIS
□ ASMARA
▫ MALABO

Other city or town
● Alexandria
○ Oran
○ Agadir
○ Kankan

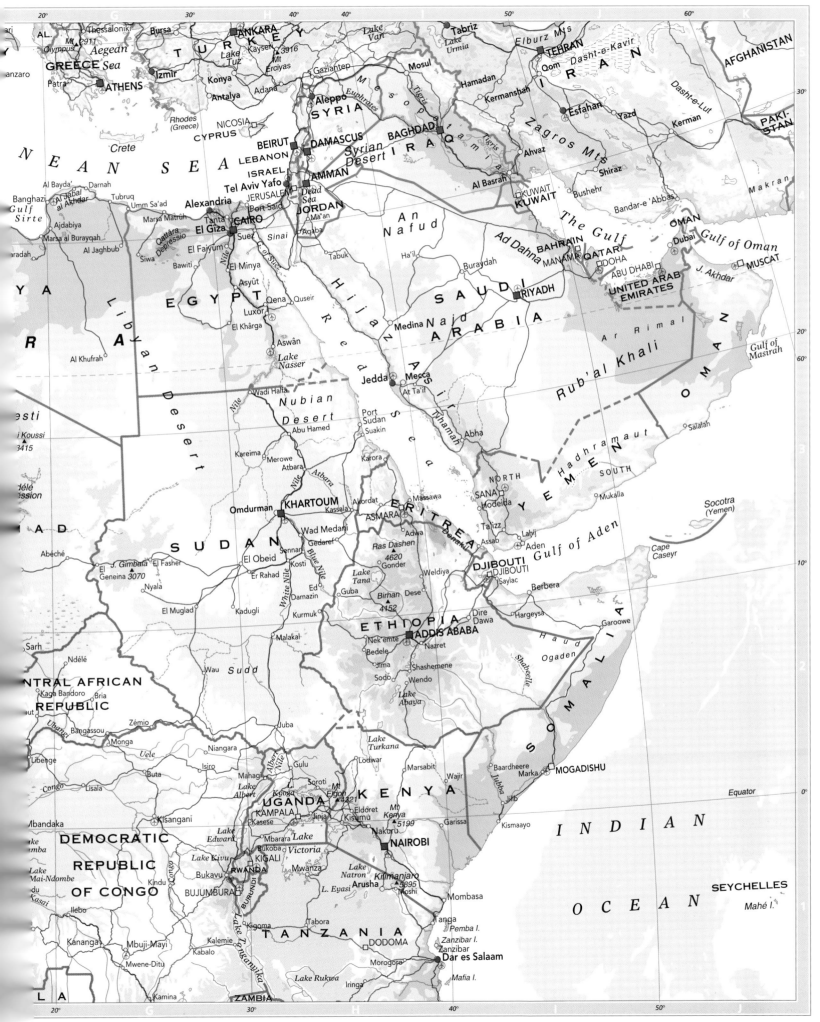

Millers Stereographic projection

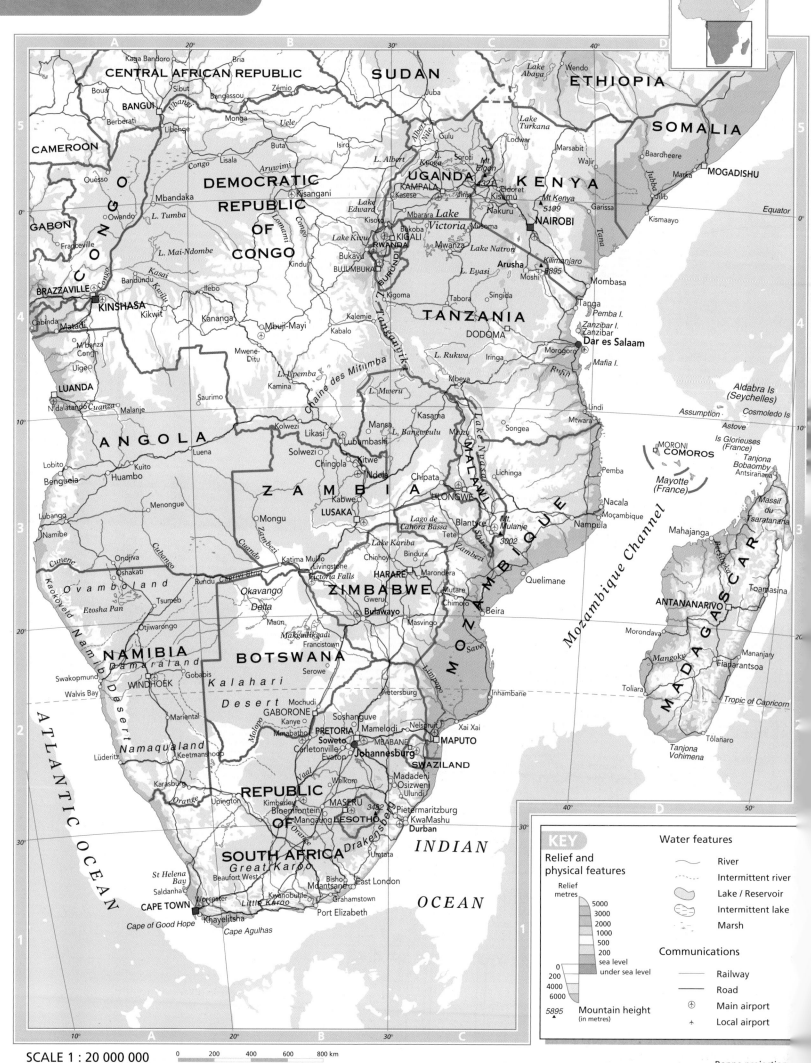

0   200   400   600   800 km

Bonne projection

KEY

Relief and physical features

Relief metres

5000
3000
2000
1000
500
200
0   sea level
     under sea level
200
4000
6000

5895   Mountain height (in metres)

Water features

~~~ River

---- Intermittent river

Lake / Reservoir

Intermittent lake

Marsh

Communications

Railway

Road

⊕ Main airport

✦ Local airport

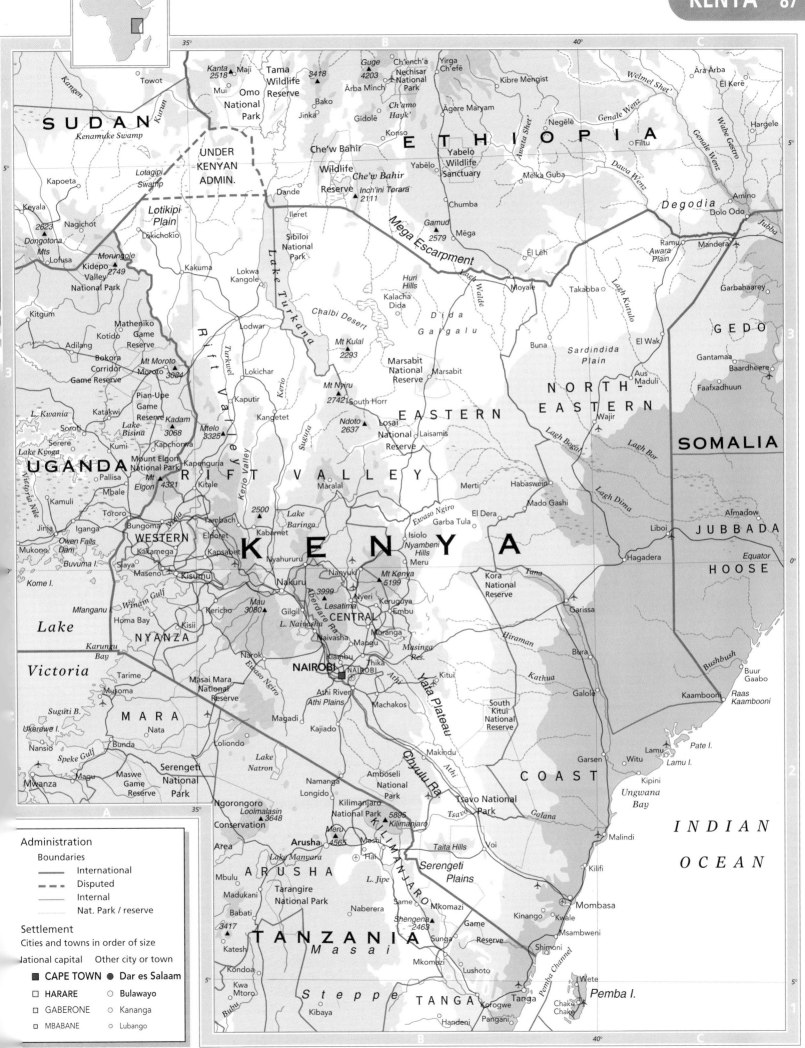

SUDAN

ETHIOPIA

UGANDA

KENYA

SOMALIA

TANZANIA

Lake Victoria

INDIAN OCEAN

UNDER KENYAN ADMIN.

RIFT VALLEY

WESTERN

NYANZA

MARA

CENTRAL

EASTERN

NORTH EASTERN

COAST

GEDO

JUBBADA HOOSE

NAIROBI

Administration
Boundaries
International
Disputed
Internal
Nat. Park / reserve

Settlement
Cities and towns in order of size
National capital   Other city or town
■ CAPE TOWN   ● Dar es Salaam
□ HARARE   ○ Bulawayo
□ GABERONE   ○ Kananga
▫ MBABANE   ○ Lubango

SCALE 1 : 5 000 000

0   50   100   150   200 km

Oblated Stereographic projection

1 POPULATION DENSITY

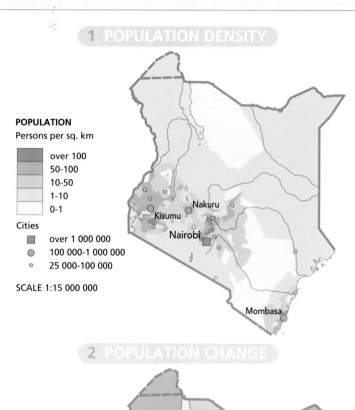

POPULATION
Persons per sq. km

- over 100
- 50-100
- 10-50
- 1-10
- 0-1

Cities
- over 1 000 000
- 100 000-1 000 000
- 25 000-100 000

SCALE 1:15 000 000

2 POPULATION CHANGE

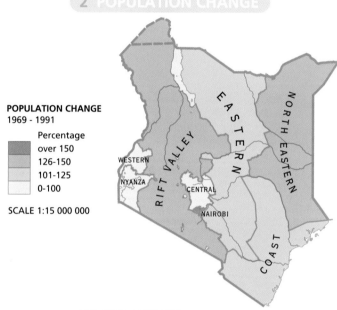

POPULATION CHANGE
1969 - 1991

Percentage
- over 150
- 126-150
- 101-125
- 0-100

SCALE 1:15 000 000

3 ECONOMIC ACTIVITY

INDUSTRY
- • Major industrial centre
- Iron / Steel
- Oil refineries
- Motor vehicles
- Mechanical engineering
- Publishing / Paper
- Chemicals
- Textiles / Clothing
- Food processing

CROPS
- Cash crop producing area

SCALE 1:15 000 000

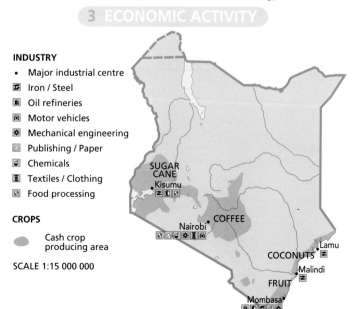

4 POPULATION GROWTH

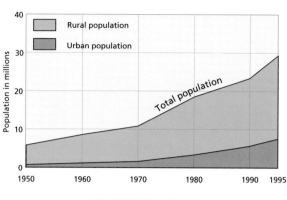

5 MAIN CITIES

City	1969 census	1991 census	% Increase
Nairobi	478 000	1 504 900	215
Mombasa	246 000	425 600	73
Kisumu	30 000	167 100	456
Nakuru	47 000	101 700	115
Machakos	4000	92 300	2300

6 TOURISM

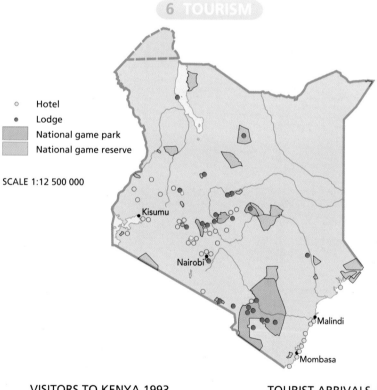

- ○ Hotel
- ● Lodge
- National game park
- National game reserve

SCALE 1:12 500 000

VISITORS TO KENYA 1993
Total 826 000

Others 25.7%
UK 16.8%
Germany 15.7%
Tanzania 11.4%
USA 6.7%
Uganda 6.7%
Italy 5%
France 4.8%
Switzerland 3.9%
Sweden 3.3%

TOURIST ARRIVALS 1984-1993

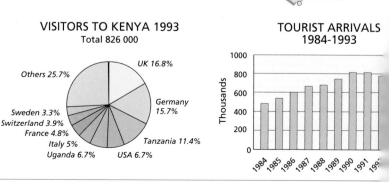

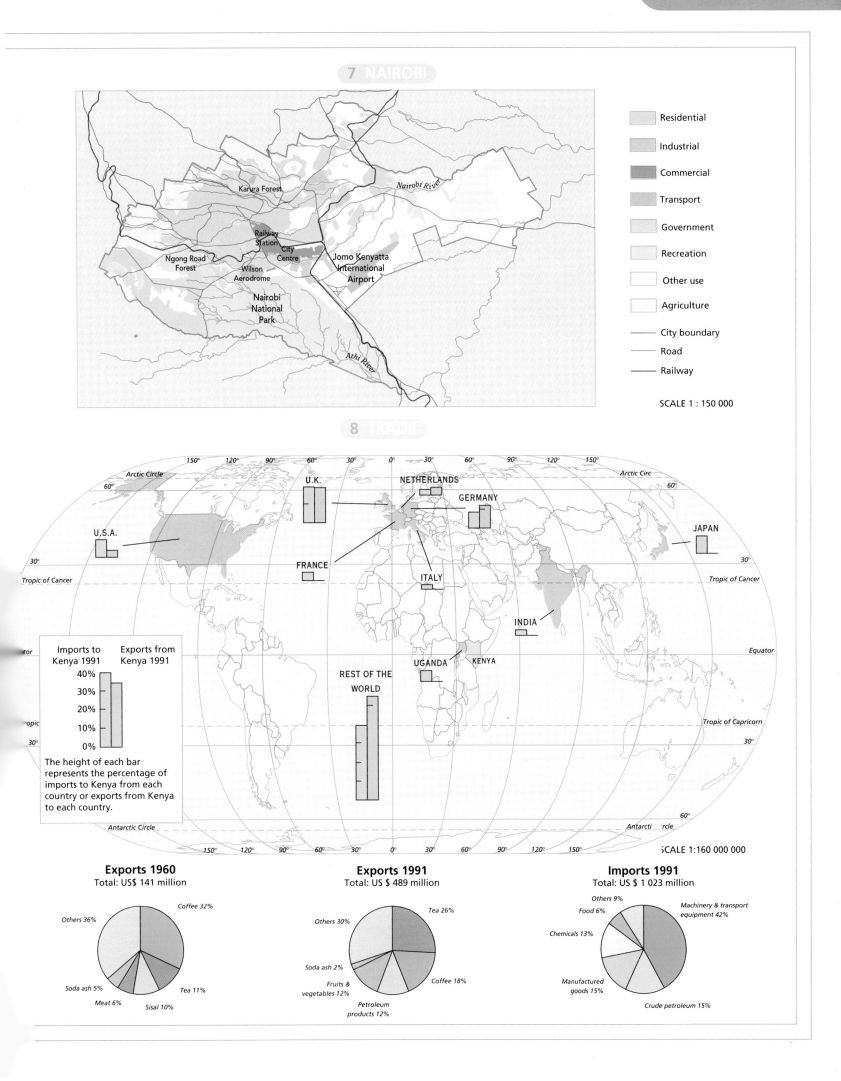

7 NAIROBI

Karura Forest

Nairobi River

Railway Station
City Centre

Ngong Road Forest
Wilson Aerodrome
Jomo Kenyatta International Airport

Nairobi National Park

Athi River

Residential
Industrial
Commercial
Transport
Government
Recreation
Other use
Agriculture
City boundary
Road
Railway

SCALE 1 : 150 000

8 TRADE

Arctic Circle
U.K.
NETHERLANDS
GERMANY
U.S.A.
JAPAN
FRANCE
ITALY
INDIA
Tropic of Cancer
Equator
UGANDA   KENYA
REST OF THE WORLD
Tropic of Capricorn
Antarctic Circle

SCALE 1:160 000 000

Imports to Kenya 1991   Exports from Kenya 1991

40%
30%
20%
10%
0%

The height of each bar represents the percentage of imports to Kenya from each country or exports from Kenya to each country.

Exports 1960
Total: US$ 141 million

Coffee 32%
Others 36%
Soda ash 5%
Meat 6%
Sisal 10%
Tea 11%

Exports 1991
Total: US $ 489 million

Tea 26%
Others 30%
Soda ash 2%
Fruits & vegetables 12%
Petroleum products 12%
Coffee 18%

Imports 1991
Total: US $ 1 023 million

Others 9%
Food 6%
Chemicals 13%
Machinery & transport equipment 42%
Manufactured goods 15%
Crude petroleum 15%

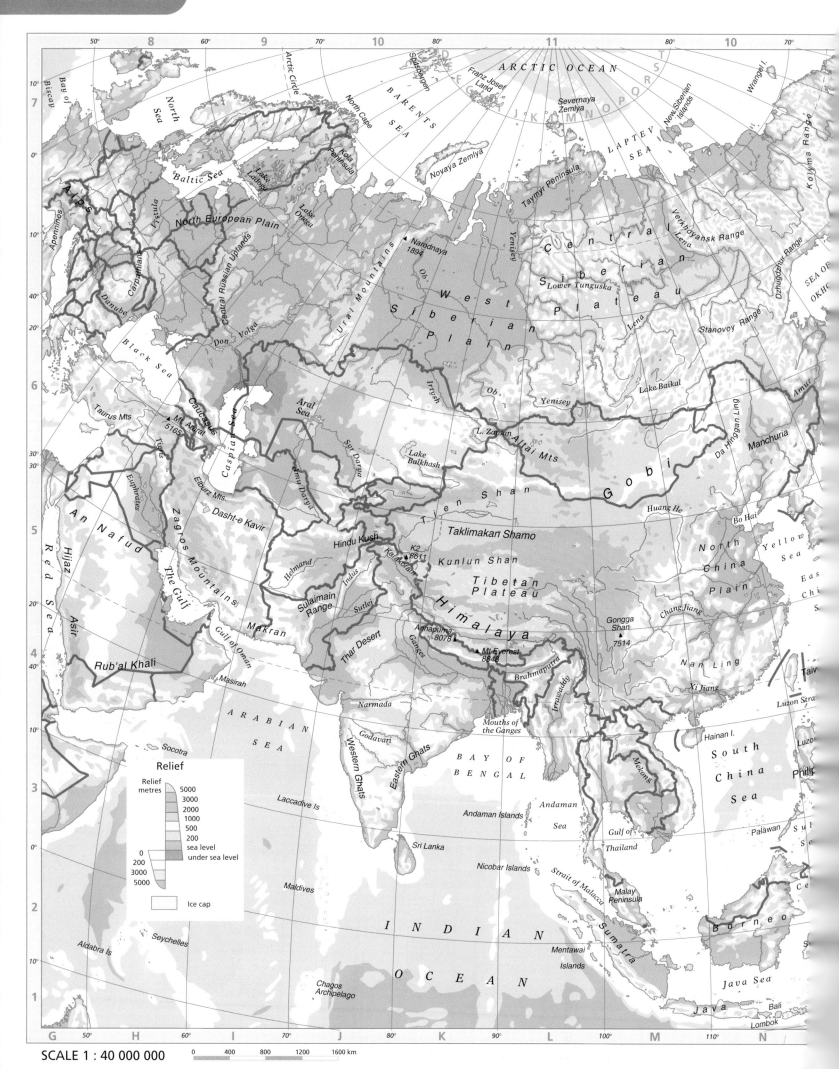

Relief

Relief metres	
5000	
3000	
2000	
1000	
500	
200	
0	sea level
	under sea level
200	
3000	
5000	

Ice cap

SCALE 1 : 40 000 000

0   400   800   1200   1600 km

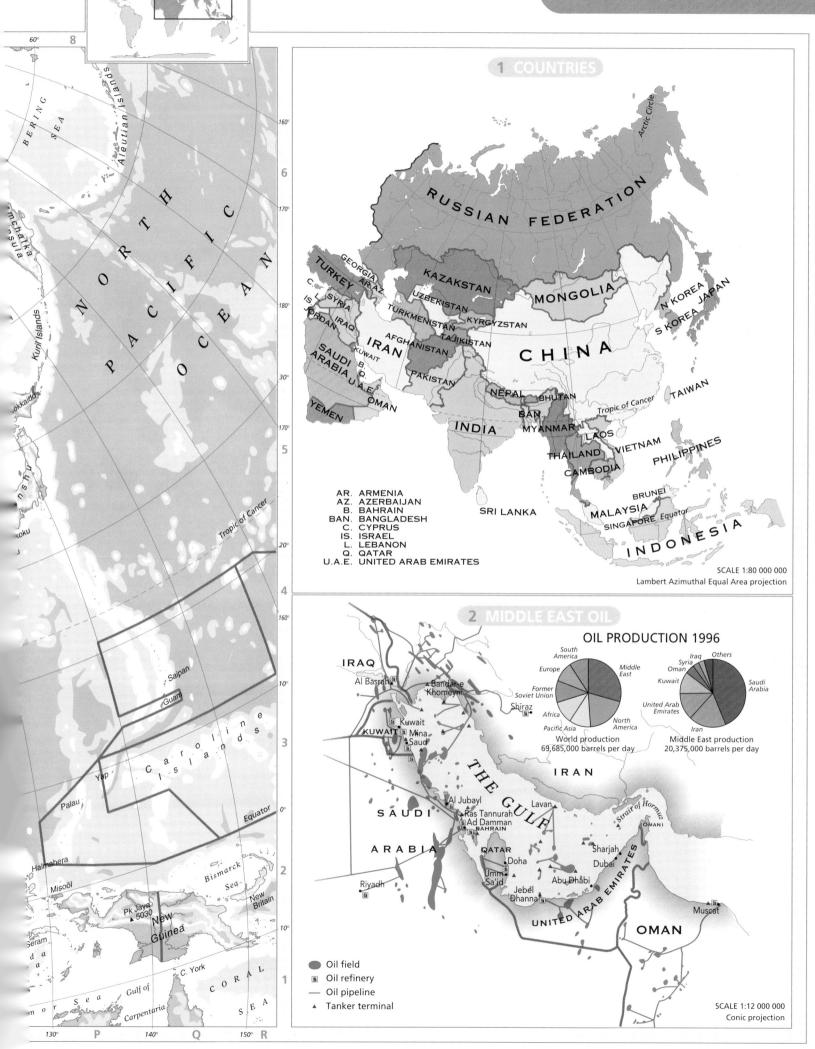

1 COUNTRIES

RUSSIAN FEDERATION

GEORGIA
TURKEY AR. AZ.
C. L. SYRIA
IS. L.
JORDAN IRAQ
SAUDI B.Q.
ARABIA U.A.E.
YEMEN OMAN

KAZAKSTAN
UZBEKISTAN
TURKMENISTAN
IRAN
AFGHANISTAN TAJIKISTAN
KUWAIT
PAKISTAN

KYRGYZSTAN

MONGOLIA

CHINA

N KOREA JAPAN
S KOREA

NEPAL BHUTAN
BAN.
INDIA MYANMAR
LAOS
THAILAND VIETNAM
CAMBODIA
PHILIPPINES

Tropic of Cancer
TAIWAN

Arctic Circle

SRI LANKA

BRUNEI
MALAYSIA
SINGAPORE Equator
INDONESIA

AR.   ARMENIA
AZ.   AZERBAIJAN
B.   BAHRAIN
BAN.   BANGLADESH
C.   CYPRUS
IS.   ISRAEL
L.   LEBANON
Q.   QATAR
U.A.E.   UNITED ARAB EMIRATES

SCALE 1:80 000 000
Lambert Azimuthal Equal Area projection

2 MIDDLE EAST OIL

OIL PRODUCTION 1996

South
America
Europe Middle
East
Former
Soviet Union
Africa North
America
Pacific Asia

Iraq
Syria Others
Oman
Kuwait Saudi
Arabia
United Arab
Emirates
Iran

World production
69,685,000 barrels per day

Middle East production
20,375,000 barrels per day

IRAQ
Al Basrah
Bandar-e
Khomeyni
Shiraz

Kuwait
KUWAIT Mina
Sa'ud

IRAN

SAUDI
Al Jubayl
Ras Tannurah
Ad Damman
BAHRAIN
Lavan

THE GULF

Strait of Hormuz
(OMAN)

ARABIA
QATAR
Doha
Umm
Sa'id
Riyadh
Jebel
Dhanna

Sharjah
Dubai

Abu Dhabi

UNITED ARAB EMIRATES

OMAN
Muscat

● Oil field
▣ Oil refinery
— Oil pipeline
▲ Tanker terminal

SCALE 1:12 000 000
Conic projection

BERING SEA
Aleutian Islands
NORTH PACIFIC OCEAN
Kuril Islands
Kamchatka Peninsula
Hokkaido
Honshu
Shikoku
Tropic of Cancer

Saipan
Guam
Caroline Islands
Yap
Palau
Equator

Halmahera
Misoöl
Seram
Bismarck Sea
New Britain
Pk Jaya 5030
New Guinea
C. York
Gulf of Carpentaria
Timor Sea
CORAL SEA

Lambert Azimuthal Equal Area projection

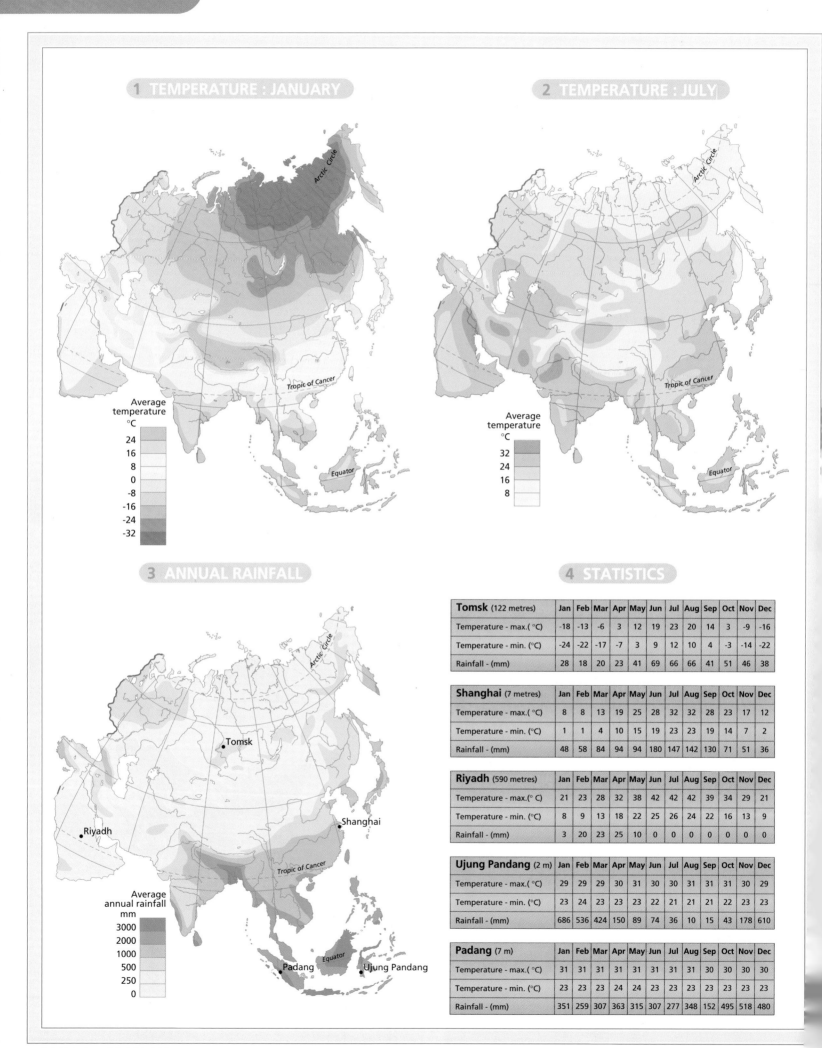

1 TEMPERATURE : JANUARY

Average temperature °C

| 24 |
| 16 |
| 8 |
| 0 |
| -8 |
| -16 |
| -24 |
| -32 |

Arctic Circle
Tropic of Cancer
Equator

2 TEMPERATURE : JULY

Average temperature °C

| 32 |
| 24 |
| 16 |
| 8 |

Arctic Circle
Tropic of Cancer
Equator

3 ANNUAL RAINFALL

Average annual rainfall mm

| 3000 |
| 2000 |
| 1000 |
| 500 |
| 250 |
| 0 |

Tomsk
Riyadh
Shanghai
Padang
Ujung Pandang

Arctic Circle
Tropic of Cancer
Equator

4 STATISTICS

Tomsk (122 metres)	Jan	Feb	Mar	Apr	May	Jun	Jul	Aug	Sep	Oct	Nov	Dec
Temperature - max.(°C)	-18	-13	-6	3	12	19	23	20	14	3	-9	-16
Temperature - min. (°C)	-24	-22	-17	-7	3	9	12	10	4	-3	-14	-22
Rainfall - (mm)	28	18	20	23	41	69	66	66	41	51	46	38

Shanghai (7 metres)	Jan	Feb	Mar	Apr	May	Jun	Jul	Aug	Sep	Oct	Nov	Dec
Temperature - max.(°C)	8	8	13	19	25	28	32	32	28	23	17	12
Temperature - min. (°C)	1	1	4	10	15	19	23	23	19	14	7	2
Rainfall - (mm)	48	58	84	94	94	180	147	142	130	71	51	36

Riyadh (590 metres)	Jan	Feb	Mar	Apr	May	Jun	Jul	Aug	Sep	Oct	Nov	Dec
Temperature - max.(° C)	21	23	28	32	38	42	42	42	39	34	29	21
Temperature - min. (°C)	8	9	13	18	22	25	26	24	22	16	13	9
Rainfall - (mm)	3	20	23	25	10	0	0	0	0	0	0	0

Ujung Pandang (2 m)	Jan	Feb	Mar	Apr	May	Jun	Jul	Aug	Sep	Oct	Nov	Dec
Temperature - max.(°C)	29	29	29	30	31	30	30	31	31	31	30	29
Temperature - min. (°C)	23	24	23	23	22	22	21	21	21	22	23	23
Rainfall - (mm)	686	536	424	150	89	74	36	10	15	43	178	610

Padang (7 m)	Jan	Feb	Mar	Apr	May	Jun	Jul	Aug	Sep	Oct	Nov	Dec
Temperature - max.(°C)	31	31	31	31	31	31	31	31	30	30	30	30
Temperature - min. (°C)	23	23	23	24	24	23	23	23	23	23	23	23
Rainfall - (mm)	351	259	307	363	315	307	277	348	152	495	518	480

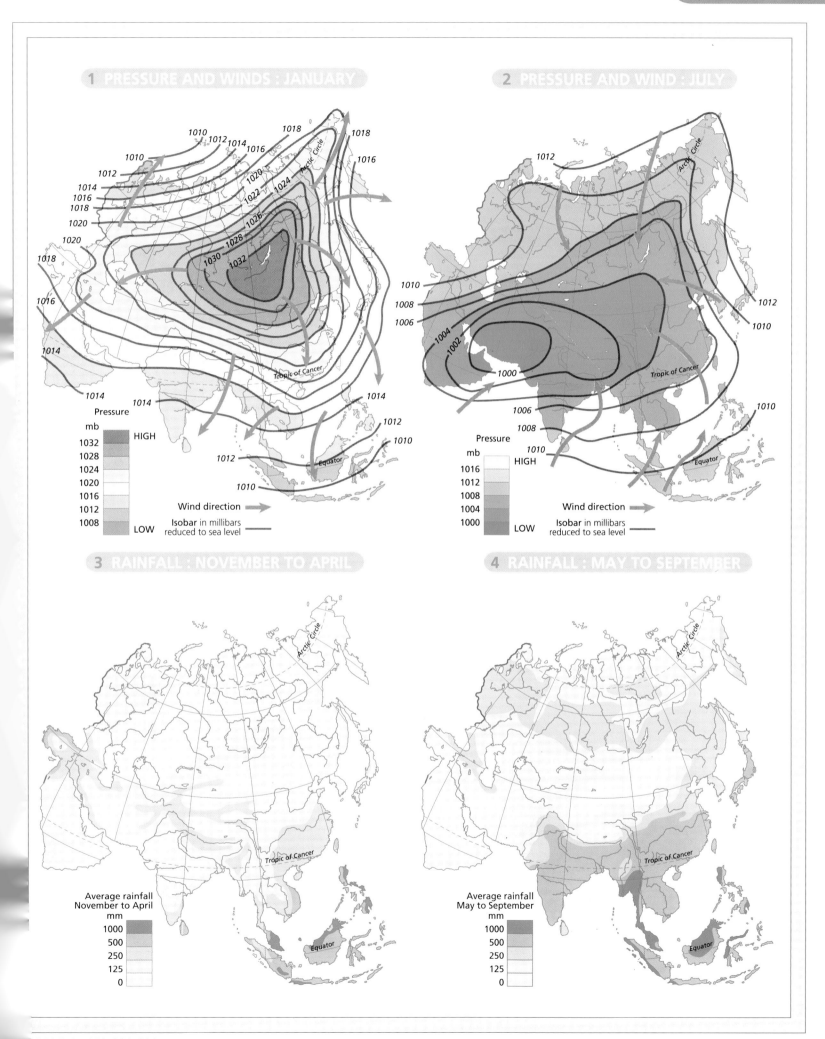

1 PRESSURE AND WINDS : JANUARY

Pressure
mb
1032 HIGH
1028
1024
1020
1016
1012
1008 LOW

Wind direction

Isobar in millibars reduced to sea level

2 PRESSURE AND WIND : JULY

Pressure
mb
1016 HIGH
1012
1008
1004
1000 LOW

Wind direction

Isobar in millibars reduced to sea level

3 RAINFALL : NOVEMBER TO APRIL

Average rainfall
November to April
mm
1000
500
250
125
0

4 RAINFALL : MAY TO SEPTEMBER

Average rainfall
May to September
mm
1000
500
250
125
0

SCALE 1 : 100 000 000

Lambert Azimuthal Equal Area projection

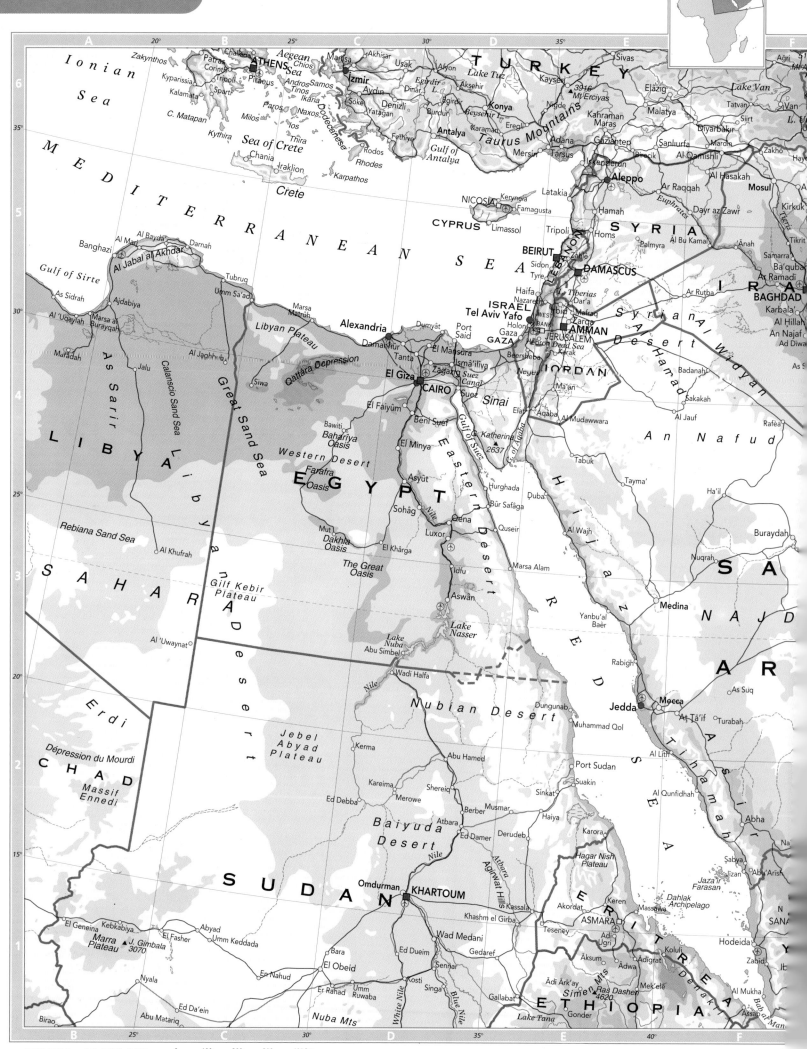

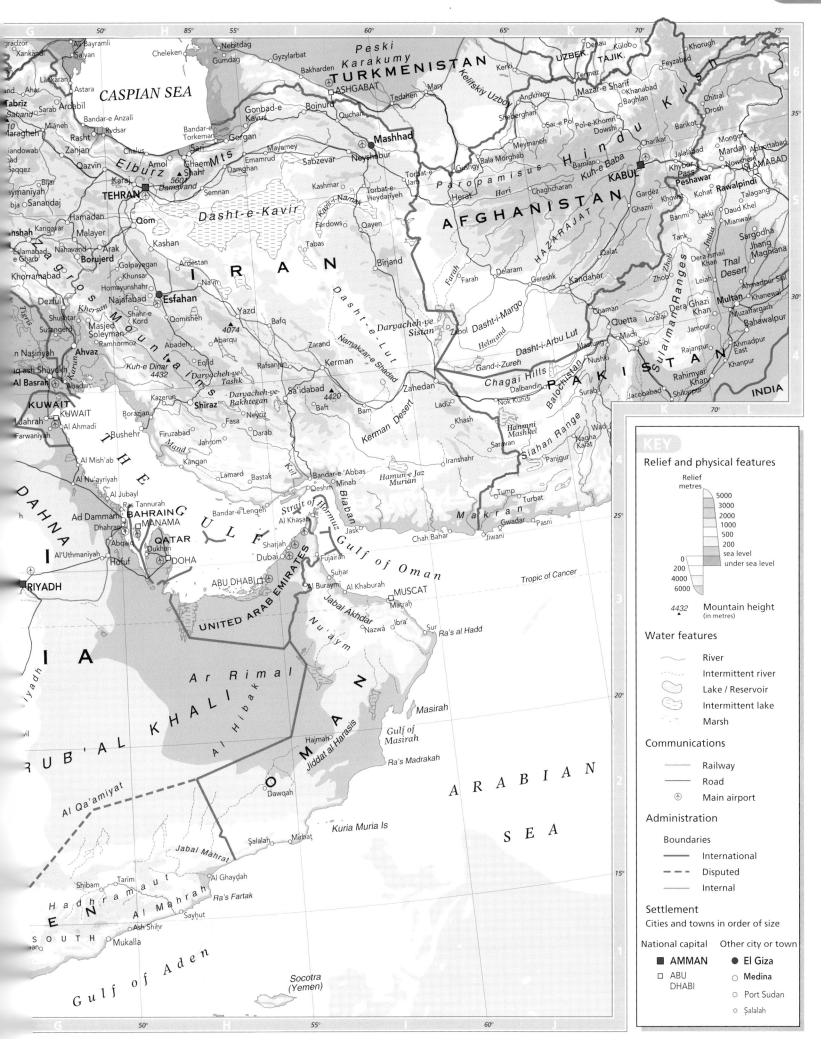

Peski Karakumy

CASPIAN SEA

TURKMENISTAN

UZBEK.   TAJIK.

ASHGABAT

Khorugh

Feyzabad

Chelekin
Nebitdag
Gyzylarbat
Gumdag

Gonbad-e Kavus

Bojnurd   Quchan

Tedzhen   Mary   Kerki

Andkhvoy   Mazar-e Sharif   Khanabad   Baghlan

Chitral   Drosh

Ar Bayramli
Xankändi
Xanlan
Salyan

Al Bayramli
Salyan

Mashhad

Bakharden

Kelifskiy Uzboy

Sheberghan   Sar-e Pol   Pol-e Khomri   Dowshi

Barikot   Mongora   Mardan   Abbottabad

Tabriz
Sahand   Ahar   Astara

Bandar-e Anzali   Rasht   Rvdsar   Chalus

Sari   Amol   Ghaem   Shahr   Mts
Emamrud   Damghan   Semnan

Sabzevar   Neyshabur   Torbat-e Jam

Gushgy   Bala Morghab

Meymaneh   Bamian   Kuh-e Baba   KABUL   Jalalabad   Mardan   Nowshera   ISLAMABAD   Rawalpindi

Khyber Pass   Peshawar   Kohat   Talagang

liandowab
Zaqqez

Zanjan
Qazvin   Karaj   5601 Damavand   Elburz

Kashmar   Torbat-e Heydariyeh

Herat   Hari   Chaghcharan   Paropamisus   Hindu Kush   Charikar   Gardez   Khowst   Banmi   Lakki   Daud Khel   Mianwali

Sanandaj   Hamadan   TEHRAN   Qom

Damghan

Ferdows   Qayen   Birjand

AFGHANISTAN   HAZARAJATAN   Ghazni   Tank   Sargodha   Jhang   Maghiana

Kangavar   Malayer   Arak   Kashan   Ardestan   Na'in   Tabas

Kermanshah   Eslamabad e Gharb   Khorramabad   Borujerd   Golpayegan   Khunsar   Homayunshahr   Esfahan

Dasht-e Kavir

Farah   Delaram   Gereshk   Qalat

Farah   Dasht-i-Margo   Kandahar   Chaman   Loralai   Dera Ghazi Khan   Muzaffargarh   Multan   Khanewal   Bahawalpur

Dezful   Shushtar   Susangerd   Masjed Soleyman   Ramhormoz   Shahr-e Kord   Najafabad   Qomisheh

Kavir-e Namak

Dasht-e-Lut

Zabol   Dasht-i-Arbu Lut   Helmand   Mastung   Quetta   Mach   Sibi   Jampur   Rahimyar Khan   Khanpur

n Nasiriyah   Ahvaz   Kuh-e Dinar 4432   Khersan   Kazerun   4074   Abarqu   Yazd   Bafq   Zarand   Kerman   Gand-i-Zureh   Nok Kundi   Surab   Jacobabad   Shikarpur   INDIA

Eqld   Darvacheh-ye Tashk   Rafsanjan

Dasht-e-Sistan   Chagai Hills   Dalbandin   Balochistan   Nushki   Rajanpur   Shikarpur

Iq ash Shuyukh   Al Basrah   Abadan

Darvacheh-ye Bakhtegan   Sa'idabad   4420   Zahedan   Ladiz   Khash   Hamni Mashkel   Saravan   Nagha Kalat

KUWAIT   KUWAIT   Shiraz   Fasa   Neyriz   Bam   Siahan Range   Panjgur

Al Jahrah   Al Ahmadi   Borazjan   Firuzabad   Jahrom   Darab   Kerman Desert   Iranshahr   Tump   Turbat

Farwaniyah   Bushehr   Kangan   Mand   Lamard   Bastak   Hamun-e Jaz Murian   Gwadar   Pasni

Al Mish'ab   Al Nu'ayriyah   Bandar-e Lengeh   Qeshm   Bandar-e 'Abbas   Minab   Jask   Chah Bahar   Jiwani

DAHNA   Al Jubayl   Ras Tannurah   BAHRAIN   Bandar-e Lengeh   Strait of Hormuz   Makran

Ad Dammam   Dhahran   MANAMA   QATAR   Al Khasab   Biaban   GULF   Gulf of Oman

Abqaiq   Al'Uthmaniyah   Dukhan   DOHA   Sharjah   Fujairah

RIYADH   Hofuf   Dubai   UNITED ARAB EMIRATES   Suhar   Matrah   MUSCAT   Tropic of Cancer

ABU DHABI   Al Buraymi   Al Khaburah

Jabal Akhdar   Ibra'   Nazwa   Sur   Ra's al Hadd

UNITED ARAB EMIRATES   Nu'aym

A   Ar Rimal   Al Hibak   Masirah

RUB' AL KHALI   O   M   A   N   Gulf of Masirah

iyadh   Hajmah   Jiddat al Harasis   Ra's Madrakah

ARABIAN

Al Qa'amiyat   Dawqah   SEA

Kuria Muria Is

Salalah   Mirbat

Jabal Mahrat

Shibam   Tarim   Al Ghaydah

Hadhramaut   Ash Shihr   Al Mahrah   Ra's Fartak   Sayhut

EN   SOUTH   Mukalla

Gulf of Aden   Socotra (Yemen)

KEY

Relief and physical features

Relief metres

5000
3000
2000
1000
500
200
sea level
0
under sea level
200
4000
6000

▲ 4432   Mountain height (in metres)

Water features

~~~ River

········ Intermittent river

Lake / Reservoir

Intermittent lake

Marsh

Communications

——— Railway

——— Road

⊕ Main airport

Administration

Boundaries

——— International

– – – Disputed

········· Internal

Settlement

Cities and towns in order of size

National capital   Other city or town

■ AMMAN   ● El Giza

□ ABU DHABI   ○ Medina

○ Port Sudan

○ Şalalah

Albers Conic Equal Area projection

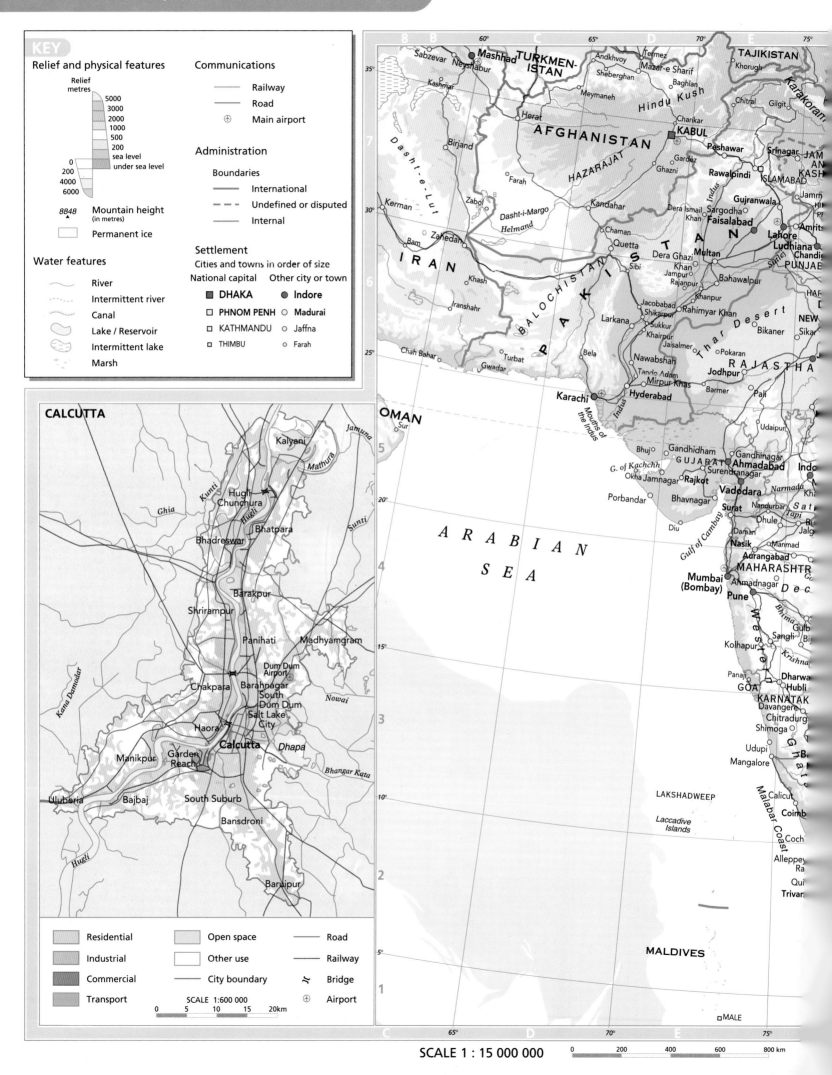

KEY

Relief and physical features

Relief metres
5000
3000
2000
1000
500
200
0 sea level
200 under sea level
4000
6000

8848 ▲ Mountain height (in metres)

Permanent ice

Water features

~~~ River
····· Intermittent river
~~~ Canal
Lake / Reservoir
Intermittent lake
Marsh

Communications

Railway
Road
⊕ Main airport

Administration

Boundaries

International
Undefined or disputed
Internal

Settlement

Cities and towns in order of size

National capital   Other city or town

■ DHAKA   ● Indore
□ PHNOM PENH   ○ Madurai
□ KATHMANDU   ○ Jaffna
□ THIMBU   ○ Farah

CALCUTTA

Kalyani
Kunti
Hugli
Chunchura
Ghia
Bhatpara
Bhadreswar
Mathura
Jamuna
Sunti
Nowai
Barakpur
Shrirampur
Panihati
Madhyamgram
Dum Dum Airport
Chakpara
Barahnagar
South Dum Dum
Salt Lake City
Haora
Calcutta
Dhapa
Manikpur
Garden Reach
Bhangar Kata
Kana Damodar
Uluberia
Bajbaj
South Suburb
Bansdroni
Hugli
Baruipur

Residential
Industrial
Commercial
Transport
Open space
Other use
City boundary
Road
Railway
≍ Bridge
⊕ Airport

SCALE 1:600 000
0 5 10 15 20km

Sabzevar
Neyshabur
Mashhad
TURKMEN-ISTAN
Andkhvoy
Termez
Mazar-e Sharif
TAJIKISTAN
Khorugh
Kashmar
Sheberghan
Baghlan
Chitral
Gilgit
Meymaneh
Hindu Kush
Karakoram
Dasht-e-Lut
Herat
Charikar
KABUL
Peshawar
Srinagar
JAMM
AN
KASH
Birjand
AFGHANISTAN
Gardez
Rawalpindi
ISLAMABAD
Jamm
HI
Kerman
Farah
Ghazni
Gujranwala
HAZARAJAT
Zabol
Kandahar
Dera Ismail Khan
Sargodha
Faisalabad
Lahore
Ludhiana
Chandi
PUNJAB
Dasht-i-Margo
Chaman
Quetta
Multan
Amrits
Zahedan
Helmand
Dera Ghazi Khan
Bahawalpur
Bam
Sibi
Jampur
Rajanpur
Khanpur
Bahawalpur
Bikaner
Sikar
NEW
Khash
Jacobabad
Rahimyar Khan
Iranshahr
Larkana
Shikarpur
Sukkur
Jaisalmer
Thar Desert
Pokaran
RAJASTHA
Chah Bahar
Khairpur
Bela
Nawabshah
Jodhpur
Turbat
Tando Adam
Mirpur Khas
Gwadar
Barmer
Pali
Karachi
Hyderabad
Mouths of the Indus
Indus
OMAN
Sur
Udaipur
Bhuj
Gandhidham
Gandhinagar
G. of Kachchh
GUJARAT
Ahmadabad
Indo
Okha Jamnagar
Surendranagar
Rajkot
Vadodara
Narmada
Porbandar
Bhavnagar
Nandurbar
Sat
Diu
Surat
Dhule
Daman
Tapi
Jalg
Gulf of Cambay
Nasik
Manmad
Aurangabad
ARABIAN
SEA
Mumbai (Bombay)
Ahmadnagar
MAHARASHTR
Go
Pune
Dec
Bhima
Gulb
Western
Bi
Kolhapur
Sangli
Krishna
Panaji
Dharwa
GOA
Hubli
KARNATAK
Davangere
Chitradurg
Shimoga
Udupi
G
Mangalore
B
Malabar Coast
LAKSHADWEEP
Calicut
Laccadive Islands
Coimb
Coch
Alleppey
Ra
Qui
Trivan
MALDIVES
□ MALE

SCALE 1 : 15 000 000
0 200 400 600 800 km

Conic projection

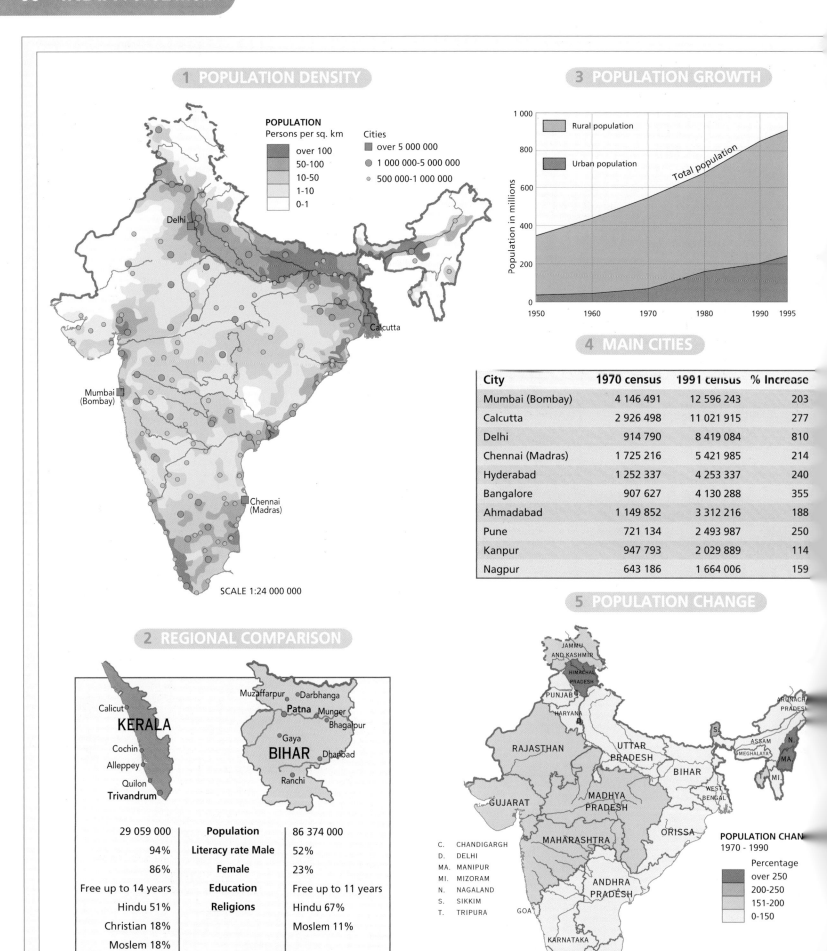

1 POPULATION DENSITY

POPULATION
Persons per sq. km
- over 100
- 50-100
- 10-50
- 1-10
- 0-1

Cities
- over 5 000 000
- 1 000 000-5 000 000
- 500 000-1 000 000

Delhi

Mumbai (Bombay)

Chennai (Madras)

Calcutta

SCALE 1:24 000 000

3 POPULATION GROWTH

Rural population
Urban population
Total population

Population in millions

0, 200, 400, 600, 800, 1 000

1950, 1960, 1970, 1980, 1990, 1995

4 MAIN CITIES

City	1970 census	1991 census	% Increase
Mumbai (Bombay)	4 146 491	12 596 243	203
Calcutta	2 926 498	11 021 915	277
Delhi	914 790	8 419 084	810
Chennai (Madras)	1 725 216	5 421 985	214
Hyderabad	1 252 337	4 253 337	240
Bangalore	907 627	4 130 288	355
Ahmadabad	1 149 852	3 312 216	188
Pune	721 134	2 493 987	250
Kanpur	947 793	2 029 889	114
Nagpur	643 186	1 664 006	159

2 REGIONAL COMPARISON

Calicut

KERALA

Cochin
Alleppey
Quilon
Trivandrum

Muzaffarpur Darbhanga
Patna Munger
Bhagalpur
Gaya
BIHAR Dhanbad
Ranchi

29 059 000	**Population**	86 374 000
94%	**Literacy rate Male**	52%
86%	**Female**	23%
Free up to 14 years	**Education**	Free up to 11 years
Hindu 51%	**Religions**	Hindu 67%
Christian 18%		Moslem 11%
Moslem 18%		
Malayalam	**Languages**	Hindi
Tamil		Urdu
Kannada		Bengali

5 POPULATION CHANGE

JAMMU AND KASHMIR
HIMACHAL PRADESH
PUNJAB
HARYANA
RAJASTHAN
UTTAR PRADESH
GUJARAT
MADHYA PRADESH
BIHAR
WEST BENGAL
ASSAM
MEGHALAYA
ARUNACHAL PRADESH
NAGALAND
MANIPUR
MIZORAM
TRIPURA
SIKKIM
MAHARASHTRA
ORISSA
ANDHRA PRADESH
GOA
KARNATAKA
TAMIL NADU
KERALA

C. CHANDIGARGH
D. DELHI
MA. MANIPUR
MI. MIZORAM
N. NAGALAND
S. SIKKIM
T. TRIPURA

POPULATION CHAN
1970 - 1990

Percentage
- over 250
- 200-250
- 151-200
- 0-150

SCALE 1:30 000 000

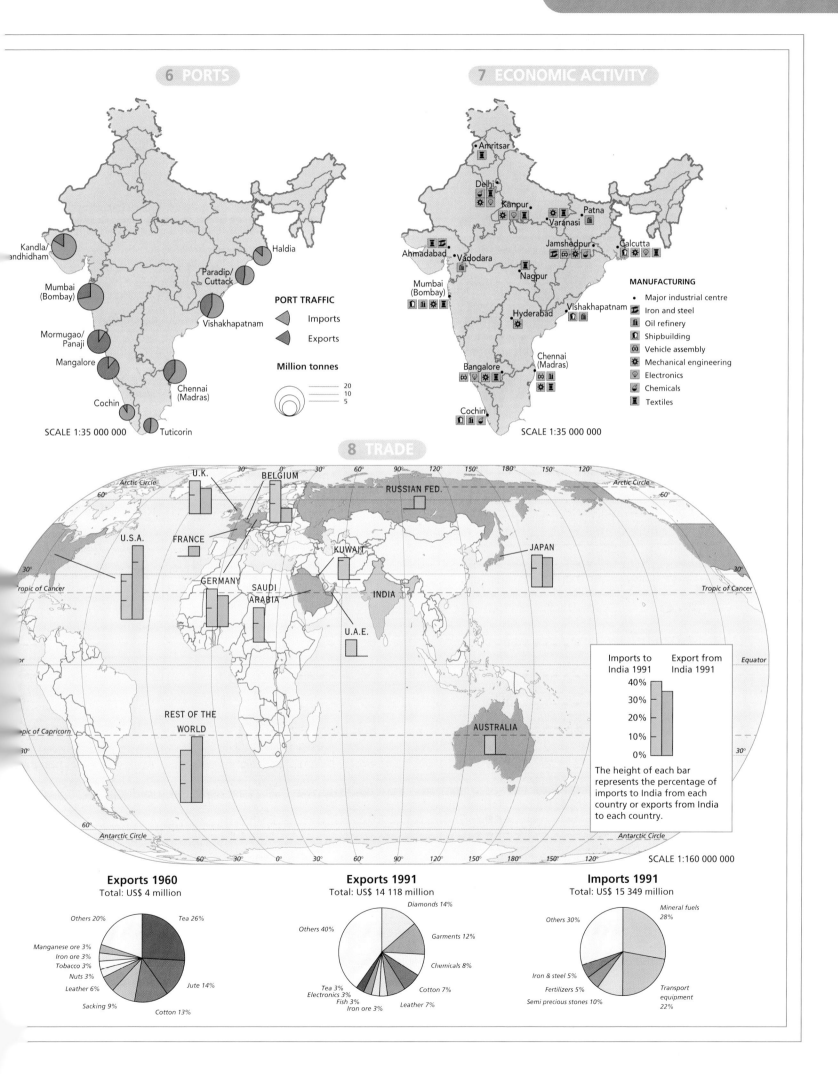

6 PORTS

Kandla/Gandhidham
Mumbai (Bombay)
Mormugao/Panaji
Mangalore
Cochin
Tuticorin
Chennai (Madras)
Vishakhapatnam
Paradip/Cuttack
Haldia

PORT TRAFFIC

Imports
Exports

Million tonnes

20
10
5

SCALE 1:35 000 000

7 ECONOMIC ACTIVITY

Amritsar
Delhi
Kanpur
Patna
Varanasi
Jamshedpur
Calcutta
Ahmadabad
Vadodara
Mumbai (Bombay)
Nagpur
Hyderabad
Vishakhapatnam
Bangalore
Chennai (Madras)
Cochin

MANUFACTURING

• Major industrial centre
Iron and steel
Oil refinery
Shipbuilding
Vehicle assembly
Mechanical engineering
Electronics
Chemicals
Textiles

SCALE 1:35 000 000

8 TRADE

Arctic Circle
Arctic Circle
U.K.
BELGIUM
RUSSIAN FED.
U.S.A.
FRANCE
JAPAN
Tropic of Cancer
GERMANY
KUWAIT
Tropic of Cancer
SAUDI ARABIA
INDIA
U.A.E.
Equator
Equator
REST OF THE WORLD
AUSTRALIA
Tropic of Capricorn
Tropic of Capricorn
Antarctic Circle
Antarctic Circle

SCALE 1:160 000 000

Imports to India 1991   Export from India 1991

40%
30%
20%
10%
0%

The height of each bar represents the percentage of imports to India from each country or exports from India to each country.

Exports 1960
Total: US$ 4 million

Others 20%
Tea 26%
Manganese ore 3%
Iron ore 3%
Tobacco 3%
Nuts 3%
Leather 6%
Jute 14%
Sacking 9%
Cotton 13%

Exports 1991
Total: US$ 14 118 million

Diamonds 14%
Others 40%
Garments 12%
Chemicals 8%
Tea 3%
Electronics 3%
Fish 3%
Iron ore 3%
Cotton 7%
Leather 7%

Imports 1991
Total: US$ 15 349 million

Mineral fuels 28%
Others 30%
Iron & steel 5%
Fertilizers 5%
Semi precious stones 10%
Transport equipment 22%

1 POPULATION DENSITY

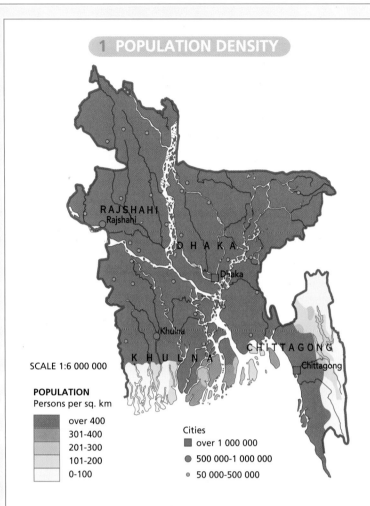

SCALE 1:6 000 000

POPULATION
Persons per sq. km

over 400
301-400
201-300
101-200
0-100

Cities

■ over 1 000 000
● 500 000-1 000 000
• 50 000-500 000

Forest
Dense forests known as the Sundarbans are found along the southwest c◼
of Bangladesh. The same green on the right of the image is wooded fore◼
found on the highlands along the border with Myanmar.

Silt laden water
The red/browm area on the satellite image is the silt laden water at the
mouth of the Ganges. Silt carried down by the rivers Ganges and
Brahmaputra is deposited at the delta which is steadily growing out into
the Bay of Bengal.

Cultivated land
When silt is deposited on the deltaic plains extremely fertile ground is le◼
This is most suitable for the growing of rice, especially floating varieties
which are adapted to cope with seasonal flooding.

Rivers
Bangladesh has two major rivers, the Ganges and the Brahmaputra or
Jamuna, whose many tributaries criss cross the country.

Reservoir
In addition to its many small natural lakes, Bangladesh has a large
reservoir, the Karnafuli Reservoir, in the hills near Chittagong.

2 MAIN CITIES

City	1974 census	1991 census	% Increase
Dhaka	1 310 972	6 105 160	366
Chittagong	416 733	2 040 663	390
Khulna	436 000	877 388	101
Rajshahi	132 909	517 136	289

3 ECONOMIC ACTIVITY

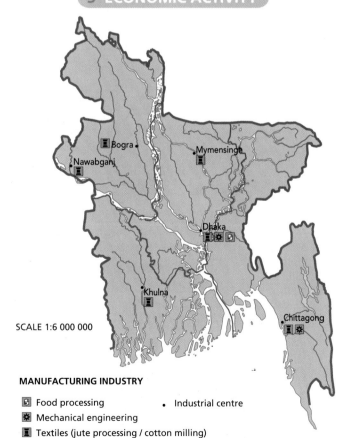

SCALE 1:6 000 000

MANUFACTURING INDUSTRY

🅖 Food processing   • Industrial centre

✴ Mechanical engineering

▤ Textiles (jute processing / cotton milling)

4 TRADE

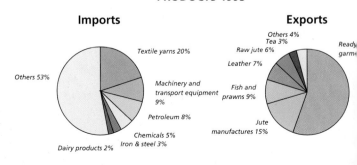

PARTNERS 1993

Imports
Total: US$ 3950 million

Japan 10.5%
S. Korea 9.4%
USA 7.0%
Hong Kong 6.8%
Singapore 6.6%
India 6.3%
China 5.3%
Yemen 3.9%
Others 44.2%

Exports
Total: US$ 2119 million

USA
Others 33.4%
Netherlands 3.2%
Japan 3.4%
Singapore 3.8%
Belgium 4.5%
Italy 5.5%
UK 7.7%
Ge◼ 9.6◼

PRODUCTS 1993

Imports

Textile yarns 20%
Machinery and transport equipment 9%
Petroleum 8%
Chemicals 5%
Iron & steel 3%
Dairy products 2%
Others 53%

Exports

Others 4%
Tea 3%
Raw jute 6%
Leather 7%
Fish and prawns 9%
Ready◼ garme◼
Jute manufactures 15%

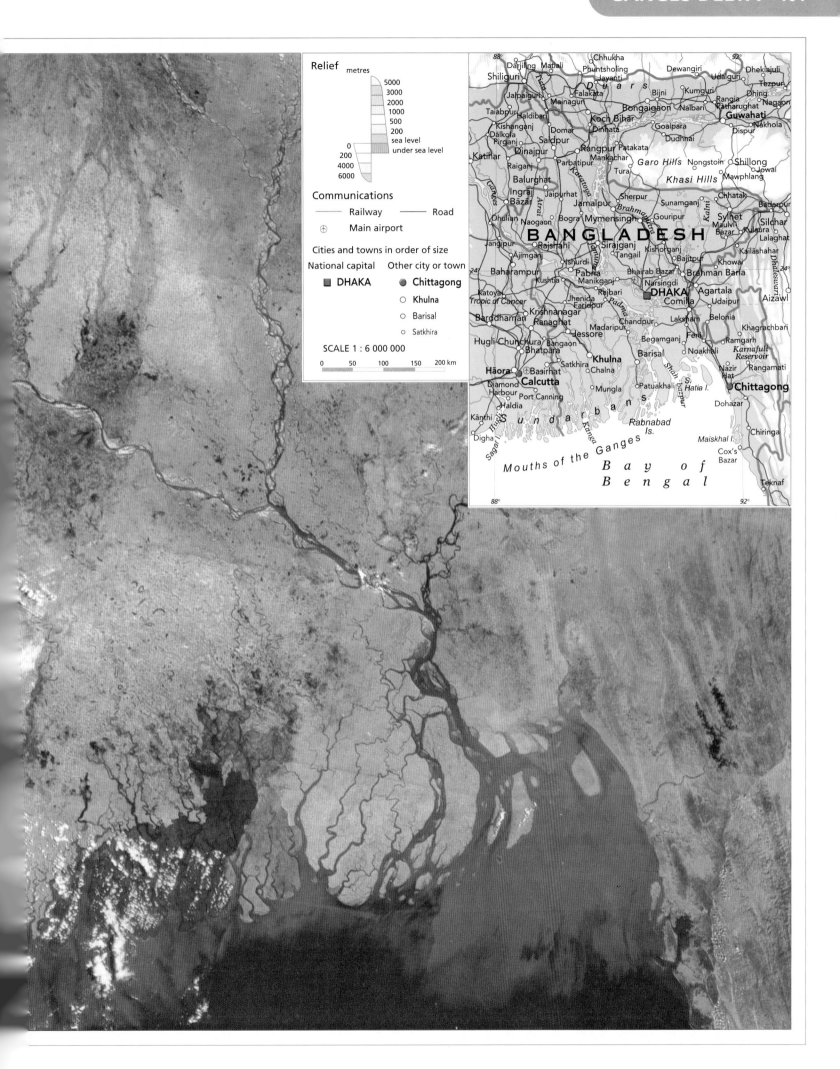

Relief

metres

5000
3000
2000
1000
500
200
0 sea level
under sea level
200
4000
6000

Communications

Railway   Road

⊕   Main airport

Cities and towns in order of size

National capital   Other city or town

◼ DHAKA   ● Chittagong

○ Khulna

○ Barisal

○ Satkhira

SCALE 1 : 6 000 000

0   50   100   150   200 km

Chhukha
Darjiling Matali   Phuntsholing   Dewangiri   Dhekiajuli
Shiliguri   Jayanti   Udalguri   Tezpur
Jalpaiguri   Falakata   Bijni Kumguri   Dhing Nagaon
Taiabpur Haldibari   Mainaguri   Bongaigaon Nalbari Rangia Patharughat   Guwahati
Kishanganj   Koch Bihar   Goalpara   Nakhola
Dalkola   Domar   Dinhata   Dudhnai   Dispur
Pirganj   Saldpur
Katihar   Dinajpur   Rangpur Patakata   Garo Hills Nongstoin   Shillong
Mankachar
Raiganj   Parbatipur   Tura   Khasi Hills   Mawphlang Jowai
Balurghat
Ingraj   Jaipurhat   Sherpur   Sunamganj   Chhatak   Badarpur
Bazar
Dhulian Naogaon   Bogra Mymensingh   Gouripur   Kalni   Sylhet Maulvi   Silchar
Jangipur   Rajshahi   Jamalpur   Brahmaputra   Bazar Kulaura Lalaghat
BANGLADESH   Sirajganj   Kishorganj   Kailashahar
Ajimganj   Tangail   Khowai   Dhalesvari
Baharampur   Ishurdi   Pabna   Bhairab Bazar Brahman Barla
Kushtia   Manikganj   Narsingdi
Katoya   Jhenida   Rajbari   DHAKA   Agartala
Tropic of Cancer   Faridpur   Comilla   Aizawl
Krishnanagar   Madaripur   Chandpur   Laksham   Belonia
Barddhaman Ranaghat   Jessore   Begamganj   Khagrachbari
Hugli-Chunchura Bangaon   Madaripur   Feni   Ramgarh
Bhatpara   Chalna   Noakhali   Karnafuli
Haora   Satkhira   Khulna   Barisal   Nazir Reservoir
Calcutta   Basirhat   Barisal   Hat Rangamati
Diamond   Port Canning   Mungla   Patuakhali   Dohazar
Harbour   Haldia   Sundarbans   Hatia I.   Chittagong
Kanthi   Sagar I.   Rabnabad   Maiskhal I.   Chiringa
Digha   Is.   Cox's Bazar
Mouths of the Ganges   Bay of
Bengal
Teknaf

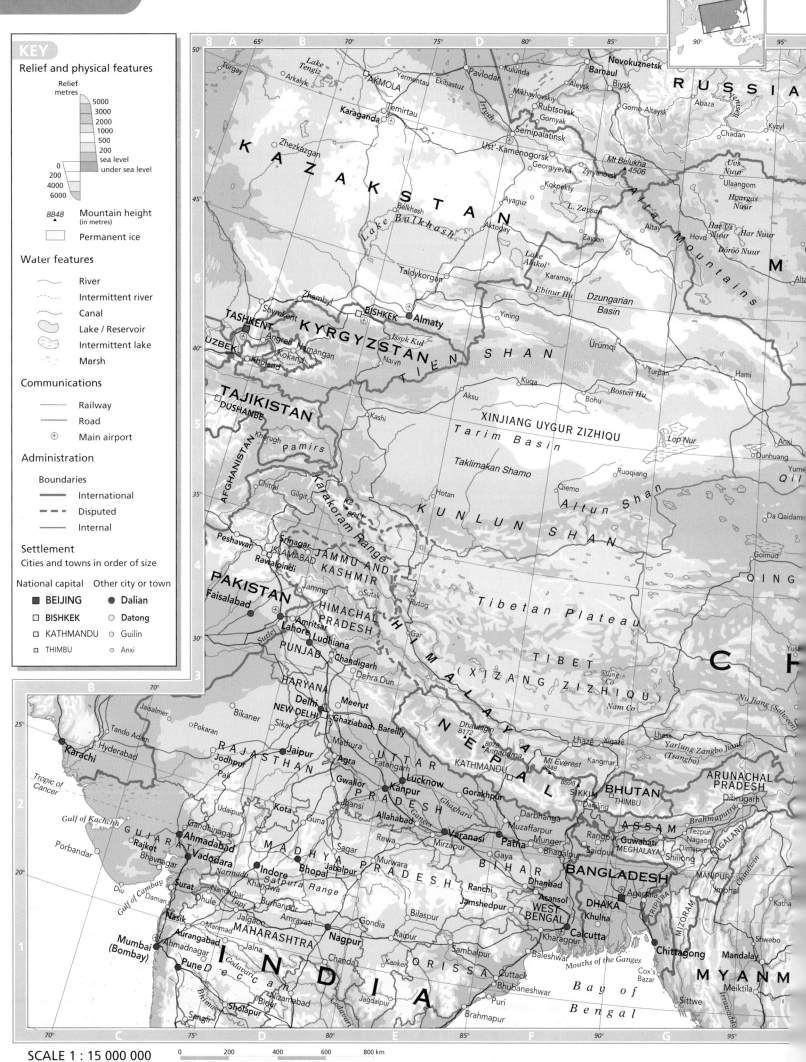

KEY

Relief and physical features

Relief
metres
5000
3000
2000
1000
500
200
sea level
0
under sea level
200
4000
6000

8848 ▲ Mountain height
(in metres)

Permanent ice

Water features

River

Intermittent river

Canal

Lake / Reservoir

Intermittent lake

Marsh

Communications

Railway

Road

⊕ Main airport

Administration

Boundaries

International

Disputed

Internal

Settlement

Cities and towns in order of size

National capital   Other city or town

■ **BEIJING**   ● Dalian

□ **BISHKEK**   ○ Datong

□ **KATHMANDU**   ○ Guilin

□ **THIMBU**   ○ Anxi

SCALE 1 : 15 000 000

0   200   400   600   800 km

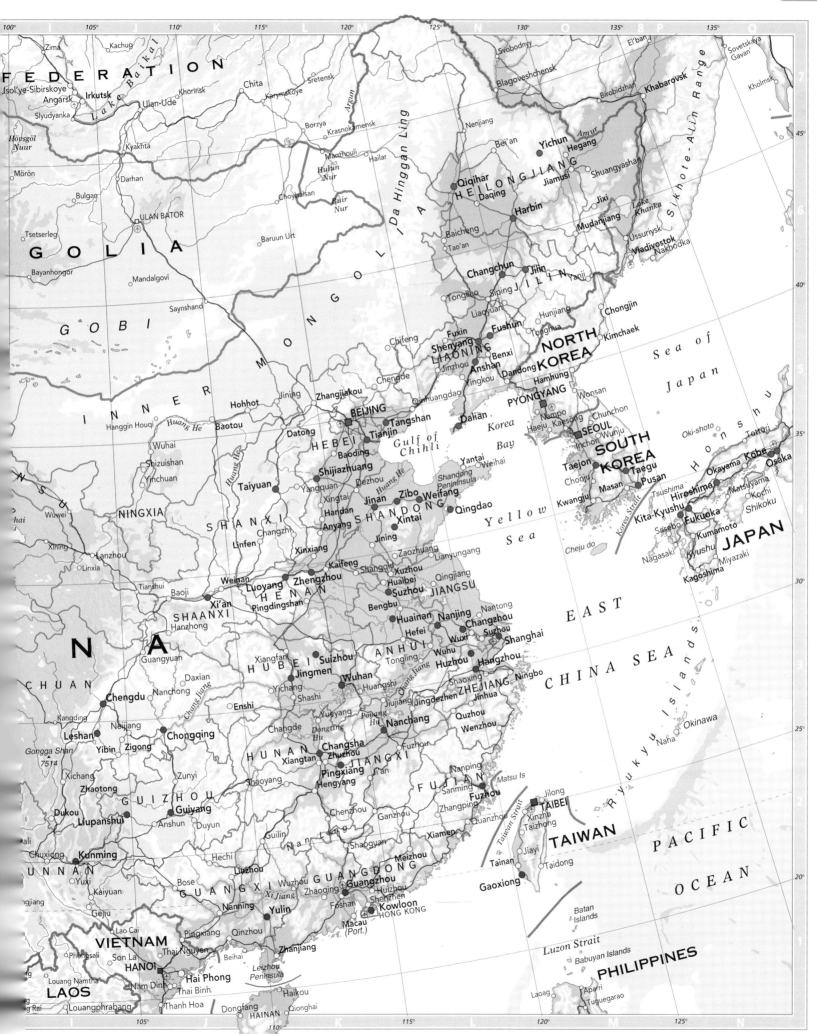

Conic projection

P A C I F I C

O C E A N

Farallon de Pajaros

Maug Islands

Asuncion

Agrihan

Pagan

Alamagan

Northern
Mariana
Islands
(U.S.A.)

Sarigan
Anatahan

Saipan

Tinian

Rota

Guam
(U.S.A.) Agana

Ulithi

Yap

Fais

Ngulu

FEDERATED STATES

OF MICRONESIA

Sorol

Woleai
Atoll

Eauripik
Atoll

PALAU

KOROR

PHILIPPINES

Catanduanes

Naga

Legaspi

Irosin

Catarman

Masbate

Calbayog

Samar

Cadiz

Tacloban

Cebu

Ormoc

Leyte

Tagbilaran

Surigao

Bohol

Butuan

Cagayan de Oro

Mindanao

Cotabato

Davao

Zamboanga

Davao
G.

Moro Gulf

General
Santos

Karakelong

Talaud Is

Sangir Is

Morotai

Manadao

Tobelo

Tondano

Ternate

Halmahera

Gorontalo

Waigeo

Equator

Bacan

Kwoka

3000

Manokwari

Biak

Biak

Pelleluhu Is

Peleng

Taliabu

Misoöl

Dampir Str.

Sorong

Doberai
Peninsula

Yapen

Serui

Wuvulu I.

Ninigo
Group

Obi

Cenderawasih
Gulf

Mamberamo

Jayapura

Vanimo

Sula Is

Seram Sea

Berau Gulf

Babo

Aitape

Wewak

Banggai
Is

Namlea

3019

Bula

Fakfak

Kaimana

Maoke Range

NEW

Buru

Ambon

Seram

Adi

5030

Pk Jaya

Pk Mandala

Wabag

Wowoni

Banda Is

Amamapare

4700

Central Ra.

PAPUA

Tari

4088

Buton

Kai Is

Wokam

IRIAN

NEW

Mt Giluwe

Tukangbesi
Is

B a n d a   S e a

Aru Is

Kobroör

JAYA

GUINEA

Trangan

Kikori

Damar

Tanimbar
Is

GUINEA

Kikori

Wetar

Roma

Saumlakki

Babar Is

A R A F U R A

Balimo

Alor

Selaru

Selaru

Fly

Daru

Dili

EAST
TIMOR

Leti Is

S E A

C. Vals

Morehead

Mutis

2960

Merauke

Timor

2427

Torres Str.

Kupang

Melville I.
(Aust.)

Croker I.
(Aust.)

C. Wessel

Prince of Wales I.

C. York

Bamaga

Roti

AUSTRALIA

Mercator projection

KEY

Relief and physical features

Relief
metres

5000
3000
2000
1000
500
200
sea level
under sea level
0
200
4000
6000

5030 ▲ Mountain height
(in metres)

Water features

~ River

Lake / Reservoir

Marsh

Communications

—— Railway

—— Road

⊕ Main airport

Administration

Boundaries

——— International

– – – Disputed

——— Internal

Settlement

Cities and towns in order of size

National capital Other city or town

■ JAKARTA ● Surabaya

□ PHNOM PENH ○ Padang

□ VIENTIANE ○ Ipoh

□ BANDAR SERI
BEGAWAN ○ Ternate

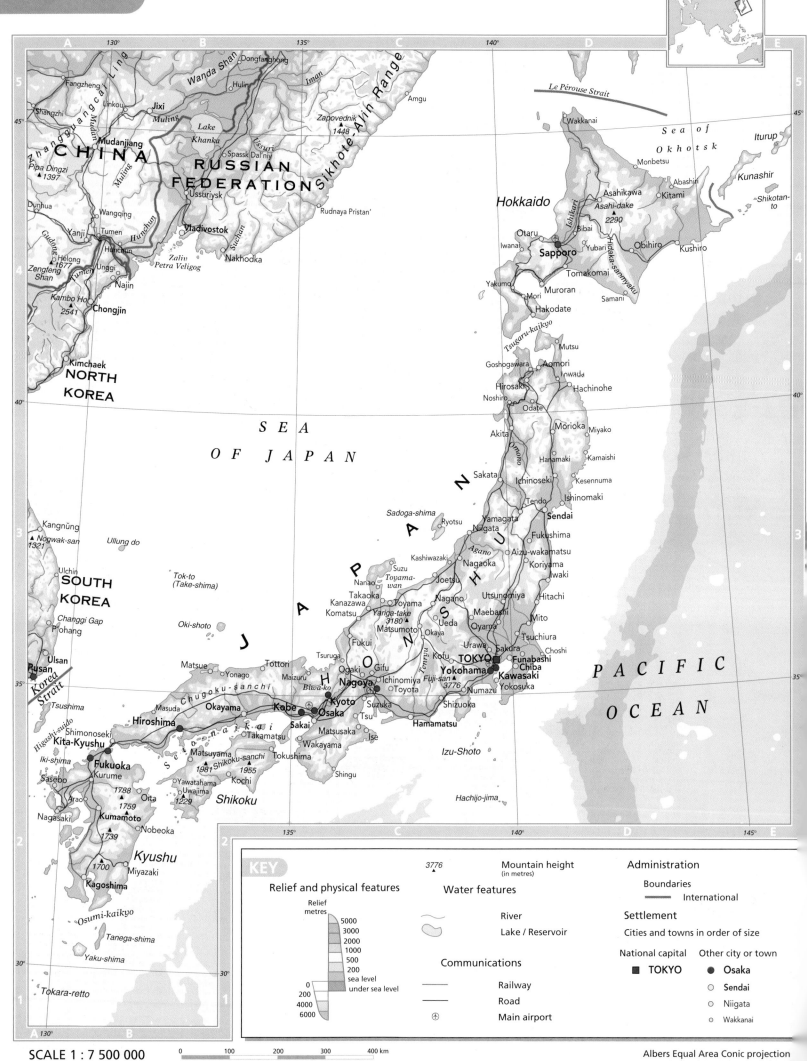

SCALE 1 : 7 500 000

0   100   200   300   400 km

Albers Equal Area Conic projection

KEY

Relief and physical features

Relief
metres
5000
3000
2000
1000
500
200
0 sea level
under sea level
200
4000
6000

3776 ▲ Mountain height
(in metres)

Water features

～ River

Lake / Reservoir

Communications

Railway

Road

⊕ Main airport

Administration

Boundaries

International

Settlement

Cities and towns in order of size

National capital   Other city or town

■ TOKYO   ● Osaka

◎ Sendai

○ Niigata

○ Wakkanai

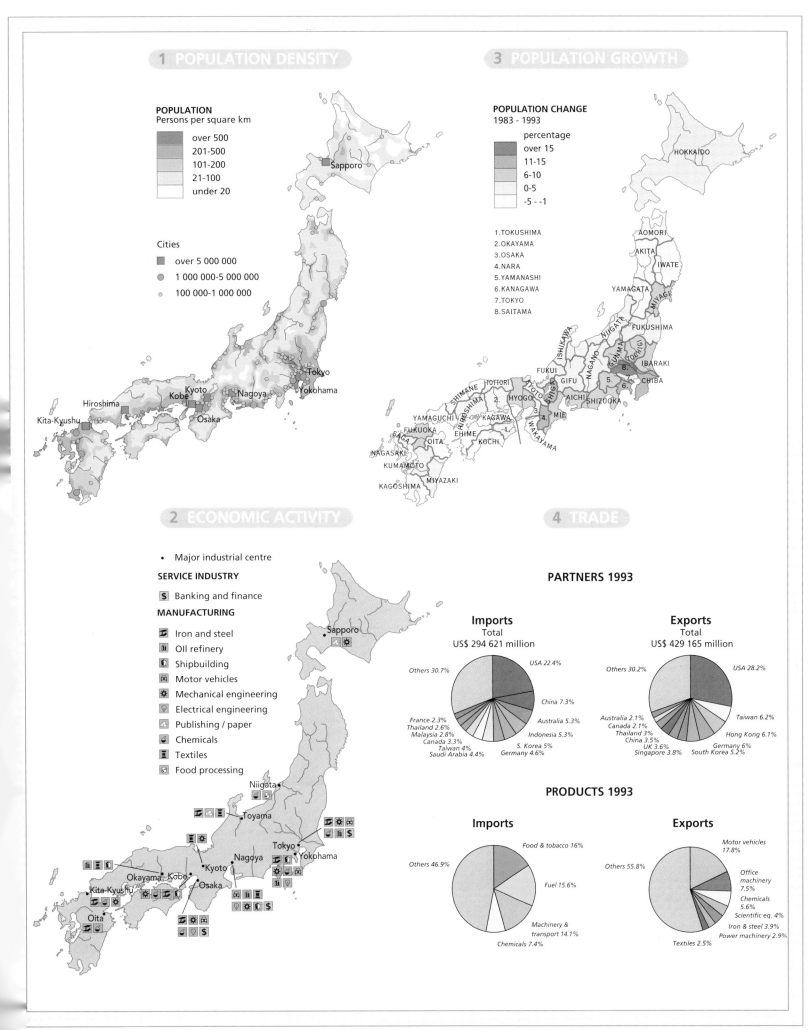

1 POPULATION DENSITY

POPULATION
Persons per square km

- over 500
- 201-500
- 101-200
- 21-100
- under 20

Cities

- over 5 000 000
- 1 000 000-5 000 000
- 100 000-1 000 000

Sapporo

Tokyo
Kyoto
Kobe
Nagoya
Yokohama
Hiroshima
Osaka
Kita-Kyushu

3 POPULATION GROWTH

POPULATION CHANGE
1983 - 1993

percentage

- over 15
- 11-15
- 6-10
- 0-5
- -5 - -1

1. TOKUSHIMA
2. OKAYAMA
3. OSAKA
4. NARA
5. YAMANASHI
6. KANAGAWA
7. TOKYO
8. SAITAMA

HOKKAIDO
AOMORI
AKITA
IWATE
YAMAGATA
MIYAGI
NIIGATA
FUKUSHIMA
ISHIKAWA
TOYAMA
NAGANO
GUNMA
TOCHIGI
IBARAKI
FUKUI
GIFU
SHIGA
CHIBA
TOTTORI
KYOTO
AICHI
SHIZUOKA
SHIMANE
HYOGO
MIE
YAMAGUCHI
HIROSHIMA
KAGAWA
WAKAYAMA
FUKUOKA
EHIME
SAGA
OITA
KOCHI
NAGASAKI
KUMAMOTO
MIYAZAKI
KAGOSHIMA

2 ECONOMIC ACTIVITY

- Major industrial centre

SERVICE INDUSTRY

- $ Banking and finance

MANUFACTURING

- Iron and steel
- Oil refinery
- Shipbuilding
- Motor vehicles
- Mechanical engineering
- Electrical engineering
- Publishing / paper
- Chemicals
- Textiles
- Food processing

Sapporo
Niigata
Toyama
Tokyo
Yokohama
Nagoya
Kyoto
Okayama Kobe
Kita-Kyushu Osaka
Oita

4 TRADE

PARTNERS 1993

Imports
Total
US$ 294 621 million

- USA 22.4%
- China 7.3%
- Australia 5.3%
- Indonesia 5.3%
- S. Korea 5%
- Germany 4.6%
- Saudi Arabia 4.4%
- Taiwan 4%
- Canada 3.3%
- Malaysia 2.8%
- Thailand 2.6%
- France 2.3%
- Others 30.7%

Exports
Total
US$ 429 165 million

- USA 28.2%
- Taiwan 6.2%
- Hong Kong 6.1%
- Germany 6%
- South Korea 5.2%
- Singapore 3.8%
- UK 3.6%
- China 3.5%
- Thailand 3%
- Canada 2.1%
- Australia 2.1%
- Others 30.2%

PRODUCTS 1993

Imports

- Food & tobacco 16%
- Fuel 15.6%
- Machinery & transport 14.1%
- Chemicals 7.4%
- Others 46.9%

Exports

- Motor vehicles 17.8%
- Office machinery 7.5%
- Chemicals 5.6%
- Scientific eq. 4%
- Iron & steel 3.9%
- Power machinery 2.9%
- Textiles 2.5%
- Others 55.8%

SCALE 1 : 15 000 000

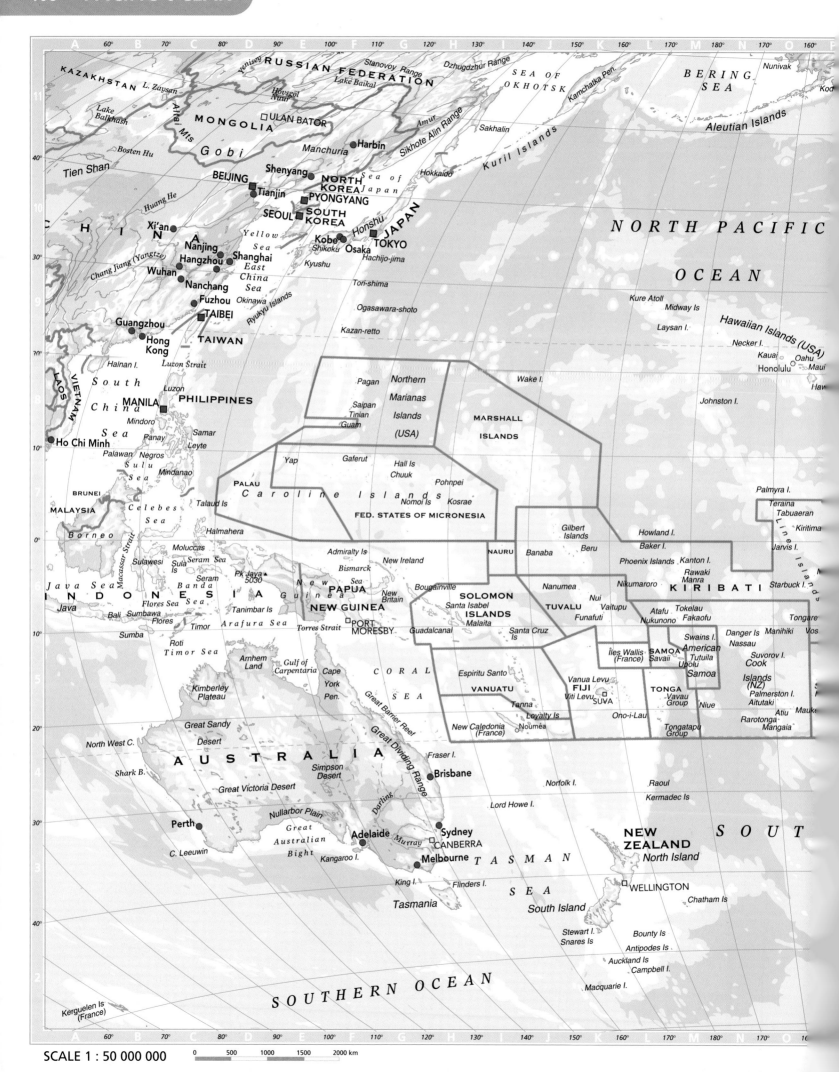

SCALE 1 : 50 000 000

0   500   1000   1500   2000 km

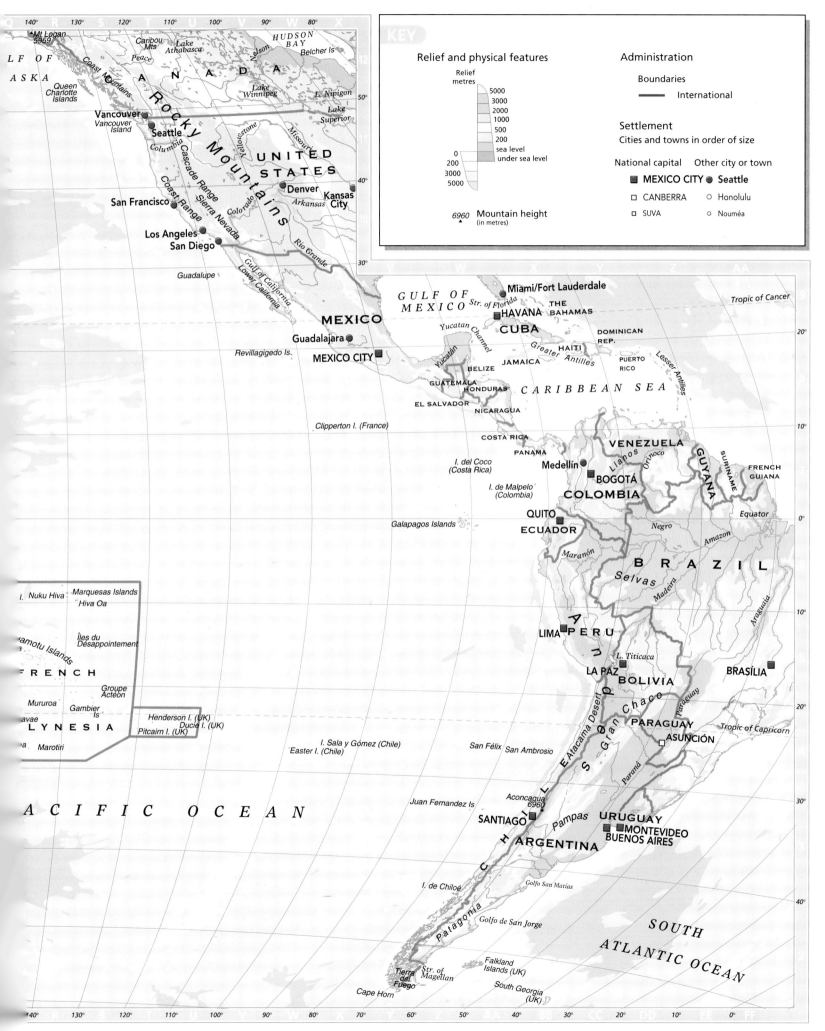

Relief and physical features

Relief
metres
5000
3000
2000
1000
500
200
sea level
0
under sea level
200
3000
5000

6960 ▲ Mountain height
(in metres)

Administration

Boundaries
International

Settlement
Cities and towns in order of size

National capital | Other city or town
■ MEXICO CITY | ● Seattle
□ CANBERRA | ○ Honolulu
□ SUVA | ○ Nouméa

Hammer - Aitoff projection

Samarinda
Palu
Makassar Strait
Towori Gulf
Sulawesi
Bt Gandadiwata 3074
Parepare
Ujung Pandang
Kabaena 2871
Salayar
Muna
Buton
Wowoni
Banggai Is
Peleng
Taliabu
Sula Is
Obi
Buru
Ambon
Banda Is
Tukangbesi Is
Seram
Seram Sea
Misoöl
Berau Gulf
3019
Cenderawasih Gulf
Jayapura
Memberamo
Maoke Range
5030 Pk Jaya
4700 Pk Mandala
NEW
GUINEA
Central Ra.
Mt Giluwe 4088
Purari
Kikori
Kerema
4073 Mt Victoria
Umboi
Lae
Balimo
Fly
PORT MORESBY
Owen Stanley Ra.
Gulf of Papua
PAPUA NEW GUINEA
New Ireland
Bismarck Sea
New Britain
Bougainville Island
Solomon Sea
Woodlark I.
D'Entrecasteaux Is
Trobriand Is
Tagula I.
Rosse

INDONESIA
Banda Sea
Kai Is
Wokam
Aru Is
Kobroör
Trangan
Tanimbar Is
C. Vals
Torres Strait
Prince of Wales I.
C. York
Flores Sea
Buru
Kabaena
Salayar
Wetar
Roma
Damar
Babar Is
Selaru
Dili 2960 EAST TIMOR
Alor
Leti Is
Timor
Sawu Sea
Raba
Endeh Flores
Waingapu
Sumba
Roti
Kupang

Arafura Sea
Timor Sea
C. Londonderry
Melville I.
Bathurst I.
Darwin
Joseph Bonaparte Gulf
Daly
Katherine
Victoria
Arnhem Land
Wessel Is
C. Wessel
C. Arnhem
Gulf of Carpentaria
Groote Eylandt
Wellesley Is
Cape York
Mitchell
Cooktown
Cairns
CORAL SEA
CORAL SEA ISLANDS
TERRITORY
Leichhardt
Normanton
Townsville
Great Barrier Reef
Great Dividing Range

Collier Bay
Wyndham
Lake Argyle
Kimberley Plateau
Mt Ord 936
Derby
Broome
Hall's Creek
Tanami Desert
NORTHERN TERRITORY
Barkly Tableland
Flinders
Mount Isa
Selwyn Range
Georgina
Mt Dalrymple 1277
Mackay
QUEENSLAND
Barcaldine
Rockhampton
Gladstone
Capricorn Channel
Sandy Cape
Bundaberg
Fraser I.
Maryborough

Eighty Mile Beach
Port Hedland
Barrow I.
Dampier
De Grey
Great Sandy Desert
Fortescue
Hamersley Range 1250
Ashburton
L. Disappointment
L. Mackay
L. Wills
L. White
WESTERN AUSTRALIA
1510 Mt Ziel
Macdonnell Ranges
Alice Springs
Gibson Desert
Ayers Rock 867
L. Amadeus
Musgrave Ranges
Simpson Desert
Warburton
Cooper Creek
Diamantina
Sturt Desert
Warrego
Toowoomba
Brisbane
Southport
Gold Coast
Coolangatta
Dirranbandi
Darling Downs
Lismore
Moree
Bourke
Grey Range
Grafton
Coffs Harbour
Round Mt 1615
Port Macquarie
Armidale
Tamworth

L. Macleod
Gascoyne
Murchison
L. Carnegie
L. Wells
L. Carey
Great Victoria Desert
L. Eyre (North)
L. Eyre (South)
L. Blanche
SOUTH AUSTRALIA
L. Frome
Broken Hill
NEW SOUTH WALES
Darling
Dubbo
Maitland
Newcastle
Gosford
Sydney
Wollongong
Geraldton
L. Barlee
L. Moore
Kalgoorlie
L. Cowan
Nullarbor Plain
L. Gairdner
L. Torrens
Flinders Range
Port Augusta
Whyalla
Port Pirie
Lachlan
Murrumbidgee
Hay
Murray
Wagga Wagga
Albury
Mt Kosciusko 2230
CANBERRA
AUST. CAP. TER.
Goulburn
Norseman
Ravensthorpe
Esperance
Great Australian Bight
Port Lincoln
Cape Carnot
Kangaroo I.
Spencer Gulf
Adelaide
Murray Bridge
Mildura
Bendigo
VICTORIA
Mt William 1167
Ballart
Melbourne
Bairnsdale
Sale
Perth
Fremantle
Bunbury
Hood Pt
C. Leeuwin
Albany
Hotham
Mt Gambier
Portland
Geelong
Wilson's Promontory
Bass Strait
Flinders I.
King I.
TASMANIA
TAS
Burnie
Devonport
Launceston
Mt Ossa 1617
Hobart
South East Cape

KEY

Relief and physical features

Relief metres
5000
3000
2000
1000
500
200
0 sea level
200 under sea level
4000
6000

3754 ▲ Mountain height (in metres)

Water features

~ River
--- Intermittent river
Lake / Reservoir
Intermittent lake
Marsh
Coral reef

Communications

Railway
Road
⊕ Main airport

Administration

Boundaries
— International
— Internal

Settlement

Cities and towns in order of size

National capital
□ CANBERRA
□ SUVA

Other city or town
● Sydney
○ Auckland
○ Newcastle
○ Darwin

SCALE 1 : 20 000 000

0 200 400 600 800 km

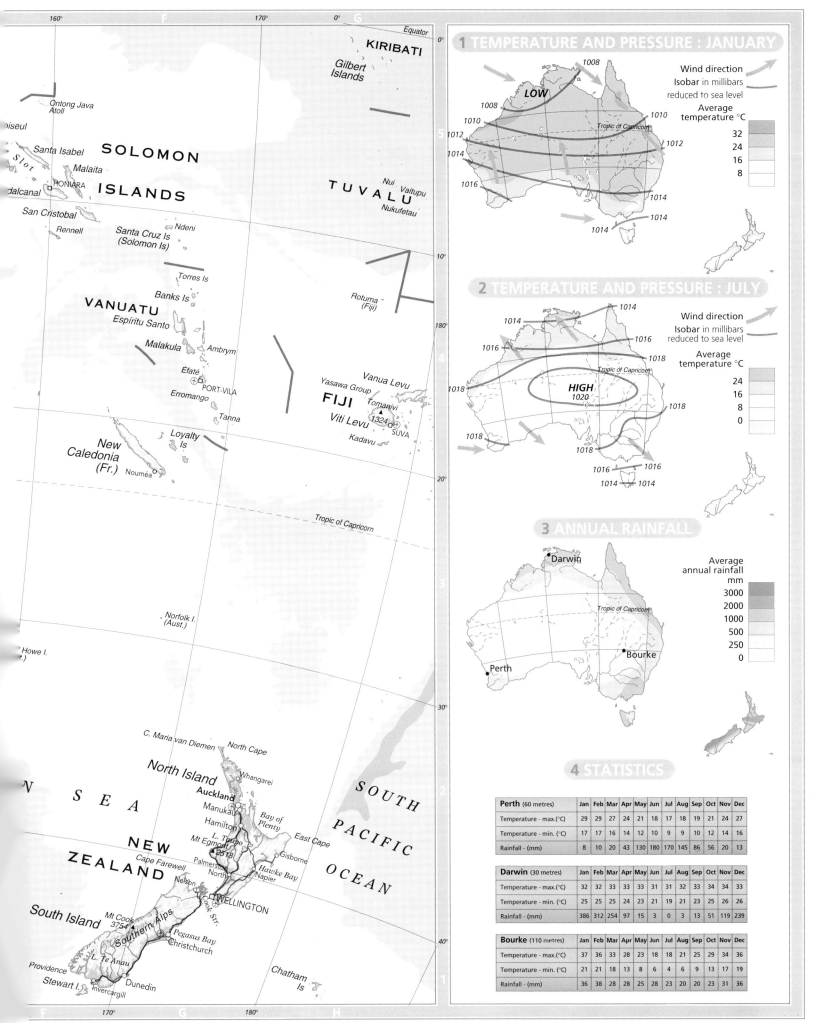

160° F 170° 0° G Equator 0°

KIRIBATI

Gilbert
Islands

Ontong Java
Atoll

SOLOMON

Santa Isabel

Malaita

HONIARA

ISLANDS

alcanal

San Cristobal

Rennell

Santa Cruz Is
(Solomon Is)

Ndeni

Nui Vaitupu

TUVALU

Nukufetau

Torres Is

Banks Is

VANUATU

Espíritu Santo

Malakula

Ambrym

Efaté

PORT-VILA

Erromango

Rotuma
(Fiji)

180°

Yasawa Group

Vanua Levu

FIJI

Tomanivi

1324

SUVA

Tanna

Viti Levu

Kadavu

New
Caledonia
(Fr.)

Loyalty
Is

Nouméa

10°

20°

Tropic of Capricorn

Norfolk I.
(Aust.)

Howe I.

30°

C. Maria van Diemen North Cape

North Island

Whangarei

N S E A

Auckland

Manukau

Bay of
Plenty

East Cape

Hamilton

L. Taupo

Mt Egmont
2518

Gisborne

NEW

Cape Farewell

Palmerston
North

Hawke Bay

Napier

SOUTH

PACIFIC

OCEAN

ZEALAND

Nelson

WELLINGTON

Cook Str.

South Island

Mt Cook
3754

Southern Alps

Pegasus Bay

Christchurch

L. Te Anau

Providence

Stewart I.

Dunedin

Invercargill

Chatham
Is

40°

170° F G 180° H

1 TEMPERATURE AND PRESSURE : JANUARY

1008

LOW

1008

1010

1012

1014

1016

Tropic of Capricorn

1010

1012

1014

1014

1014

Wind direction
Isobar in millibars
reduced to sea level

Average
temperature °C

	32
	24
	16
	8

2 TEMPERATURE AND PRESSURE : JULY

1014

1014

1016

1016

1018

Tropic of Capricorn

HIGH
1020

1018

1018

1018

1018

1016 1016

1014 1014

Wind direction
Isobar in millibars
reduced to sea level

Average
temperature °C

	24
	16
	8
	0

3 ANNUAL RAINFALL

Darwin

Tropic of Capricorn

Bourke

Perth

Average
annual rainfall
mm

	3000
	2000
	1000
	500
	250
	0

4 STATISTICS

Perth (60 metres)	Jan	Feb	Mar	Apr	May	Jun	Jul	Aug	Sep	Oct	Nov	Dec
Temperature - max.(°C)	29	29	27	24	21	18	17	18	19	21	24	27
Temperature - min. (°C)	17	17	16	14	12	10	9	9	10	12	14	16
Rainfall - (mm)	8	10	20	43	130	180	170	145	86	56	20	13

Darwin (30 metres)	Jan	Feb	Mar	Apr	May	Jun	Jul	Aug	Sep	Oct	Nov	Dec
Temperature - max.(°C)	32	32	33	33	33	31	31	32	33	34	34	33
Temperature - min. (°C)	25	25	25	24	23	21	19	21	23	25	26	26
Rainfall - (mm)	386	312	254	97	15	3	0	3	13	51	119	239

Bourke (110 metres)	Jan	Feb	Mar	Apr	May	Jun	Jul	Aug	Sep	Oct	Nov	Dec
Temperature - max.(°C)	37	36	33	28	23	18	18	21	25	29	34	36
Temperature - min. (°C)	21	21	18	13	8	6	4	6	9	13	17	19
Rainfall - (mm)	36	38	28	28	25	28	23	20	20	23	31	36

Lambert Azimuthal Equal Area projection

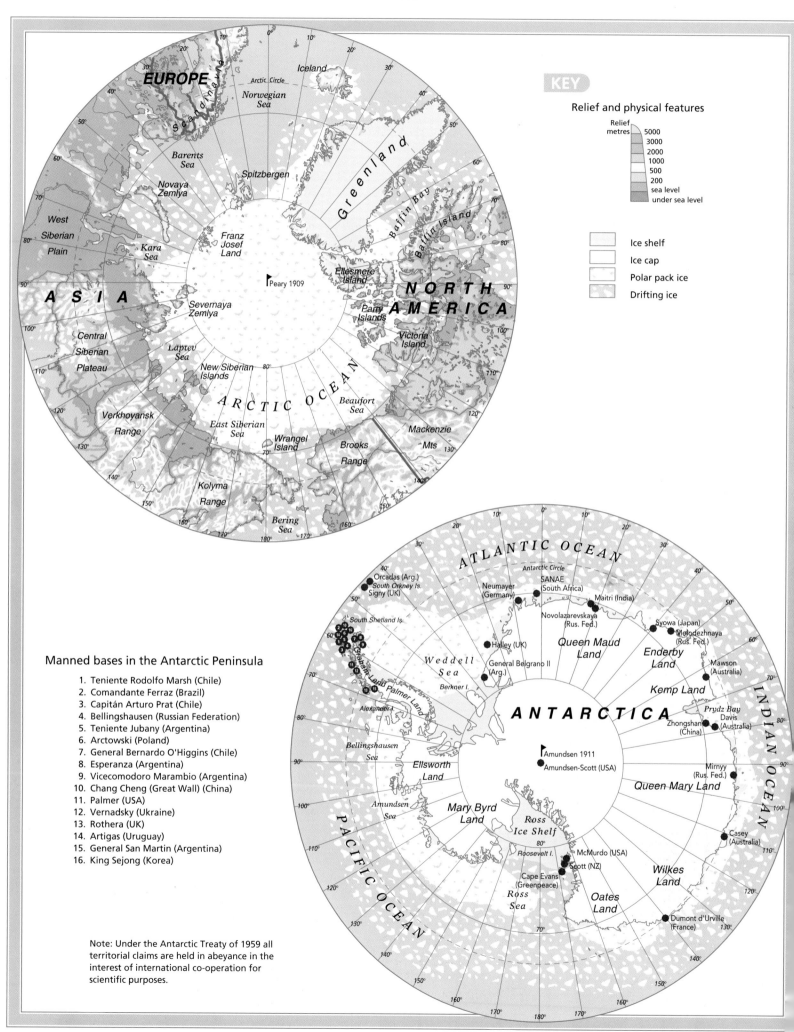

KEY

Relief and physical features

Relief metres

	5000
	3000
	2000
	1000
	500
	200
	sea level
	under sea level

Ice shelf

Ice cap

Polar pack ice

Drifting ice

Manned bases in the Antarctic Peninsula

1. Teniente Rodolfo Marsh (Chile)
2. Comandante Ferraz (Brazil)
3. Capitán Arturo Prat (Chile)
4. Bellingshausen (Russian Federation)
5. Teniente Jubany (Argentina)
6. Arctowski (Poland)
7. General Bernardo O'Higgins (Chile)
8. Esperanza (Argentina)
9. Vicecomodoro Marambio (Argentina)
10. Chang Cheng (Great Wall) (China)
11. Palmer (USA)
12. Vernadsky (Ukraine)
13. Rothera (UK)
14. Artigas (Uruguay)
15. General San Martin (Argentina)
16. King Sejong (Korea)

Note: Under the Antarctic Treaty of 1959 all territorial claims are held in abeyance in the interest of international co-operation for scientific purposes.

SCALE 1 : 50 000 000

0   500   1000   1500   2000 km

Polar Stereographic projection

1 TIME ZONES

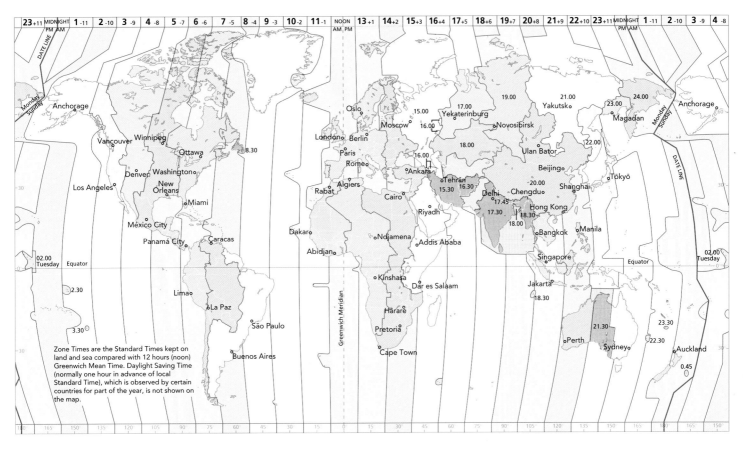

| 23 +11 | 1 -11 | 2 -10 | 3 -9 | 4 -8 | 5 -7 | 6 -6 | 7 -5 | 8 -4 | 9 -3 | 10 -2 | 11 -1 | NOON | 13 +1 | 14 +2 | 15 +3 | 16 +4 | 17 +5 | 18 +6 | 19 +7 | 20 +8 | 21 +9 | 22 +10 | 23 +11 | 1 -11 | 2 -10 | 3 -9 | 4 -8 |

Zone Times are the Standard Times kept on land and sea compared with 12 hours (noon) Greenwich Mean Time. Daylight Saving Time (normally one hour in advance of local Standard Time), which is observed by certain countries for part of the year, is not shown on the map.

2 INTERNATIONAL ORGANIZATIONS

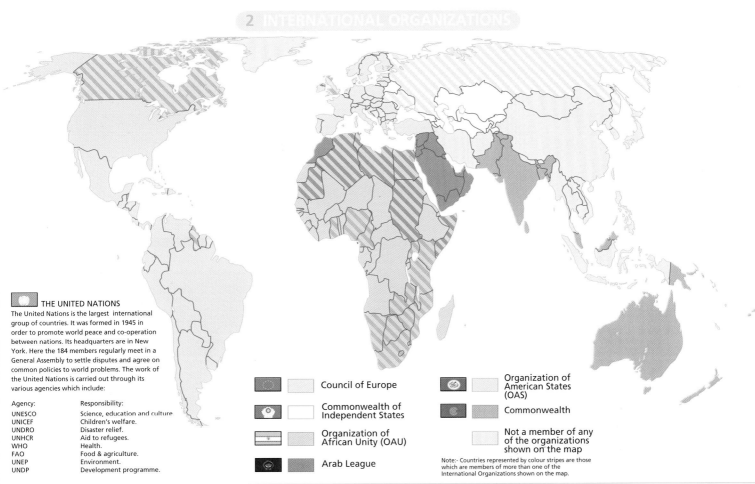

THE UNITED NATIONS

The United Nations is the largest international group of countries. It was formed in 1945 in order to promote world peace and co-operation between nations. Its headquarters are in New York. Here the 184 members regularly meet in a General Assembly to settle disputes and agree on common policies to world problems. The work of the United Nations is carried out through its various agencies which include:

Agency:	Responsibility:
UNESCO	Science, education and culture
UNICEF	Children's welfare.
UNDRO	Disaster relief.
UNHCR	Aid to refugees.
WHO	Health.
FAO	Food & agriculture.
UNEP	Environment.
UNDP	Development programme.

Council of Europe

Commonwealth of Independent States

Organization of African Unity (OAU)

Arab League

Organization of American States (OAS)

Commonwealth

Not a member of any of the organizations shown on the map

Note:- Countries represented by colour stripes are those which are members of more than one of the International Organizations shown on the map.

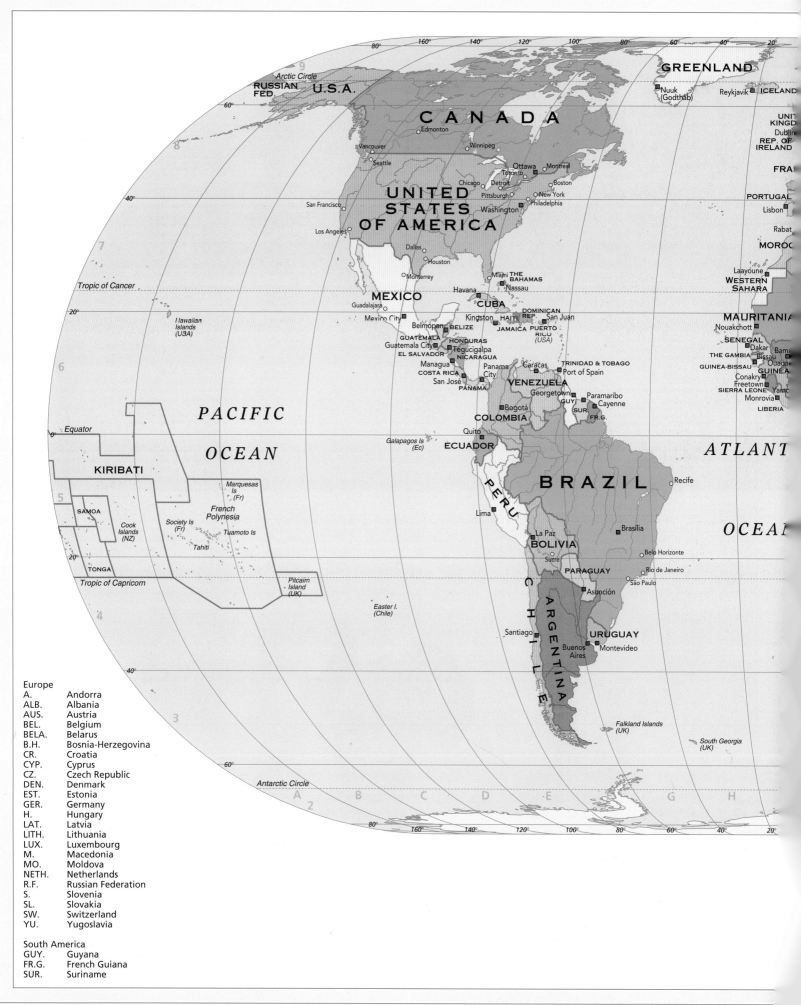

SCALE 1 : 80 000 000

0   800   1600   2400   3200 km

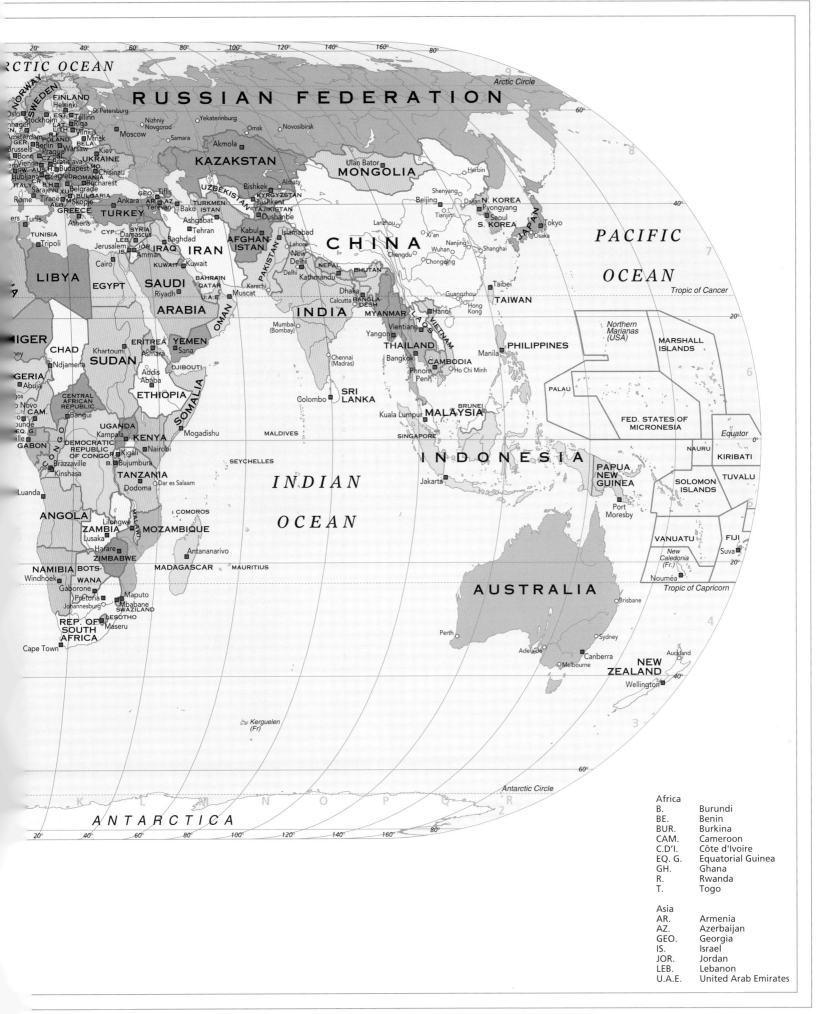

Africa
B.	Burundi
BE.	Benin
BUR.	Burkina
CAM.	Cameroon
C.D'I.	Côte d'Ivoire
EQ. G.	Equatorial Guinea
GH.	Ghana
R.	Rwanda
T.	Togo

Asia
AR.	Armenia
AZ.	Azerbaijan
GEO.	Georgia
IS.	Israel
JOR.	Jordan
LEB.	Lebanon
U.A.E.	United Arab Emirates

Eckert iv projection

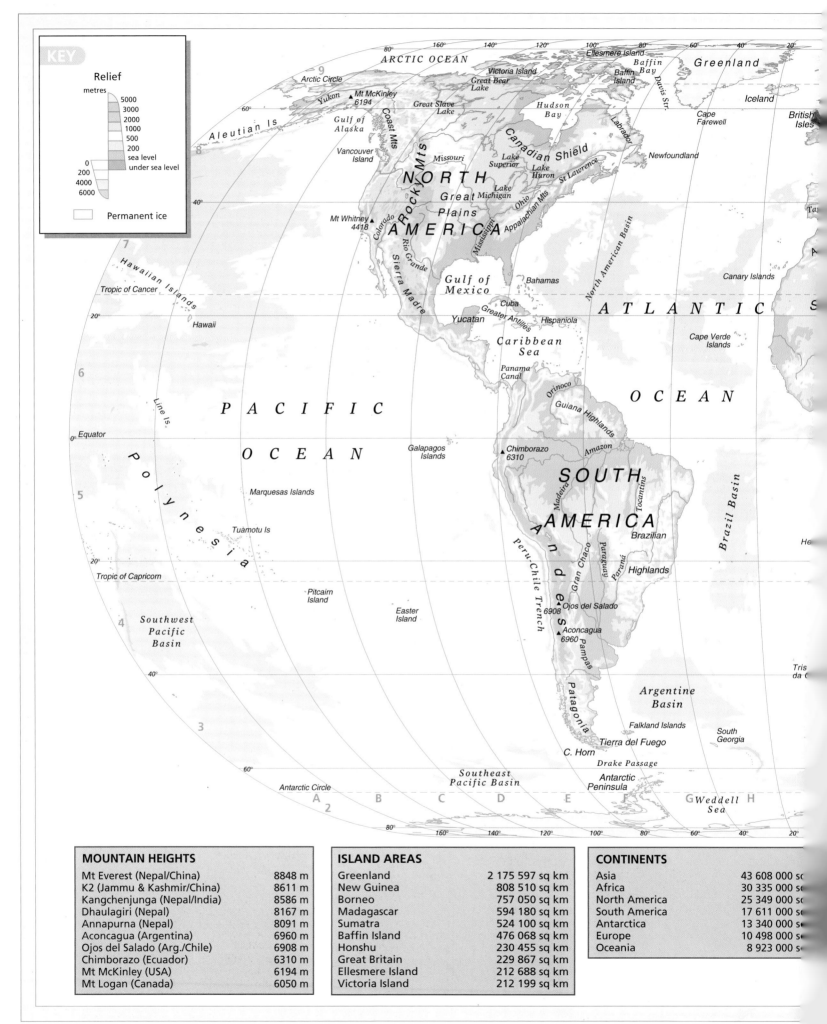

KEY

Relief

metres

5000
3000
2000
1000
500
200
0
sea level
200
under sea level
4000
6000

Permanent ice

ARCTIC OCEAN

Arctic Circle

Ellesmere Island

Victoria Island

Great Bear
Lake

Baffin
Island

Baffin
Bay

Greenland

Davis Str.

Iceland

Yukon ▲ Mt McKinley
6194

Great Slave
Lake

Hudson
Bay

Cape
Farewell

British
Isles

Aleutian Is

Gulf of
Alaska

Coast Mts

Canadian Shield

Labrador

Newfoundland

Vancouver
Island

Missouri

Lake
Superior

Lake
Huron

St Lawrence

NORTH

Lake
Michigan

Rocky Mts

Great

Mt Whitney ▲
4418

Colorado

Plains

Ohio

Appalachian Mts

North American Basin

AMERICA

Mississippi

Sierra Madre

Rio Grande

Gulf of
Mexico

Bahamas

Canary Islands

Tropic of Cancer

Hawaiian Islands

Hawaii

Yucatan

Cuba

Greater Antilles

Hispaniola

A T L A N T I C

Cape Verde
Islands

*Caribbean
Sea*

Panama
Canal

O C E A N

6

P A C I F I C

Galapagos
Islands

Orinoco

Guiana Highlands

Line Is

Equator

O C E A N

SOUTH

Chimborazo ▲
6310

Amazon

P
o
l
y
n
e
s
i
a

Marquesas Islands

5

Madeira

Tocantins

Brazil Basin

Tuamotu Is

AMERICA

Brazilian

Peru-Chile Trench

Gran Chaco

Paraguay

Paraná

Highlands

Tropic of Capricorn

Pitcairn
Island

Easter
Island

A
n
d
e
s

Ojos del Salado
6908 ▲

Aconcagua
6960 ▲

*Southwest
Pacific
Basin*

4

Pampas

*Argentine
Basin*

3

Patagonia

Falkland Islands

South
Georgia

Antarctic Circle

Tierra del Fuego

C. Horn

Drake Passage

*Southeast
Pacific Basin*

*Antarctic
Peninsula*

Weddell
Sea

A   B   C   D   E   F   G   H

2

MOUNTAIN HEIGHTS		**ISLAND AREAS**		**CONTINENTS**	
Mt Everest (Nepal/China)	8848 m	Greenland	2 175 597 sq km	Asia	43 608 000 sq
K2 (Jammu & Kashmir/China)	8611 m	New Guinea	808 510 sq km	Africa	30 335 000 sq
Kangchenjunga (Nepal/India)	8586 m	Borneo	757 050 sq km	North America	25 349 000 sq
Dhaulagiri (Nepal)	8167 m	Madagascar	594 180 sq km	South America	17 611 000 sq
Annapurna (Nepal)	8091 m	Sumatra	524 100 sq km	Antarctica	13 340 000 sq
Aconcagua (Argentina)	6960 m	Baffin Island	476 068 sq km	Europe	10 498 000 sq
Ojos del Salado (Arg./Chile)	6908 m	Honshu	230 455 sq km	Oceania	8 923 000 sq
Chimborazo (Ecuador)	6310 m	Great Britain	229 867 sq km		
Mt McKinley (USA)	6194 m	Ellesmere Island	212 688 sq km		
Mt Logan (Canada)	6050 m	Victoria Island	212 199 sq km		

SCALE 1 : 80 000 000

0   800   1600   2400   3200 km

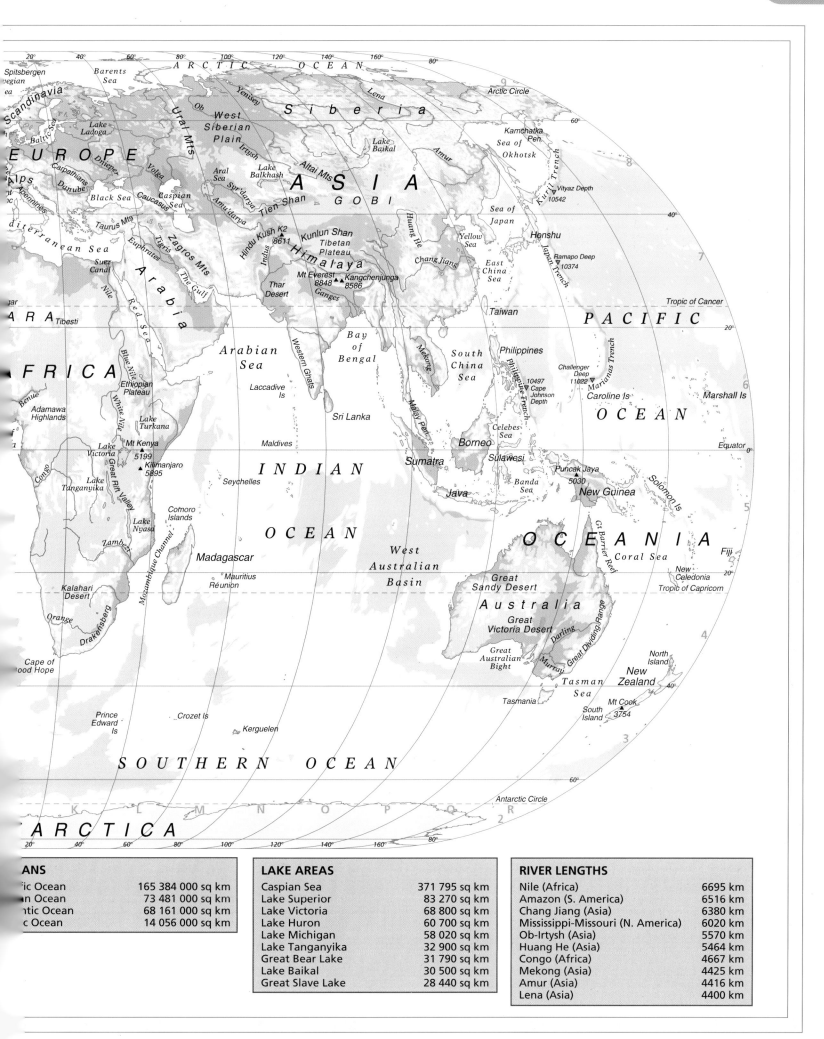

ARCTIC OCEAN
Spitsbergen
Barents Sea
Scandinavia
Lake Ladoga
Baltic Sea
EUROPE
Alps
Apennines
Carpathians
Dnieper
Danube
Black Sea
Caucasus
Taurus Mts
Mediterranean Sea
Suez Canal
Nile
Red Sea
Arabia
The Gulf
Zagros Mts
Euphrates
Tigris
Hindu Kush
K2 8611
Indus
Thar Desert
Kunlun Shan
Tibetan Plateau
Himalaya
Mt Everest 8848
Kangchenjunga 8586
Ganges
Caspian Sea
Aral Sea
Syr darya
Amu darya
Tien Shan
Altai Mts
Lake Balkhash
West Siberian Plain
Ob
Irtysh
Yenisey
Lena
Siberia
ASIA
GOBI
Lake Baikal
Amur
Kamchatka Pen.
Sea of Okhotsk
Kuril Trench
Vityaz Depth 10542
Sea of Japan
Honshu
Ramapo Deep 10374
Japan Trench
Huang He
Chang Jiang
Yellow Sea
East China Sea
Taiwan
PACIFIC
Tropic of Cancer
OCEAN
SAHARA
Tibesti
AFRICA
Benue
Adamawa Highlands
Ethiopian Plateau
Blue Nile
White Nile
Lake Turkana
Mt Kenya 5199
Kilimanjaro 5895
Lake Victoria
Great Rift Valley
Lake Tanganyika
Lake Nyasa
Zambezi
Mozambique Channel
Comoro Islands
Madagascar
Mauritius
Réunion
Kalahari Desert
Orange
Drakensberg
Cape of Good Hope
Arabian Sea
Laccadive Is
Maldives
Sri Lanka
Seychelles
Western Ghats
Bay of Bengal
INDIAN
OCEAN
West Australian Basin
Mekong
Malay Pen.
South China Sea
Philippines
Challenger Deep 11022
Cape Johnson Depth 10497
Philippine Trench
Celebes Sea
Borneo
Sumatra
Java
Sulawesi
Banda Sea
Mariana Trench
Caroline Is
Marshall Is
OCEAN
Equator
Puncak Jaya 5030
New Guinea
Solomon Is
OCEANIA
Gt Barrier Reef
Coral Sea
Fiji
New Caledonia
Great Sandy Desert
Australia
Great Victoria Desert
Great Australian Bight
Darling
Murray
Great Dividing Range
North Island
New Zealand
Mt Cook 3754
South Island
Tasman Sea
Tasmania
Tropic of Capricorn
Prince Edward Is
Crozet Is
Kerguelen
SOUTHERN OCEAN
Antarctic Circle
ANTARCTICA
Arctic Circle

OCEANS	
Pacific Ocean	165 384 000 sq km
Indian Ocean	73 481 000 sq km
Atlantic Ocean	68 161 000 sq km
Arctic Ocean	14 056 000 sq km

LAKE AREAS	
Caspian Sea	371 795 sq km
Lake Superior	83 270 sq km
Lake Victoria	68 800 sq km
Lake Huron	60 700 sq km
Lake Michigan	58 020 sq km
Lake Tanganyika	32 900 sq km
Great Bear Lake	31 790 sq km
Lake Baikal	30 500 sq km
Great Slave Lake	28 440 sq km

RIVER LENGTHS	
Nile (Africa)	6695 km
Amazon (S. America)	6516 km
Chang Jiang (Asia)	6380 km
Mississippi-Missouri (N. America)	6020 km
Ob-Irtysh (Asia)	5570 km
Huang He (Asia)	5464 km
Congo (Africa)	4667 km
Mekong (Asia)	4425 km
Amur (Asia)	4416 km
Lena (Asia)	4400 km

Eckert iv projection

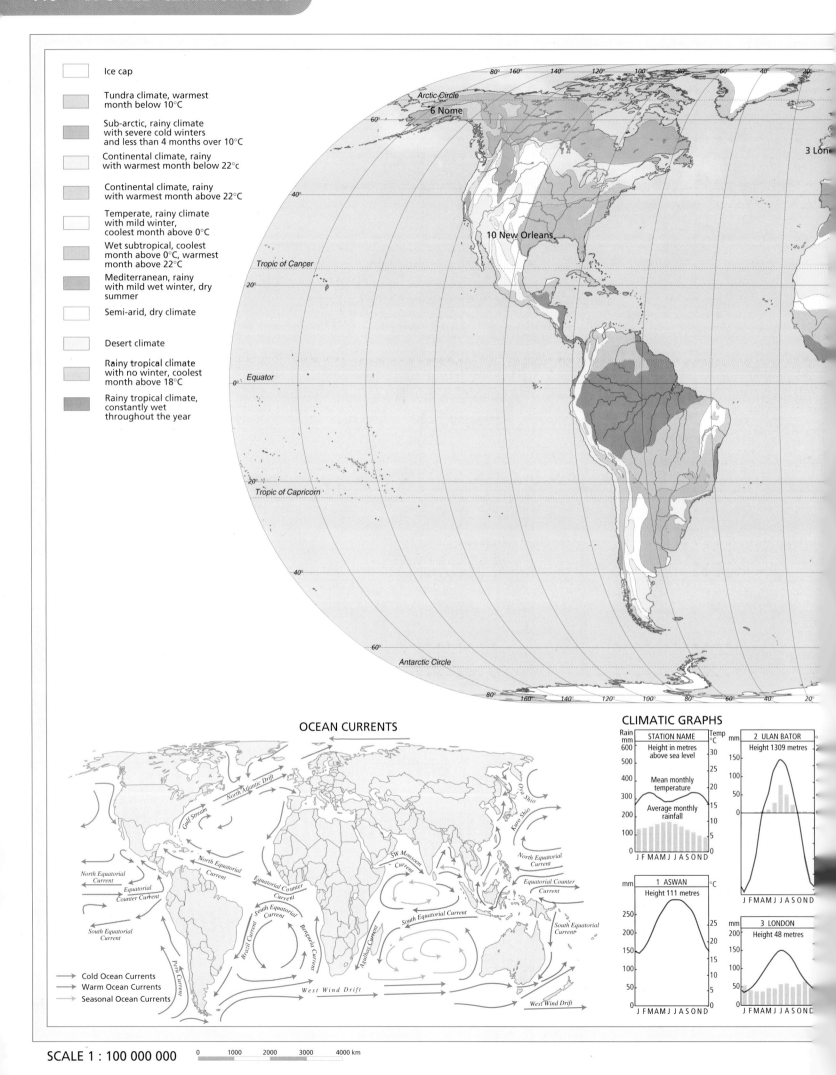

Ice cap

Tundra climate, warmest month below 10°C

Sub-arctic, rainy climate with severe cold winters and less than 4 months over 10°C

Continental climate, rainy with warmest month below 22°c

Continental climate, rainy with warmest month above 22°C

Temperate, rainy climate with mild winter, coolest month above 0°C

Wet subtropical, coolest month above 0°C, warmest month above 22°C

Mediterranean, rainy with mild wet winter, dry summer

Semi-arid, dry climate

Desert climate

Rainy tropical climate with no winter, coolest month above 18°C

Rainy tropical climate, constantly wet throughout the year

OCEAN CURRENTS

North Atlantic Drift
Gulf Stream
North Equatorial Current
North Equatorial Current
Equatorial Counter Current
Equatorial Counter Current
South Equatorial Current
South Equatorial Current
Oya Shio
Karo Shio
North Equatorial Current
Equatorial Counter Current
SW Monsoon Current
South Equatorial Current
South Equatorial Current
Brazil Current
Benguela Current
Agulhas Current
Peru Current
West Wind Drift
West Wind Drift

→ Cold Ocean Currents
→ Warm Ocean Currents
→ Seasonal Ocean Currents

CLIMATIC GRAPHS

Rain mm / STATION NAME / Temp °C
600
500 — 30
Height in metres above sea level
400 — 25
300 — 20
Mean monthly temperature
— 15
Average monthly rainfall
200 — 10
100 — 5
0
J F M A M J J A S O N D

2 ULAN BATOR
mm Height 1309 metres
150
100
50
0
J F M A M J J A S O N D

mm 1 ASWAN °C
Height 111 metres
25
250
20
200
150 — 15
J F M A M J J A S O N D

3 LONDON
mm Height 48 metres
200
150
100
50
0
J F M A M J J A S O N D

SCALE 1 : 100 000 000

0   1000   2000   3000   4000 km

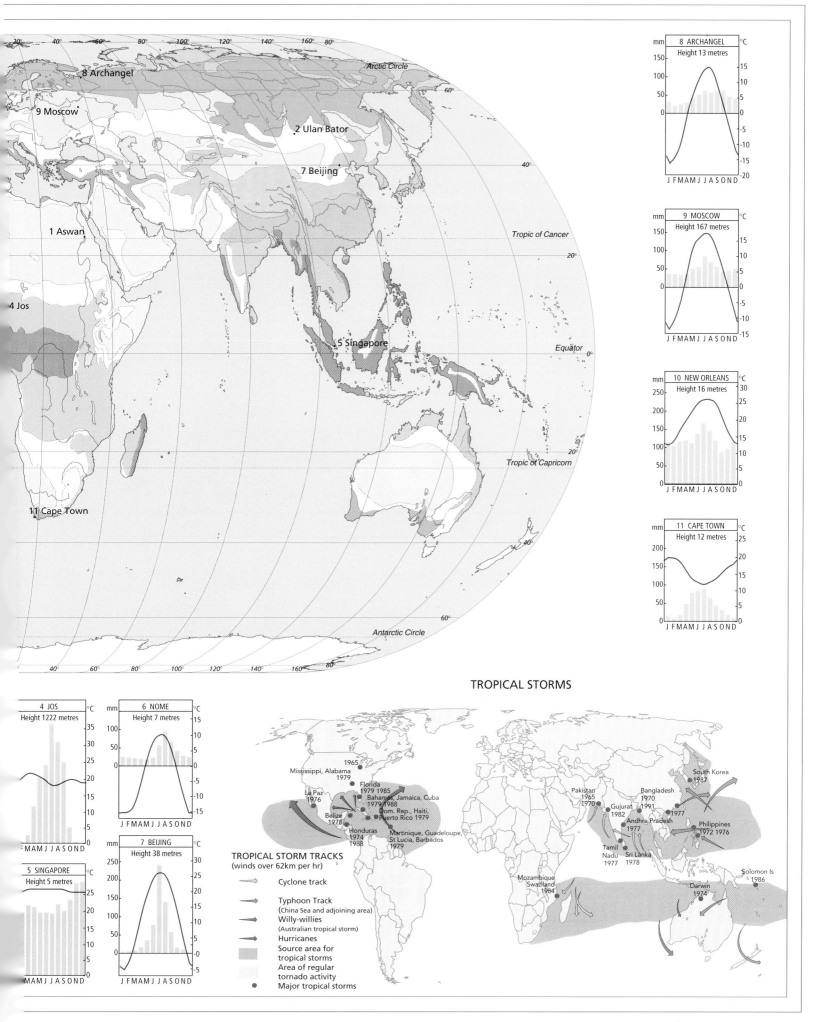

Eckert IV projection

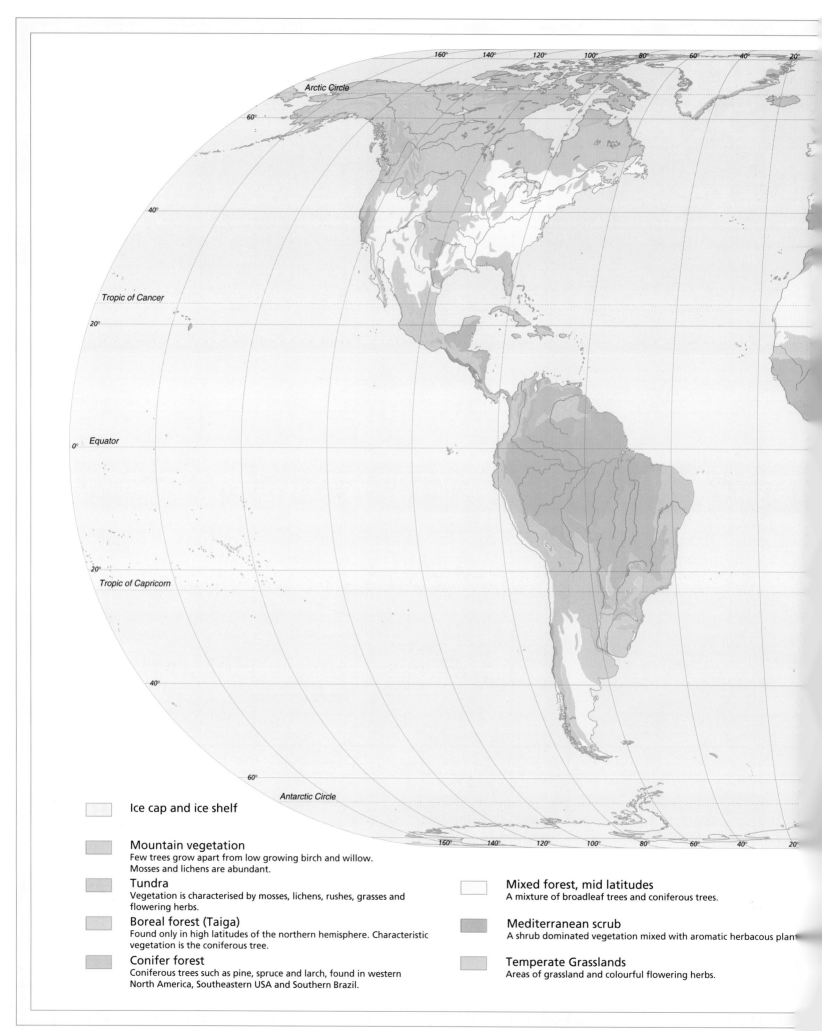

Ice cap and ice shelf

Mountain vegetation
Few trees grow apart from low growing birch and willow.
Mosses and lichens are abundant.

Tundra
Vegetation is characterised by mosses, lichens, rushes, grasses and
flowering herbs.

Boreal forest (Taiga)
Found only in high latitudes of the northern hemisphere. Characteristic
vegetation is the coniferous tree.

Conifer forest
Coniferous trees such as pine, spruce and larch, found in western
North America, Southeastern USA and Southern Brazil.

Mixed forest, mid latitudes
A mixture of broadleaf trees and coniferous trees.

Mediterranean scrub
A shrub dominated vegetation mixed with aromatic herbacous plant

Temperate Grasslands
Areas of grassland and colourful flowering herbs.

SCALE 1 : 80 000 000

0   800   1600   2400   3200 km

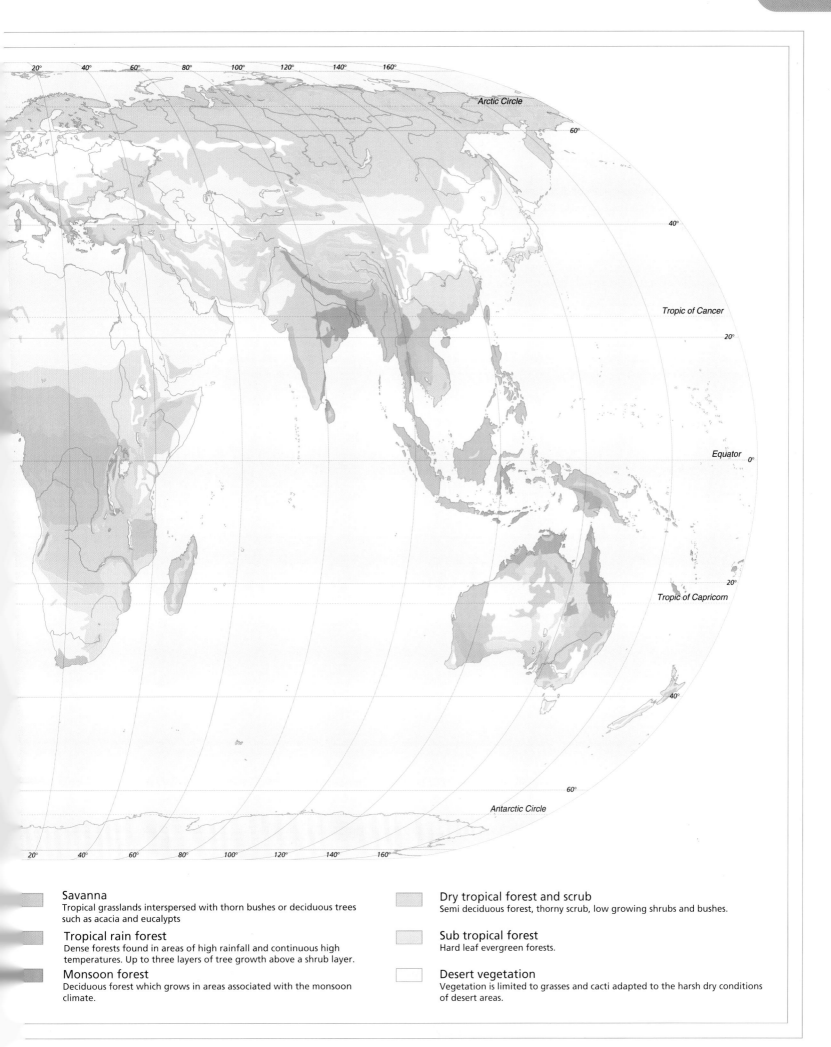

Savanna
Tropical grasslands interspersed with thorn bushes or deciduous trees such as acacia and eucalypts

Tropical rain forest
Dense forests found in areas of high rainfall and continuous high temperatures. Up to three layers of tree growth above a shrub layer.

Monsoon forest
Deciduous forest which grows in areas associated with the monsoon climate.

Dry tropical forest and scrub
Semi deciduous forest, thorny scrub, low growing shrubs and bushes.

Sub tropical forest
Hard leaf evergreen forests.

Desert vegetation
Vegetation is limited to grasses and cacti adapted to the harsh dry conditions of desert areas.

Eckert IV projection

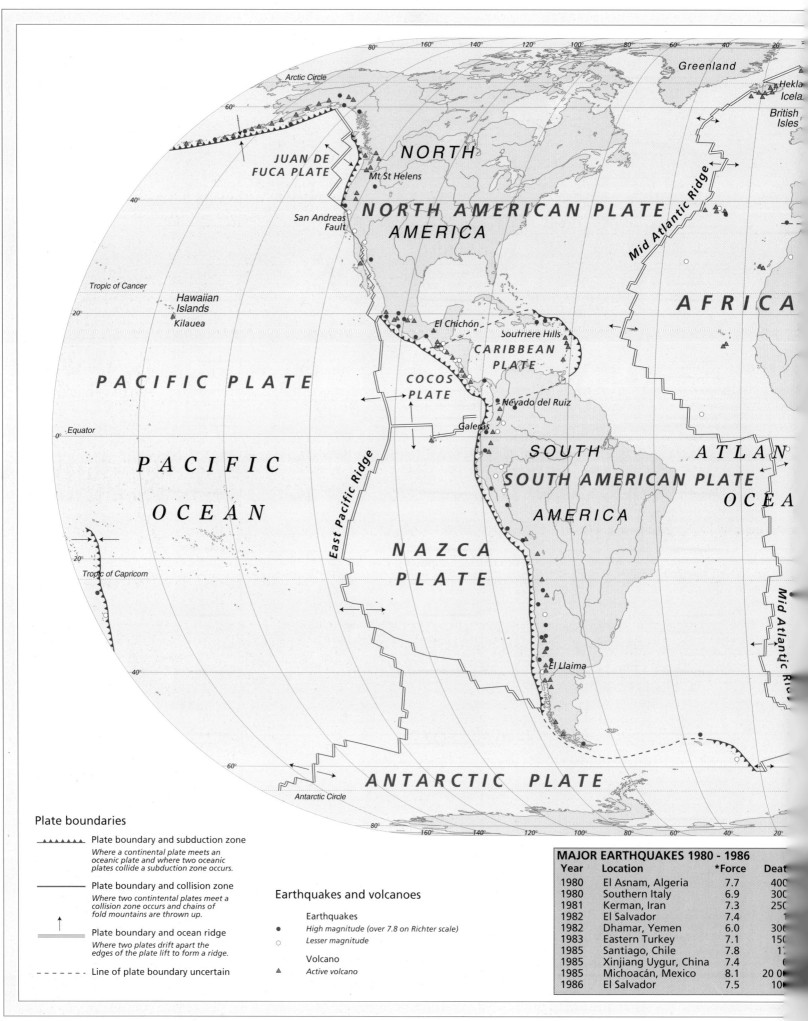

Greenland

Hekla
Icela

British
Isles

Arctic Circle

60°

NORTH

JUAN DE
FUCA PLATE

NORTH AMERICAN PLATE

Mt St Helens

AMERICA

San Andreas
Fault

Tropic of Cancer

AFRICA

Mid Atlantic Ridge

Hawaiian
Islands

El Chichón

Kilauea

Soutriere Hills

CARIBBEAN
PLATE

PACIFIC PLATE

COCOS
PLATE

Nevado del Ruiz

Equator

Galeras

SOUTH

ATLAN

PACIFIC

SOUTH AMERICAN PLATE

OCEA

OCEAN

AMERICA

NAZCA

East Pacific Ridge

Tropic of Capricorn

PLATE

El Llaima

Mid Atlantic Ri

ANTARCTIC PLATE

Antarctic Circle

Plate boundaries

⌃⌃⌃⌃⌃ Plate boundary and subduction zone

Where a continental plate meets an oceanic plate and where two oceanic plates collide a subduction zone occurs.

──── Plate boundary and collision zone

Where two contintental plates meet a collision zone occurs and chains of fold mountains are thrown up.

═══ Plate boundary and ocean ridge

Where two plates drift apart the edges of the plate lift to form a ridge.

------- Line of plate boundary uncertain

Earthquakes and volcanoes

Earthquakes

● *High magnitude (over 7.8 on Richter scale)*

○ *Lesser magnitude*

Volcano

▲ *Active volcano*

MAJOR EARTHQUAKES 1980 - 1986			
Year	Location	*Force	Deat
1980	El Asnam, Algeria	7.7	400
1980	Southern Italy	6.9	300
1981	Kerman, Iran	7.3	250
1982	El Salvador	7.4	1
1982	Dhamar, Yemen	6.0	300
1983	Eastern Turkey	7.1	150
1985	Santiago, Chile	7.8	1
1985	Xinjiang Uygur, China	7.4	6
1985	Michoacán, Mexico	8.1	20 0
1986	El Salvador	7.5	10

SCALE 1 : 80 000 000

0   800   1600   2400   3200 km

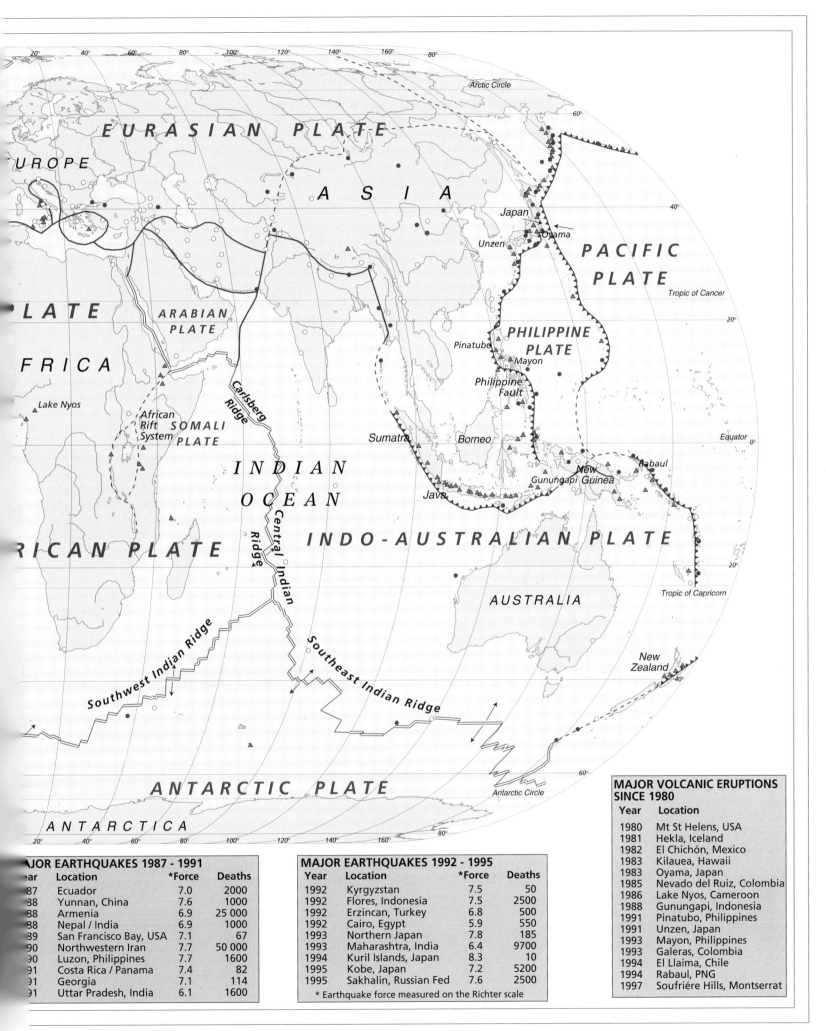

EURASIAN PLATE

EUROPE

ASIA

PACIFIC PLATE

Japan
Unzen
Oyama

PHILIPPINE PLATE

Pinatubo
Mayon

Philippine Fault

PLATE

ARABIAN PLATE

AFRICA

Lake Nyos

African Rift System

SOMALI PLATE

Carlsberg Ridge

Sumatra

Borneo

INDIAN OCEAN

Central Indian Ridge

AFRICAN PLATE

INDO-AUSTRALIAN PLATE

Java

Gunungapi

New Guinea

Rabaul

New Zealand

AUSTRALIA

Southwest Indian Ridge

Southeast Indian Ridge

ANTARCTIC PLATE

Antarctic Circle

ANTARCTICA

Arctic Circle

Tropic of Cancer

Equator

Tropic of Capricorn

Eckert iv projection

MAJOR EARTHQUAKES 1987 - 1991

Year	Location	*Force	Deaths
87	Ecuador	7.0	2000
88	Yunnan, China	7.6	1000
88	Armenia	6.9	25 000
88	Nepal / India	6.9	1000
89	San Francisco Bay, USA	7.1	67
90	Northwestern Iran	7.7	50 000
90	Luzon, Philippines	7.7	1600
91	Costa Rica / Panama	7.4	82
91	Georgia	7.1	114
91	Uttar Pradesh, India	6.1	1600

MAJOR EARTHQUAKES 1992 - 1995

Year	Location	*Force	Deaths
1992	Kyrgyzstan	7.5	50
1992	Flores, Indonesia	7.5	2500
1992	Erzincan, Turkey	6.8	500
1992	Cairo, Egypt	5.9	550
1993	Northern Japan	7.8	185
1993	Maharashtra, India	6.4	9700
1994	Kuril Islands, Japan	8.3	10
1995	Kobe, Japan	7.2	5200
1995	Sakhalin, Russian Fed	7.6	2500

* Earthquake force measured on the Richter scale

MAJOR VOLCANIC ERUPTIONS SINCE 1980

Year	Location
1980	Mt St Helens, USA
1981	Hekla, Iceland
1982	El Chichón, Mexico
1983	Kilauea, Hawaii
1983	Oyama, Japan
1985	Nevado del Ruiz, Colombia
1986	Lake Nyos, Cameroon
1988	Gunungapi, Indonesia
1991	Pinatubo, Philippines
1991	Unzen, Japan
1993	Mayon, Philippines
1993	Galeras, Colombia
1994	El Llaima, Chile
1994	Rabaul, PNG
1997	Soufriére Hills, Montserrat

POPULATION DISTRIBUTION

Persons per sq km

	over 100
	40-100
	10-40
	2-10
	0-2

POPULATION STRUCTURE

USA 1989

MEXICO 1990

Male	Female
	75+
65-69	70-74
55-59	60-64
45-49	50-54
35-39	40-44
25-29	30-34
15-19	20-24
5-9	10-14
	0-4

10 8 6 4 2 0 2 4 6 8 10%

Each full square represents 1% of the total population

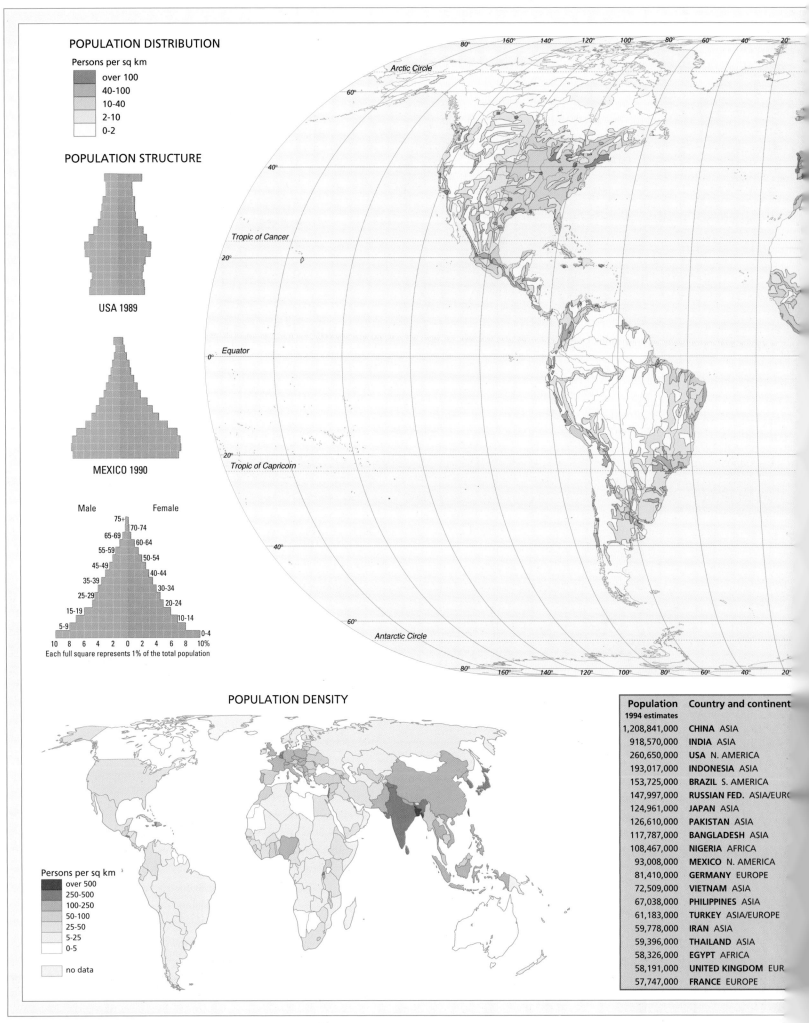

Arctic Circle

Tropic of Cancer

Equator

Tropic of Capricorn

Antarctic Circle

POPULATION DENSITY

Persons per sq km

	over 500
	250-500
	100-250
	50-100
	25-50
	5-25
	0-5
	no data

Population 1994 estimates	Country and continent
1,208,841,000	**CHINA** ASIA
918,570,000	**INDIA** ASIA
260,650,000	**USA** N. AMERICA
193,017,000	**INDONESIA** ASIA
153,725,000	**BRAZIL** S. AMERICA
147,997,000	**RUSSIAN FED.** ASIA/EURO
124,961,000	**JAPAN** ASIA
126,610,000	**PAKISTAN** ASIA
117,787,000	**BANGLADESH** ASIA
108,467,000	**NIGERIA** AFRICA
93,008,000	**MEXICO** N. AMERICA
81,410,000	**GERMANY** EUROPE
72,509,000	**VIETNAM** ASIA
67,038,000	**PHILIPPINES** ASIA
61,183,000	**TURKEY** ASIA/EUROPE
59,778,000	**IRAN** ASIA
59,396,000	**THAILAND** ASIA
58,326,000	**EGYPT** AFRICA
58,191,000	**UNITED KINGDOM** EUR
57,747,000	**FRANCE** EUROPE

SCALE 1 : 100 000 000

0   1000   2000   3000   4000 km

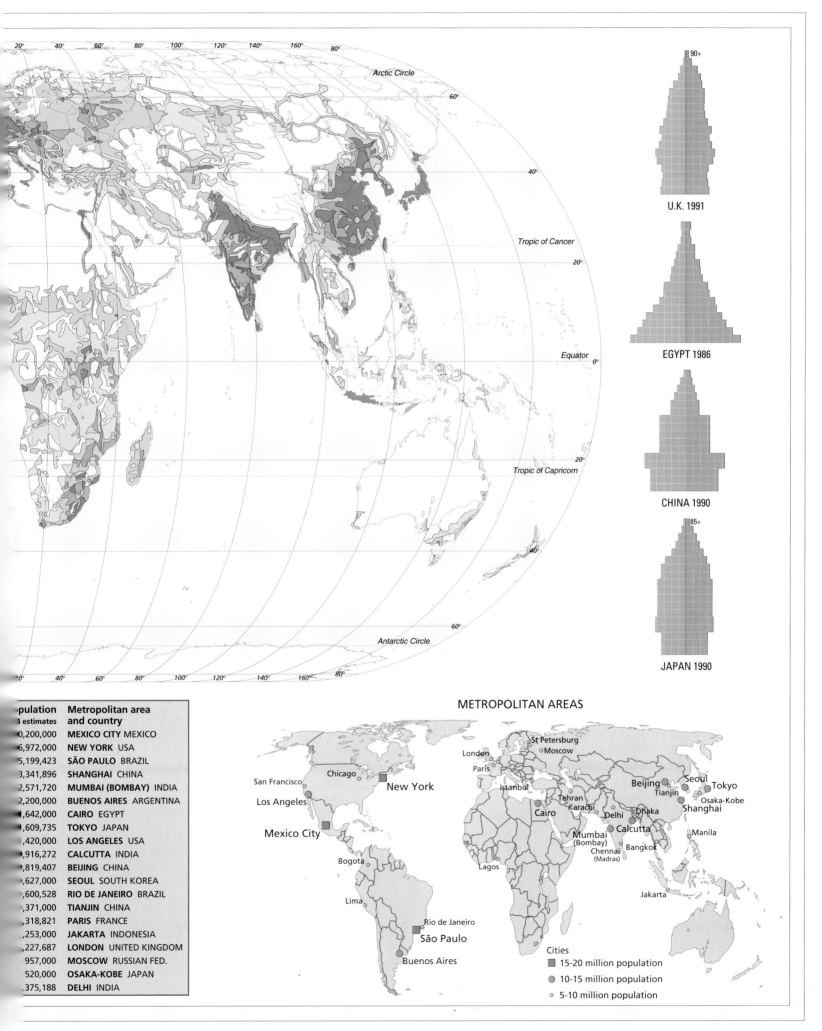

U.K. 1991

EGYPT 1986

CHINA 1990

JAPAN 1990

pulation estimates	Metropolitan area and country
0,200,000	**MEXICO CITY** MEXICO
6,972,000	**NEW YORK** USA
5,199,423	**SÃO PAULO** BRAZIL
3,341,896	**SHANGHAI** CHINA
2,571,720	**MUMBAI (BOMBAY)** INDIA
2,200,000	**BUENOS AIRES** ARGENTINA
1,642,000	**CAIRO** EGYPT
1,609,735	**TOKYO** JAPAN
1,420,000	**LOS ANGELES** USA
1,916,272	**CALCUTTA** INDIA
1,819,407	**BEIJING** CHINA
1,627,000	**SEOUL** SOUTH KOREA
1,600,528	**RIO DE JANEIRO** BRAZIL
1,371,000	**TIANJIN** CHINA
1,318,821	**PARIS** FRANCE
1,253,000	**JAKARTA** INDONESIA
1,227,687	**LONDON** UNITED KINGDOM
957,000	**MOSCOW** RUSSIAN FED.
520,000	**OSAKA-KOBE** JAPAN
375,188	**DELHI** INDIA

METROPOLITAN AREAS

Cities
- ■ 15-20 million population
- ● 10-15 million population
- · 5-10 million population

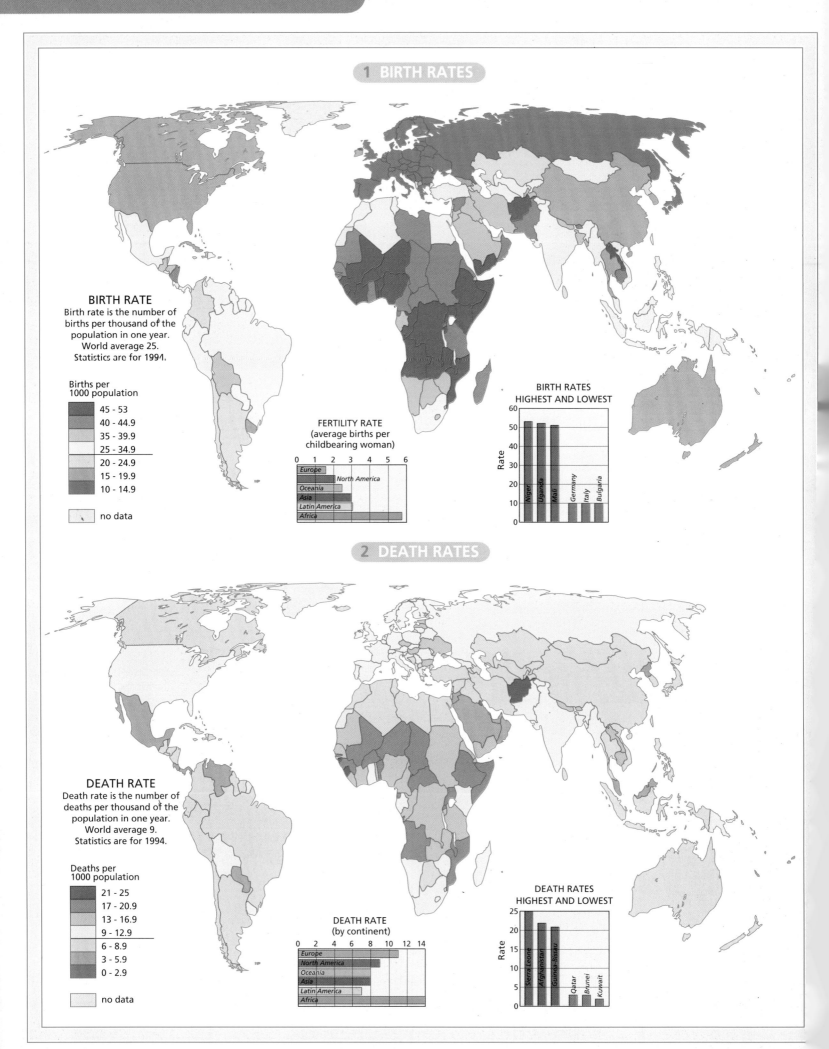

1 BIRTH RATES

BIRTH RATE
Birth rate is the number of births per thousand of the population in one year.
World average 25.
Statistics are for 1994.

Births per 1000 population

- 45 - 53
- 40 - 44.9
- 35 - 39.9
- 25 - 34.9
- 20 - 24.9
- 15 - 19.9
- 10 - 14.9

no data

FERTILITY RATE
(average births per childbearing woman)

Europe
North America
Oceania
Asia
Latin America
Africa

BIRTH RATES HIGHEST AND LOWEST

Niger, Uganda, Mali, Germany, Italy, Bulgaria

2 DEATH RATES

DEATH RATE
Death rate is the number of deaths per thousand of the population in one year.
World average 9.
Statistics are for 1994.

Deaths per 1000 population

- 21 - 25
- 17 - 20.9
- 13 - 16.9
- 9 - 12.9
- 6 - 8.9
- 3 - 5.9
- 0 - 2.9

no data

DEATH RATE
(by continent)

Europe
North America
Oceania
Asia
Latin America
Africa

DEATH RATES HIGHEST AND LOWEST

Sierra Leone, Afghanistan, Guinea-Bissau, Qatar, Brunei, Kuwait

SCALE 1 : 140 000 000

Eckert IV projection

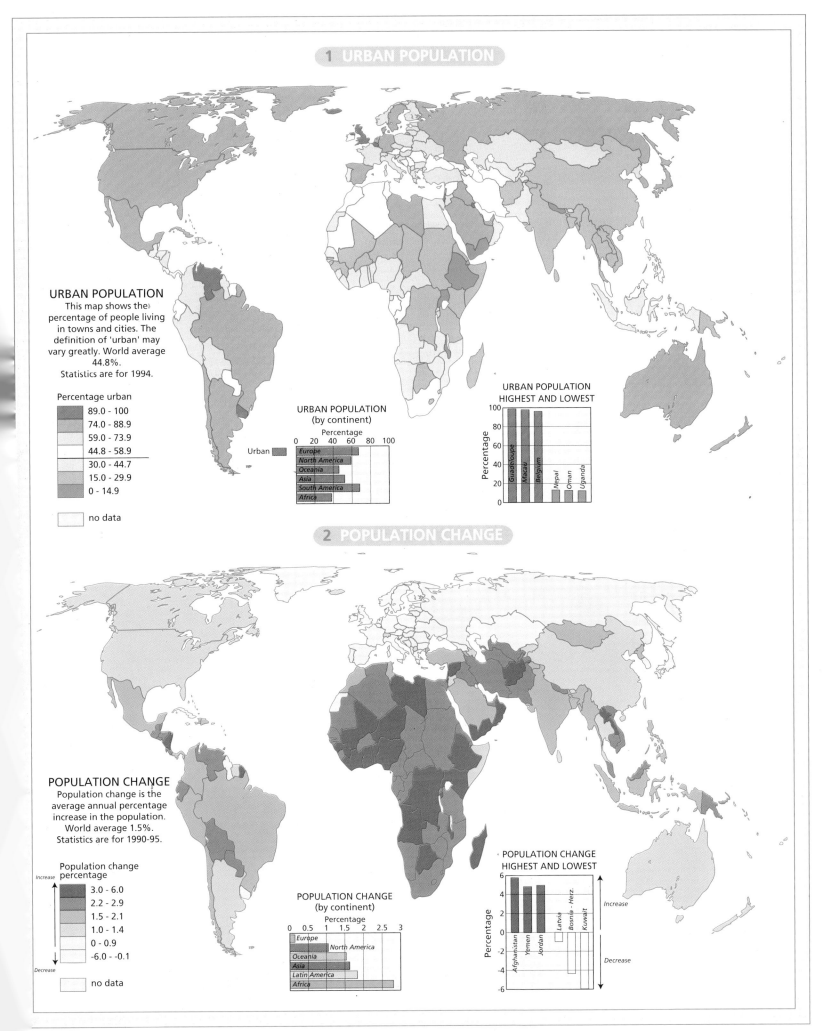

1 URBAN POPULATION

URBAN POPULATION

This map shows the percentage of people living in towns and cities. The definition of 'urban' may vary greatly. World average 44.8%.
Statistics are for 1994.

Percentage urban

	89.0 - 100
	74.0 - 88.9
	59.0 - 73.9
	44.8 - 58.9
	30.0 - 44.7
	15.0 - 29.9
	0 - 14.9

| | no data |

URBAN POPULATION
(by continent)

Percentage
0   20   40   60   80   100

Urban

- Europe
- North America
- Oceania
- Asia
- South America
- Africa

URBAN POPULATION
HIGHEST AND LOWEST

Percentage
0 20 40 60 80 100

Guadeloupe
Macau
Belgium
Nepal
Oman
Uganda

2 POPULATION CHANGE

POPULATION CHANGE

Population change is the average annual percentage increase in the population.
World average 1.5%.
Statistics are for 1990-95.

Population change percentage

Increase ↑

	3.0 - 6.0
	2.2 - 2.9
	1.5 - 2.1
	1.0 - 1.4
	0 - 0.9
	-6.0 - -0.1

Decrease ↓

| | no data |

POPULATION CHANGE
(by continent)

Percentage
0   0.5   1   1.5   2   2.5   3

- Europe
- North America
- Oceania
- Asia
- Latin America
- Africa

POPULATION CHANGE
HIGHEST AND LOWEST

Percentage
6
4
2
0
-2
-4
-6

Increase →

Afghanistan
Yemen
Jordan
Latvia
Bosnia - Herz.
Kuwait

Decrease →

SCALE 1 : 140 000 000

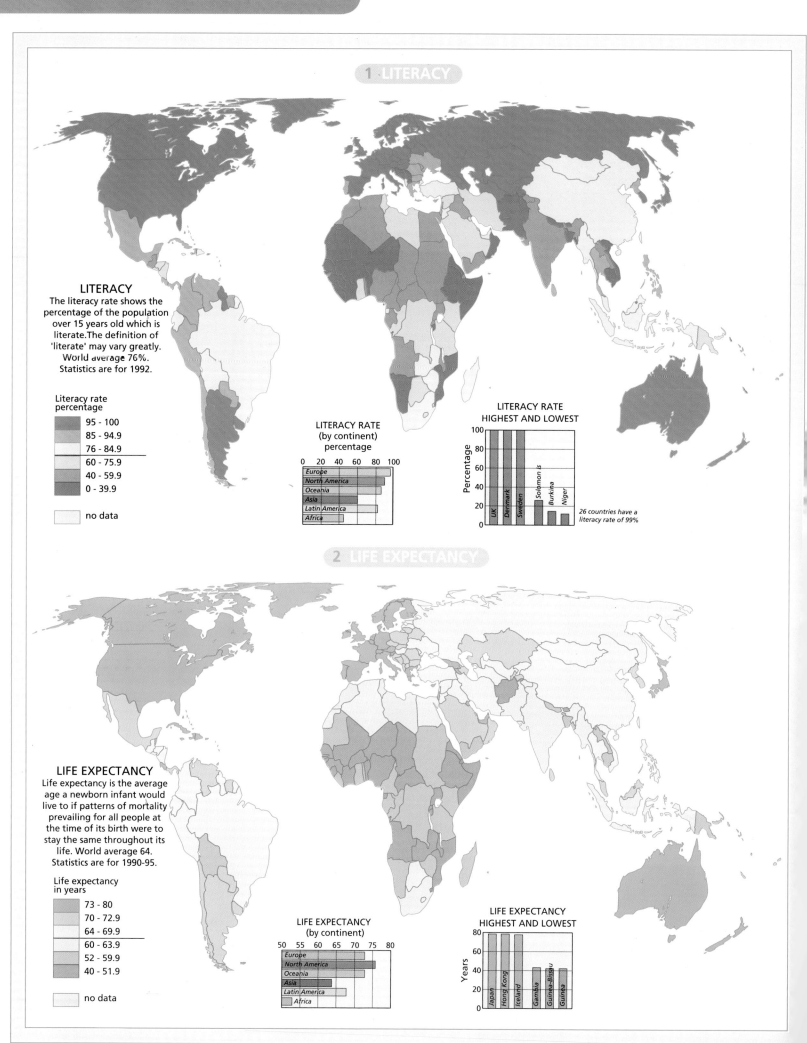

1 LITERACY

LITERACY
The literacy rate shows the percentage of the population over 15 years old which is literate. The definition of 'literate' may vary greatly. World average 76%. Statistics are for 1992.

Literacy rate percentage
- 95 - 100
- 85 - 94.9
- 76 - 84.9
- 60 - 75.9
- 40 - 59.9
- 0 - 39.9

no data

LITERACY RATE
(by continent)
percentage

0 20 40 60 80 100
- Europe
- North America
- Oceania
- Asia
- Latin America
- Africa

LITERACY RATE
HIGHEST AND LOWEST

Percentage — UK, Denmark, Sweden, Solomon Is, Burkina, Niger

26 countries have a literacy rate of 99%

2 LIFE EXPECTANCY

LIFE EXPECTANCY
Life expectancy is the average age a newborn infant would live to if patterns of mortality prevailing for all people at the time of its birth were to stay the same throughout its life. World average 64. Statistics are for 1990-95.

Life expectancy in years
- 73 - 80
- 70 - 72.9
- 64 - 69.9
- 60 - 63.9
- 52 - 59.9
- 40 - 51.9

no data

LIFE EXPECTANCY
(by continent)

50 55 60 65 70 75 80
- Europe
- North America
- Oceania
- Asia
- Latin America
- Africa

LIFE EXPECTANCY
HIGHEST AND LOWEST

Years — Japan, Hong Kong, Iceland, Gambia, Guinea-Bissau, Guinea

SCALE 1 : 140 000 000

Eckert IV projection

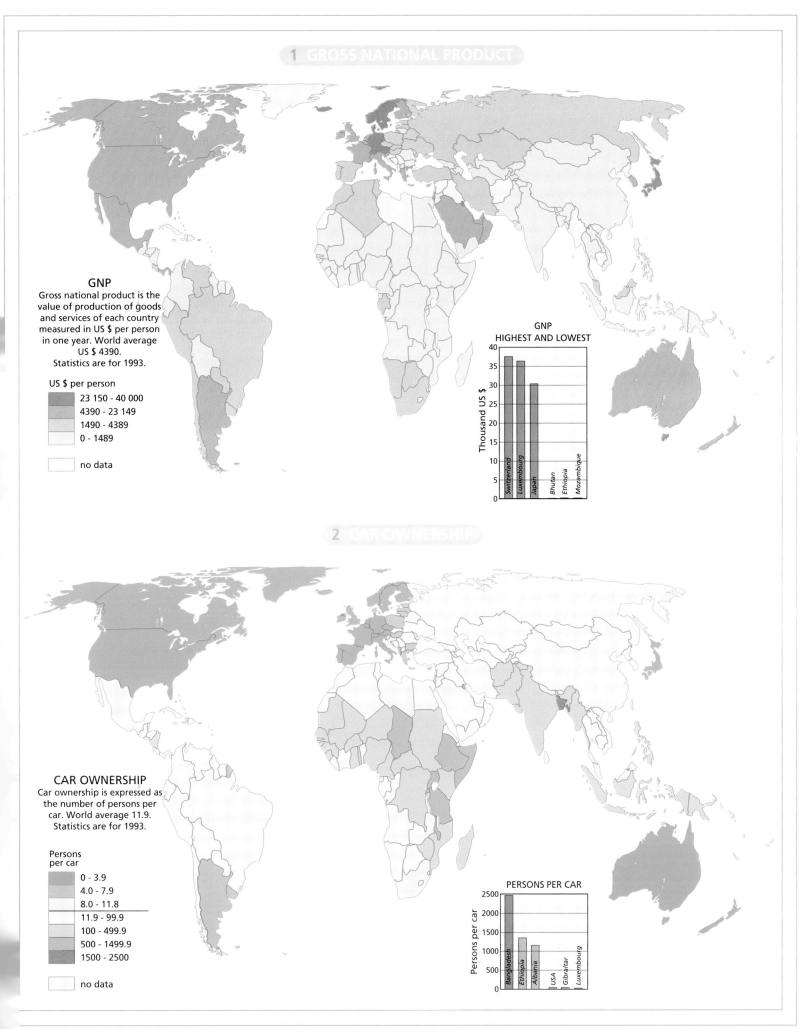

1 GROSS NATIONAL PRODUCT

GNP

Gross national product is the value of production of goods and services of each country measured in US $ per person in one year. World average US $ 4390.
Statistics are for 1993.

US $ per person

- 23 150 - 40 000
- 4390 - 23 149
- 1490 - 4389
- 0 - 1489

no data

GNP HIGHEST AND LOWEST

Thousand US $

Switzerland, Luxembourg, Japan, Bhutan, Ethiopia, Mozambique

2 CAR OWNERSHIP

CAR OWNERSHIP

Car ownership is expressed as the number of persons per car. World average 11.9.
Statistics are for 1993.

Persons per car

- 0 - 3.9
- 4.0 - 7.9
- 8.0 - 11.8
- 11.9 - 99.9
- 100 - 499.9
- 500 - 1499.9
- 1500 - 2500

no data

PERSONS PER CAR

Persons per car

Bangladesh, Ethiopia, Albania, USA, Gibraltar, Luxembourg

SCALE 1 : 140 000 000

Eckert IV projection

THREATS TO THE ENVIRONMENT

- *Forest
- Severe marine pollution
- Partial marine pollution
- ~ River pollution
- ~ Forest areas under threat
- ★ Forest above global average of deforestation
- ☢ Current nuclear test site
- ☣ Former nuclear test site
- • Major city with air pollution problem due to industry and vehicle exhaust
- ▲ Offshore oil production

*Includes Tropical rain forest, Monsoon forest and Dry tropical scrub. See World Natural Vegetation pp120-121.

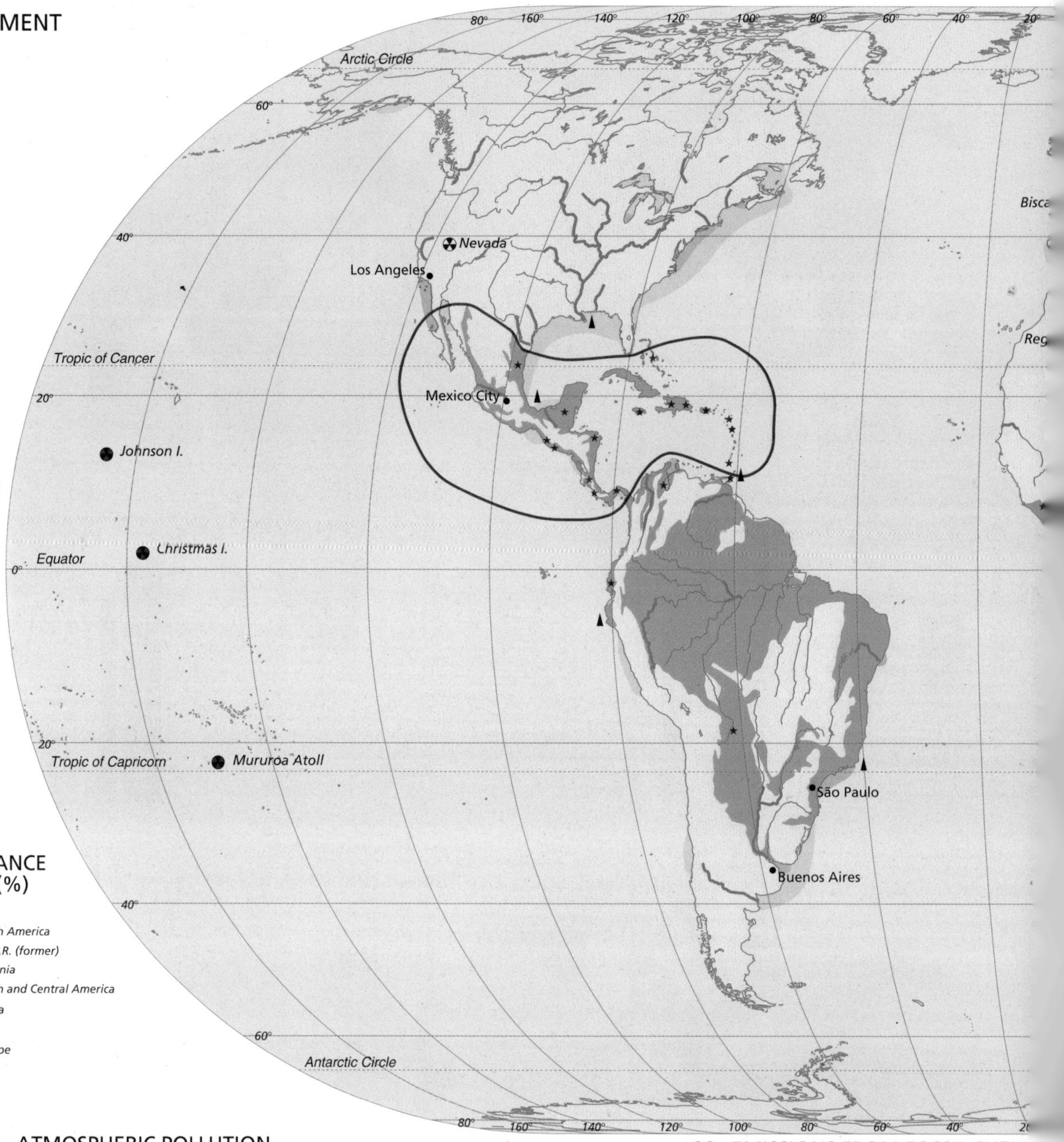

Map labels

Arctic Circle
Nevada
Los Angeles
Tropic of Cancer
Mexico City
Johnson I.
Christmas I.
Equator
Tropic of Capricorn
Mururoa Atoll
São Paulo
Buenos Aires
Bisca
Reg
Antarctic Circle

DEGREE OF HUMAN DISTURBANCE TO NATURAL LAND COVER (%)

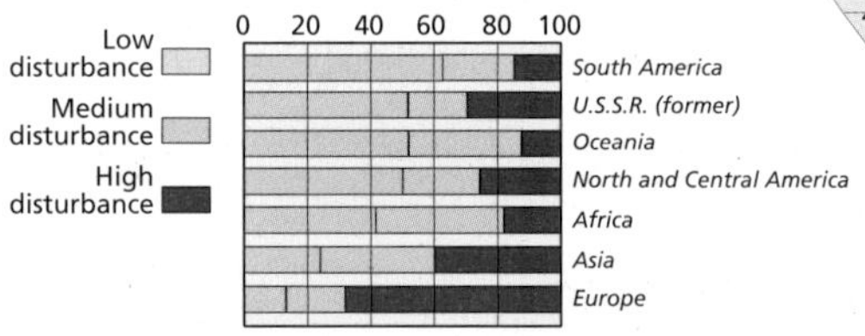

Low disturbance
Medium disturbance
High disturbance

0 20 40 60 80 100

- South America
- U.S.S.R. (former)
- Oceania
- North and Central America
- Africa
- Asia
- Europe

ATMOSPHERIC POLLUTION
(National greenhouse gas emissions)

Share of global emissions (%)
- 10-20
- 5-10
- 2.5-5
- 1.25-2.5
- 1-1.25
- 0.75-1
- 0-0.75

CO₂ EMISSIONS FROM FOSSIL FUEL CONSUMPTION 1955-1991

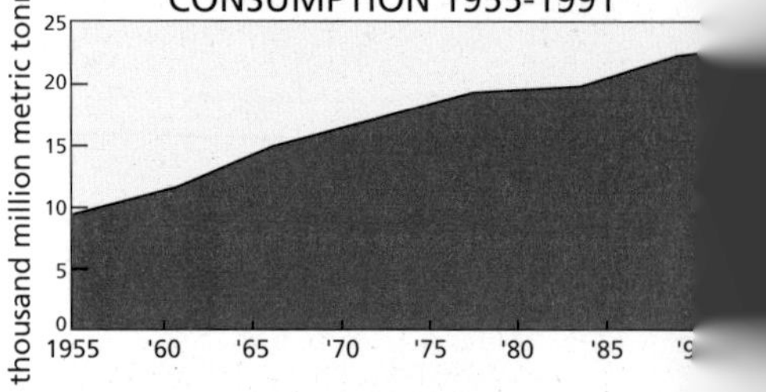

thousand million metric tonnes

25
20
15
10
5

1955 '60 '65 '70 '75 '80 '85 '9

GREENHOUSE EMISSIONS 1991

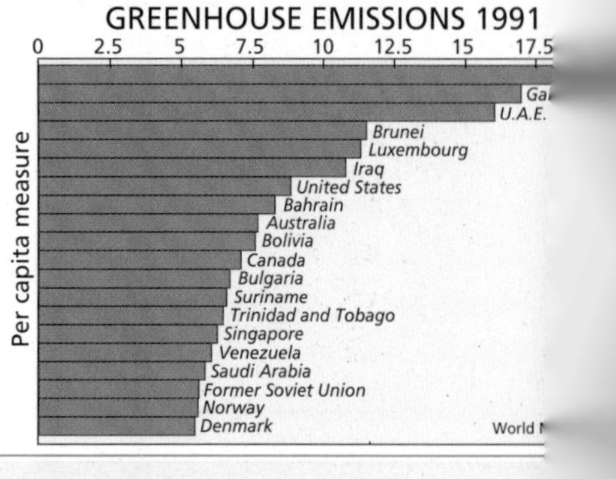

0 2.5 5 7.5 10 12.5 15 17.5

Per capita measure

Ga
U.A.E.
Brunei
Luxembourg
Iraq
United States
Bahrain
Australia
Bolivia
Canada
Bulgaria
Suriname
Trinidad and Tobago
Singapore
Venezuela
Saudi Arabia
Former Soviet Union
Norway
Denmark
World

SCALE 1 : 100 000 000

0 1000 2000 3000 4000 km

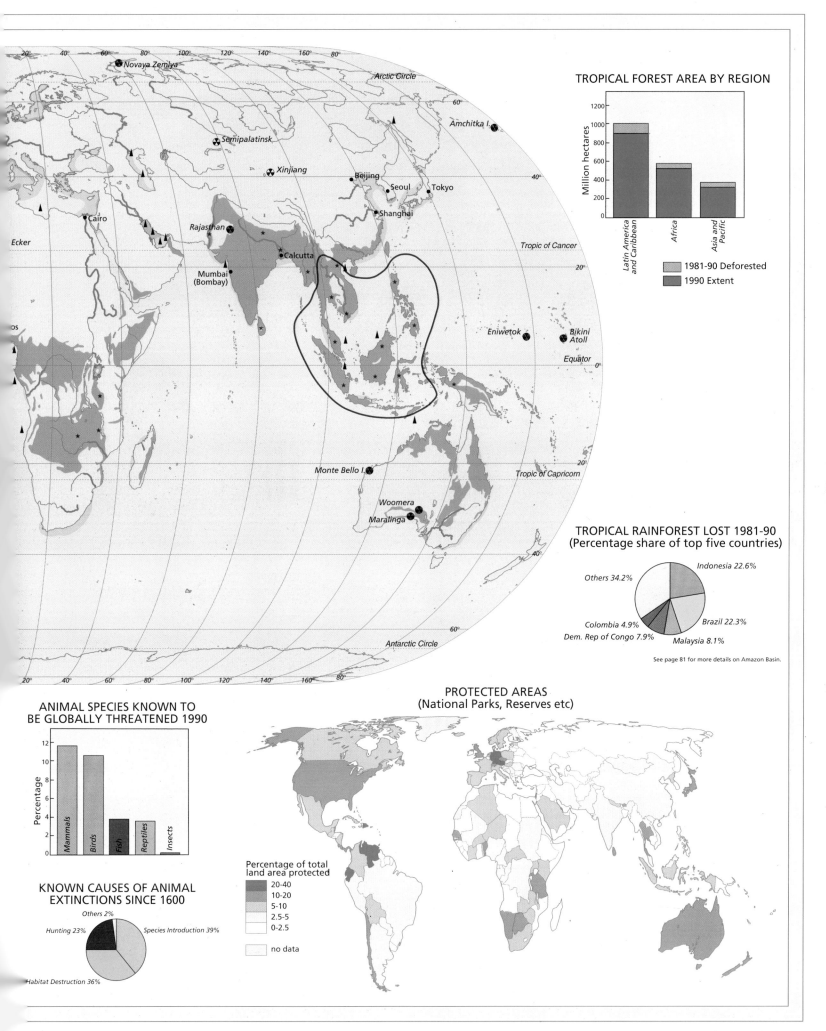

TROPICAL FOREST AREA BY REGION

Million hectares

- 1981-90 Deforested
- 1990 Extent

Latin America and Caribbean
Africa
Asia and Pacific

TROPICAL RAINFOREST LOST 1981-90
(Percentage share of top five countries)

- Others 34.2%
- Indonesia 22.6%
- Brazil 22.3%
- Malaysia 8.1%
- Dem. Rep of Congo 7.9%
- Colombia 4.9%

See page 81 for more details on Amazon Basin.

ANIMAL SPECIES KNOWN TO BE GLOBALLY THREATENED 1990

Percentage

- Mammals
- Birds
- Fish
- Reptiles
- Insects

KNOWN CAUSES OF ANIMAL EXTINCTIONS SINCE 1600

- Others 2%
- Hunting 23%
- Species Introduction 39%
- Habitat Destruction 36%

PROTECTED AREAS
(National Parks, Reserves etc)

Percentage of total land area protected
- 20-40
- 10-20
- 5-10
- 2.5-5
- 0-2.5

no data

Map labels
Novaya Zemlya
Arctic Circle
Amchitka I.
Semipalatinsk
Xinjiang
Beijing
Seoul
Tokyo
Shanghai
Cairo
Rajasthan
Tropic of Cancer
Calcutta
Mumbai (Bombay)
Eniwetok
Bikini Atoll
Equator
Monte Bello I.
Tropic of Capricorn
Woomera
Maralinga
Antarctic Circle

Ecker

Eckert IV projection

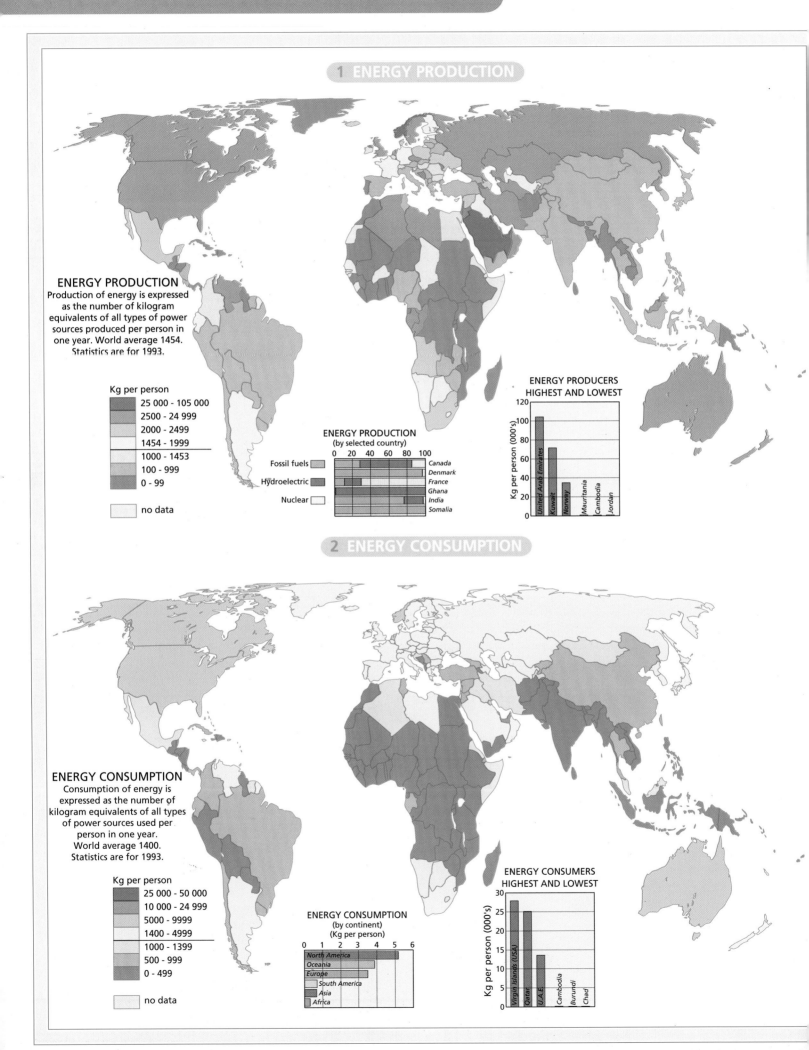

1 ENERGY PRODUCTION

ENERGY PRODUCTION
Production of energy is expressed as the number of kilogram equivalents of all types of power sources produced per person in one year. World average 1454. Statistics are for 1993.

Kg per person

- 25 000 - 105 000
- 2500 - 24 999
- 2000 - 2499
- 1454 - 1999
- 1000 - 1453
- 100 - 999
- 0 - 99

no data

ENERGY PRODUCTION
(by selected country)

0 20 40 60 80 100

- Fossil fuels
- Hydroelectric
- Nuclear

Canada
Denmark
France
Ghana
India
Somalia

ENERGY PRODUCERS
HIGHEST AND LOWEST

Kg per person (000's)

United Arab Emirates, Kuwait, Norway, Mauritania, Cambodia, Jordan

2 ENERGY CONSUMPTION

ENERGY CONSUMPTION
Consumption of energy is expressed as the number of kilogram equivalents of all types of power sources used per person in one year. World average 1400. Statistics are for 1993.

Kg per person

- 25 000 - 50 000
- 10 000 - 24 999
- 5000 - 9999
- 1400 - 4999
- 1000 - 1399
- 500 - 999
- 0 - 499

no data

ENERGY CONSUMPTION
(by continent)
(Kg per person)

0 1 2 3 4 5 6

North America
Oceania
Europe
South America
Asia
Africa

ENERGY CONSUMERS
HIGHEST AND LOWEST

Kg per person (000's)

Virgin Islands (USA), Qatar, U.A.E., Cambodia, Burundi, Chad

SCALE 1 : 140 000 000

Eckert IV projection

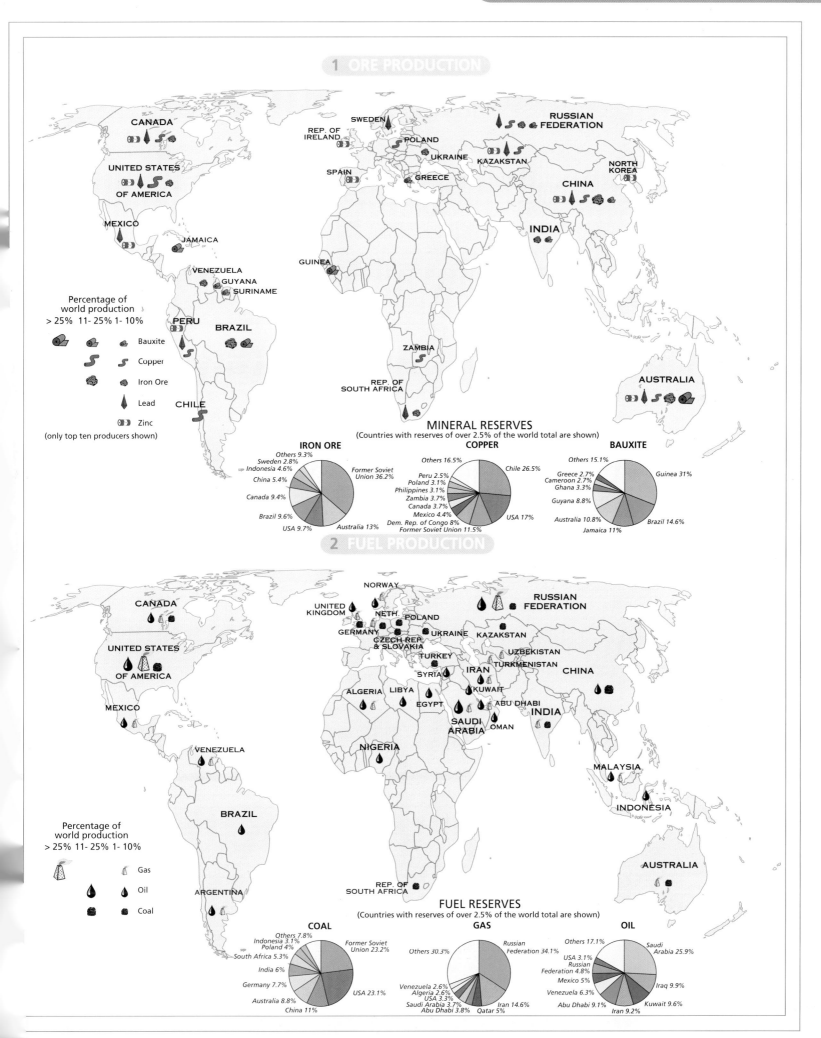

1 ORE PRODUCTION

CANADA
UNITED STATES OF AMERICA
MEXICO
JAMAICA
VENEZUELA
GUYANA
SURINAME
PERU
BRAZIL
CHILE

SWEDEN
REP. OF IRELAND
POLAND
UKRAINE
SPAIN
GREECE
GUINEA
ZAMBIA
REP. OF SOUTH AFRICA

RUSSIAN FEDERATION
KAZAKSTAN
NORTH KOREA
CHINA
INDIA
AUSTRALIA

Percentage of world production
> 25% 11- 25% 1- 10%

Bauxite
Copper
Iron Ore
Lead
Zinc

(only top ten producers shown)

MINERAL RESERVES
(Countries with reserves of over 2.5% of the world total are shown)

IRON ORE
Others 9.3%
Sweden 2.8%
Indonesia 4.6%
China 5.4%
Canada 9.4%
Brazil 9.6%
USA 9.7%
Australia 13%
Former Soviet Union 36.2%

COPPER
Others 16.5%
Peru 2.5%
Poland 3.1%
Philippines 3.1%
Zambia 3.7%
Canada 3.7%
Mexico 4.4%
Dem. Rep. of Congo 8%
Former Soviet Union 11.5%
Chile 26.5%
USA 17%

BAUXITE
Others 15.1%
Greece 2.7%
Cameroon 2.7%
Ghana 3.3%
Guyana 8.8%
Australia 10.8%
Jamaica 11%
Guinea 31%
Brazil 14.6%

2 FUEL PRODUCTION

CANADA
UNITED STATES OF AMERICA
MEXICO
VENEZUELA
BRAZIL
ARGENTINA

NORWAY
UNITED KINGDOM
NETH.
GERMANY
POLAND
CZECH REP. & SLOVAKIA
UKRAINE
TURKEY
SYRIA
ALGERIA
LIBYA
EGYPT
IRAN
KUWAIT
ABU DHABI
SAUDI ARABIA
OMAN
NIGERIA
REP. OF SOUTH AFRICA

RUSSIAN FEDERATION
KAZAKSTAN
UZBEKISTAN
TURKMENISTAN
CHINA
INDIA
MALAYSIA
INDONESIA
AUSTRALIA

Percentage of world production
> 25% 11- 25% 1- 10%

Gas
Oil
Coal

FUEL RESERVES
(Countries with reserves of over 2.5% of the world total are shown)

COAL
Others 7.8%
Indonesia 3.1%
Poland 4%
South Africa 5.3%
India 6%
Germany 7.7%
Australia 8.8%
China 11%
Former Soviet Union 23.2%
USA 23.1%

GAS
Others 30.3%
Venezuela 2.6%
Algeria 2.6%
USA 3.3%
Saudi Arabia 3.7%
Abu Dhabi 3.8%
Qatar 5%
Iran 14.6%
Russian Federation 34.1%

OIL
Others 17.1%
USA 3.1%
Russian Federation 4.8%
Mexico 5%
Venezuela 6.3%
Abu Dhabi 9.1%
Iran 9.2%
Kuwait 9.6%
Iraq 9.9%
Saudi Arabia 25.9%

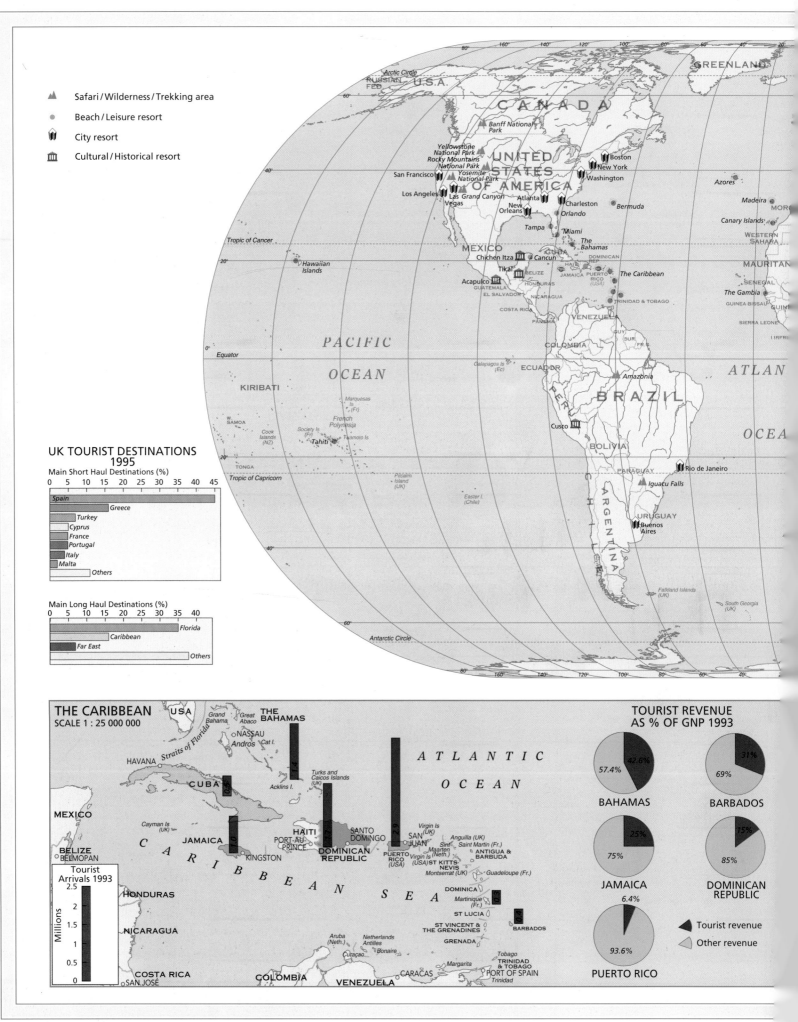

Legend
- ▲ Safari / Wilderness / Trekking area
- ● Beach / Leisure resort
- ⬗ City resort
- 🏛 Cultural / Historical resort

UK TOURIST DESTINATIONS 1995

Main Short Haul Destinations (%)

0 5 10 15 20 25 30 35 40 45

- Spain
- Greece
- Turkey
- Cyprus
- France
- Portugal
- Italy
- Malta
- Others

Main Long Haul Destinations (%)

0 5 10 15 20 25 30 35 40

- Florida
- Caribbean
- Far East
- Others

THE CARIBBEAN
SCALE 1 : 25 000 000

Tourist Arrivals 1993
Millions
2.5 / 2 / 1.5 / 1 / 0.5 / 0

TOURIST REVENUE AS % OF GNP 1993

BAHAMAS — 42.6% Tourist revenue / 57.4% Other revenue

BARBADOS — 31% / 69%

JAMAICA — 25% / 75%

DOMINICAN REPUBLIC — 15% / 85%

PUERTO RICO — 6.4% / 93.6%

- ◆ Tourist revenue
- ◇ Other revenue

SCALE 1 : 100 000 000

0 1000 2000 3000 4000 km

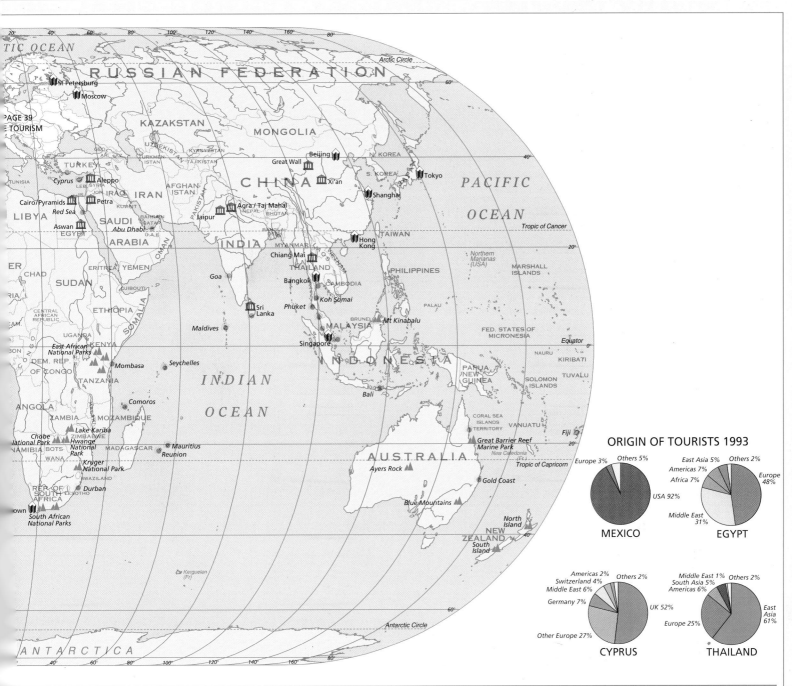

RUSSIAN FEDERATION

St Petersburg
Moscow

PAGE 39
E TOURISM

KAZAKSTAN
MONGOLIA
Beijing
N. KOREA
Great Wall
CHINA
Xi'an
Tokyo
S. KOREA
Shanghai
PACIFIC
OCEAN
TURKEY
Cyprus
Aleppo
IRAQ IRAN
ISTAN
Cairo/Pyramids
Petra
Red Sea
Aswan
SAUDI
Abu Dhabi
EGYPT
ARABIA
LIBYA
Agra / Taj Mahal
Jaipur
INDIA
Tropic of Cancer
TAIWAN
Hong Kong
Chiang Mai
THAILAND
Goa
Bangkok
CAMBODIA
PHILIPPINES
Koh Samui
Sri Lanka
Phuket
Maldives
Mt Kinabalu
MALAYSIA
Singapore
INDONESIA
East African National Parks
KENYA
Mombasa
Seychelles
INDIAN
OCEAN
TANZANIA
Comoros
Bali
ZAMBIA MOZAMBIQUE
Lake Kariba
ZIMBABWE
Hwange National Park
Mauritius
Reunion
MADAGASCAR
Kruger National Park
AUSTRALIA
Durban
Ayers Rock
South African National Parks
Blue Mountains
Gold Coast
ANTARCTICA
NEW ZEALAND
North Island
South Island

ORIGIN OF TOURISTS 1993

MEXICO
- USA 92%
- Europe 3%
- Others 5%

EGYPT
- Europe 48%
- Middle East 31%
- Africa 7%
- Americas 7%
- East Asia 5%
- Others 2%

CYPRUS
- UK 52%
- Other Europe 27%
- Germany 7%
- Middle East 6%
- Switzerland 4%
- Others 2%
- Americas 2%

THAILAND
- East Asia 61%
- Europe 25%
- Americas 6%
- South Asia 5%
- Middle East 1%
- Others 2%

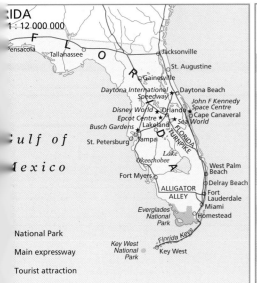

FLORIDA
1 : 12 000 000

Pensacola
Tallahassee
Jacksonville
St. Augustine
Gainesville
Daytona International Speedway
Daytona Beach
Disney World
Orlando
John F Kennedy Space Centre
Epcot Centre
Cape Canaveral
Busch Gardens
Lakeland
Sea World
Tampa
St. Petersburg
Gulf of Mexico
Lake Okeechobee
West Palm Beach
Fort Myers
Delray Beach
ALLIGATOR ALLEY
Fort Lauderdale
Everglades National Park
Miami
Homestead
National Park
Key West National Park
Florida Keys
Key West
Main expressway
Tourist attraction

	GROWTH IN TOURISM - Tourist Arrivals (1000's)										Importance of tourism 1993
Country	1984	1985	1986	1987	1988	1989	1990	1991	1992	1993	Income as % of GNP
Bermuda	417	407	460	478	427	418	435	386	375	413	28.7
Cuba	207	240	276	282	298	315	327	418	455	544	36.0
Cyprus	666	770	828	949	1112	1378	1561	1385	1991	1841	21.2
Dom. Rep.	562	660	747	902	1116	1400	1533	1321	1524	1691	15.0
Egypt	N/A	1407	1236	1671	1833	2351	2411	2112	2944	2291	3.6
France	35 379	36 748	36 080	36 974	38 288	49 549	52 497	55 041	59 710	60 100	1.8
Greece	5523	6574	7025	7564	7923	8082	8873	8036	9331	9413	4.3
Martinique	184	193	183	234	280	312	282	315	321	366	8.3
Mexico	4654	4207	4625	5407	5692	14 962	17 174	16 066	17 273	16 534	2.0
Spain	27 176	27 477	29 910	32 900	35 000	38 867	37 441	38 539	39 638	40 085	3.5
Thailand	2347	2438	2818	3483	4231	4810	5299	5087	5136	5761	4.2
Trinidad & Tobago	191	187	191	202	188	190	195	220	235	249	1.6

KEY INFORMATION

POPULATION

FLAG	COUNTRY	CAPITAL CITY	TOTAL (in '000s 1996)	DENSITY (persons per sq km 1996)	BIRTH RATE (per 1000 population 1994)	DEATH RATE (per 1000 population 1994)	LIFE EXPEC-TANCY (in years 1996)	POP. CHANGE (average % per annum 1990 - 1995)	URBAN POP. (% 1996)
	AFGHANISTAN	Kabul	20 883	32	50	22	45	5.83	20
	ALBANIA	Tiranë	3401	118.3	24	6	71	0.9	38
	ALGERIA	Algiers	29 168	12.2	29	6	68	2.27	57
	ANGOLA	Luanda	11 185	9	51	19	47	3.72	32
	ARGENTINA	Buenos Aires	35 220	12.7	20	8	73	1.22	88
	ARMENIA	Yerevan	3764	126.3	21	6	71	1.42	69
	AUSTRALIA	Canberra	18 289	2.4	15	7	78	1.37	85
	AUSTRIA	Vienna	8106	96.7	12	11	77	0.67	64
	AZERBAIJAN	Baku	7554	87.2	23	6	71	1.2	56
	BAHAMAS	Nassau	284	20.4	19	5	73	1.51	87
	BAHRAIN	Manama	599	866.9	28	4	73	2.8	91
	BANGLADESH	Dhaka	120 073	833.9	35	12	57	2.16	19
	BARBADOS	Bridgetown	261	607	16	9	76	0.35	48
	BELARUS	Minsk	10 247	49.4	12	12	70	-0.14	72
	BELGIUM	Brussels	10 159	332.9	12	11	77	0.32	97
	BELIZE	Belmopan	222	9.7	35	5	74	2.64	47
	BENIN	Porto Novo	5514	49	49	18	54	3.1	39
	BHUTAN	Thimbu	1812	38.9	40	15	52	1.18	6
	BOLIVIA	La Paz	7588	6.9	36	10	61	2.41	62
	BOSNIA-HERZEGOVINA	Sarajevo	3628	71	13	7	73	-4.39	43
	BOTSWANA	Gaborone	1490	2.6	37	7	52	3.06	63
	BRAZIL	Brasília	157 872	18.5	25	7	67	1.72	79
	BRUNEI	Bandar Seri Begawan	300	52	24	3	75	2.06	70
	BULGARIA	Sofia	8468	76.3	10	13	71	-0.5	69
	BURKINA	Ouagadougou	10 780	39.3	47	18	46	2.76	16
	BURUNDI	Bujumbura	6088	218.7	46	16	46	3	8
	CAMBODIA	Phnom Penh	10 273	56.8	44	14	53	2.96	21
	CAMEROON	Yaoundé	13 560	28.5	41	12	56	2.76	46
	CANADA	Ottawa	29 964	3	15	8	79	1.17	77
	CAPE VERDE	Praia	396	98.2	36	9	66	2.77	56
	CENTRAL AFRICAN REPUBLIC	Bangui	3344	5.4	42	17	49	2.49	40
	CHAD	Ndjamena	6515	5.1	44	18	47	2.71	23
	CHILE	Santiago	14 419	19	22	6	75	1.62	84
	CHINA	Beijing	1 232 083	128.9	19	7	69	1.11	31
	COLOMBIA	Bogotá	35 626	31.2	24	6	71	1.66	73
	COMOROS	Moroni	632	339.4	48	12	57	3.68	31
	CONGO	Brazzaville	2668	7.8	45	15	51	2.98	59
	CONGO, DEM. REP. OF	Kinshasa	46 812	20	48	14	53	3.19	29
	COSTA RICA	San José	3398	66.5	26	4	77	2.41	50
	CÔTE D'IVOIRE	Yamoussoukro	14 781	45.8	50	15	51	3.48	44
	CROATIA	Zagreb	4501	79.6	11	12	72	-0.1	56
	CUBA	Havana	11 018	99.4	17	7	76	0.82	76
	CYPRUS	Nicosia	756	81.7	19	8	77	1.11	54
	CZECH REPUBLIC	Prague	10 315	130.8	13	13	73	-0.02	66

LAND

EDUCATION AND HEALTH

DEVELOPMENT

AREA ('000s sq km)	CULTIV-ATED AREA ('000s sq km 1993)	FOREST ('000s sq km 1993)	ADULT LITERACY (% 1992)	SCHOOL ENROL-MENT (Secondary, gross % 1993)	PEOPLE PER DOCTOR (1991)	FOOD INTAKE (calories per capita per day 1992)	ENERGY CONSU-MPTION (kg per cap oil eq 1993)	TRADE BALANCE (millions US $ 1994)	GNP PER CAPITA (US $ 1995 or earlier)	COUNTRY	TIME ZONES (+ OR - GMT)
652	81	19	28.9	6	5452	1523	30	-428	280	AFGHANISTAN	+4½
29	7	10	85	79	583	2605	305		670	ALBANIA	+1
2382	79	40	57.4	59	1262	2897	1058	2489	1600	ALGERIA	+1
1247	35	519	42.5		15 298	1839	61	1849	410	ANGOLA	+1
2767	272	509	95.9	74	337	2880	1428	-5868	8030	ARGENTINA	-3
30	6	4	98.8		241		334	-56	730	ARMENIA	+4
7682	465	1450	99	83	467	3179	5310	-5853	18 720	AUSTRALIA	+8 to +10½
84	15	32	99	105.5	347	3497	2934	-10 313	26 890	AUSTRIA	+1
87	20	10	96.3		259		1768	-102	480	AZERBAIJAN	+4
14		3	98	93		2624	2134	-284	11 940	BAHAMAS	-5
0.691			83.5	99	758		12 325	-283	7840	BAHRAIN	+3
144	97	19	36.4	18.5	6615	2019	65	-2051	240	BANGLADESH	+6
0.43			97	87		3207	1315	-427	6560	BARBADOS	-4
208	62	70	97.9		254		2928	-32	2070	BELARUS	+2
31	8	7	99	102.5	307	3681	4698	7275	24 710	BELGIUM	+1
23	1	21	96			2662	436	-114	2630	BELIZE	-6
113	19	34	32.9	12	19 899	2532	32	-110	370	BENIN	+1
47	1	31	39.2		10 643		35		420	BHUTAN	+6
1099	24	580	80.7	34	2331	2094	290	-177	800	BOLIVIA	-4
51	9	20					190			BOSNIA-HERZEGOVINA	+1
581	4	265	67.2	54	8276	2266			3020	BOTSWANA	+2
8512	490	4880	81.9	33.5	729	2824	580	7561	3640	BRAZIL	-2 to -5
6		5	86.4	71.5	1556	2745	10 533	601	14 240	BRUNEI	+8
111	43	39	93	70	324	2831	2598	-733	1330	BULGARIA	+2
274	36	138	17.4	8.5	32 146	2387	20	-431	230	BURKINA	GMT
28	14	1	32.9	6.5		1941	14	-118	160	BURUNDI	+2
181	24	116	37.8		27 215	2021	17		270	CAMBODIA	+7
475	70	359	59.6	27.5	14 206	1981	68	640	650	CAMEROON	+1
9971	455	4940	99	107	463	3094	7624	10 427	19 380	CANADA	-3½ to -8
4			66.4	19.5		2805	97	-150	960	CAPE VERDE	-1
622	20	467	53.9	12	18 530	1690	26	-41	340	C.A.R.	+1
1284	33	324	44.9	7.5	60 415	1989	5	-77	180	CHAD	+1
757	43	165	94.5	70	946	2582	931	-286	4160	CHILE	-4 to -6
9562	960	1305	79.3	53.5	642	2727	603	5343	620	CHINA	+8
1142	55	500	90.3	61.5	1124	2677	583	-3484	1910	COLOMBIA	-5
2	1		55.6	18.5		1897	36	-47	470	COMOROS	+3
342	2	211	70.7		4542	2296	236	602	680	CONGO	+1
2345	79	1738	74.1	22.5	26 982	2060	42	-39	120	CONGO, DEM. REP. OF	+1 to +2
51	5	16	94.3	47	1179	2883	457	-810	2610	COSTA RICA	-6
322	37	71	36.6	24	23 900	2491	196	974	660	CÔTE D'IVOIRE	GMT
57	13	21					1394	-970	3250	CROATIA	+1
111	33	26	94.9	84	305	2833	809	-135	1170	CUBA	-5
9	2	1	94	94.5	604	3779	2059	-2053	10 380	CYPRUS	+2
79	33	26	99			3156	3849	-471	3870	CZECH REPUBLIC	+1

KEY INFORMATION

POPULATION

FLAG	COUNTRY	CAPITAL CITY	TOTAL (in '000s 1996)	DENSITY (persons per sq km 1996)	BIRTH RATE (per 1000 population 1994)	DEATH RATE (per 1000 population 1994)	LIFE EXPEC-TANCY (in years 1996)	POP. CHANGE (average % per annum 1990 - 1995)	URBAN POP. (% 1996)
	DENMARK	Copenhagen	5262	122.2	12	12	75	0.16	85
	DJIBOUTI	Djibouti	617	26.6	38	16	50	2.2	82
	DOMINICAN REPUBLIC	Santo Domingo	8052	166.2	27	6	71	1.91	63
	ECUADOR	Quito	11 698	43	28	6	70	2.2	60
	EGYPT	Cairo	60 603	60.6	29	8	65	2.22	45
	EL SALVADOR	San Salvador	5796	275.5	33	7	69	2.18	45
	EQUATORIAL GUINEA	Malabo	410	14.6	43	18	49	2.55	44
	ERITREA	Asmara	3280	27.9	43	15	50	2.72	18
	ESTONIA	Tallinn	1470	32.5	11	13	69	-0.58	73
	ETHIOPIA	Addis Ababa	58 506	51.6	48	18	49	2.98	16
	FIJI	Suva	797	43.5	24	5	72	1.52	41
	FINLAND	Helsinki	5124	15.2	13	10	76	0.48	63
	FRANCE	Paris	58 375	107.3	13	10	79	0.44	75
	GABON	Libreville	1106	4.1	37	15	55	2.83	51
	GAMBIA	Banjul	1141	101	44	19	46	3.83	30
	GEORGIA	Tiflis	5411	77.6	16	9	73	0.14	59
	GERMANY	Berlin	81 912	228.9	10	12	76	0.55	87
	GHANA	Accra	17 832	74.8	42	12	57	3	36
	GREECE	Athens	10 475	79.4	10	10	78	0.41	59
	GUATEMALA	Guatemala City	10 928	100.4	39	8	66	2.88	39
	GUINEA	Conakry	7518	30.6	51	20	46	3.04	30
	GUINEA-BISSAU	Bissau	1091	30.2	43	21	44	2.14	22
	GUYANA	Georgetown	838	3.9	25	7	64	0.94	36
	HAITI	Port-au-Prince	7336	264.4	35	12	54	2.03	32
	HONDURAS	Tegucigalpa	6140	54.8	37	6	69	2.95	44
	HUNGARY	Budapest	10 193	109.6	12	15	69	-0.49	65
	ICELAND	Reykjavik	271	2.6	18	7	79	1.06	92
	INDIA	New Delhi	944 580	287.3	29	10	62	1.91	27
	INDONESIA	Jakarta	196 813	102.5	25	8	64	1.55	36
	IRAN	Tehran	61 128	37.1	35	7	69	2.65	60
	IRAQ	Baghdad	20 607	47	38	7	61	2.46	75
	IRELAND, REPUBLIC OF	Dublin	3521	50.1	15	9	76	0.28	58
	ISRAEL	Jerusalem	5696	274.2	21	7	77	3.78	90
	ITALY	Rome	57 399	190.5	10	10	78	0.06	67
	JAMAICA	Kingston	2491	226.6	22	6	74	0.68	54
	JAPAN	Tokyo	125 761	332.9	10	8	80	0.25	78
	JORDAN	Amman	5581	62.6	39	5	69	4.89	72
	KAZAKSTAN	Akmola	16 526	6.1	20	8	68	0.52	60
	KENYA	Nairobi	31 806	54.6	45	12	54	3.59	30
	KUWAIT	Kuwait	1687	94.7	24	2	76	-6.52	100
	KYRGYZSTAN	Bishkek	4575	23	29	7	68	1.68	39
	LAOS	Vientiane	5035	21.3	45	15	53	3	21
	LATVIA	Riga	2491	39.1	11	13	68	-0.87	73
	LEBANON	Beirut	3084	295.1	27	7	69	3.27	87

AREA ('000s sq km)	CULTIVATED AREA ('000s sq km 1993)	FOREST ('000s sq km 1993)	ADULT LITERACY (% 1992)	SCHOOL ENROLMENT (Secondary, gross % 1993)	PEOPLE PER DOCTOR (1991)	FOOD INTAKE (calories per capita per day 1992)	ENERGY CONSUMPTION (kg per cap oil eq 1993)	TRADE BALANCE (millions US $ 1994)	GNP PER CAPITA (US $ 1995 or earlier)	COUNTRY	TIME ZONES (+ OR - GMT)
43	25	4	99	110	376	3664	3522	5979	29 890	DENMARK	+1
23	2		43.2	13.5		2338	767	-203	780	DJIBOUTI	+3
48	15	6	80.7	50.5	978	2286	469	-2124	1460	DOMINICAN REPUBLIC	-4
272	30	156	88.4	56	977	2583	534	75	1390	ECUADOR	-5 to -6
1000	28		49.1	79.5	725	3335	486	-6808	790	EGYPT	+2
21	7	1	69.8	26.5	1641	2663	313	-1185	1610	EL SALVADOR	-6
28	2	13	75.3		69 600		111	2	380	EQUATORIAL GUINEA	+1
117	13	20				1610			100	ERITREA	+3
45	11	20	99	91	208		3288	-364	2860	ESTONIA	+2
1134	127	250	32.7	10.5	38 255	1610	21	-683	100	ETHIOPIA	+3
18	3	12	90.1	60.5		3089	334	-279	2440	FIJI	+12
338	26	232	99	124	519	3018	4786	6436	20 580	FINLAND	+2
544	194	149	99	102	393	3633	3800	5743	24 990	FRANCE	+1
268	5	199	58.9		2074	2500	622	1443	3490	GABON	+1
11	2	3	35.6	20.5	13 045	2360	67	-166	320	GAMBIA	GMT
70	10	27	99		178		696	-121	440	GEORGIA	+4
358	121	107	99	97	365	3344	4054	42 127	27 510	GERMANY	+1
239	43	79	60.7	38.5	25 047	2199	98	-257	390	GHANA	GMT
132	35	26	93.8	98	304	3815	2276	-13 235	8210	GREECE	+2
109	19	58	54.2	18.5	2570	2255	171	-1308	1340	GUATEMALA	-6
246	7	145	33	11.5	9065	2389	58		550	GUINEA	GMT
36	3	11	51.7	6.5	7910	2556	73	-30	250	GUINEA-BISSAU	GMT
215	5	165	97.5	57.5	7171	2384	426	-89	590	GUYANA	-4
28	9	1	42.6	21.5	6871	1706	31	-232	250	HAITI	-5
112	20	60	70.7	30.5	1879	2305	192	-213	600	HONDURAS	-6
93	50	18	99	82	323	3503	2316	-3916	4120	HUNGARY	+1
103		1	99	92	378	3058	4935	151	24 950	ICELAND	GMT
3287	1697	685	49.9	48.5	2494	2395	247	-1751	340	INDIA	+5½
1919	310	1118	82.5	43	7767	2752	331	8069	980	INDONESIA	+7 to +9
1648	182	114	64.9	62	3228	2860	1215	-2481	1033	IRAN	+3½
438	55	2	54.6	42.5	4273	2121	1145		1036	IRAQ	+3
70	9	3	99	103	676	3847	2904	8939	14 710	REPUBLIC OF IRELAND	GMT
21	4	1	95	86	392	3050	2297	-6892	15 920	ISRAEL	+2
301	119	68	97.4	77	235	3561	2820	21 971	19 020	ITALY	+1
11	2	2	83.7	62.5	2157	2607	1035	-1061	1510	JAMAICA	-5
378	45	251	99	97	613	2903	3357	121 825	39 640	JAPAN	+9
89	4	1	83.9	53	891	3022	709	-1958	1510	JORDAN	+2
2717	348	96	97.5		254		4763	581	1330	KAZAKSTAN	+4 to +6
583	45	168	74.5	27	7358	2075	81	-598	280	KENYA	+3
18			76.9	55	739	2523	6337	5285	17 390	KUWAIT	+3
199	14	7	97		295		782	0	700	KYRGYZSTAN	+5
237	8	125	53.5	22	7418	2259	25	-81	350	LAOS	+7
64	17	28	99	85	200		1712	-251	2270	LATVIA	+2
10	3	1	91.4	69	770	3317	1028		2660	LEBANON	+2

KEY INFORMATION			POPULATION						
FLAG	COUNTRY	CAPITAL CITY	TOTAL (in '000s 1996)	DENSITY (persons per sq km 1996)	BIRTH RATE (per 1000 population 1994)	DEATH RATE (per 1000 population 1994)	LIFE EXPEC- TANCY (in years 1996)	POP. CHANGE (average % per annum 1990 - 1995)	URBAN POP. (% 1996)
	LESOTHO	Maseru	2078	68.5	37	10	58	2.69	25
	LIBERIA	Monrovia	2820	25.3	47	14	48	3.32	48
	LIBYA	Tripoli	5593	3.2	42	8	65	3.47	86
	LITHUANIA	Vilnius	3710	56.9	13	11	70	-0.06	72
	LUXEMBOURG	Luxembourg	412	159.3	13	11	76	1.26	90
	MACEDONIA	Skopje	2163	84.1	15	7	72	1.11	60
	MADAGASCAR	Antananarivo	15 353	26.2	44	12	58	3.21	27
	MALAWI	Lilongwe	10 114	85.4	51	20	41	3.45	14
	MALAYSIA	Kuala Lumpur	20 581	61.8	29	5	72	2.37	54
	MALDIVES	Male	263	882.6	42	9	64	3.31	27
	MALI	Bamako	11 134	9	51	19	47	3.17	28
	MALTA	Valletta	373	1180.4	15	8	77	0.67	89
	MAURITANIA	Nouakchott	2351	2.3	40	14	53	2.54	53
	MAURITIUS	Port Louis	1134	555.9	21	7	71	1.1	41
	MEXICO	Mexico City	96 578	49	28	5	72	2.06	74
	MICRONESIA	Palikir	126	179.7				2.77	29
	MOLDOVA	Chişinau	4237	125.7	16	10	68	0.32	52
	MONGOLIA	Ulan Bator	2354	1.5	28	7	65	2.03	61
	MOROCCO	Rabat	27 623	61.9	29	8	66	2.1	53
	MOZAMBIQUE	Maputo	17 796	22.3	45	18	47	2.41	35
	MYANMAR	Yangon	45 922	67.9	33	11	59	2.14	26
	NAMIBIA	Windhoek	1575	1.9	37	11	56	2.65	37
	NEPAL	Kathmandu	21 127	143.5	39	13	56	2.59	11
	NETHERLANDS	Amsterdam	15 517	373.7	13	9	78	0.72	89
	NEW ZEALAND	Wellington	3570	13.2	17	8	77	1.24	86
	NICARAGUA	Managua	4238	32.6	40	7	68	3.74	63
	NIGER	Niamey	9465	7.5	53	19	48	3.37	19
	NIGERIA	Abuja	115 020	124.5	45	15	52	3	41
	NORTH KOREA	Pyongyang	22 466	186.4	24	5	72	1.88	62
	NORWAY	Oslo	4381	13.5	14	11	77	0.45	73
	OMAN	Muscat	2302	7.4	44	5	70	4.23	78
	PAKISTAN	Islamabad	134 146	166.9	41	9	63	2.83	35
	PANAMA	Panama City	2674	34.7	25	5	74	1.86	56
	PAPUA NEW GUINEA	Port Moresby	4400	9.5	33	11	57	2.27	16
	PARAGUAY	Asunción	4955	12.2	33	5	69	2.78	53
	PERU	Lima	23 947	18.6	27	7	68	1.93	71
	PHILIPPINES	Manila	71 899	239.7	30	6	68	2.12	55
	POLAND	Warsaw	38 618	123.5	13	10	71	0.14	64
	PORTUGAL	Lisbon	9808	110.3	12	11	75	-0.09	36
	QATAR	Doha	558	48.8	21	3	71	2.53	92
	ROMANIA	Bucharest	22 608	95.2	11	11	70	-0.32	56
	RUSSIAN FEDERATION	Moscow	147 739	8.7	11	12	65	-0.12	76
	RWANDA	Kigali	5397	204.9	44	17	36	2.59	6
	SÃO TOMÉ & PRÍNCIPE	São Tomé	135	140			69	2.2	44

LAND			EDUCATION AND HEALTH				DEVELOPMENT				
AREA ('000s sq km)	CULTIVATED AREA ('000s sq km 1993)	FOREST ('000s sq km 1993)	ADULT LITERACY (% 1992)	SCHOOL ENROLMENT (Secondary, gross % 1993)	PEOPLE PER DOCTOR (1991)	FOOD INTAKE (calories per capita per day 1992)	ENERGY CONSUMPTION (kg per cap oil eq 1993)	TRADE BALANCE (millions US $ 1994)	GNP PER CAPITA (US $ 1995 or earlier)	COUNTRY	TIME ZONES (+ OR - GMT)
30	3		68.6	26.5		2201			770	LESOTHO	+2
111	4	17	35.4	21.5	29 292	1640	41	124	450	LIBERIA	GMT
1760	22	8	72.4		862	3308	2163	5857	5310	LIBYA	+1
65	30	20	98.4	78.5	218		2368	185	1900	LITHUANIA	+2
3			99	71	537	3681	9694		41 210	LUXEMBOURG	+1
26	7	10					1567	-144	860	MACEDONIA	+1
587	31	232	81.4	15.5	9081	2135	26	-173	230	MADAGASCAR	+3
118	17	37	53.9	4	31 637	1825	26	-226	170	MALAWI	+2
333	49	223	81.5	60	2847	2888	1236	-826	3890	MALAYSIA	+8
0.298				92.6		2580	151	-176	990	MALDIVES	+5
1240	25	69	27.2	7.5	23 370	2278	17	-93	250	MALI	GMT
0.316			87	85		3486	1562	-930	7970	MALTA	+1
1031	2	44	36.2	15	11 912	2685	432	215	460	MAURITANIA	GMT
2	1		81.1	54		2690	456	-571	3380	MAURITIUS	+4
1973	247	487	88.6	56	663	3146	1311	-18 542	3320	MEXICO	-6 to -8
0.701									1890	MICRONESIA	+10 to +11
34	22	4	96		255		1267	-7	920	MOLDOVA	+2
1565	14	138	81.1	91	413	1899	1079		310	MONGOLIA	+8
447	99	90	40.6	34.5	5067	2984	274	-3198	1110	MOROCCO	GMT
799	32	140	36.9	7	45 778	1680	23	-823	80	MOZAMBIQUE	+2
677	101	324	82	23	3947	2598	38	-114	220	MYANMAR	+6½
824	7	180	40	52.5	6338	2134			2000	NAMIBIA	+1
147	24	58	25.6	35.5	21 520	1957	22	-489	200	NEPAL	5¾
42	9	4	99	116.5	417	3222	5167	15 313	24 000	NETHERLANDS	+1
271	38	74	99	91.5	373	3669	3871	283	14 340	NEW ZEALAND	+12 to +12¾
130	13	32	64.7	42.5	1856	2293	304	-479	380	NICARAGUA	-6
1267	36	25	12.4	6.5	48 325	2257	41	-43	220	NIGER	+1
924	324	113	52.5	23.5	5997	2124	160	2402	260	NIGERIA	+1
121	20	74	95		377	2833	3031		970	NORTH KOREA	+9
324	9	83	99	110.5	328	3244	5020	7380	31 250	NORWAY	+1
310	1		35	64.5	1079		1947	1630	4820	OMAN	+4
804	213	35	35.7	21	1874	2315	204	-1535	460	PAKISTAN	+5
77	7	33	89.6	61.5	857	2242	576	-1871	2750	PANAMA	-5
463	4	420	69.7	12.5	13 071	2613	190	1109	1160	PAPUA NEW GUINEA	+10
407	23	129	91.2	33.5	1687	2670	260	-1004	1690	PARAGUAY	-4
1285	34	848	87.3	63	989	1882	328	-2239	2310	PERU	-5
300	92	136	94	73	1195	2257	290	-4341	1050	PHILIPPINES	+8
313	147	88	99	84	482	3301	2529	-4143	2790	POLAND	+1
89	32	33	86.2	81	381	3634	1463	-9084	9740	PORTUGAL	GMT
11			78.1	88.5	646		25 210	1290	11 600	QATAR	+3
238	99	67	96.9	82	553	3051	1828	-294	1480	ROMANIA	+2
17 075	1339	7785	98.7		215	3332	4856	24 593	2240	RUSSIAN FED.	+2 to +12
26	12	6	56.8	10		1821	24	-220	180	RWANDA	+2
0.964			60			2129	197		350	SÃO TOMÉ & PRINCIPE	GMT

KEY INFORMATION

FLAG	COUNTRY	CAPITAL CITY

POPULATION

FLAG	COUNTRY	CAPITAL CITY	TOTAL (in '000s 1996)	DENSITY (persons per sq km 1996)	BIRTH RATE (per 1000 population 1994)	DEATH RATE (per 1000 population 1994)	LIFE EXPEC-TANCY (in years 1996)	POP. CHANGE (average % per annum 1990 - 1995)	URBAN POP. (% 1996)
	SAUDI ARABIA	Riyadh	18 836	8.6	35	5	71	2.16	84
	SENEGAL	Dakar	8572	43.6	43	16	51	2.52	44
	SIERRA LEONE	Freetown	4297	59.9	49	25	37	2.4	34
	SINGAPORE	Singapore	3044	4763.7	16	6	77	1.03	100
	SLOVAKIA	Bratislava	5374	109.6	14	11	71	0.36	59
	SLOVENIA	Ljubljana	1991	98.3	11	11	73	0.29	52
	SOLOMON ISLANDS	Honiara	391	13.8	37	4	71	3.32	18
	SOMALIA	Mogadishu	9822	15.4	50	18	48	1.28	26
	SOUTH AFRICA, REPUBLIC OF	Pretoria / Cape Town	42 393	34.8	31	9	65	2.24	50
	SOUTH KOREA	Seoul	45 545	458.8	16	6	72	0.97	82
	SPAIN	Madrid	39 270	77.8	10	9	78	0.18	77
	SRI LANKA	Colombo	18 300	278.9	21	6	73	1.27	22
	ST LUCIA	Castries	144	233.8			71	1.35	38
	ST VINCENT & THE GRENADINES	Kingstown	113	290.5			72	0.88	50
	SUDAN	Khartoum	27 291	10.9	40	13	54	2.67	32
	SURINAME	Paramaribo	432	2.6	25	6	71	1.1	50
	SWAZILAND	Mbabane	938	54	38	11	59	2.78	32
	SWEDEN	Stockholm	8843	19.7	14	11	78	0.51	83
	SWITZERLAND	Bern	7074	171.3	13	9	78	1.05	61
	SYRIA	Damascus	14 574	78.7	41	6	68	3.43	53
	TAIWAN	Taibei	21 211	586.3	15	6	76		75
	TAJIKISTAN	Dushanbe	5919	41.4	37	6	67	2.86	32
	TANZANIA	Dodoma	30 799	32.6	43	14	51	2.96	25
	THAILAND	Bangkok	60 003	116.9	19	6	69	1.12	20
	TOGO	Lomé	4201	74	45	13	50	3.18	31
	TRINIDAD & TOBAGO	Port of Spain	1297	252.8	21	6	73	1.1	72
	TUNISIA	Tunis	9156	55.8	26	6	69	1.92	63
	TURKEY	Ankara	62 697	80.4	27	7	68	1.98	71
	TURKMENISTAN	Ashgabat	4569	9.4	32	8	65	2.28	45
	UGANDA	Kampala	20 256	84	52	19	41	3.42	13
	UKRAINE	Kiev	51 094	84.6	11	13	69	-0.1	71
	UNITED ARAB EMIRATES	Abu Dhabi	2260	29.1	23	3	75	2.62	84
	UNITED KINGDOM	London	58 144	238.2	13	11	77	0.29	89
	UNITED STATES OF AMERICA	Washington	266 557	27.2	16	9	76	1.04	76
	URUGUAY	Montevideo	3203	18.2	17	10	73	0.58	90
	UZBEKISTAN	Tashkent	22 912	51.2	31	6	68	2.24	41
	VANUATU	Port-Vila	174	14.3	35	7	67	2.49	19
	VENEZUELA	Caracas	22 710	24.9	27	5	72	2.27	86
	VIETNAM	Hanoi	75 181	228.1	31	8	67	2.23	19
	WESTERN SAMOA	Apia	166	58.6	37	6	69	1.07	22
	YEMEN	Sana	15 919	30.2	49	15	57	4.97	34
	YUGOSLAVIA	Belgrade	10 574	103.5	14	10	72	1.32	57
	ZAMBIA	Lusaka	8275	11	45	15	43	2.97	43
	ZIMBABWE	Harare	11 908	30.5	39	12	49	2.57	33

AREA ('000s sq km)	CULTIVATED AREA ('000s sq km 1993)	FOREST ('000s sq km 1993)	ADULT LITERACY (% 1992)	SCHOOL ENROLMENT (Secondary, gross % 1993)	PEOPLE PER DOCTOR (1991)	FOOD INTAKE (calories per capita per day 1992)	ENERGY CONSUMPTION (kg per cap oil eq 1993)	TRADE BALANCE (millions US $ 1994)	GNP PER CAPITA (US $ 1995 or earlier)	COUNTRY	TIME ZONES (+ OR - GMT)
2200	37	18	60.6	51	969	2735	4092	1979	7040	SAUDI ARABIA	+3
197	24	105	30.5	17	18 002	2262	116	-489	600	SENEGAL	GMT
72	5	20	28.7	16.5	13 837	1694	31	-34	180	SIERRA LEONE	GMT
0.639			89.9	70.5	950		6371	-5841	26 730	SINGAPORE	+8
49	16	20	99			3156	3019	29	2950	SLOVAKIA	+1
20	3	10					2396	-428	8200	SLOVENIA	+1
28	1	25	24	15.5		2173	147	-5	910	SOLOMON ISLANDS	+11
638	10	160	27	7	16 660	1499		-28	120	SOMALIA	+3
1219	132	82	80.6	71	1597	2695	1888		3160	SOUTH AFRICA, REP. OF	+2
99	21	65	97.4	92.5	1076	3285	2438	-6305	9700	SOUTH KOREA	+9
505	197	161	98	108.5	280	3708	2031	-19 205	13 580	SPAIN	+1
66	19	21	89.3	74.5	7337	2273	104	-1290	700	SRI LANKA	+5½
0.616			93			2588	403	-190	3370	ST LUCIA	-4
0.389			98			2347	264	-92	2280	ST VINCENT	+4
2506	130	442	42.7	21	11 620	2202	43	-551	480	SUDAN	+2
164	1	150	92.2	54	1927	2547	1374	0	880	SURINAME	-3
17	2	1	74	49.5		2706			1170	SWAZILAND	+2
450	28	280	99	95.5	322	2972	4561	9669	23 750	SWEDEN	+1
41	5	13	99	91.5	334	3379	3321	2158	40 630	SWITZERLAND	+1
185	58	7	67.7	48.5	1439	3175	986	-1822	1120	SYRIA	+2
36			91		974					TAIWAN	+8
143	8	5	96.7		366		1067	28	340	TAJIKISTAN	+5
945	35	335	64.4	5.5	24 070	2018	26	-778	120	TANZANIA	+3
513	208	135	93.5	33	5080	2432	675	-8885	2740	THAILAND	+7
57	24	9	47.9	23.5	15 352	2242	53	-60	310	TOGO	GMT
5	1	2	97.4	79	1197	2585	4993	164	3770	TRINIDAD & TOBAGO	-4
164	50	7	62.8	49	1897	3330	608	-1900	1820	TUNISIA	+1
779	275	202	80.5	50	1201	3429	793	-5155	2780	TURKEY	+2
488	15	40	97.7		296		3380	548	920	TURKMENISTAN	+5
241	68	55	58.6	12	26 850	2159	19	-459	240	UGANDA	+3
604	344	103	95		234		3733	-281	1630	UKRAINE	+2 to +3
78			77.7	72.5	673	3384	13 667	9415	17 400	U.A.E.	+4
244	61	24	99	86.5	623	3317	3910	-22 183	18 700	UNITED KINGDOM	GMT
9809	1878	2862	99	94	408	3732	7570	-176 694	26 980	UNITED STATES	-5 to -10
176	13	9	96.9	61.5	348	2750	585	-860	5170	URUGUAY	-3
447	45	13	97.2		292	2079		-121	970	UZBEKISTAN	+5
12	1	9	65			2739	124	-65	1200	VANUATU	+11
912	39	300	90.4	34.5	605	2618	2379	7488	3020	VENEZUELA	-4
330	67	97	91.9	42.5	3108	2250	106	70	240	VIETNAM	+7
3	1	1	98			2828	269	-76	1120	WESTERN SAMOA	-11
528	15	20	41.4			2203	222	-1277	260	YEMEN	+3
102	40	27				3551	856			YUGOSLAVIA	+1
753	53	287	75.2	19.5	9787	1931	137	187	400	ZAMBIA	+2
391	29	88	83.4	47	7537	1985	462	-775	540	ZIMBABWE	+2

How to use the Index

All the names on the maps in this atlas, except some of those on the special topic maps, are included in the index.

The names are arranged in **alphabetical order.** Where the name has more than one word the separate words are considered as one to decide the position of the name in the index:

Thetford
Thetford Mines
The Trossachs
The Wash
The Weald
Thiers

Where there is more than one place with the same name, the country name is used to decide the order:

London Canada
London England

If both places are in the same country, the county or state name is also used:

Avon *r.* Bristol England
Avon *r.* Dorset England

Each entry in the index starts with the name of the place or feature, followed by the name of the country or region in which it is located. This is followed by the number of the most appropriate page on which the name appears, usually the largest scale map. Next comes the alphanumeric reference followed by the latitude and longitude.

Names of physical features such as rivers, capes, mountains etc are followed by a description. The descriptions are usually shortened to one or two letters, these abbreviations are keyed below. Town names are followed by a description only when the name may be confused with that of a physical feature:

Big Spring *town*

To help to distinguish the different parts of each entry, different styles of type are used:

place name	country name or region name	alphanumeric grid reference
description (if any)	page number	latitude/ longitude

Thames *r.* England **15** **C2** 51.30N 0.05E

To use the **alphanumeric grid reference** to find a feature on the map, first find the correct page and then look at the white letters printed in the blue frame along the top and bottom of the map and the white numbers printed in the blue frame at the sides of the map. When you have found the correct letter and number follow the grid boxes up and along until you find the correct grid box in which the feature appears. You must then search the grid box until you find the name of the feature.

The **latitude and longitude reference** gives a more exact description of the position of the feature.

Page 6 of the atlas describes lines of latitude and lines of longitude, and explains how they are numbered and divided into degrees and minutes. Each name in the index has a different latitude and longitude reference, so the feature can be located accurately. The lines of latitude and lines of longitude shown on each map are numbered in degrees. These numbers are printed black along the top, bottom and sides of the map.

The drawing above shows part of the map on page 20 and the lines of latitude and lines of longitude.

The index entry for Wexford is given as follows

Wexford Rep. of Ire. **20** **E2** 52.20N 6.28W

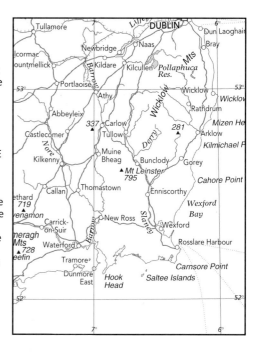

To locate Wexford, first find latitude 52N and estimate 20 minutes north from 52 degrees to find 52.20N, then find longitude 6W and estimate 28 minutes west from 6 degrees to find 6.28W. The symbol for the town of Wexford is where latitude 52.20N and longitude 6.28W meet.

On maps at a smaller scale than the map of Ireland, it is not possible to show every line of latitude and longitude. Only every 5 or 10 degrees of latitude and longitude may be shown. On these maps you must estimate the degrees and minutes to find the exact location of a feature.

Abbreviations

A. and B.	Argyll and Bute
Afghan.	Afghanistan
Ala.	Alabama
b., **B.**	bay, Bay
Bangla.	Bangladesh
Bosnia.	Bosnia-Herzegovina
B.V.Is.	British Virgin Islands
c., **C.**	cape, Cape
Cambs.	Cambridgeshire
C.A.R.	Central African Republic
Carib. Sea	Caribbean Sea
Colo.	Colorado
Czech Rep.	Czech Republic
d.	internal division eg. county, state
D. and G.	Dumfries and Galloway
Del.	Delaware
Derbys.	Derbyshire
des.	desert
Dom. Rep.	Dominican Republic
Equat. Guinea	Equatorial Guinea
E. Sussex	East Sussex
E. Yorks.	East Riding of Yorkshire
est.	estuary
f.	physical feature eg. valley, plain, geographic district
Fla.	Florida
g., **G.**	Gulf
Ga.	Georgia
Glos.	Gloucestershire
Hants.	Hampshire
Herts.	Hertfordshire
High.	Highland

i., **I.**, *is.*, **Is.**	island, Island, islands, Islands
Ill.	Illinois
I.o.M.	Isle of Man
I.o.W.	Isle of Wight
l., **L.**	lake, Lake
La.	Louisiana
Lancs.	Lancashire
Leics.	Leicestershire
Liech.	Liechtenstein
Lincs.	Lincolnshire
Lux.	Luxembourg
Man.	Manitoba
Med. Sea	Mediterranean Sea
Miss.	Mississippi
Mt.	Mount
mtn., **Mtn.**	mountain, Mountain
mts., **Mts.**	mountains, Mountains
N. Ayr.	North Ayrshire
N.C.	North Carolina
N. Cal.	New Caledonia
Neth.	Netherlands
Neth. Ant.	Netherlands Antilles
Nev.	Nevada
Nfld.	Newfoundland
N. Korea	North Korea
N. Mex.	New Mexico
Northum.	Northumberland
Notts.	Nottinghamshire
N.Y.	New York
Oc.	Ocean
Oreg.	Oregon
Oxon.	Oxfordshire
P. and K.	Perth and Kinross

Pem.	Pembrokeshire
pen., **Pen.**	peninsula, Peninsula
Phil.	Philadelphia
P.N.G.	Papua New Guinea
Pt.	Point
r., **R.**	river, River
Rep.of Ire.	Republic of Ireland
Resr.	Reservoir
R.S.A.	Republic of South Africa
Russian Fed.	Russian Federation
Sd.	Sound
S.C.	South Carolina
Shrops.	Shropshire
S. Korea	South Korea
Staffs.	Staffordshire
str., **Str.**	strait, Strait
Switz.	Switzerland
Tex.	Texas
U.A.E.	United Arab Emirates
U.K.	United Kingdom
U.S.A.	United States of America
U.S. V.Is.	United States Virgin Islands
Va.	Virginia
Warwicks.	Warwickshire
W. Isles	Western Isles
W. Sahara	Western Sahara
W. Sussex	West Sussex
W. Va.	West Virginia
Wilts.	Wiltshire
Wyo.	Wyoming
Yugo.	Yugoslavia

A

Aachen Germany **48 C4** 50.46N 6.06E
Aalen Germany **48 E3** 48.50N 10.05E
Aalst Belgium **42 D2** 50.57N 4.03E
Abadan Iran **95 G5** 30.21N 48.15E
Abadeh Iran **95 H5** 31.10N 52.40E
Abadla Algeria **84 D5** 31.01N 2.45W
Abakan Russian Fed. **59 L3** 53.43N 91.25E
Abancay Peru **76 C3** 13.35S 72.55W
Abarqu Iran **95 H5** 31.09N 53.18E
Abashiri Japan **106 D4** 44.02N 144.17E
Abaya, L. Ethiopia **85 H2** 6.20N 38.00E
Abaza Russian Fed. **102 G8** 52.44N 90.12E
Abbeville France **44 D7** 50.06N 1.51E
Abbeyfeale Rep. of Ire. **20 B2** 52.24N 9.18W
Abbey Head Scotland **17 F2** 54.45N 3.58W
Abbeyleix Rep. of Ire. **20 D2** 52.55N 7.20W
Abbottabad Pakistan **95 L5** 34.12N 73.15E
Abéché Chad **85 G3** 13.49N 20.49E
Åbenrå Denmark **43 B1** 55.03N 9.26E
Abeokuta Nigeria **84 E2** 7.10N 3.26E
Aberaeron Wales **12 C4** 52.15N 4.16W
Aberchirder Scotland **19 G2** 57.33N 2.38W
Aberdare Wales **12 D3** 51.43N 3.27W
Aberdare Range *mts.* Kenya **87 B2** 0.20S 36.07E
Aberdeen Scotland **19 G2** 57.08N 2.07W
Aberdeen U.S.A. **64 G6** 45.28N 98.30W
Aberdeen City *d.* Scotland **8 D5** 57.08N 2.07W
Aberdeenshire *d.* Scotland **8 D5** 57.22N 2.35W
Aberfeldy Scotland **17 F4** 56.38N 3.52W
Aberford England **15 F2** 53.51N 1.20W
Aberfoyle Scotland **16 E4** 56.11N 4.23W
Abergavenny Wales **12 D3** 51.49N 3.01W
Abergele Wales **12 D5** 53.17N 3.34W
Aberporth Wales **12 C4** 52.08N 4.33W
Abersoch Wales **12 C4** 52.50N 4.31W
Abertillery Wales **12 D3** 51.44N 3.09W
Aberystwyth Wales **12 C4** 52.25N 4.06W
Abha Saudi Arabia **94 F2** 18.13N 42.30E
Abidjan Côte d'Ivoire **84 D2** 5.19N 4.01W
Abilene U.S.A. **64 G3** 32.27N 99.45W
Abingdon England **10 D2** 51.40N 1.17W
Abington Scotland **17 F3** 55.29N 3.42W
Abitibi, L. Canada **65 K6** 48.42N 79.45W
Aboyne Scotland **19 G2** 57.05N 2.49W
Abqaiq Saudi Arabia **95 G4** 25.55N 49.40E
Abu' Arish Saudi Arabia **94 F2** 16.58N 42.50E
Abu Dhabi U.A.E. **95 H3** 24.27N 54.23E
Abu Hamed Sudan **85 H3** 19.32N 33.20E
Abuja Nigeria **84 E2** 9.12N 7.11E
Abu Matariq Sudan **94 C1** 10.58N 26.17E
Abunã *r.* Brazil **76 D4** 9.41S 65.20W
Abu Simbel Egypt **94 D3** 22.18N 31.40E
Abyad Sudan **94 C1** 13.46N 26.28E
Acapulco Mexico **70 E4** 16.51N 99.56W
Acarigua Venezuela **71 K2** 9.35N 69.12W
Accra Ghana **84 D2** 5.33N 0.15W
Accrington England **15 E2** 53.46N 2.22W
Acheloös *r.* Greece **56 E3** 38.20N 21.04E
Achill I. Rep. of Ire. **20 A3** 53.57N 10.00W
Achinsk Russian Fed. **59 L3** 56.10N 90.10E
A'Chralaig *mtn.* Scotland **18 D2** 57.11N 5.09W
Acklins I. The Bahamas **71 J5** 22.30N 74.10W
Acle England **11 G3** 52.38N 1.33E
Aconcagua *mtn.* Argentina **75 B3** 32.37S 70.00W
A Coruña Spain **46 A5** 43.22N 8.24W
Acre *r.* Brazil **76 D4** 8.45S 67.23W
Acre *d.* Brazil **76 C4** 8.50S 71.30W
Actéon, Groupe *is.* French Polynesia **109 Q4** 22.00S 136.00W
Adaja *r.* Spain **46 C4** 41.32N 4.52W
Adamawa Highlands Nigeria/Cameroon **84 F2** 7.05N 12.00E
Adana Turkey **57 L2** 37.00N 35.19E
Adda *r.* Italy **50 C6** 45.08N 9.55E
Ad Dahna *des.* Saudi Arabia **95 G2** 26.00N 47.00E
Ad Dakhla W. Sahara **84 C4** 23.43N 15.57W
Ad Dammam Saudi Arabia **95 H4** 26.23N 50.08E
Adderbury England **10 D3** 52.01N 1.19W
Ad Dir'īyah Saudi Arabia **95 G4** 24.45N 46.32E
Addis Ababa Ethiopia **85 H2** 9.03N 38.42E
Ad Dīwanīyah Iraq **94 F5** 31.59N 44.57E
Adelaide Australia **110 C2** 34.56S 138.36E
Aden Yemen **94 F1** 12.50N 45.00E
Aden, G. of Indian Oc. **85 I3** 13.00N 50.00E
Adi *i.* Indonesia **105 I3** 4.10S 133.10E
Adī Ārk'ay Ethiopia **94 E1** 13.35N 37.57E
Adige *r.* Italy **50 E6** 45.10N 12.20E
Ādīgrat Ethiopia **94 E1** 14.18N 39.31E
Adilang Uganda **87 A3** 2.44N 33.28E
Ādī Ugri Eritrea **94 E1** 14.55N 38.53E
Adıyaman Turkey **57 N2** 37.46N 38.15E
Admiralty Is. P.N.G. **108 J6** 2.30S 147.20E
Adour *r.* France **44 C3** 43.28N 1.35W
Adriatic Sea Med. Sea **50 F5** 42.30N 16.00E
Adwa Ethiopia **85 H3** 14.12N 38.56E
Aegean Sea Med. Sea **56 G3** 39.00N 25.00E
Afghanistan Asia **95 K5** 33.00N 65.30E
Afmadow Somalia **87 C3** 0.27N 42.05E
Africa 82
Afyon Turkey **57 J3** 38.46N 30.32E
Agadez Niger **84 E3** 17.00N 7.56E
Agadir Morocco **84 D5** 30.26N 9.36W
Agana Guam **105 K6** 13.28N 144.45E
Agano *r.* Japan **106 C3** 37.58N 139.02E
Agartala India **97 I5** 23.49N 91.15E
Agde France **44 E3** 43.19N 3.28E
Agen France **44 D4** 44.12N 0.38E
Agere Maryam Ethiopia **87 B4** 5.40N 38.11E
Aghla Mtn. Rep. of Ire. **16 A2** 54.50N 8.10W
Agios Efstratios *i.* Greece **56 G3** 39.30N 25.00E
Agirwat Hills Sudan **94 E2** 16.00N 35.10E
Agra India **97 F6** 27.09N 78.00E
Ağri Turkey **94 F6** 39.44N 43.04E
Agrigento Italy **50 E2** 37.19N 13.36E
Agrihan *i.* N. Mariana Is. **105 L7** 18.44N 145.39E
Aguascalientes Mexico **70 D5** 21.51N 102.18W
Aguascalientes *d.* Mexico **70 D4** 22.00N 102.18W
Aguilar de Campóo Spain **46 C5** 42.55N 4.15W
Águilas Spain **46 E2** 37.25N 1.35W
Agulhas, C. R.S.A. **86 B1** 34.50S 20.00E
Agulhas Negras *mtn.* Brazil **72 F4** 22.20S 44.43W
Ahar Iran **95 G6** 38.25N 47.07E
Ahaus Germany **42 G4** 52.04N 7.01E
Ahmadabad India **96 E5** 23.03N 72.40E
Ahmadnagar India **96 E4** 19.08N 74.48E
Ahmadpur East Pakistan **95 L4** 29.09N 71.16E
Ahmadpur Sial Pakistan **95 L5** 30.41N 71.46E
Ahvaz Iran **95 G5** 31.17N 48.44E
Aigina *i.* Greece **56 F2** 37.43N 23.30E
Ailsa Craig *i.* Scotland **16 D3** 55.15N 5.07W
Aïn Beïda Algeria **52 E4** 35.50N 7.27E
Aïn Sefra Algeria **84 D5** 32.45N 0.35W
Aïr *mts.* Niger **84 E3** 18.30N 8.30E
Airdrie Canada **62 G3** 51.20N 114.00W
Airdrie Scotland **17 F3** 55.52N 3.59W
Aisne *r.* France **44 E6** 49.27N 2.51E
Aitape P.N.G. **105 K3** 3.10S 142.17E
Aitutaki *i.* Cook Is. **108 P5** 18.52S 159.46W
Aix-en-Provence France **44 F3** 43.31N 5.27E
Aizu-wakamatsu Japan **106 C3** 37.30N 139.58E
Ajaccio France **44 H2** 41.55N 8.43E
Ajdabiya Libya **85 G5** 30.48N 20.15E
Akhdar, Al Jabal al *mts.* Libya **85 G5** 32.10N 22.00E
Akhdar, Jabal *mts.* Oman **95 I3** 23.10N 57.25E
Akhisar Turkey **57 H3** 38.54N 27.49E
Akimiski I. Canada **63 J3** 53.00N 81.20W
Akita Japan **106 D3** 39.44N 140.05E
Akkajaure *l.* Sweden **43 D4** 67.40N 17.30E
Akmola Kazakstan **102 C8** 51.10N 71.28E
Akobo *r.* Sudan/Ethiopia **82 G5** 8.30N 33.15E
Akordat Eritrea **85 H3** 15.35N 37.55E
Akpatok I. Canada **63 L4** 60.30N 68.30W
Akranes Iceland **43 X2** 64.19N 22.05W
Akron U.S.A. **65 J5** 41.04N 81.31W
Aksaray Turkey **94 D5** 38.22N 34.02E
Akşehir Turkey **57 J3** 38.22N 31.24E
Aksu China **102 E6** 42.10N 80.00E
Āksum Ethiopia **94 E1** 14.08N 38.48E
Aktau Kazakstan **58 H2** 43.37N 51.11E
Aktogay Kazakstan **102 D7** 46.59N 79.42E
Aktyubinsk Kazakstan **58 H3** 50.16N 57.13E
Akureyri Iceland **43 Y2** 65.41N 18.04W
Alabama *r.* U.S.A. **65 I3** 31.05N 87.55W
Alabama *d.* U.S.A. **65 I3** 33.00N 87.00W
Alagoas *d.* Brazil **77 G4** 9.30S 37.00W
Alagoinhas Brazil **77 G3** 12.09S 38.21W
Al Ahmadi Kuwait **95 G4** 29.05N 48.04E
Alakol', L. Kazakstan **102 E7** 46.00N 81.40E
Alakurtti Russian Fed. **43 G4** 67.00N 30.23E
Alamagan *i.* N. Mariana Is. **105 L7** 17.35N 145.50E
Åland *is.* Finland **43 E3** 60.20N 20.00E
Alanya Turkey **57 J2** 36.32N 32.02E
Al Artawīyah Saudi Arabia **95 G4** 26.31N 45.21E
Alaska *d.* U.S.A. **62 C4** 65.00N 153.00W
Alaska, G. of U.S.A. **62 D3** 58.45N 145.00W
Alaska Pen. U.S.A. **62 C3** 56.00N 160.00W
Alaska Range *mts.* U.S.A. **62 C4** 62.10N 152.00W
Alausí Ecuador **76 C4** 2.00S 78.50W
Alavus Finland **43 E3** 62.35N 23.37E
Alaw Resr. Wales **12 C5** 53.20N 4.25W
Albacete Spain **46 E3** 39.00N 1.52W
Alba Iulia Romania **56 F7** 46.04N 23.33E
Albania Europe **56 E4** 41.00N 20.00E
Albany Australia **110 A2** 34.57S 117.54E
Albany Ga. U.S.A. **65 J3** 31.37N 84.10W
Albany N.Y. U.S.A. **65 L5** 42.40N 73.49W
Albany *r.* Canada **63 J3** 52.10N 82.00W
Al Basrah Iraq **95 G5** 30.33N 47.50E
Al Bayda' Libya **85 G5** 32.50N 21.50E
Albenga Italy **50 C6** 44.03N 8.13E
Alberche *r.* Spain **46 C4** 40.00N 4.45W
Albert France **42 B1** 50.00N 2.40E
Albert, L. Africa **86 C5** 1.45N 31.00E
Alberta *d.* Canada **62 G3** 55.00N 115.00W
Albert Lea U.S.A. **65 H5** 43.39N 93.22W
Albert Nile *r.* Uganda **85 H2** 3.30N 32.00E
Albi France **44 E3** 43.56N 2.08E
Al Biyadah *f.* Saudi Arabia **95 G3** 22.00N 47.00E
Alboran, Isla de *i.* Spain **46 D1** 35.55N 3.10W
Ålborg Denmark **43 B2** 57.03N 9.56E
Āl Bu Kamal Syria **94 F5** 34.27N 40.55E
Albuquerque U.S.A. **64 E4** 35.05N 106.38W
Al Buraymi U.A.E. **95 I3** 24.15N 55.45E
Albury Australia **110 D2** 36.03S 146.53E
Alcalá de Henares Spain **46 D4** 40.28N 3.22W
Alcalá la Real Spain **46 D2** 37.28N 3.55W
Alcañiz Spain **46 E4** 41.03N 0.09W
Alcázar de San Juan Spain **46 D3** 39.24N 3.12W
Alcester England **10 D3** 52.13N 1.52W
Alcoy Spain **46 E3** 38.42N 0.29W
Alcúdia Spain **46 G3** 39.51N 3.09E
Aldabra Is. Indian Oc. **86 D4** 9.00S 47.00E
Aldan Russian Fed. **59 O3** 58.44N 125.22E
Aldan *r.* Russian Fed. **59 P4** 63.30N 130.00E
Aldbrough England **15 G2** 53.50N 0.07W
Aldeburgh England **11 G3** 52.09N 1.35E
Alderley Edge England **15 E2** 53.18N 2.15W
Alderney *i.* Channel Is. **13 Z9** 49.42N 2.11W
Aldershot England **10 E2** 51.15N 0.47W
Aldingham England **14 D3** 54.08N 3.08W
Aldridge England **10 D3** 52.36N 1.55W
Aleksandrovsk-Sakhalinskiy Russian Fed. **59 Q3** 50.55N 142.12E
Aleksin Russian Fed. **55 O6** 54.31N 37.07E
Alençon France **44 D6** 48.25N 0.05E
Aleppo Syria **94 E6** 36.14N 37.10E
Alès France **44 F4** 44.08N 4.05E
Alessandria Italy **50 C6** 44.54N 8.37E
Ålesund Norway **43 A3** 62.28N 6.11E
Aleutian Is. U.S.A. **108 N12** 52.00N 176.00W
Aleutian Range *mts.* U.S.A. **62 C3** 58.00N 156.00W
Alexander Archipelago *is.* U.S.A. **62 E3** 56.30N 134.30W
Alexander I. Antarctica **112** 72.00S 70.00W
Alexandra, C. South Georgia **75 F1** 54.05S 37.58W
Alexandria Egypt **94 C5** 31.13N 29.55E
Alexandria Scotland **16 E3** 55.59N 4.35W
Alexandria La. U.S.A. **65 H3** 31.19N 92.29W
Alexandria Va. U.S.A. **65 K4** 38.48N 77.03W
Alexandroupoli Greece **56 G4** 40.50N 25.53E
Aleysk Russian Fed. **102 E8** 52.32N 82.17E
Al Farwanīyah Kuwait **95 G4** 29.04N 47.50E
Alford England **15 H2** 53.17N 0.11E
Alfreton England **15 F2** 53.06N 1.22W
Algarve *f.* Portugal **46 A2** 37.20N 8.00W
Algeciras Spain **46 C2** 36.08N 5.27W
Algeria Africa **84 E4** 28.00N 2.00E
Al Ghaydah Yemen **95 H2** 16.12N 52.16E
Alghero Italy **50 C4** 40.33N 8.20E
Algiers Algeria **84 E5** 36.50N 3.00E
Al Hamad *des.* Asia **94 E5** 31.45N 39.00E
Al Hamadah al Hamra' *f.* Libya **52 F2** 29.00N 12.00E
Al Hasakah Syria **94 F6** 36.29N 40.45E
Al Hibak *f.* Saudi Arabia **95 H3** 21.00N 53.30E
Al Hillah Iraq **94 F5** 32.28N 44.29E
Al Hoceima Morocco **46 D1** 35.15N 3.55W
Aliakmonas *r.* Greece **56 F4** 40.30N 22.38E
Ali Bayramli Azerbaijan **95 G6** 39.56N 48.55E
Alicante Spain **46 E3** 38.21N 0.29W
Alice Springs *town* Australia **110 C3** 23.42S 133.52E
Alingsås Sweden **43 C2** 57.55N 12.30E
Al Jaghbub Libya **85 E4** 29.42N 24.38E
Al Jaharah Kuwait **95 G4** 29.20N 47.41E
Al Jauf Saudi Arabia **94 E4** 29.49N 39.52E
Al Jawsh Libya **52 F3** 32.00N 11.40E
Al Jubayl Saudi Arabia **95 G4** 26.59N 49.40E
Al Khaburah Oman **95 I3** 23.58N 57.10E
Al Khasab Oman **95 I4** 26.14N 56.15E
Al Khufrah Libya **85 G4** 24.09N 23.19E
Al Khums Libya **53 F3** 32.39N 14.15E
Alkmaar Neth. **42 D4** 52.37N 4.44E
Al Kut Iraq **95 G5** 32.30N 45.51E
Allahabad India **97 G6** 25.57N 81.50E
Allegheny Mts. U.S.A. **65 K5** 38.00N 81.00W
Allendale Town England **15 E3** 54.54N 2.15W
Allen, Lough Rep. of Ire. **20 C4** 54.07N 8.04W
Allentown U.S.A. **65 K5** 40.37N 75.30W
Alleppey India **96 F2** 9.30N 76.22E
Aller *r.* Germany **48 D5** 52.57N 9.11E
Alliance U.S.A. **64 F5** 42.08N 103.00W
Allier *r.* France **44 E5** 46.58N 3.04E
Al Lith Saudi Arabia **94 F3** 20.09N 40.16E
Alloa Scotland **17 F4** 56.07N 3.49W
Al Mahrah *f.* Yemen **95 H2** 15.30N 51.00E
Almansa Spain **46 E3** 38.52N 1.06W
Almanzor *mtn.* Spain **46 C4** 40.20N 5.22W
Al Marj Libya **53 H3** 32.30N 20.50E
Almaty Kazakstan **102 D6** 43.19N 76.55E
Almeirim Brazil **77 E4** 1.30S 52.35W
Almelo Neth. **42 F4** 52.21N 6.40E
Almería Spain **46 D2** 36.50N 2.26W
Almina, Punta *c.* Morocco **46 C1** 35.54N 5.17W
Al Mish'ab Saudi Arabia **95 G4** 28.00N 48.48E
Almodôvar Portugal **46 A2** 37.31N 8.03W
Almond *r.* Scotland **17 F4** 56.25N 3.28W
Al Mudawwara Jordan **94 E5** 29.20N 36.00E
Al Mukha Yemen **94 F1** 13.19N 43.15E
Almuñécar Spain **46 D2** 36.44N 3.41W
Al Nu'ayriyah Saudi Arabia **95 G4** 27.27N 48.17E
Alnwick England **15 F4** 55.25N 1.41W
Alor *i.* Indonesia **105 G2** 8.20S 124.30E
Alpes Maritimes *mts.* France **44 G4** 44.07N 7.08E
Alpine U.S.A. **64 F3** 30.22N 103.40W
Alps *mts.* Europe **34 E2** 46.00N 7.30E
Al Qa'amiyat *f.* Saudi Arabia **95 G2** 18.30N 49.00E
Al Qaddahiyah Libya **53 G3** 31.24N 15.12E
Al Qamishlī Syria **94 F6** 37.05N 41.11E
Al Qunfidhah Saudi Arabia **94 F2** 19.08N 41.15E
Alsager England **15 E2** 53.07N 2.20W
Alston England **15 E3** 54.48N 2.26W
Alta *r.* Norway **43 E5** 70.00N 23.15E
Altai Mts. Mongolia **102 G7** 46.30N 93.30E
Altamira Brazil **77 E4** 3.12S 52.12W
Altamura Italy **50 G4** 40.50N 16.32E
Altay China **102 F7** 47.48N 88.07E
Altay Mongolia **102 H7** 46.20N 97.00E
Altenburg Germany **48 F4** 50.59N 12.27E
Altiplano *f.* Bolivia **76 D3** 18.00S 67.30W
Altiplano Mexicano *mts.* N. America **60 I4** 24.00N 105.00W
Alton England **10 E2** 51.08N 0.59W
Altoona U.S.A. **65 K5** 40.32N 78.23W
Altrincham England **15 E2** 53.25N 2.21W
Altun Shan *mts.* China **102 F5** 38.10N 87.50E
Al'Uqaylah Libya **53 G3** 30.15N 19.12E
Alur Setar Malaysia **104 C5** 6.06N 100.23E
Al'Uthmanīyah Saudi Arabia **95 G4** 25.16N 49.24E
Al'Uwaynat Libya **94 B3** 21.53N 24.51E
Alva U.S.A. **64 G4** 36.48N 98.40W
Älvdalen Sweden **43 C3** 61.14N 14.05E
Alveley England **10 C3** 52.28N 2.20W
Älvsbyn Sweden **43 E4** 65.41N 21.00E
Al Wajh Saudi Arabia **94 E4** 26.16N 36.28E
Alwen Resr. Wales **12 D5** 53.05N 3.35W
Al Widyan *f.* Iraq/Saudi Arabia **94 F5** 31.00N 42.00E
Alyth Scotland **17 F4** 56.38N 3.14W
Alytus Lithuania **55 I6** 54.24N 24.03E
Amadeus, L. Australia **110 C3** 24.50S 130.45E
Amadjuak L. Canada **63 K4** 65.00N 71.00W
Amadora Portugal **46 A3** 38.45N 9.13W
Åmål Sweden **43 C2** 59.04N 12.41E
Amamapare Indonesia **105 J3** 4.56S 136.43E
Amapá *d.* Brazil **77 E5** 2.00N 52.00W
Amarillo U.S.A. **64 F4** 35.14N 101.50W
Amasya Turkey **57 L4** 40.37N 35.50E
Amazon *r.* Brazil **77 E4** 2.00S 50.00W
Amazonas *d.* Brazil **76 D4** 4.50S 64.00W
Amazon Delta *f.* Brazil **77 F5** 0.00 50.00W
Ambarchik Russian Fed. **59 S4** 69.39N 162.27E
Ambato Ecuador **76 C4** 1.18S 78.36W
Ambergate England **15 F2** 53.03N 1.29W
Ambergris Cay *i.* Belize **70 G4** 18.00N 87.58W
Amble England **15 F4** 55.20N 1.34W
Ambleside England **14 E3** 54.26N 2.58W
Ambon Indonesia **105 H3** 3.50S 128.10E
Amboseli Nat. Park Kenya **87 B2** 2.40S 37.10E
Ambrym *i.* Vanuatu **111 F4** 16.15S 168.10E
Ameland *i.* Neth. **42 E5** 53.28N 5.48E
American Samoa *is.* Pacific Oc. **108 O5** 14.20S 170.00W
Amersfoort Neth. **42 E4** 52.10N 5.23E
Amersham England **11 E2** 51.40N 0.38W
Amesbury England **10 D2** 51.10N 1.46W
Amgu Russian Fed. **106 C5** 45.48N 137.36E
Amgun *r.* Russian Fed. **59 P3** 53.10N 139.47E
Amiens France **44 E6** 49.54N 2.18E
Amino Ethiopia **87 C3** 4.25N 41.52E
Amlwch Wales **12 C5** 53.24N 4.21W
Amman Jordan **94 E5** 31.57N 35.56E
Ammanford Wales **12 C3** 51.48N 4.00W
Amol Iran **95 H6** 36.26N 52.24E
Amorgos *i.* Greece **56 G2** 36.49N 25.54E
Amos Canada **63 K2** 48.35N 78.05W
Ampthill England **11 E3** 52.03N 0.30W
Amravati India **97 F5** 20.58N 77.50E
Amritsar India **96 E7** 31.35N 74.56E
Amstelveen Neth. **42 D4** 52.18N 4.51E
Amsterdam Neth. **42 D4** 52.22N 4.54E
Amudar'ya *r.* Asia **90 H7** 43.50N 59.00E
Amund Ringnes I. Canada **63 I5** 78.00N 96.00W
Amundsen G. Canada **62 F5** 70.30N 122.00W
Amundsen Sea Antarctica **112** 70.00S 110.00W
Amuntai Indonesia **104 F3** 2.24S 115.14E
Amur *r.* Russian Fed. **59 P3** 53.17N 140.00E
Anabar *r.* Russian Fed. **59 N5** 72.40N 113.30E
Anadyr Russian Fed. **59 T4** 64.40N 177.32E
Anadyr *r.* Russian Fed. **59 T4** 65.00N 176.00E
Anadyr, G. of Russian Fed. **59 U4** 64.30N 177.50W
'Ānah Iraq **94 F5** 34.29N 41.57E
Anambas Is. Indonesia **104 D4** 3.00N 106.10E
Anamur Turkey **57 K2** 36.06N 32.49E
Anápolis Brazil **77 F3** 16.19S 48.58W
Anatahan *i.* N. Mariana Is. **105 L7** 16.22N 145.38E
Anatolia *f.* Turkey **57 J3** 38.30N 32.00E
Anchorage U.S.A. **62 D4** 61.10N 150.00W
Ancona Italy **50 E5** 43.37N 13.33E
Åndalsnes Norway **43 A3** 62.33N 7.43E
Andaman Is. India **97 I3** 12.00N 93.00E
Andaman Sea Indian Oc. **97 J3** 11.00N 96.00E
Anderlecht Belgium **42 D2** 50.51N 4.18E
Anderson U.S.A. **62 D4** 64.25N 149.10W
Anderson *r.* Canada **62 F4** 69.45N 129.00W
Andes *mts.* S. America **74 B5** 15.00S 74.00W
Andfjorden *est.* Norway **43 D5** 69.10N 16.20E
Andhra Pradesh *d.* India **97 F4** 17.00N 79.00E
Andkhvoy Afghan. **95 K6** 36.56N 65.05E
Andorra Europe **46 F5** 42.30N 1.32E
Andorra La Vella Andorra **46 F5** 42.30N 1.31E
Andover England **10 D2** 51.13N 1.29W
Andøya *i.* Norway **43 C5** 69.00N 15.30E
Andreas I.o.M. **14 C3** 54.22N 4.26W
Andreas, C. Cyprus **57 L1** 35.40N 34.35E
Andros *i.* Greece **56 G2** 37.50N 24.50E
Andros *i.* The Bahamas **71 I5** 24.30N 78.00W
Andújar Spain **46 C3** 38.02N 4.03W
Anegada *i.* B.V.Is. **71 L4** 18.46N 64.24W
Aneto, Pico de *mtn.* Spain **46 F5** 42.40N 0.19E
Angara *r.* Russian Fed. **59 L3** 58.00N 93.00E
Angarsk Russian Fed. **103 I8** 52.31N 103.55E
Ånge Sweden **43 C3** 62.31N 15.40E
Angel de la Guarda *i.* Mexico **70 B6** 29.10N 113.20W
Ängelholm Sweden **43 C2** 56.15N 12.50E
Angers France **44 C5** 47.29N 0.32W
Angola Africa **86 A3** 12.00S 18.00E
Angola Basin *f.* Atlantic Oc. **117 J5**
Angoulême France **44 D4** 45.40N 0.10E
Angren Uzbekistan **102 C6** 41.01N 70.10E
Anguilla *i.* Leeward Is. **71 L4** 18.14N 63.05W
Angus *d.* Scotland **8 D5** 56.45N 3.00W
Anhui *d.* China **103 L4** 31.30N 116.45E
Ankara Turkey **57 K3** 39.55N 32.50E
Anlaby England **15 G2** 53.45N 0.27W
Annaba Algeria **84 E5** 36.55N 7.47E
An Nafud *des.* Saudi Arabia **94 F4** 28.40N 41.30E
An Najaf Iraq **94 F5** 31.59N 44.19E
Annalee *r.* Rep. of Ire. **20 D4** 54.08N 7.25W
Annalong N. Ireland **16 D2** 54.06N 5.55W
Annan Scotland **17 F2** 54.59N 3.16W
Annan *r.* Scotland **17 F3** 54.58N 3.16W
Annapurna *mtn.* Nepal **97 G6** 28.34N 83.50E
Ann Arbor U.S.A. **65 J5** 42.18N 83.45W
An Nasirīyah Iraq **95 G5** 31.04N 46.16E
An Nawfaliyah Libya **53 G3** 30.47N 17.50E
Annecy France **44 G4** 45.54N 6.07E
Ansbach Germany **48 E3** 49.18N 10.36E
Anshan China **103 M6** 41.05N 122.58E
Anshun China **103 J3** 26.15N 105.51E
Anstruther Scotland **17 G4** 56.14N 2.42W
Antakya Turkey **57 M2** 36.12N 36.10E
Antalya Turkey **57 J2** 36.53N 30.42E
Antalya, G. of Turkey **57 J2** 36.38N 31.00E
Antananarivo Madagascar **86 D3** 18.52S 47.30E
Antarctica 112
Antarctic Pen. *f.* Antarctica **116 F2** 65.00S 64.00W
An Teallach *mtn.* Scotland **18 D2** 57.48N 5.16W
Antequera Spain **46 C2** 37.01N 4.34W
Antibes France **44 G3** 43.35N 7.07E
Anticosti, Île d' Canada **63 L2** 49.20N 63.00W
Antigua *i.* Leeward Is. **71 L4** 17.09N 61.49W
Antigua and Barbuda Leeward Is. **71 L4** 17.30N 61.49W
Antikythira *i.* Greece **56 F1** 35.52N 23.18E
Antipodes Is. Pacific Oc. **108 M2** 49.42S 178.50E
Antofagasta Chile **76 C2** 23.40S 70.23W
Antrim N. Ireland **16 C2** 54.43N 6.14W
Antrim *d.* N. Ireland **20 E4** 54.45N 6.15W
Antrim Hills N. Ireland **16 C2** 55.00N 6.10W
Antsirañana Madagascar **86 D3** 12.19S 49.17E
Antwerpen Belgium **42 D3** 51.13N 4.25E
Antwerpen *d.* Belgium **42 D3** 51.16N 4.45E
Anxi China **102 H6** 40.32N 95.57E
Anyang China **103 K5** 36.04N 114.20E
Anzhero-Sudzhensk Russian Fed. **58 K3** 56.10N 86.10E
Aomori Japan **106 D4** 40.50N 140.43E
Aosta Italy **50 B6** 45.43N 7.19E
Apa *r.* Brazil/Paraguay **77 E2** 22.08S 57.55W
Apalachee B. U.S.A. **65 J2** 29.30N 84.00W
Apaporis *r.* Colombia **76 D4** 1.40S 69.20W
Aparri Phil. **105 G7** 18.22N 121.40E
Apatity Russian Fed. **43 H4** 67.32N 33.21E
Apeldoorn Neth. **42 E4** 52.13N 5.57E
Apennines *mts.* Italy **50 D6** 44.00N 11.00E
Aporé *r.* Brazil **77 E3** 19.30S 50.55W
Appalachian Mts. U.S.A. **65 K4** 39.30N 78.00W
Appleby-in-Westmorland England **15 E3** 54.35N 2.29W
Appledore England **13 C3** 51.03N 4.12W
Appleton U.S.A. **65 I5** 44.16N 88.25W
Apucarana Brazil **77 E2** 23.34S 51.28W
Apurimac *r.* Peru **76 C3** 10.43S 73.55W
Aqaba Jordan **94 E4** 29.32N 35.00E
Aqaba, G. of Asia **94 D4** 28.45N 34.45E
Āra Ārba Ethiopia **87 C4** 5.50N 41.30E
Arabia Asia **117 L2** 25.00N 45.00E
Arabian Sea Asia **96 C4** 19.00N 65.00E
Aracaju Brazil **77 G3** 10.54S 37.07W
Araçatuba Brazil **77 E2** 21.12S 50.24W
Aracena, Sierra de *mts.* Spain **46 B2** 37.50N 7.00W
Arad Romania **54 G2** 46.12N 21.19E

Arafura Sea Austa. **105 I2** 9.00S 135.00E
Aragón *r.* Spain **46 E5** 42.20N 1.45W
Araguaia *r.* Brazil **77 F4** 5.30S 48.05W
Araguaína Brazil **77 F4** 7.16S 48.18W
Araguari Brazil **77 F3** 18.38S 48.13W
Arak Iran **95 G5** 34.06N 49.44E
Arakan Yoma *mts.* Myanmar **97 I5** 20.00N 94.00E
Aral Sea Asia **58 H2** 45.00N 60.00E
Aralsk Kazakstan **58 I2** 46.56N 61.43E
Aranda de Duero Spain **46 D4** 41.40N 3.41W
Aran I. Rep. of Ire. **20 C5** 55.00N 8.32W
Aran Is. Rep. of Ire. **20 B3** 53.07N 9.38W
Aranjuez Spain **46 D4** 40.02N 3.37W
Arao Japan **106 B2** 33.00N 130.26E
Arapiraca Brazil **77 G4** 9.45S 36.40W
Arapkir Turkey **57 N3** 39.03N 38.29E
Araraquara Brazil **77 F2** 21.46S 48.08W
Ararat, Mt. Turkey **90 G7** 39.45N 44.15E
Ārba Minch Ethiopia **87 B4** 6.02N 37.33E
Arbil Iraq **94 F6** 36.12N 44.01E
Arboga Sweden **43 C2** 59.24N 15.51E
Arbroath Scotland **17 G4** 56.34N 2.35W
Arcachon France **44 C4** 44.40N 1.11W
Archangel Russian Fed. **58 G4** 64.32N 41.10E
Arctic Bay *town* Canada **63 J5** 73.05N 85.20W
Arctic Ocean **112**
Arctic Red *r.* Canada **62 E4** 67.26N 133.48W
Ardabil Iran **95 G6** 38.15N 48.18E
Ardas *r.* Greece **56 H4** 41.39N 26.30E
Ardèche *r.* France **44 F4** 44.31N 4.40E
Ardennes *mts.* Belgium **42 E2** 50.10N 5.30E
Ardestan Iran **95 H5** 33.22N 52.25E
Ardglass N. Ireland **16 D2** 54.16N 5.37W
Ardila *r.* Portugal **46 B3** 38.10N 7.30W
Ardnamurchan, Pt. of Scotland **18 C1** 56.44N 6.14W
Ardrishaig Scotland **16 D3** 56.00N 5.26W
Ardrossan Scotland **16 E3** 55.38N 4.49W
Ards Pen. N. Ireland **16 D2** 54.30N 5.30W
Ardvasar Scotland **18 D2** 57.03N 5.54W
Arena, Pt. U.S.A. **64 B4** 38.58N 123.44W
Arendal Norway **43 B2** 58.27N 8.56E
Arenig Fawr *mtn.* Wales **12 D4** 52.55N 3.45W
Arequipa Peru **76 C3** 16.25S 71.32W
Arezzo Italy **50 D5** 43.27N 11.52E
Arganda Spain **46 D4** 40.19N 3.26W
Argentan France **44 C6** 48.45N 0.01W
Argentina S. America **75 C3** 35.00S 65.00W
Argentino, L. Argentina **75 B1** 50.15S 72.25W
Argenton France **44 D5** 46.36N 1.30E
Argos Greece **56 F2** 37.37N 22.45E
Argun *r.* Russian Fed. **103 M8** 53.30N 121.48E
Argyle, L. Australia **110 B4** 16.20S 128.14E
Argyll *f.* Scotland **16 D4** 56.12N 5.15W
Argyll and Bute *d.* Scotland **8 C5** 56.15N 5.30W
Århus Denmark **43 B2** 56.10N 10.13E
Arica Chile **76 C3** 18.30S 70.20W
Ariège *r.* France **44 D3** 43.31N 1.25E
Arienas, Loch Scotland **16 D4** 56.38N 5.45W
Arinos *r.* Brazil **77 E3** 10.20S 57.35W
Aripuanã *r.* Brazil **77 D4** 5.05S 60.30W
Ariquemes Brazil **76 D4** 9.56S 63.04W
Arisaig Scotland **18 D1** 56.55N 5.51W
Arisaig, Sd. of Scotland **18 D1** 56.51N 5.50W
Arizona *d.* U.S.A. **64 D3** 34.00N 112.00W
Arkaig, Loch Scotland **18 D1** 56.59N 5.10W
Arkalyk Kazakstan **102 B8** 50.17N 66.51E
Arkansas *r.* U.S.A. **65 H3** 33.50N 91.00W
Arkansas *d.* U.S.A. **65 H4** 35.00N 92.00W
Arkansas City U.S.A. **64 G4** 37.03N 97.02W
Arklow Rep. of Ire. **20 E2** 52.47N 6.10W
Arles France **44 F3** 43.41N 4.38E
Arlit Niger **84 E3** 19.00N 7.35E
Arlon Belgium **42 E1** 49.41N 5.49E
Armagh N. Ireland **16 C2** 54.21N 6.40W
Armagh *d.* N. Ireland **20 E4** 54.15N 6.45W
Armavir Russian Fed. **53 L5** 44.59N 41.10E
Armenia Asia **58 G2** 40.00N 45.00E
Armenia Colombia **74 B7** 4.32N 75.40W
Armidale Australia **110 E2** 30.32S 151.40E
Armoy N. Ireland **16 C3** 55.08N 6.20W
Arnauti, C. Cyprus **57 K1** 35.06N 32.17E
Arnhem Neth. **42 E3** 52.00N 5.55E
Arnhem, C. Australia **110 C4** 12.10S 137.00E
Arnhem Land *f.* Australia **110 C4** 13.00S 132.30E
Arno *r.* Italy **50 D5** 43.43N 10.17E
Ar Ramadī Iraq **94 F5** 33.27N 43.19E
Arran *i.* Scotland **16 D3** 55.35N 5.14W
Ar Raqqah Syria **94 E6** 35.57N 39.03E
Arras France **44 E7** 50.17N 2.46E
Arrecife Canary Is. **46 Z2** 28.57N 13.32W
Ar Rimal *f.* Saudi Arabia **95 H3** 22.00N 53.00E
Arrochar Scotland **16 E4** 56.12N 4.44W
Ar Ruṭba Iraq **94 F5** 33.03N 40.18E
Arta Greece **56 E3** 39.10N 20.57E
Artigas Uruguay **77 E1** 30.24S 56.28W
Artois *f.* France **42 B2** 50.16N 2.50E
Aruba *i.* Neth. Ant. **71 J3** 12.30N 70.00W
Aru Is. Indonesia **105 I2** 6.00S 134.30E
Arunachal Pradesh *d.* India **97 I6** 28.40N 94.60E
Arundel England **11 E1** 50.52N 0.32W
Arusha Tanzania **86 B2** 3.21S 36.40E
Aruwimi *r.* Dem. Rep. of Congo **86 B5** 1.20N 23.26E
Arviat Canada **63 I4** 61.10N 94.15W
Arvidsjaur Sweden **43 D4** 65.37N 19.10E
Arvika Sweden **43 C2** 59.41N 12.38E
Asahi-dake *mtn.* Japan **106 D4** 43.42N 142.54E
Asahikawa Japan **106 D4** 43.46N 142.23E
Asansol India **97 H5** 23.40N 87.00E
Ascension I. Atlantic Oc. **82 B4** 8.00S 14.00W
Ascoli Piceno Italy **50 E5** 42.52N 13.36E
Åsele Sweden **43 D4** 64.10N 17.20E
Ashbourne England **15 F2** 53.02N 1.44W
Ashbourne Rep. of Ire. **20 E3** 53.31N 6.25W
Ashburton England **13 D2** 50.31N 3.45W
Ashburton *r.* Australia **110 A3** 21.15S 115.00E
Ashby de la Zouch England **10 D3** 52.45N 1.29W
Ashford England **11 F2** 51.08N 0.53E
Ashgabat Turkmenistan **95 I6** 37.58N 58.24E
Ashington England **15 F4** 55.11N 1.34W
Ashland U.S.A. **65 H6** 46.34N 90.45W
Ash Shiḥr Yemen **95 G1** 14.45N 49.36E
Ashton-under-Lyne England **15 E2** 53.30N 2.08W
Asia **90-91**
Asilah Morocco **46 B1** 35.32N 6.00W
Asinara, G. of Med. Sea **50 C4** 41.00N 8.32E
Asir *f.* Saudi Arabia **94 F2** 19.00N 42.00E
Askern England **15 F2** 53.37N 1.09W
Askim Norway **43 B2** 59.33N 11.20E
Asmara Eritrea **85 H3** 15.20N 38.58E
Åsnen *l.* Sweden **43 C2** 56.40N 14.50E
Aspang Markt Austria **54 E2** 47.34N 16.06E
Aspatria England **14 D3** 54.45N 3.20W
Assab Eritrea **85 I3** 13.01N 42.47E
Assam *d.* India **97 I6** 26.30N 93.00E
As Samawah Iraq **94 G5** 31.18N 45.18E
As Sarir *f.* Libya **53 H2** 27.00N 21.20E
Assen Neth. **42 F4** 53.00N 6.34E
As Sidrah Libya **53 G3** 30.31N 18.34E
Assiniboine, Mt. Canada **62 G3** 50.51N 115.39W
As Sulaymanīyah Iraq **95 G6** 35.32N 45.27E
As Sulayyil Saudi Arabia **95 G3** 20.27N 45.34E
Assumption *i.* Indian Oc. **86 D4** 9.30S 47.20E
As Suq Saudi Arabia **94 F3** 21.55N 42.02E
Assynt, Loch Scotland **18 D3** 58.11N 5.03W
Astara Azerbaijan **95 G6** 38.27N 48.53E
Asti Italy **50 C6** 44.54N 8.13E
Astorga Spain **46 B5** 42.30N 6.02W
Astoria U.S.A. **64 B6** 46.12N 123.50W
Astove *i.* Indian Oc. **86 D3** 10.05S 47.40E
Astrakhan' Russian Fed. **58 G2** 46.22N 48.00E
Asunción Paraguay **77 E2** 25.15S 57.40W
Asuncion *i.* N. Mariana Is. **105 L7** 19.34N 145.24E
Aswân Egypt **94 D3** 24.05N 32.56E
Asyût Egypt **94 D4** 27.14N 31.07E
Atacama Desert S. America **76 D2** 20.00S 69.00W
Atafu Pacific Oc. **108 N6** 8.40S 172.40W
Atâr Mauritania **84 C4** 20.32N 13.08W
Ataturk Resr. Turkey **57 N2** 37.30N 38.40E
Atbara Sudan **85 H3** 17.42N 34.00E
Atbara *r.* Sudan **85 H3** 17.47N 34.00E
Ath Belgium **42 C2** 50.38N 3.45E
Athabasca *r.* Canada **62 G3** 58.30N 111.00W
Athabasca, L. Canada **62 H3** 59.30N 109.00W
Athboy Rep. of Ire. **20 E3** 53.37N 6.55W
Athenry Rep. of Ire. **20 C3** 53.18N 8.48W
Athens Greece **56 F2** 37.59N 23.42E
Atherstone England **10 D3** 52.35N 1.32W
Athi *r.* Kenya **87 B2** 2.59S 38.29E
Athi Plains *f.* Kenya **87 B2** 1.30S 36.50E
Athi River *town* Kenya **87 B2** 1.28S 36.58E
Athlone Rep. of Ire. **20 D3** 53.26N 7.57W
Athos, Mt. Greece **56 G4** 40.09N 24.19E
Athy Rep. of Ire. **20 E2** 53.00N 7.00W
Ati Chad **85 F3** 13.11N 18.20E
Atlanta U.S.A. **65 J3** 33.45N 84.23W
Atlantic City U.S.A. **65 L4** 39.23N 74.27W
Atlantic Ocean **116**
Atlas Mts. Africa **82 C8** 33.00N 4.00W
Aṭ Ṭā'if Saudi Arabia **94 F3** 21.15N 40.21E
Attleborough England **11 G3** 52.31N 1.01E
Atui *i.* Cook Is. **108 P4** 20.00S 158.07W
Atyrau Kazakstan **58 H2** 47.08N 51.59E
Aube *r.* France **44 E6** 48.30N 3.37E
Auchterarder Scotland **17 F4** 56.18N 3.43W
Auchtermuchty Scotland **17 F4** 56.17N 3.15W
Auckland New Zealand **111 G2** 36.52S 174.45E
Auckland Is. Pacific Oc. **108 L1** 50.35S 166.00E
Audlem England **15 E1** 52.59N 2.31W
Aughton England **15 F2** 53.22N 1.18W
Augsburg Germany **48 E3** 48.21N 10.54E
Augusta Ga. U.S.A. **65 J3** 33.29N 82.00W
Augusta Maine U.S.A. **65 M5** 44.20N 69.50W
Aulnoye-Aymeries France **42 C2** 50.12N 3.50E
Aurangabad India **96 F4** 19.52N 75.22E
Aurich Germany **42 G5** 53.28N 7.29E
Aurora Colo. U.S.A. **64 F4** 39.44N 104.52W
Aurora Ill. U.S.A. **65 I5** 41.45N 88.20W
Auskerry *i.* Scotland **19 G4** 59.02N 2.34W
Aus Maduli Kenya **87 C3** 2.16N 40.36E
Austin U.S.A. **64 G3** 30.18N 97.47W
Australia Austa. **110 B3** 25.00S 135.00E
Australian Capital Territory *d.* Australia **110 D2** 35.30S 149.00E
Austria Europe **54 C2** 47.30N 14.00E
Auvergne *f.* France **44 E4** 45.20N 2.40E
Auxerre France **44 E5** 47.48N 3.35E
Avallon France **44 E5** 47.30N 3.54E
Avanos Turkey **57 L3** 38.44N 34.51E
Aveiro Portugal **46 A4** 40.40N 8.35W
Avellino Italy **50 F4** 40.55N 14.46E
Avesta Sweden **43 D3** 60.09N 16.10E
Aveyron *r.* France **44 D4** 44.09N 1.10E
Avezzano Italy **50 E5** 42.03N 13.26E
Aviemore Scotland **19 F2** 57.11N 3.51W
Avignon France **44 F3** 43.56N 4.48E
Ávila Spain **46 C4** 40.39N 4.42W
Avilés Spain **46 C5** 43.33N 5.55W
Avon *r.* Bristol England **10 C2** 51.30N 2.43W
Avon *r.* Dorset England **10 D1** 50.43N 1.45W
Avon *r.* Glos. England **10 C3** 52.00N 2.10W
Avon *r.* Scotland **19 F2** 57.25N 3.23W
Avonmouth England **10 C2** 51.30N 2.42W
Awara Plain *f.* Kenya **87 C3** 3.45N 41.05E
Awata Shet' *r.* Ethiopia **87 B3** 4.55N 39.25E
Awe, Loch Scotland **16 D4** 56.18N 5.24W
Axe *r.* England **13 D2** 50.42N 3.03W
Axel Heiberg I. Canada **63 I5** 79.30N 90.00W
Axminster England **13 E2** 50.47N 3.01W
Ayacucho Peru **76 C3** 13.10S 74.15W
Ayaguz Kazakstan **102 E7** 47.59N 80.27E
Ayan Russian Fed. **59 P3** 56.29N 138.00E
Aydın Turkey **57 H2** 37.52N 27.50E
Ayers Rock *mtn.* Australia **110 C3** 25.20S 131.01E
Aylesbury England **10 E2** 51.48N 0.49W
Aylesham England **11 G2** 51.14N 1.12E
Aylsham England **11 G3** 52.48N 1.16E
Ayr Scotland **16 E3** 55.28N 4.37W
Ayr *r.* Scotland **16 E3** 55.28N 4.38W
Ayr, Pt. of Wales **12 D5** 53.21N 3.20W
Ayre, Pt. of I.o.M. **14 C3** 54.25N 4.22W
Ayutthaya Thailand **104 C6** 14.25N 100.30E
Ayvalık Turkey **56 H3** 39.19N 26.42E
Azerbaijan Asia **58 G2** 40.10N 47.50E
Azogues Ecuador **76 C4** 2.35S 78.00W
Azores *is.* Atlantic Oc. **82 A8** 38.00N 28.00W
Azov, Sea of Ukraine **53 K6** 46.00N 36.30E
Azrou Morocco **52 B3** 33.27N 5.14W
Azuero Pen. Panama **71 H2** 7.30N 80.30W
Azul, Cordillera *mts.* Peru **76 C4** 9.00S 76.30W

B

Baardeere Somalia **87 C3** 2.18N 42.18E
Bab al Mandab *str.* Asia **94 F1** 13.00N 43.10E
Babar Is. Indonesia **105 H2** 8.00S 129.30E
Babati Tanzania **87 B2** 4.14S 35.45E
Babbacombe B. England **13 D2** 50.30N 3.28W
Babia Gora *mtn.* Slovakia/Poland **54 F3** 49.38N 19.38E
Babo Indonesia **105 I3** 2.33S 133.25E
Baboua C.A.R. **84 F2** 5.49N 14.51E
Babruysk Belarus **55 K5** 53.08N 29.10E
Babuyan Is. Phil. **105 G7** 19.20N 121.30E
Bacabal Brazil **77 F4** 4.15S 44.45W
Bacan *i.* Indonesia **105 H3** 0.30S 127.30E
Bacău Romania **55 J2** 46.32N 26.59E
Back *r.* Canada **63 I4** 66.37N 96.00W
Backwater Resr. Scotland **19 F1** 56.45N 3.16W
Bac Liêu Vietnam **104 D5** 9.17N 105.44E
Bacolod Phil. **105 G6** 10.38N 122.58E
Badajoz Spain **46 B3** 38.53N 6.58W
Badanah Saudi Arabia **94 F5** 30.59N 41.02E
Baden-Baden Germany **48 D3** 48.45N 8.15E
Bad Neuenahr-Ahrweiler Germany **42 G2** 50.33N 7.08E
Badulla Sri Lanka **97 G2** 6.59N 81.03E
Baffin B. Canada **63 L5** 74.00N 70.00W
Baffin I. Canada **63 L4** 68.50N 70.00W
Bafoussam Cameroon **84 F2** 5.31N 10.25E
Bafq Iran **95 I5** 31.35N 55.21E
Bafra Turkey **57 L4** 41.34N 35.56E
Baft Iran **95 I4** 29.12N 56.36E
Bagé Brazil **77 E1** 31.22S 54.06W
Baggy Pt. England **13 C3** 51.08N 4.15W
Baghdad Iraq **94 F5** 33.20N 44.26E
Baghlan Afghan. **95 K6** 36.11N 68.44E
Baguio Phil. **104 G7** 16.25N 120.37E
Baharîya Oasis Egypt **94 C4** 28.10N 29.00E
Bahawalpur Pakistan **96 E6** 29.24N 71.47E
Bahia *d.* Brazil **77 F3** 12.30S 42.30W
Bahía Blanca Argentina **75 C3** 38.45S 62.15W
Bahrain Asia **95 H4** 26.00N 50.35E
Baia Mare Romania **55 H2** 47.40N 23.35E
Baicheng China **103 M7** 45.40N 122.52E
Baie Comeau Canada **63 L2** 49.12N 68.10W
Baie-du-Poste *see* Mistissini Canada **63**
Baikal, L. Russian Fed. **59 M3** 53.30N 108.00E
Bailieborough Rep. of Ire. **20 E3** 53.55N 6.58W
Bain *r.* England **15 G2** 53.04N 0.12W
Bairnsdale Australia **110 D2** 37.51S 147.38E
Baiyuda Desert Sudan **94 D2** 17.10N 32.30E
Baja Hungary **54 F2** 46.12N 18.58E
Baja California Norte *d.* Mexico **70 B6** 30.00N 115.00W
Baja California Sur *d.* Mexico **70 B6** 26.00N 112.00W
Baker U.S.A. **64 C5** 44.46N 117.50W
Baker I. Kiribati **108 N6** 0.14N 176.28W
Baker L. Canada **63 I4** 64.10N 95.30W
Baker Lake *town* Canada **63 I4** 64.20N 96.10W
Baker, Mt. U.S.A. **64 B6** 48.48N 121.10W
Bakersfield U.S.A. **64 C4** 35.25N 119.00W
Bakharden Turkmenistan **95 I6** 38.25N 57.24E
Bakırköy Turkey **57 I4** 40.59N 28.52E
Bako Ethiopia **87 B4** 5.50N 36.40E
Baku Azerbaijan **58 G2** 40.22N 49.53E
Bala Wales **12 D4** 52.54N 3.36W
Balabac Str. Malaysia/Phil. **104 F5** 7.30N 117.00E
Bala, Cerros de *mts.* Bolivia **76 D3** 14.00S 68.00W
Bala L. Wales **12 D4** 52.53N 3.38W
Bala Morghab Afghan. **95 J6** 35.34N 63.20E
Balaton Hungary **54 E2** 46.55N 17.50E
Balbina Reser. Brazil **77 E4** 1.30S 60.00W
Balbriggan Rep. of Ire. **20 E3** 53.36N 6.12W
Baldock England **11 E2** 51.59N 0.11W
Balearic Is. Spain **46 G3** 39.30N 2.30E
Baleia, Punta da *c.* Brazil **77 G3** 17.41S 39.07W
Baleine *r.* Canada **63 L3** 58.00N 67.50W
Baleshwar India **97 H5** 21.31N 86.59E
Bali *i.* Indonesia **104 F2** 8.30S 115.05E
Balige Indonesia **104 B4** 2.20N 99.01E
Balıkesir Turkey **57 H3** 39.38N 27.51E
Balikpapan Indonesia **104 F3** 1.15S 116.50E
Balimo P.N.G. **105 K2** 7.55S 143.20E
Balintore Scotland **19 F2** 57.45N 3.55W
Bali Sea Indonesia **104 F2** 7.30S 115.15E
Balkan Mts. Bulgaria **56 G5** 42.50N 24.30E
Balkhash Kazakstan **102 D7** 46.51N 75.00E
Balkhash, L. Kazakstan **102 D7** 46.40N 75.00E
Ballagan Pt. Rep. of Ire. **16 C1** 54.00N 6.07W
Ballantrae Scotland **16 E3** 55.06N 5.01W
Ballarat Australia **110 D2** 37.36S 143.58E
Ballater Scotland **19 F2** 57.03N 3.04W
Ballena, Punta *c.* Chile **76 C2** 22.50S 70.48W
Ballina Rep. of Ire. **20 B4** 54.08N 9.10W
Ballinasloe Rep. of Ire. **20 C3** 53.20N 8.15W
Ballybay Rep. of Ire. **16 C2** 54.08N 6.56W
Ballybofey Rep. of Ire. **16 B2** 54.47N 7.48W
Ballybunnion Rep. of Ire. **20 B2** 52.36N 9.40W
Ballycastle N. Ireland **16 C3** 55.12N 6.16W
Ballyclare N. Ireland **16 D2** 54.45N 6.00W
Ballyhaunis Rep. of Ire. **20 C3** 53.46N 8.46W
Ballymena N. Ireland **16 C2** 54.52N 6.17W
Ballymoney N. Ireland **16 C3** 55.04N 6.32W
Ballynahinch N. Ireland **16 D2** 54.24N 5.54W
Ballyquintin Pt. N. Ireland **16 D2** 54.20N 5.30W
Ballyshannon Rep. of Ire. **20 C4** 54.30N 8.11W
Balochistan *f.* Pakistan **96 D6** 29.00N 66.00E
Balsas *r.* Mexico **70 D4** 18.10N 102.05W
Bălţi Moldova **55 J2** 47.45N 27.59E
Baltic Sea Europe **43 D1** 56.30N 19.00E
Baltimore U.S.A. **65 K4** 39.18N 76.38W
Baltiysk Russian Fed. **54 F6** 54.41N 19.59E
Bam Iran **95 I4** 29.07N 58.20E
Bamako Mali **84 B3** 12.40N 7.59W
Bamberg Germany **48 E3** 49.54N 10.53E
Bamīan Afghan. **95 K5** 34.52N 67.45E
Bampton Devon England **13 D2** 51.00N 3.29W
Bampton Oxon. England **10 D2** 51.44N 1.33W
Banaba *i.* Kiribati **108 M6** 0.52S 169.35E
Banagher Rep. of Ire. **20 D3** 53.11N 7.58W
Bananal, Ilha do *f.* Brazil **77 E3** 11.30S 50.15W
Banbridge N. Ireland **16 C2** 54.21N 6.16W
Banbury England **10 D3** 52.04N 1.21W
Banchory Scotland **19 G2** 57.04N 2.28W
Banco Chinchorro *is.* Mexico **70 G4** 18.30N 87.20W
Banda Aceh Indonesia **104 B5** 5.35N 95.20E
Banda Is. Indonesia **105 H3** 4.30S 129.55E
Bandar-e' Abbas Iran **95 I4** 27.10N 56.15E
Bandar-e Anzalī Iran **95 G6** 37.26N 49.29E
Bandar-e Lengeh Iran **95 H4** 26.34N 54.53E
Bandar-e Torkeman Iran **95 H6** 36.55N 54.05E
Bandar Seri Begawan Brunei **104 E4** 4.56N 114.58E
Banda Sea Indonesia **105 H2** 5.00S 128.00E
Bandeiras *mtn.* Brazil **77 F2** 20.25S 41.45W
Banderas B. Mexico **70 C5** 20.27N 105.30W
Bandırma Turkey **57 H4** 40.22N 28.00E
Bandon Rep. of Ire. **20 C1** 51.45N 8.45W
Bandon *r.* Rep. of Ire. **20 C1** 51.43N 8.38W
Bandundu Dem. Rep. of Congo **86 A4** 3.20S 17.24E
Bandung Indonesia **104 D2** 6.57S 107.34E
Banff Canada **64 C7** 51.10N 115.34W
Banff Scotland **19 G2** 57.40N 2.31W
Bangalore India **96 F3** 12.58N 77.35E
Bangassou C.A.R. **85 G2** 4.41N 22.48E
Banggai Is. Indonesia **105 G3** 1.30S 123.10E
Banghazi Libya **85 G5** 32.07N 20.05E
Bangka *i.* Indonesia **104 D3** 2.20S 106.10E
Bangkok Thailand **104 C6** 13.45N 100.35E
Bangladesh Asia **97 H5** 24.00N 90.00E
Bangor N. Ireland **16 D2** 54.39N 5.41W
Bangor U.S.A. **65 M5** 44.49N 68.47W
Bangor Wales **12 C5** 53.13N 4.09W
Bangui C.A.R. **85 F2** 4.23N 18.37E
Bangweulu, L. Zambia **86 B3** 11.15S 29.45E
Ban Hat Yai Thailand **104 C5** 7.00N 100.28E
Bani *r.* Mali **82 C6** 14.30N 4.15W
Bani Walid Libya **53 F3** 31.43N 14.01E
Banja Luka Bosnia. **56 C6** 44.47N 17.10E
Banjarmasin Indonesia **104 E3** 3.22S 114.36E
Banjul The Gambia **84 C3** 13.28N 16.39W
Banks I. Canada **62 F5** 73.00N 122.00W
Banks Is. Vanuatu **111 F4** 13.50S 167.30E
Banmi Pakistan **95 L5** 32.59N 70.38E
Bann *r.* N. Ireland **16 C3** 55.10N 6.47W
Banská Bystrica Slovakia **54 F3** 48.44N 19.07E
Bantry Rep. of Ire. **20 B1** 51.41N 9.27W
Bantry B. Rep. of Ire. **20 B1** 51.40N 9.40W
Baoding China **103 L5** 38.54N 115.26E
Baoji China **103 J4** 34.23N 107.10E
Baoshan China **103 H3** 25.07N 99.08E
Baotou China **103 J6** 40.38N 109.59E
Ba'qubah Iraq **94 F5** 33.45N 44.38E
Baquerizo Moreno Galapagos Is. **76 B4** 0.54S 89.37W
Bar Yugo. **56 D5** 42.05N 19.06E
Bara Sudan **94 D1** 13.42N 30.22E
Baranavichi Belarus **55 I5** 53.09N 26.00E
Barbacena Brazil **77 F2** 21.13S 43.47W
Barbados Lesser Antilles **71 M3** 13.20N 59.40W
Barbuda *i.* Leeward Is. **71 L4** 17.41N 61.48W
Barcaldine Australia **110 D3** 23.31S 145.15E
Barcelona Spain **46 G4** 41.25N 2.10E
Barcelona Venezuela **71 L3** 10.08N 64.43W
Barcelos Brazil **76 D4** 0.59S 62.58W
Bárdharbunga *mtn.* Iceland **43 Y2** 64.38N 17.34W
Bardney England **15 G2** 53.13N 0.19W
Bardsey *i.* Wales **12 C4** 52.45N 4.48W
Bardsey Sd. Wales **12 C4** 52.45N 4.48W
Bareilly India **97 F6** 28.20N 79.24E
Barents Sea Arctic Oc. **58 F5** 73.00N 40.00E
Barham England **11 G2** 51.12N 1.07E
Bari Italy **50 G4** 41.08N 16.52E
Barikot Afghan. **95 L6** 35.18N 71.36E
Barinas Venezuela **71 J2** 8.36N 70.15W
Baringo, L. Kenya **87 B3** 0.35N 36.04E
Barisan Range *mts.* Indonesia **104 C3** 3.30S 102.30E
Barkly Tableland *f.* Australia **110 C4** 19.00S 136.40E
Bârlad Romania **55 J2** 46.14N 27.40E
Barlee, L. Australia **110 A3** 29.30S 119.30E
Barletta Italy **50 G4** 41.20N 16.15E
Barmer India **96 E6** 24.45N 71.23E
Barmouth Wales **12 C4** 52.44N 4.03W
Barmouth B. Wales **12 C4** 52.42N 4.05W
Barnard Castle *town* England **15 F3** 54.33N 1.55W
Barnaul Russian Fed. **58 K3** 53.21N 83.15E
Barnet England **11 E2** 51.39N 0.11W
Barnoldswick England **15 E2** 53.55N 2.11W
Barnsley England **15 F2** 53.33N 1.29W
Barnstaple England **13 C3** 51.05N 4.03W
Barnstaple B. England **13 C3** 51.04N 4.20W
Barquisimeto Venezuela **71 K3** 10.03N 69.18W
Barra *i.* Scotland **18 B1** 56.59N 7.28W
Barra, Sd. of Scotland **18 B2** 57.03N 7.25W
Barra do Corda Brazil **77 F4** 5.30S 45.15W
Barranquilla Colombia **71 J3** 11.00N 74.50W
Barretos Brazil **77 F2** 20.37S 48.38W
Barrhead Scotland **16 E3** 55.47N 4.24W
Barrow U.S.A. **62 C5** 71.16N 156.50W
Barrow *r.* Rep. of Ire. **20 D2** 52.17N 7.00W
Barrow I. Australia **110 A3** 20.40S 115.27E
Barrow-in-Furness England **14 D3** 54.08N 3.15W
Barrow, Pt. U.S.A. **62 C5** 71.30N 156.00W
Barry Wales **13 D3** 51.23N 3.19W
Barstow U.S.A. **64 C3** 34.55N 117.01W
Bartın Turkey **57 K4** 41.37N 32.20E
Barton-upon-Humber England **15 G2** 53.41N 0.27W
Bartoszyce Poland **54 G6** 54.16N 20.49E
Baru *mtn.* Panama **71 H2** 8.48N 82.33W
Baruun Urt Mongolia **103 K7** 46.48N 113.18E
Barysaw Belarus **55 K6** 54.09N 28.30E
Baschurch England **10 C3** 52.48N 2.51W
Basel Switz. **44 G5** 47.33N 7.36E
Basilan *i.* Phil. **105 G5** 6.40N 122.10E
Basildon England **11 F2** 51.34N 0.25E
Basingstoke England **10 D2** 51.15N 1.05W
Bassein Myanmar **97 I4** 16.45N 94.30E
Bassenthwaite L. England **14 D3** 54.40N 3.13W
Bass Rock *i.* Scotland **17 G4** 56.05N 2.38W
Bass Str. Australia **110 D2** 39.45S 146.00
Bastak Iran **95 H4** 27.15N 54.26
Bastia France **44 H3** 42.41N 9.26
Bastogne Belgium **42 E2** 50.00N 5.43
Bata Equat. Guinea **84 E2** 1.51N 9.49
Batabanó, G. of Cuba **71 H5** 23.15N 82.30
Batang China **103 H3** 30.02N 99.01
Batangas Phil. **105 G6** 13.46N 121.01
Batan Is. Phil. **105 G8** 20.50N 121.55
Batdâmbâng Cambodia **104 C6** 13.06N 103.13
Bath England **10 C2** 51.22N 2.22
Bath and North East Somerset *d.* England **9 D2** 51.20N 2.30
Bathgate Scotland **17 F3** 55.55N 3.38
Bathurst Australia **110 D2** 33.27S 149.35

Břeclav Czech Rep. 54 E3 48.46N 16.53E
Brecon Wales 12 D3 51.57N 3.23W
Brecon Beacons *mts.* Wales 12 D3 51.53N 3.27W
Breda Neth. 42 D3 51.35N 4.46E
Bredhafjördhur *est.* Iceland 43 X2 65.15N 23.00W
Breidhdalsvik Iceland 43 Z2 64.48N 14.00W
Bremen Germany 48 D5 53.05N 8.48E
Bremerhaven Germany 48 D5 53.33N 8.35E
Brenner Pass Italy/Austria 50 D7 47.00N 11.30E
Brentwood England 11 F2 51.38N 0.18E
Brescia Italy 50 D6 45.33N 10.12E
Bressay *i.* Scotland 19 Y9 60.08N 1.05W
Bressuire France 44 C5 46.50N 0.28W
Brest Belarus 55 H5 52.08N 23.40E
Brest France 44 A6 48.23N 4.30W
Bretton Wales 12 E5 53.10N 3.00W
Bria C.A.R. 85 G2 6.32N 21.59E
Briançon France 44 G4 44.53N 6.39E
Bride *r.* Rep. of Ire. 20 D2 52.06N 7.50W
Bridgend Wales 13 D3 51.30N 3.35W
Bridgend *d.* Wales 9 D2 51.33N 3.35W
Bridgeport U.S.A. 65 L5 41.12N 73.12W
Bridgetown Barbados 71 M3 13.06N 59.37W
Bridgnorth England 10 C3 52.33N 2.25W
Bridgwater England 13 D3 51.08N 3.00W
Bridgwater B. England 13 D3 51.15N 3.10W
Bridlington England 15 G3 54.06N 0.11W
Bridlington B. England 15 G3 54.03N 0.10W
Bridport England 10 C1 50.43N 2.45W
Brig Switz. 44 G5 46.19N 8.00E
Brigg England 15 G2 53.33N 0.30W
Brighstone England 10 D1 50.38N 1.24W
Brightlingsea England 11 G2 51.49N 1.01E
Brighton England 11 E1 50.50N 0.09W
Brighton and Hove *d.* England 9 E2 50.50N 0.09W
Brindisi Italy 50 G4 40.38N 17.57E
Brisbane Australia 110 E3 27.30S 153.00E
Bristol England 10 C2 51.26N 2.35W
Bristol *d.* England 9 D2 51.26N 2.35W
Bristol B. U.S.A. 62 C3 58.00N 158.50W
Bristol Channel England/Wales 13 D3 51.17N 3.20W
British Columbia *d.* Canada 62 F3 55.00N 125.00W
British Isles Europe 34 C3 54.00N 5.00W
Briton Ferry *town* Wales 12 D3 51.37N 3.50W
Brittany *f.* France 44 B6 48.00N 3.00W
Brive-la-Gaillarde France 44 D4 45.09N 1.32E
Brixham England 13 D2 50.24N 3.31W
Brno Czech Rep. 54 E3 49.11N 16.39E
Broad B. Scotland 18 C3 58.15N 6.15W
Broad Law *mtn.* Scotland 17 F3 55.30N 3.21W
Broadstairs England 11 G2 51.22N 1.27E
Broadview Canada 64 F7 50.20N 102.30W
Broadway England 10 D3 52.02N 1.50W
Broadwey England 10 C1 50.39N 2.29W
Broadwindsor England 10 C1 50.49N 2.48W
Brockenhurst England 10 D1 50.49N 1.34W
Brock I. Canada 62 G5 78.00N 114.30W
Brodeur Pen. Canada 63 J5 73.00N 88.00W
Brodick Scotland 16 D3 55.34N 5.09W
Broken Hill *town* Australia 110 D2 31.57S 141.30E
Bromley England 11 F2 51.24N 0.02E
Bromsgrove England 10 C3 52.20N 2.03W
Bromyard England 10 C3 52.12N 2.30W
Brønderslev Denmark 43 B2 57.16N 9.58E
Brønnøysund Norway 43 C4 65.38N 12.15E
Brooke England 11 G3 52.32N 1.25E
Brooke's Point *town* Phil. 104 F5 8.50N 117.52E
Brooks Range *mts.* U.S.A. 62 C4 68.50N 152.00W
Broome Australia 110 B4 17.58S 122.15E
Broom, Loch Scotland 18 D2 57.55N 5.15W
Brora Scotland 19 F3 58.01N 3.52W
Brora *r.* Scotland 19 F3 57.59N 3.51W
Brosna *r.* Rep. of Ire. 20 D3 53.12N 7.59W
Brotton England 15 G3 54.34N 0.55W
Brough Cumbria England 15 E3 54.32N 2.19W
Brough E.Yorks. England 15 G2 53.42N 0.34W
Brough Head Scotland 19 F4 59.09N 3.19W
Brough Ness *c.* Scotland 19 G3 58.44N 2.57W
Broughshane N. Ireland 16 C2 54.54N 6.12W
Brownhills England 10 D3 52.38N 1.57W
Broxburn Scotland 17 F3 55.57N 3.29W
Bruay-en-Artois France 42 B2 50.29N 2.36E
Brue *r.* England 13 E3 51.13N 3.00W
Brugge Belgium 42 C3 51.13N 3.14E
Brunei Asia 104 E4 4.56N 114.58E
Brunflo Sweden 43 C3 63.04N 14.50E
Brunswick U.S.A. 65 J3 31.09N 81.21W
Brussels Belgium 42 D2 50.50N 4.23E
Bruton England 13 E3 51.06N 2.28W
Bryansk Russian Fed. 55 N5 53.15N 34.09E
Bryher *i.* England 13 A1 49.57N 6.21W
Brynamman Wales 12 D3 51.49N 3.52W
Brynmawr Wales 12 D3 51.48N 3.10W
Buca Turkey 56 H3 38.22N 27.10E
Bucaramanga Colombia 71 J2 7.08N 73.01W
Bucharest Romania 56 H6 44.25N 26.06E
Buckhaven Scotland 17 F4 56.11N 3.03W
Buckie Scotland 19 G2 57.40N 2.58W
Buckingham England 10 E2 52.00N 0.59W
Buckinghamshire *d.* England 9 E2 51.50N 0.48W
Buckley Wales 12 D5 53.11N 3.04W
Budapest Hungary 54 F2 47.30N 19.03E
Buddon Ness *c.* Scotland 17 G4 56.29N 2.42W
Bude England 13 C2 50.49N 4.33W
Bude B. England 13 C2 50.45N 4.40W
Buenaventura Colombia 74 B7 3.54N 77.02W
Buenos Aires Argentina 75 D3 34.40S 58.30W
Buffalo N.Y. U.S.A. 65 K5 42.52N 78.55W
Buffalo Wyo. U.S.A. 64 E5 44.21N 106.40W
Bug *r.* Poland 54 G5 52.29N 21.11E
Bug *r.* Ukraine 55 L2 46.55N 31.59E
Buhayrat al Asad *l.* Syria 57 N2 36.10N 38.20E
Builth Wells Wales 12 D4 52.09N 3.24W
Buir Nur *l.* Mongolia 103 L7 47.50N 117.40E
Bujumbura Burundi 86 B4 3.22S 29.21E
Bukavu Dem. Rep. of Congo 86 B4 2.30S 28.49E
Bukittinggi Indonesia 104 C3 0.18S 100.20E
Bukoba Tanzania 86 C4 1.20S 31.49E
Bula Indonesia 105 I3 3.07S 130.27E
Bulawayo Zimbabwe 86 B2 20.10S 28.43E
Bulgan Mongolia 103 I7 48.34N 103.12E
Bulgaria Europe 56 G5 42.30N 25.00E
Bulukumba Indonesia 104 G2 5.35S 120.13E
Bulun Russian Fed. 59 O5 70.50N 127.20E
Buna Kenya 87 B3 2.49N 39.27E
Bunbury Australia 110 A2 33.20S 115.34E
Bunclody Rep. of Ire. 20 E2 52.39N 6.39W
Buncrana Rep. of Ire. 20 D5 55.08N 7.28W
Bunda Tanzania 87 A2 2.00S 33.57E
Bundaberg Australia 110 E3 24.50S 152.21E
Bundoran Rep. of Ire. 20 C4 54.28N 8.20W
Bungay England 11 G3 52.27N 1.26E
Bungoma Kenya 87 A3 0.33N 34.33E
Buôn Mê Thuột Vietnam 104 D6 12.41N 108.02E
Bura Kenya 87 B2 1.09S 39.55E
Buraydah Saudi Arabia 94 F4 26.18N 43.58E
Burbage England 10 D2 51.22N 1.40W
Burdur Turkey 57 J2 37.44N 30.17E
Bure *r.* England 11 G3 52.36N 1.44E
Burford England 10 D2 51.48N 1.38W
Burgas Bulgaria 56 H5 42.30N 27.29E
Burgess Hill *town* England 11 E1 50.57N 0.07W
Burghead Scotland 19 F2 57.42N 3.30W
Burgh le Marsh England 15 H2 53.10N 0.15E
Burgos Spain 46 D5 42.21N 3.41W
Burhanpur India 96 F5 21.18N 76.08E
Burkina Africa 84 D3 12.15N 1.30W
Burley U.S.A. 64 D5 42.32N 113.48W
Burlington U.S.A. 65 L5 44.25N 73.14W
Burnham England 10 E2 51.35N 0.39W
Burnham-on-Crouch England 11 F2 51.37N 0.50E
Burnham-on-Sea England 13 D3 51.15N 3.00W
Burnie Australia 110 D1 41.03S 145.55E
Burniston England 15 G3 54.19N 0.27W
Burnley England 15 E2 53.47N 2.15W
Burns Lake *town* Canada 62 F3 54.14N 125.45W
Burntisland Scotland 17 F4 56.03N 3.15W
Burntwood Green England 10 D3 52.42N 1.54W
Burray *i.* Scotland 19 G3 58.51N 2.54W
Burrow Head Scotland 16 E2 54.41N 4.24W
Burry Inlet Wales 12 C3 51.40N 4.11W
Burry Port Wales 12 C3 51.41N 4.17W
Bursa Turkey 57 I4 40.11N 29.04E
Bûr Safâga Egypt 94 D4 26.45N 33.55E
Burscough Bridge England 14 E2 53.37N 2.51W
Burton-in-Kendal England 14 E3 54.12N 2.43W
Burton Latimer England 10 E3 52.23N 0.41W
Burton upon Trent England 10 D3 52.48N 1.39W
Buru *i.* Indonesia 105 H3 3.30S 126.30E
Burundi Africa 86 B4 3.30S 30.00E
Burwash Landing Canada 62 E4 61.21N 139.01W
Burwell England 11 F3 52.17N 0.20E
Burwick Scotland 19 G3 58.44N 2.57W
Bury England 15 E2 53.36N 2.19W
Bury St. Edmunds England 11 F3 52.15N 0.42E
Bush *r.* N. Ireland 16 C3 55.13N 6.33W
Bushbush *r.* Somalia 87 C2 1.08S 41.52E
Bushehr Iran 95 H4 28.57N 50.52E
Bushmills N. Ireland 16 C3 55.12N 6.32W
Buta Dem. Rep. of Congo 86 B5 2.49N 24.50E
Bute *i.* Scotland 16 D3 55.51N 5.07W
Bute, Sd. of Scotland 16 D3 55.44N 5.10W
Buton *i.* Indonesia 105 G2 5.00S 122.50E
Butte U.S.A. 64 D6 46.00N 112.31W
Butterworth Malaysia 104 C5 5.24N 100.22E
Buttevant Rep. of Ire. 20 C2 52.13N 8.40W
Butt of Lewis *c.* Scotland 18 C3 58.31N 6.15W
Butuan Phil. 105 H5 8.56N 125.31E
Buur Gaabo Somalia 87 C2 1.10S 41.50E
Buvuma I. Uganda 87 A3 0.12N 33.17E
Buxton England 15 F2 53.16N 1.54W
Buzău Romania 56 H6 45.10N 26.49E
Byarezina *r.* Belarus 55 L5 52.30N 30.20E
Bydgoszcz Poland 54 E5 53.16N 18.00E
Byfield England 10 D3 52.10N 1.15W
Bylot I. Canada 63 K5 73.00N 78.30W
Byrranga Mts. Russian Fed. 59 M5 74.50N 101.00E
Bytom Poland 54 F4 50.22N 18.54E

C

Caacupé Paraguay 77 E2 25.23S 57.05W
Cabanatuan Phil. 104 G7 15.30N 120.58E
Caban Coch Resr. Wales 12 D4 52.17N 3.34W
Cabimas Venezuela 71 J3 10.26N 71.27W
Cabinda Angola 84 F1 5.34S 12.12E
Cabonga, Resr. Canada 65 K6 47.20N 76.35W
Cabot Str. Canada 63 M2 47.00N 59.00W
Cabrera, Sierra *mts.* Spain 46 B5 42.10N 6.30W
Cabriel *r.* Spain 46 E3 39.13N 1.07W
Cáceres Brazil 77 E3 16.05S 57.40W
Cáceres Spain 46 B3 39.29N 6.23W
Cachimbo, Serra do *mts.* Brazil 77 E4 8.30S 55.00W
Cachoeiro de Itapemirin Brazil 77 F2 20.51S 41.07W
Cadera, C. Venezuela 71 K3 10.40N 66.05W
Cadillac U.S.A. 65 I5 44.15N 85.23W
Cadiz Phil. 105 G6 10.57N 123.18E
Cádiz Spain 46 B2 36.32N 6.18W
Cádiz, G. of Spain 46 B2 37.00N 7.10W
Caen France 44 C6 49.11N 0.22W
Caerleon Wales 12 E3 51.36N 2.57W
Caernarfon Wales 12 C5 53.08N 4.17W
Caernarfon B. Wales 12 C5 53.05N 4.25W
Caerphilly Wales 12 D3 51.34N 3.13W
Caerphilly *d.* Wales 9 D2 51.34N 3.13W
Cagayan de Oro Phil. 105 G5 8.29N 124.40E
Cagliari Italy 50 C3 39.14N 9.07E
Cagliari, G. of Med. Sea 50 C3 39.07N 9.15E
Caha Mts. Rep. of Ire. 20 B1 51.44N 9.45W
Cahirciveen Rep. of Ire. 20 A1 51.51N 10.14W
Cahora Bassa, Lago de *l.* Mozambique 86 C3 15.33S 32.42E
Cahore Pt. Rep. of Ire. 20 E2 52.33N 6.11W
Cahors France 44 D4 44.28N 0.26E
Cahul Moldova 55 K1 45.58N 28.10E
Caiabis, Serra dos *mts.* Brazil 77 E3 12.00S 56.30W
Caiapó, Serra do *mts.* Brazil 77 E3 17.10S 52.00W
Caicos Is. Turks & Caicos Is. 71 J5 21.30N 72.00W
Cairn Gorm *mtn.* Scotland 19 F2 57.06N 3.39W
Cairngorm Mts. Scotland 19 F2 57.04N 3.30W
Cairnryan Scotland 16 D2 54.58N 5.02W
Cairns Australia 110 D4 16.51S 145.43E
Cairn Toul *mtn.* Scotland 19 F2 57.04N 3.44W
Cairo Egypt 94 D4 30.03N 31.15E
Caister-on-Sea England 11 G3 52.38N 1.43E
Caistor England 15 G2 53.29N 0.20W
Caithness *f.* Scotland 19 F3 58.25N 3.25W
Calabar Nigeria 84 E2 4.56N 8.22E
Calais France 44 D7 50.57N 1.50E
Calama Chile 76 D2 22.30S 68.55W
Calamian Group *is.* Phil. 104 G6 12.00N 120.05E
Calamocha Spain 46 E4 40.54N 1.18W
Calanscio Sand Sea *f.* Libya 53 H2 27.00N 23.00E
Calapan Phil. 104 G6 13.23N 121.10E
Călăraşi Romania 56 H6 44.11N 27.21E
Calatayud Spain 46 E4 41.21N 1.39W
Calbayog Phil. 105 G6 12.04N 124.58E
Calcanhar, Punta do *c.* Brazil 77 G4 5.06S 35.30W
Calcutta India 97 H5 22.35N 88.21E
Caldas da Rainha Portugal 46 A3 39.24N 9.08W
Caldey Island Wales 12 C3 51.38N 4.43W
Caldicot Wales 12 E3 51.36N 2.45W
Calf of Man *i.* I.o.M. 14 C3 54.03N 4.49W
Calgary Canada 62 G3 51.05N 114.05W
Cali Colombia 74 B7 3.24N 76.30W
Calicut India 96 F3 11.15N 75.45E
Caliente U.S.A. 64 D4 37.36N 114.31W
California *d.* U.S.A. 64 B4 37.00N 120.00W
California, G. of Mexico 70 B6 28.30N 112.30W
Callan Rep. of Ire. 20 D2 52.33N 7.23W
Callander Scotland 16 E4 56.15N 4.13W
Callanish Scotland 18 C3 58.12N 6.45W
Callao Peru 76 C3 12.05S 77.08W
Callington England 13 C2 50.30N 4.19W
Calne England 10 D2 51.26N 2.00W
Caltanissetta Italy 50 F2 37.30N 14.05E
Calvi France 44 H3 42.34N 8.44E
Cam *r.* England 11 F3 52.34N 0.21E
Camaçari Brazil 77 G3 12.44S 38.16W
Camagüey Cuba 71 I5 21.25N 77.55W
Camagüey, Archipelago de Cuba 71 I5 22.30N 78.00W
Cambay, G. of India 96 E5 20.30N 72.00E
Camberley England 10 E2 51.21N 0.45W
Cambodia Asia 104 C6 12.00N 105.00E
Camborne England 13 B2 50.12N 5.19W
Cambrai France 42 C2 50.10N 3.14E
Cambrian Mts. Wales 12 D4 52.33N 3.33W
Cambridge England 11 F3 52.13N 0.08E
Cambridge Bay *town* Canada 62 H4 69.09N 105.00W
Cambridgeshire *d.* England 9 E3 52.15N 0.05W
Camelford England 13 C2 50.37N 4.41W
Cameroon Africa 84 F2 6.00N 12.30E
Cameroun, Mt. Cameroon 84 E2 4.20N 9.05E
Cametá Brazil 77 F4 2.12S 49.30W
Campbell I. Pacific Oc. 108 L1 52.30S 169.02E
Campbell River *town* Canada 62 F3 50.00N 125.18W
Campbellton Canada 65 M6 48.00N 66.40W
Campbeltown Scotland 16 D3 55.25N 5.36W
Campeche Mexico 70 F4 19.50N 90.30W
Campeche *d.* Mexico 70 F4 19.00N 90.00W
Campeche B. Mexico 70 F4 19.30N 94.00W
Campina Grande Brazil 77 G4 7.15S 35.53W
Campinas Brazil 77 F2 22.54S 47.06W
Campobasso Italy 50 F4 41.34N 14.39E
Campo Grande Brazil 77 E2 20.24S 54.35W
Campos Brazil 77 F2 21.46S 41.21W
Cam Ranh Vietnam 104 D6 11.54N 109.14E
Camrose Wales 12 B3 51.50N 5.01W
Canada N. America 62 H3 60.00N 105.00W
Canadian *r.* U.S.A. 64 G4 35.20N 95.40W
Canadian Shield *f.* N. America 60 K7 50.00N 80.00W
Çanakkale Turkey 56 H4 40.09N 26.26E
Canal du Midi France 44 D3 43.18N 2.00E
Canary Is. Atlantic Oc. 46 X2 29.00N 15.00W
Canaveral, C. U.S.A. 65 J2 28.28N 80.28W
Canberra Australia 110 D2 35.18S 149.08E
Cancún Mexico 70 G5 21.26N 86.51W
Caniapiscau *r.* Canada 63 L3 57.40N 69.30W
Caniapiscau, Résr. Canada 63 K3 55.05N 72.40W
Canindé *r.* Brazil 77 F4 6.14S 42.51W
Canisp *mtn.* Scotland 18 D3 58.07N 5.03W
Çankaya Turkey 57 K3 39.52N 32.52E
Çankırı Turkey 57 K4 40.35N 33.37E
Canna *i.* Scotland 18 C2 57.03N 6.30W
Cannes France 44 G3 43.33N 7.00E
Cannock England 10 C3 52.42N 2.02W
Canõas Brazil 77 E2 29.55S 51.10W
Canon City U.S.A. 64 E4 38.27N 105.14W
Cantabrian Mts. Spain 46 B5 43.00N 6.00W
Canterbury England 11 G2 51.17N 1.05E
Cân Tho Vietnam 104 D6 10.03N 105.46E
Canvey Island *town* England 11 F2 51.32N 0.35E
Cao Bang Vietnam 104 D8 22.40N 106.16E
Capbreton France 44 C3 43.38N 1.15W
Cape Breton I. Canada 63 L2 46.00N 61.00W
Capel St. Mary England 11 G2 51.59N 1.02E
Cape Town R.S.A. 86 A1 33.56S 18.28E
Cape Verde Atlantic Oc. 84 B3 16.00N 24.00W
Cape York Pen. Australia 110 D4 12.40S 142.20E
Cap Haïtien *town* Haiti 71 J4 19.47N 72.17W
Capim *r.* Brazil 77 F4 1.40S 47.47W
Capraia *i.* Italy 50 C5 43.03N 9.50E
Caprera *i.* Italy 50 C4 41.48N 9.27E
Capri *i.* Italy 50 F4 40.33N 14.13E
Capricorn Channel *str.* Australia 110 E3 23.00S 152.00E
Caprivi Strip *f.* Namibia 86 B3 17.50S 23.10E
Caquetá *r.* Colombia 76 C4 1.20S 70.50W
Carabay, Cordillera de *mts.* Peru 76 C3 13.50S 71.00W
Caracal Romania 56 G6 44.08N 24.18E
Caracas Venezuela 71 K3 10.35N 66.56W
Carajás, Serra dos *mts.* Brazil 77 E4 5.00S 51.00W
Caratasca Lagoon Honduras 71 H4 15.10N 84.00W
Caratinga Brazil 77 F3 19.50S 42.06W
Caravaca de la Cruz Spain 46 E3 38.06N 1.51W
Carbonara, C. Italy 50 C3 39.06N 9.32E
Carcassonne France 44 E3 43.13N 2.21E
Cardiff Wales 13 D3 51.28N 3.11W
Cardiff *d.* Wales 9 D2 51.30N 3.12W
Cardigan Wales 12 C4 52.06N 4.41W
Cardigan B. Wales 12 C4 52.30N 4.30W
Carei Romania 54 H2 47.42N 22.28E
Carey, L. Australia 110 B3 29.05S 122.15E
Cariacica Brazil 77 F2 20.15S 40.23W
Caribbean Sea C. America 71 I4 15.00N 75.00W
Caribou Mts. Canada 62 G3 58.30N 115.00W
Cark Mtn. Rep. of Ire. 16 B2 54.53N 7.53W
Carletonville R.S.A. 86 B2 26.21S 27.23E
Carlingford Lough Rep. of Ire./N. Ireland 16 C2 54.03N 6.09W
Carlisle England 14 E3 54.54N 2.55W
Carlow Rep. of Ire. 20 E2 52.50N 6.54W
Carlow *d.* Rep. of Ire. 20 E2 52.43N 6.50W
Carluke Scotland 17 E3 55.44N 3.51W
Carmacks Canada 62 E4 62.04N 136.21W
Carmarthen Wales 12 C3 51.52N 4.20W
Carmarthen B. Wales 12 C3 51.40N 4.30W
Carmarthenshire *d.* Wales 9 C2 52.00N 4.17W
Carmel Head Wales 12 C5 53.24N 4.35W
Carndonagh Rep. of Ire. 16 B3 55.15N 7.15W
Carnedd Llywelyn *mtn.* Wales 12 D5 53.10N 3.58W
Carnedd y Filiast *mtn.* Wales 12 D4 52.56N 3.40W
Carnegie, L. Australia 110 B3 26.15S 123.00E
Carn Eighe *mtn.* Scotland 18 D2 57.17N 5.07W
Carnforth England 14 E3 54.08N 2.47W
Carnic Alps *mts.* Italy/Austria 50 E7 46.40N 12.48E
Car Nicobar *i.* India 104 A5 9.06N 92.57E
Carnlough N. Ireland 16 D2 54.58N 6.00W
Carn nan Gabhar *mtn.* Scotland 19 F1 56.49N 3.44W
Carnot C.A.R. 84 F2 4.59N 15.56E
Carnot, C. Australia 110 C2 34.57S 135.38E
Carnoustie Scotland 17 G4 56.30N 2.44W
Carnsore Pt. Rep. of Ire. 20 E2 52.10N 6.21W
Caroline I. Kiribati 109 Q6 10.00S 150.30W
Caroline Is. Pacific Oc. 108 J7 5.00N 150.00E
Carpathian Mts. Europe 34 F2 48.45N 23.45E
Carpentaria, G. of Australia 110 C4 14.00S 140.00E
Carpentras France 44 F4 44.03N 5.03E
Carra, Lough Rep. of Ire. 20 B3 53.40N 9.15W
Carrara Italy 50 D6 44.04N 10.06E
Carrauntuohill *mtn.* Rep. of Ire. 20 B2 52.00N 9.45W
Carrickfergus N. Ireland 16 D2 54.43N 5.49W
Carrickmacross Rep. of Ire. 20 E3 53.59N 6.44W
Carrick-on-Shannon Rep. of Ire. 20 C3 53.57N 8.06W
Carrick-on-Suir Rep. of Ire. 20 D2 52.21N 7.26W
Carron *r.* Falkirk Scotland 17 F4 56.01N 3.44W
Carron *r.* High. Scotland 19 E2 57.53N 4.22W
Carrowmore Lake Rep. of Ire. 20 B4 54.11N 9.48W
Carson City U.S.A. 64 C4 39.10N 119.46W
Carsphairn Scotland 16 E3 55.13N 4.15W
Cartagena Colombia 71 I3 10.24N 75.33W
Cartagena Spain 46 E2 37.36N 0.59W
Carter Bar *pass* Scotland/England 17 G3 55.21N 2.27W
Carterton England 10 D2 51.46N 1.35W
Cartmel England 14 E3 54.12N 2.57W
Caruarú Brazil 77 G4 8.15S 35.55W
Carvin France 42 B2 50.30N 2.58E
Casablanca Morocco 84 D5 33.39N 7.35W
Cascade Range *mts.* U.S.A. 64 B5 44.00N 121.30W
Cascavel Brazil 77 E2 24.59S 53.29W
Caserta Italy 50 F4 41.06N 14.21E
Caseyr, C. Somalia 85 J3 12.00N 51.30E
Cashel Rep. of Ire. 20 D2 52.31N 7.54W
Casper U.S.A. 64 E5 42.50N 106.20W
Caspian Depression *f.* Russian Fed./Kazakstan 58 G2 47.00N 48.00E
Caspian Sea Asia 90 H7 42.00N 51.00E
Cassiar Mts. Canada 62 F3 60.00N 131.00W
Cassley *r.* Scotland 18 E3 57.58N 4.35W
Castanhal Brazil 77 F4 1.16S 47.51W
Castelló de la Plana Spain 46 E3 39.59N 0.03W
Castlebar Rep. of Ire. 20 B3 53.52N 9.19W
Castleblayney Rep. of Ire. 20 E4 54.08N 6.46W
Castle Cary England 13 E3 51.06N 2.31W
Castlecomer Rep. of Ire. 20 D2 52.48N 7.12W
Castleconnell Rep. of Ire. 20 C2 52.43N 8.30W
Castlederg N. Ireland 16 B2 54.43N 7.37W
Castle Donnington England 10 D3 52.51N 1.19W
Castle Douglas Scotland 17 F2 54.56N 3.56W
Castleford England 15 F2 53.43N 1.21W
Castleisland *town* Rep. of Ire. 20 B2 52.14N 9.29W
Castletown I.o.M. 14 C3 54.04N 4.38W
Castres France 44 E3 43.36N 2.14E
Castries St. Lucia 71 L3 14.01N 60.59W
Catamarca Argentina 76 D2 28.28S 65.46W
Catanduanes *i.* Phil. 105 G6 13.45N 124.20E
Catania Italy 50 F2 37.31N 15.05E
Catanzaro Italy 50 G3 38.55N 16.35E
Catarman Phil. 105 G6 12.28N 124.50E
Caterham England 11 E2 51.17N 0.04W
Cat I. The Bahamas 71 I5 24.30N 75.30W
Catoche, C. Mexico 70 G5 21.38N 87.08W
Catterick England 15 F3 54.23N 1.38W
Cauca *r.* Colombia 71 J2 8.57N 74.30W
Caucaia Brazil 77 G4 3.45S 38.45W
Caucasus *mts.* Europe 58 G2 43.00N 44.00E
Caudry France 42 C2 50.07N 3.25E
Cavan Rep. of Ire. 20 D3 53.59N 7.22W
Cavan *d.* Rep. of Ire. 20 D3 54.00N 7.15W
Cawston England 11 G3 52.46N 1.10E
Caxias Brazil 77 F4 4.53S 43.20W
Caxias do Sul Brazil 77 E2 29.14S 51.10W
Cayenne French Guiana 74 D7 4.55N 52.18W
Cayman Brac *i.* Cayman Is. 71 I4 19.44N 79.48W
Cayman Is. C. America 71 H4 19.00N 81.00W
Cayos Miskito *is.* Nicaragua 71 H3 14.30N 82.40W
Ceará *d.* Brazil 77 G4 4.50S 39.00W
Cebu Phil. 105 G6 10.17N 123.56E
Cebu *i.* Phil. 105 G6 10.15N 123.45E
Cedar *r.* U.S.A. 65 H5 41.15N 91.20W
Cedar City U.S.A. 64 D4 37.40N 113.04W
Cedar Rapids *town* U.S.A. 65 H5 41.59N 91.31W
Cedros *i.* Mexico 64 C2 28.15N 115.15W
Cefalù Italy 50 F3 38.01N 14.03E
Cegléd Hungary 54 F2 47.10N 19.48
Celaya Mexico 70 D5 20.32N 100.48W
Celebes Sea Indonesia 105 G4 3.00N 122.00
Celje Slovenia 54 D2 46.15N 15.16
Celle Germany 48 E5 52.37N 10.05
Cenderawasih G. Indonesia 105 J3 2.30S 135.20
Central *d.* Kenya 87 B2 1.00S 37.00
Central African Republic Africa 85 F2 6.30N 20.00
Central, Cordillera *mts.* Bolivia 76 D3 20.00S 65.00
Central, Cordillera *mts.* Colombia 74 B7 5.00N 75.20
Central, Cordillera *mts.* Peru 76 C4 7.00S 79.00
Central Range *mts.* P.N.G. 105 K3 5.00S 142.00
Central Russian Uplands *f.* Russian Fed. 55 O5 53.00N 37.00
Central Siberian Plateau *f.* Russian Fed. 59 M4 66.00N 108.00
Ceredigion *d.* Wales 9 C3 52.15N 4.00
Cernavodă Romania 57 I6 44.20N 28.02
Cerralvo *i.* Mexico 70 C5 24.17N 109.52
Cerro de Pasco Peru 76 C3 10.43S 76.15
Cervo Spain 46 B5 43.40N 7.25
České Budějovice Czech Rep. 54 D3 49.00N 14.3
Ceuta Spain 46 C1 35.53N 5.19
Cévennes *mts.* France 44 E4 44.25N 3.3
Ceyhan *r.* Turkey 57 L2 36.54N 34.5
Chad Africa 85 F3 13.00N 19.0

Criciúma Brazil **77 F2** 28.40S 49.23W
Crickhowell Wales **12 D3** 51.52N 3.08W
Crieff Scotland **17 F4** 56.23N 3.52W
Criffell *mtn.* Scotland **17 F2** 54.57N 3.38W
Crimea *pen.* Ukraine **55 N1** 45.30N 34.00E
Crimond Scotland **19 H2** 57.36N 1.55W
Cristóbal Colón *mtn.* Colombia **71 J3** 10.53N 73.48W
Croatia Europe **56 C6** 45.30N 17.00E
Cromarty Scotland **19 E2** 57.40N 4.01W
Cromarty Firth *est.* Scotland **19 E2** 57.41N 4.10W
Cromdale, Hills of Scotland **19 F2** 57.18N 3.30W
Cromer England **11 G3** 52.56N 1.18E
Cronamuck Mtn. Rep. of Ire. **16 B2** 54.54N 7.52W
Crook England **15 F3** 54.43N 1.45W
Crooked I. The Bahamas **71 J5** 22.45N 74.00W
Crooked Island Passage The Bahamas **71 J5** 22.45N 74.40W
Croom Rep. of Ire. **20 C2** 52.30N 8.42W
Crosby England **14 D2** 53.30N 3.02W
Cross Fell *mtn.* England **15 E3** 54.43N 2.28W
Crossgar N. Ireland **16 D2** 54.24N 5.45W
Crossmaglen N. Ireland **16 C2** 54.05N 6.37W
Crotone Italy **50 G3** 39.05N 17.06E
Crouch *r.* England **11 F2** 51.37N 0.45E
Crowborough England **11 F2** 51.03N 0.09E
Crowland England **11 E3** 52.41N 0.10W
Crowle England **15 G2** 53.36N 0.49W
Crowthorne England **10 E2** 51.23N 0.49W
Croyde England **13 C3** 51.07N 4.13W
Croydon England **11 E2** 51.23N 0.06W
Crozet Is. Indian Oc. **117 L2** 47.00S 52.00E
Cruden Bay *town* Scotland **19 H2** 57.24N 1.51W
Crumlin N. Ireland **16 C2** 54.38N 6.13W
Crummock Water *l.* England **14 D3** 54.33N 3.19W
Cruz, Cabo *c.* Cuba **71 I4** 19.52N 77.44W
Cruzeiro do Sul Brazil **76 C4** 7.40S 72.39W
Cuando *r.* Africa **86 B3** 18.30S 23.30E
Cuanza *r.* Angola **86 A4** 9.22S 13.09E
Cuba C. America **71 I5** 22.00N 79.00W
Cubango *r.* Botswana **86 B3** 18.30S 22.04E
Cuckfield England **11 E2** 51.00N 0.00W
Cúcuta Colombia **71 J2** 7.55N 72.31W
Cuddalore India **97 F3** 11.43N 79.46E
Cuddapah India **97 F3** 14.30N 78.30E
Cuenca Ecuador **76 C4** 2.54S 79.00W
Cuenca Spain **46 D4** 40.04N 2.07W
Cuenca, Serrania de *mts.* Spain **46 E4** 40.25N 2.00W
Cuernavaca Mexico **70 E4** 18.57N 99.15W
Cuiabá Brazil **77 E3** 15.32S 56.05W
Cuiabá *r.* Brazil **77 E3** 18.00S 57.25W
Cuilcagh *mtn.* Rep. of Ire. **16 B2** 54.12N 7.50W
Cuillin Hills Scotland **18 C2** 57.12N 6.13W
Culiacán Mexico **70 C5** 24.50N 107.23W
Cullen Scotland **19 G2** 57.42N 2.50W
Cullera Spain **46 E3** 39.10N 0.15W
Cullin Sound Scotland **18 C2** 57.05N 6.20W
Cullompton England **13 D2** 50.52N 3.23W
Cullybackey N. Ireland **16 C2** 54.53N 6.21W
Cul Mor *mtn.* Scotland **18 D3** 58.04N 5.10W
Culuene *r.* Brazil **77 E3** 12.56S 52.51W
Culzean B. Scotland **16 E3** 55.21N 4.50W
Cumaná Venezuela **71 L3** 10.29N 64.12W
Cumbal *mtn.* Colombia **76 C5** 0.59N 77.53W
Cumberland Sd. Canada **63 L4** 65.00N 65.30W
Cumbernauld Scotland **17 F3** 55.57N 4.00W
Cumbria *d.* England **9 D4** 54.40N 3.00W
Cumnock Scotland **16 E3** 55.27N 4.15W
Cunene *r.* Angola **86 A3** 17.15S 11.50E
Cuneo Italy **50 B6** 44.22N 7.32E
Cupar Scotland **17 F4** 56.19N 3.01W
Cupica, G. of Colombia **71 I2** 6.35N 77.25W
Curaçao *i.* Neth. Ant. **71 K3** 12.15N 69.00W
Curaray *r.* Peru **76 C4** 2.20S 74.05W
Curitiba Brazil **77 F2** 25.24S 49.16W
Curuá *r.* Brazil **77 E4** 5.23S 54.22W
Cushendall N. Ireland **16 C3** 55.05N 6.04W
Cuttack India **97 H5** 20.26N 85.56E
Cuxhaven Germany **48 D5** 53.52N 8.42E
Cuzco Peru **76 C3** 13.32S 72.10W
Cwmbran Wales **12 D3** 51.39N 3.01W
Cyclades *is.* Greece **56 G2** 37.00N 25.00E
Cyprus Asia **57 K1** 35.00N 33.00E
Cyrenaica *f.* Libya **53 H2** 28.00N 22.10E
Czech Republic Europe **54 D3** 49.30N 15.00
Częstochowa Poland **54 F4** 50.49N 19.07E

D

Dabrowa Gornicza Poland **54 F4** 50.22N 19.20E
Dagupan Phil. **104 G7** 16.02N 120.21E
Da Hinggan Ling *mts.* China **103 M7** 50.00N 122.10E
Dahlak Archipelago *is.* Eritrea **94 F2** 15.45N 40.30E
Dailly Scotland **16 E3** 55.18N 4.43W
Dakar Senegal **84 C3** 14.38N 17.27W
Dakhla Oasis Egypt **94 C4** 25.30N 29.00E
Dakol'ka *r.* Belarus **55 K5** 52.10N 29.00E
Dakovica Yugo. **56 E5** 42.22N 20.26E
Dalaman Turkey **57 I2** 36.47N 28.47E
Da Lat Vietnam **104 D6** 11.56N 108.25E
Dalbandin Pakistan **95 J4** 28.53N 64.25E
Dalbeattie Scotland **17 F2** 54.55N 3.49W
Dali China **103 I3** 25.42N 100.11E
Dalian China **103 M5** 38.53N 121.37E
Dalkeith Scotland **17 F3** 55.54N 3.04W
Dallas U.S.A. **64 G3** 32.47N 96.48W
Dalmally Scotland **16 E4** 56.25N 4.58W
Dalmatia *f.* Croatia **56 C5** 43.30N 17.00E
Dalmellington Scotland **16 E3** 55.19N 4.24W
Daloa Côte d'Ivoire **84 D2** 6.56N 6.28W
Dalry D. and G. Scotland **16 E3** 55.07N 4.10W
Dalry N.Ayr. Scotland **16 E3** 55.43N 4.43W
Dalrymple Scotland **16 E3** 55.24N 4.35W
Dalrymple, Mt. Australia **110 D3** 21.02S 148.38E
Dalton-in-Furness England **14 D3** 54.10N 3.11W
Daly *r.* Australia **110 C4** 13.20S 130.19E
Daman India **96 E5** 20.25N 72.58E
Damanhûr Egypt **94 D5** 31.03N 30.28E
Damar *i.* Indonesia **105 H2** 7.10S 128.30E
Damaraland *f.* Namibia **86 A2** 22.20S 16.00E
Damascus Syria **94 E5** 33.30N 36.19E
Damavand *mtn.* Iran **95 H6** 35.47N 52.04E
Damghan Iran **95 H6** 36.09N 54.22E
Dampier Australia **110 A3** 20.40S 116.42E
Dampir Str. Pacific Oc. **105 I3** 0.30S 130.50E
Da Nang Vietnam **104 D7** 16.04N 108.14E
Dande Ethiopia **87 B3** 4.53N 36.20E
Dandong China **103 M6** 40.06N 124.25E
Dane *r.* England **15 E2** 53.16N 2.30W
Danger Is. Cook Is. **108 O5** 10.53S 165.49W
Dankov Russian Fed. **55 P5** 53.15N 39.08E
Danube *r.* Europe **35 F2** 45.26N 29.38E
Danube, Mouths of the *f.* Romania **55 K1** 45.05N 29.45E
Danville U.S.A. **65 K4** 36.34N 79.25W
Dapaong Togo **84 E3** 10.58N 0.07E
Da Qaidam China **102 H5** 37.44N 95.08E
Daqing China **103 N7** 46.40N 125.00E
Dar'a Syria **94 E5** 32.37N 36.06E
Darab Iran **95 H4** 28.45N 54.34E
Darabani Romania **55 J3** 48.11N 26.35E
Daravica *mtn.* Yugo. **56 E5** 42.32N 20.08E
Darbhanga India **97 H6** 26.10N 85.54E
Dardanelles *str.* Turkey **56 H4** 40.15N 26.30E
Dar es Salaam Tanzania **86 C4** 6.51S 39.18E
Darhan Mongolia **103 J7** 49.34N 106.23E
Darién, G. of Colombia **71 I2** 9.20N 77.00W
Darjiling India **97 H6** 27.02N 88.20E
Darling *r.* Australia **110 D2** 34.05S 141.57E
Darling Downs *f.* Australia **110 D3** 28.00S 149.45E
Darlington England **15 F3** 54.33N 1.33W
Darlington *d.* England **9 E4** 54.33N 1.33W
Darmstadt Germany **48 D3** 49.52N 8.30E
Darnah Libya **85 G5** 32.45N 22.39E
Dart *r.* England **13 D2** 50.24N 3.41W
Dartford England **11 F2** 51.27N 0.14E
Dartmoor *hills* England **13 D2** 50.33N 3.55W
Dartmouth England **13 D2** 50.21N 3.35W
Darton England **15 F2** 53.36N 1.32W
Daru P.N.G. **105 K2** 9.05S 143.10E
Darwen England **15 E2** 53.42N 2.29W
Darwin Australia **110 C4** 12.23S 130.44E
Daryacheh-ye-Bakhtegan *l.* Iran **95 H4** 29.20N 54.05E
Daryacheh-ye Sistan *f.* Iran **95 J5** 31.00N 61.15E
Daryacheh-ye-Tashk *l.* Iran **95 H5** 30.05N 54.00E
Dasht-e-Kavir *des.* Iran **95 H6** 34.40N 55.00E
Dasht-e-Lut *des.* Iran **95 I5** 31.30N 58.00E
Dasht-i-Arbu Lut *des.* Afghan. **95 J5** 30.00N 65.00E
Dasht-i-Margo *des.* Afghan. **95 J5** 30.45N 63.00E
Datong China **103 K5** 40.12N 113.12E
Daud Khel Pakistan **95 L5** 32.53N 71.34E
Daugava *r.* Europe **43 F2** 57.03N 24.00E
Daugavpils Latvia **43 F1** 55.52N 26.31E
Dauphin Canada **62 H3** 51.09N 100.05W
Dauphiné *f.* France **44 F4** 45.00N 5.45E
Davangere India **96 F3** 14.30N 75.52E
Davao Phil. **105 H5** 7.05N 125.38E
Davao G. Phil. **105 H5** 6.30N 126.00E
Davenport U.S.A. **65 H5** 41.40N 90.36W
Daventry England **10 D3** 52.16N 1.10W
David Panama **71 H2** 8.26N 82.26W
Davis Str. N. America **63 M4** 66.00N 58.00W
Dawa Wenz *r.* Ethiopia **87 C3** 4.11N 42.06E
Dawlish England **13 D2** 50.34N 3.28W
Dawqah Oman **95 H2** 18.38N 54.05E
Dawson Canada **62 E4** 64.04N 139.24W
Dawson Creek *town* Canada **62 F3** 55.44N 120.15W
Daxian China **103 J4** 31.10N 107.28E
Dayr az Zawr Syria **94 F6** 35.20N 40.08E
Dayton U.S.A. **65 J4** 39.45N 84.10W
Daytona Beach *town* U.S.A. **65 J2** 29.11N 81.01W
Dead Sea Jordan **94 E5** 31.25N 35.30E
Deal England **11 G2** 51.13N 1.25E
Death Valley *f.* U.S.A. **64 C4** 36.00N 116.45W
Debak Malaysia **104 E4** 1.30N 111.28E
Debar Macedonia **56 E4** 41.31N 20.30E
Debenham England **11 G3** 52.14N 1.10E
Debrecen Hungary **54 G2** 47.30N 21.37E
Decatur U.S.A. **65 I4** 39.44N 88.57W
Deccan *f.* India **96 F4** 18.00N 76.30E
Děčín Czech Rep. **54 D4** 50.48N 14.15E
Dee *r.* Scotland **19 G2** 57.07N 2.04W
Dee *r.* Wales **12 D5** 53.13N 3.05W
Deele *r.* Rep. of Ire. **16 B2** 54.51N 7.29W
Degodia *f.* Ethiopia **87 C3** 4.15N 41.30E
De Grey *r.* Australia **110 A3** 20.12S 119.11E
Dehra Dun India **97 F7** 30.19N 78.00E
Dej Romania **55 H2** 47.08N 23.55E
Delano Peak *mtn.* U.S.A. **64 D4** 38.23N 112.22W
Delaram Afghan. **95 J5** 32.11N 63.25E
Delaware *d.* U.S.A. **65 K4** 39.00N 75.30W
Delft Neth. **42 D4** 52.01N 4.23E
Delfzijl Neth. **42 F5** 53.20N 6.56E
Delhi India **96 F6** 28.40N 77.14E
Deliçe *r.* Turkey **57 L4** 40.27N 34.07E
De Longa Str. Russian Fed. **59 T5** 70.00N 178.00E
Del Rio U.S.A. **64 F2** 29.23N 100.56W
Demirkazik *mtn.* Turkey **57 L2** 37.50N 35.10E
Democratic Republic of Congo Africa **86 B4** 2.00S 22.00E
Dempo *mtn.* Indonesia **104 C3** 4.02S 103.07E
Denakil *f.* Ethiopia/Eritrea **85 I3** 13.00N 41.00E
Denau Uzbekistan **95 K6** 38.20N 67.54E
Denbigh Wales **12 D5** 53.11N 3.25W
Denbighshire *d.* Wales **9 D3** 53.07N 3.20W
Den Burg Neth. **42 D5** 53.03N 4.47E
Dendermonde Belgium **42 D3** 51.01N 4.07E
Den Helder Neth. **42 D4** 52.58N 4.46E
Denizli Turkey **57 I2** 37.46N 29.05E
Denmark Europe **43 B1** 56.00N 9.00E
Denmark Str. Greenland/Iceland **63 P4** 66.00N 25.00W
Denny Scotland **17 F4** 56.02N 3.55W
Denpasar Indonesia **104 F2** 8.40S 115.14E
D'Entrecasteaux Is. P.N.G. **110 E5** 9.30S 150.40E
Denver U.S.A. **64 F4** 39.45N 104.58W
Dêqên China **102 H3** 28.45N 98.58E
Dera Ghazi Khan Pakistan **96 E7** 30.05N 70.44E
Dera Ismail Khan Pakistan **96 E7** 31.51N 70.56E
Derby Australia **110 B4** 17.19S 123.38E
Derby England **10 D3** 52.55N 1.28W
Derby *d.* England **9 E3** 52.55N 1.28W
Derbyshire *d.* England **9 E3** 53.12N 1.28W
Derg *r.* N. Ireland **16 B2** 54.44N 7.27W
Derg, Lough Donegal Rep. of Ire. **20 D4** 54.37N 7.55W
Derg, Lough Tipperary Rep. of Ire. **20 C2** 52.57N 8.18W
Derry *r.* Rep. of Ire. **20 E2** 52.35N 6.38W
Derryveagh Mts. Rep. of Ire. **20 C4** 55.00N 8.10W
Dersingham England **11 F3** 52.51N 0.30E
Derudeb Sudan **94 E2** 17.32N 36.06E
Derwent *r.* England **15 G2** 53.44N 0.57W
Derwent Resr. Derbys. England **15 F2** 53.24N 1.44W
Derwent Resr. Durham England **15 F3** 54.51N 2.00W
Derwent Water *l.* England **14 D3** 54.35N 3.09W
Desaguadero *r.* Argentina **75 C3** 34.00S 66.40W
Desappointement, Îles du *is.* Pacific Oc. **109 R5** 14.02S 141.24W
Desaquadero *r.* Bolivia **76 D3** 18.24S 67.05W
Dese Ethiopia **85 H3** 11.05N 39.40E
Deseado Argentina **75 C2** 47.44S 65.56W
Des Moines U.S.A. **65 H5** 41.35N 93.35W
Desna *r.* Russian Fed./Ukraine **55 L4** 50.32N 30.37E
Dessau Germany **48 F4** 51.51N 12.15E
Desvres France **42 A2** 50.40N 1.50E
Detroit U.S.A. **65 J5** 42.23N 83.05W
Deva Romania **54 H1** 45.54N 22.55E
Deventer Neth. **42 F4** 52.15N 6.10E
Deveron *r.* Scotland **19 G2** 57.40N 2.30W
Devils Lake *town* U.S.A. **64 G6** 48.08N 98.50W
Devizes England **10 D2** 51.21N 2.00W
Devon *r.* England **15 G2** 53.04N 0.50W
Devon *r.* Scotland **17 F4** 56.07N 3.52W
Devon *d.* England **9 D2** 50.50N 3.40W
Devon I. Canada **63 J5** 75.00N 86.00W
Devonport Australia **110 D1** 41.09S 146.16E
Devrez *r.* Turkey **57 L4** 41.07N 34.25E
Dewsbury England **15 F2** 53.42N 1.38W
Dezful Iran **95 G5** 32.24N 48.27E
Dezhou China **103 L5** 37.29N 116.11E
Dhahran Saudi Arabia **95 H4** 26.18N 50.08E
Dhaka Bangla. **97 I5** 23.42N 90.22E
Dhamar Yemen **94 F1** 14.33N 44.24E
Dhanbad India **97 H5** 23.47N 86.32E
Dhaulagiri *mtn.* Nepal **97 G6** 28.39N 83.28E
Dhule India **96 E5** 20.52N 74.50E
Diamantina *r.* Australia **110 C3** 26.45S 139.10E
Dibrugarh India **97 I6** 27.29N 94.56E
Dickinson U.S.A. **64 F6** 46.54N 102.48W
Dida Galgalu *f.* Kenya **87 B3** 3.00N 38.00E
Didcot England **10 D2** 51.36N 1.14W
Dieppe France **44 D6** 49.55N 1.05E
Diest Belgium **42 E2** 50.59N 5.03E
Digby Canada **65 M5** 44.30N 65.47W
Digne-les-Bains France **44 G4** 44.05N 0.14E
Dijon France **44 F5** 47.20N 5.02E
Diksmuide Belgium **42 B3** 51.01N 2.52E
Dili Indonesia **105 H2** 8.35S 125.35E
Dillon U.S.A. **64 D6** 45.14N 112.38W
Dimapur India **97 I6** 25.54N 93.45E
Dimitrovgrad Bulgaria **56 G5** 42.01N 25.34E
Dinan France **44 B6** 48.27N 2.02W
Dinant Belgium **42 D2** 50.16N 4.55E
Dinar Turkey **57 J3** 38.05N 30.09E
Dinard France **44 B6** 48.38N 2.04W
Dinaric Alps *mts.* Bosnia./Croatia **56 C6** 44.00N 16.30E
Dindigul India **97 F3** 10.23N 78.00E
Dingle Rep. of Ire. **20 A2** 52.08N 10.19W
Dingle B. Rep. of Ire. **20 A2** 52.05N 10.12W
Dingwall Scotland **19 E2** 57.35N 4.26W
Dipolog Phil. **105 G5** 8.34N 123.28E
Dire Dawa Ethiopia **85 I2** 9.35N 41.50E
Dirranbandi Australia **110 D3** 28.35S 148.10E
Disappointment, C. South Georgia **75 F1** 54.53S 36.08W
Disappointment, L. Australia **110 B3** 23.30S 122.55E
Disko I. Greenland **63 M4** 69.45N 53.00W
Diss England **11 G3** 52.23N 1.06E
Distington England **14 D3** 54.36N 3.32W
District of Columbia *d.* U.S.A. **65 K4** 38.55N 77.00W
Distrito Federal *d.* Brazil **77 F3** 15.45S 47.50W
Distrito Federal *d.* Mexico **70 E4** 19.20N 99.10W
Diu India **96 E5** 20.41N 70.59E
Divinópolis Brazil **77 F2** 20.08S 44.55W
Divriği Turkey **57 N3** 39.23N 38.06E
Dixon Entrance *str.* Canada/U.S.A. **62 E3** 54.10N 133.30W
Diyarbakır Turkey **94 F6** 37.55N 40.14E
Djado Plateau *f.* Niger **84 F4** 22.00N 12.30E
Djelfa Algeria **84 E5** 34.43N 3.14E
Djibouti Africa **85 I3** 12.00N 42.50E
Djibouti *town* Djibouti **85 I3** 11.35N 43.11E
Dnieper *r.* Europe **55 M2** 46.30N 32.25E
Dniestr *r.* Europe **55 K2** 46.21N 30.20E
Dniprodzerzhyns'k Ukraine **55 N3** 48.30N 34.37E
Dnipropetrovs'k Ukraine **55 N3** 48.29N 35.00E
Dniprorudne Ukraine **55 N2** 47.23N 34.57E
Doberai Pen. Indonesia **105 I3** 1.10S 132.30E
Doboj Bosnia. **56 D6** 44.44N 18.02E
Dobrich Bulgaria **57 H5** 43.34N 27.52E
Dobrovelychkivka Ukraine **55 L3** 48.23N 31.11E
Dochart *r.* Scotland **16 E4** 56.30N 4.17W
Docking England **11 F3** 52.55N 0.39E
Dodecanese *is.* Greece **53 I4** 37.00N 27.00E
Dodge City U.S.A. **64 F4** 37.45N 100.02W
Dodman Pt. England **13 C2** 50.13N 4.48W
Dodoma Tanzania **86 C4** 6.10S 35.40E
Doetinchem Neth. **42 F3** 51.57N 6.17E
Doha Qatar **95 H4** 25.15N 51.34E
Dokkum Neth. **42 F5** 53.20N 6.00E
Dolbenmaen Wales **12 C4** 52.58N 4.14W
Dole France **44 F5** 47.05N 5.30E
Dolgellau Wales **12 D4** 52.44N 3.53W
Dolomites *mts.* Italy **50 D7** 46.25N 11.50E
Dolo Odo Ethiopia **87 C3** 4.13N 42.08E
Dolyna Ukraine **55 H3** 49.00N 23.59E
Dolyns'ka Ukraine **55 M3** 48.06N 32.46E
Dominica Windward Is. **71 L4** 15.30N 61.30W
Dominican Republic C. America **71 J4** 18.00N 70.00W
Don *r.* Russian Fed. **35 G2** 47.06N 39.16E
Don *r.* Scotland **19 G2** 57.10N 2.05W
Donaghadee N. Ireland **16 D2** 54.39N 5.34W
Don Benito Spain **46 C3** 38.57N 5.52W
Doncaster England **15 F2** 53.31N 1.09W
Donegal Rep. of Ire. **20 C4** 54.39N 8.06W
Donegal *d.* Rep. of Ire. **20 C4** 54.52N 8.00W
Donegal B. Rep. of Ire. **20 C4** 54.32N 8.18W
Donegal Pt. Rep. of Ire. **20 B2** 52.42N 9.38W
Donets'k Ukraine **55 O2** 48.00N 37.50E
Dongfang China **103 J1** 19.04N 108.39E
Dongfangbong China **106 B5** 46.20N 133.10E
Dong Hoi Vietnam **104 D7** 17.32N 106.35E
Dongotona Mts. Sudan **87 A3** 4.00N 33.00E
Dongting Hu *l.* China **103 K3** 29.40N 113.00E
Donostia-San Sebastián Spain **46 E5** 43.19N 1.59W
Doon *r.* Scotland **16 E3** 55.26N 4.38W
Doon, Loch Scotland **16 E3** 55.15N 4.23W
Dorchester England **10 C1** 50.43N 2.28W
Dordogne *r.* France **44 C4** 45.03N 0.34W
Dordrecht Neth. **42 D3** 51.48N 4.40E
Dore, Mont *mtn.* France **44 E4** 45.32N 2.49E
Dorking England **11 E2** 51.14N 0.20W
Dornbirn Austria **54 A2** 47.25N 9.44E
Dornoch Scotland **19 E2** 57.52N 4.02W
Dornoch Firth *est.* Scotland **19 E2** 57.50N 4.04W
Döröö Nuur *l.* Mongolia **102 G7** 47.40N 93.30E
Dorset *d.* England **9 D2** 50.48N 2.25W
Dortmund Germany **48 C4** 51.32N 7.27E
Dothan U.S.A. **65 I3** 31.12N 85.25W
Douai France **44 E7** 50.22N 3.05E
Douala Cameroon **84 E2** 4.05N 9.43E
Douglas I.o.M. **14 C3** 54.09N 4.29W
Douglas Scotland **17 F3** 55.33N 3.51W
Doullens France **42 B2** 50.09N 2.21E
Doune Scotland **16 E4** 56.11N 4.04W
Dounreay Scotland **19 F3** 58.33N 3.45W
Dourados Brazil **77 E2** 22.09S 54.52W
Douro *r.* Portugal **46 A4** 41.10N 8.40W
Dove *r.* Derbys. England **10 D3** 52.50N 1.34W
Dove *r.* Suffolk England **11 G3** 52.21N 1.14E
Dover England **11 G2** 51.07N 1.19E
Dover U.S.A. **65 K4** 39.10N 75.32W
Dover, Str. of U.K./France **11 G1** 51.00N 1.30E
Down *d.* N. Ireland **20 F4** 54.20N 6.00W
Downham Market England **11 F3** 52.36N 0.22E
Downpatrick N. Ireland **16 D2** 54.21N 5.43W
Downpatrick Head Rep. of Ire. **20 B4** 54.20N 9.21W
Downton England **10 D1** 51.00N 1.44W
Dowshī Afghan. **95 K6** 35.38N 68.43E
Drachten Neth. **42 F5** 53.05N 6.06E
Drăgășani Romania **56 G6** 44.40N 24.16E
Draguignan France **44 G3** 43.32N 6.28E
Drakensberg *mts.* R.S.A. **86 B1** 30.00S 29.00E
Drama Greece **56 G4** 41.09N 24.11E
Drammen Norway **43 B2** 59.45N 10.15E
Dranmore Rep. of Ire. **20 C3** 53.16N 8.56W
Draperstown N. Ireland **16 C2** 54.48N 6.46W
Drau *r. see* **Drava** *r.* Austria **54**
Drava *r.* Yugo. **56 D6** 45.34N 18.56E
Drenthe *d.* Neth. **42 F4** 52.52N 6.30E
Dresden Germany **48 F4** 51.03N 13.45E
Dreux France **44 D6** 48.44N 1.23E
Drobeta-Turnu-Severin Romania **56 F6** 44.37N 22.39E
Drogheda Rep. of Ire. **20 E3** 53.43N 6.23W
Droitwich England **10 C3** 52.16N 2.10W
Dromore N. Ireland **16 C2** 54.24N 6.10W
Dronfield England **15 F2** 53.18N 1.29W
Drosh Pakistan **95 L6** 35.33N 71.48E
Drumheller Canada **62 G3** 51.28N 112.40W
Drummore Scotland **16 E2** 54.41N 4.54W
Druskininkai Lithuania **55 I5** 53.58N 23.58E
Druts' *r.* Belarus **55 L5** 53.03N 30.42E
Drygarn Fawr *mtn.* Wales **12 D4** 52.13N 3.39W
Drymen Scotland **16 E4** 56.04N 4.27W
Duarte, Pico Dom. Rep. **71 J4** 19.02N 70.59W
Ḍuba Saudi Arabia **94 E4** 27.21N 35.40E
Dubai U.A.E. **95 I4** 25.13N 55.17E
Dubawnt L. Canada **62 H4** 62.50N 102.00W
Dubbo Australia **110 D2** 32.16S 148.41E
Dublin Rep. of Ire. **20 E3** 53.21N 6.18W
Dublin *d.* Rep. of Ire. **20 E3** 53.20N 6.18W
Dublin B. Rep. of Ire. **20 E3** 53.20N 6.09W
Dubno Ukraine **55 I4** 50.28N 25.40E
Dubrovnik Croatia **56 D5** 42.40N 18.07E
Dubrovytsya Ukraine **55 J4** 51.38N 26.40E
Ducie I. Pacific Oc. **109 S4** 24.40S 124.48W
Dudinka Russian Fed. **59 K4** 69.27N 86.13E
Dudley England **10 C3** 52.30N 2.05W
Duero *r. see* Douro *r.* Spain **46**
Dufftown Scotland **19 F2** 57.27N 3.11W
Dugi Otok *i.* Croatia **56 B6** 44.04N 15.00E
Duisburg Germany **48 C4** 51.26N 6.45E
Dukhan Qatar **95 H4** 25.24N 50.47E
Dukou China **103 I3** 26.30N 101.40E
Dulce *r.* Argentina **76 D1** 30.40S 62.00W
Duluth U.S.A. **65 H6** 46.50N 92.10W
Dulverton England **13 D3** 51.02N 3.33W
Dumbarton Scotland **16 E3** 55.57N 4.35W
Dumfries Scotland **17 F3** 55.04N 3.37W
Dumfries and Galloway *d.* Scotland **8 D4** 55.05N 3.40W
Dumyât Egypt **94 D5** 31.26N 31.48E
Dunaff Head Rep. of Ire. **16 B3** 55.17N 7.31W
Dunany Pt. Rep. of Ire. **20 E3** 53.51N 6.15W
Dunbar Scotland **17 G4** 56.00N 2.31W
Dunblane Scotland **17 F4** 56.12N 3.59W
Duncansby Head Scotland **19 F3** 58.39N 3.01W
Dunchurch England **10 D3** 52.21N 1.19W
Dundalk Rep. of Ire. **20 E3** 54.01N 6.24W
Dundalk B. Rep. of Ire. **20 E3** 53.55N 6.17W
Dundee Scotland **17 F4** 56.28N 3.00W
Dundee City *d.* Scotland **8 D5** 56.28N 3.00W
Dundonald N. Ireland **16 D2** 54.36N 5.48W
Dundrum B. N. Ireland **16 D2** 54.12N 5.46W
Dunedin New Zealand **111 G1** 45.53S 170.31E
Dunfermline Scotland **17 F4** 56.04N 3.29W
Dungannon N. Ireland **16 C2** 54.30N 6.47W
Dungarvan Rep. of Ire. **20 D2** 52.06N 7.39W
Dungeness *c.* England **11 F1** 50.55N 0.58E
Dungiven N. Ireland **16 C2** 54.56N 6.57W
Dungun Malaysia **104 C4** 4.44N 103.26E
Dungunab Sudan **94 E3** 21.06N 37.05E
Dunholme England **15 G2** 53.18N 0.29W
Dunhua China **106 A4** 43.25N 128.20E
Dunhuang China **102 G6** 40.00N 94.40E
Dunkerque France **44 E7** 51.02N 2.23E
Dunkery Beacon *hill* England **13 D3** 51.11N 3.35W
Dun Laoghaire Rep. of Ire. **20 E3** 53.17N 6.09W
Dunleer Rep. of Ire. **20 E3** 53.49N 6.24W
Dunloy N. Ireland **16 C3** 55.02N 6.24W
Dunmore East Rep. of Ire. **20 D2** 52.09N 7.00W
Dunmurry N. Ireland **16 D2** 54.33N 6.00W
Dunnet B. Scotland **19 F3** 58.38N 3.25W
Dunnet Head Scotland **19 F3** 58.40N 3.23W
Dunoon Scotland **16 E3** 55.57N 4.57W
Duns Scotland **17 G3** 55.47N 2.20W
Dunstable England **11 E2** 51.53N 0.32W
Dunvegan, Loch Scotland **18 C2** 57.30N 6.40W
Durance *r.* France **44 F3** 43.55N 4.48
Durango Mexico **70 D5** 24.01N 104.00W
Durango *d.* Mexico **70 D5** 24.00N 104.00W
Durban R.S.A. **86 C2** 29.53S 31.00
Düren Germany **42 F2** 50.48N 6.30
Durham England **15 F3** 54.47N 1.34W

Gretna Scotland **17 F2** 55.00N 3.04W
Grey Range *mts.* Australia **110 D3** 28.30S 142.15E
Grimsby England **15 G2** 53.35N 0.05W
Grímsey *i.* Iceland **43 Y2** 66.33N 18.00W
Grímsvötn *mtn.* Iceland **43 Y2** 64.30N 17.10W
Grodno Belarus **55 H5** 53.40N 23.50E
Grodzisk Wielkopolski Poland **54 E5** 52.14N 16.22E
Groningen Neth. **42 F5** 53.13N 6.35E
Groningen *d.* Neth. **42 F5** 53.15N 6.45E
Groote Eylandt *i.* Australia **110 C4** 14.00S 136.30E
Grosseto Italy **50 D5** 42.46N 11.08E
Gross Glockner *mtn.* Austria **54 C2** 47.05N 12.50E
Groundhog *r.* Canada **63 J3** 49.40N 82.06W
Groznyy Russian Fed. **58 G2** 43.21N 45.42E
Grudziądz Poland **54 F5** 53.29N 18.45E
Gruinard B. Scotland **18 D2** 57.52N 5.26W
Guadalajara Mexico **70 D5** 20.30N 103.20W
Guadalajara Spain **46 D4** 40.37N 3.10W
Guadalcanal *i.* Solomon Is. **111 E5** 9.30S 160.00E
Guadalete *r.* Spain **46 B2** 36.37N 6.15W
Guadalope *r.* Spain **46 E4** 41.15N 0.03W
Guadalquivir *r.* Spain **46 B2** 36.50N 6.20W
Guadalupe *i.* Mexico **64 C2** 29.00N 118.25W
Guadalupe, Sierra de *mts.* Spain **46 C3** 39.30N 5.25W
Guadarrama, Sierra de *mts.* Spain **46 D4** 41.00N 3.50W
Guadeloupe C. America **71 L4** 16.20N 61.40W
Guadiana *r.* Portugal **46 B2** 37.10N 7.36W
Guadix Spain **46 D2** 37.19N 3.08W
Guajira Pen. Colombia **71 J3** 12.00N 72.00W
Guam *i.* Pacific Oc. **105 K6** 13.30N 144.40E
Guanajuato Mexico **70 D5** 21.00N 101.16W
Guanajuato *d.* Mexico **70 D5** 21.00N 101.00W
Guanare Venezuela **71 K2** 9.04N 69.45W
Guangdong *d.* China **103 K2** 23.00N 113.00E
Guangxi *d.* China **103 J2** 23.50N 109.00E
Guangyuan China **103 J4** 32.29N 105.55E
Guangzhou China **103 K2** 23.20N 113.30E
Guanipa *r.* Venezuela **71 L2** 10.00N 62.20W
Guantánamo Cuba **71 I5** 20.09N 75.14W
Guaporé *r.* Brazil **76 D3** 12.00S 65.15W
Guarapuava Brazil **77 E2** 25.22S 51.28W
Guara, Sierra de *mts.* Spain **46 E5** 42.20N 0.00
Guarda Portugal **46 B4** 40.32N 7.17W
Guatemala C. America **70 F4** 15.40N 90.00W
Guatemala City Guatemala **70 F3** 14.38N 90.22W
Guaviare *r.* Colombia **74 C7** 4.00N 67.35W
Guayaquil Ecuador **76 C4** 2.13S 79.54W
Guayaquil, Golfo de *g.* Ecuador **76 B4** 2.30S 80.00W
Guaymas Mexico **70 B6** 27.59N 110.54W
Guba Ethiopia **85 H3** 11.17N 35.20E
Gubkin Russian Fed. **55 O4** 51.18N 37.32E
Gudbrandsdalen *f.* Norway **43 B3** 62.00N 9.10E
Guelma Algeria **52 E4** 36.28N 7.26E
Guelmine Morocco **84 D4** 28.56N 10.04W
Guéret France **44 D5** 46.10N 1.52E
Guernsey *i.* Channel Is. **13 Y9** 49.27N 2.35W
Guerrero *d.* Mexico **70 D4** 18.00N 100.00W
Guge *mtn.* Ethiopia **87 B4** 6.16N 37.25E
Guiana Highlands S. America **74 D7** 4.00N 59.00W
Guildford England **11 E2** 51.14N 0.35W
Guilin China **103 K3** 25.21N 110.11E
Guinea Africa **84 C3** 10.30N 10.30W
Guinea, G. of Africa **82 D5** 3.00N 3.00E
Guinea-Bissau Africa **84 C3** 12.00N 15.30W
Guînes France **42 A2** 50.52N 1.52E
Güiria Venezuela **71 L3** 10.37N 62.21W
Guisborough England **15 F3** 54.32N 1.02W
Guise France **42 C1** 49.54N 3.39E
Guiyang China **103 J3** 26.35N 106.40E
Guizhou *d.* China **103 J3** 27.00N 106.30E
Gujarat *d.* India **96 E5** 22.45N 71.30E
Gujranwala Pakistan **96 E7** 32.06N 74.11E
Gulbarga India **96 F4** 17.22N 76.47E
Gullane Scotland **17 G4** 56.02N 2.49W
Gulu Uganda **86 C5** 2.46N 32.21E
Gumdag Turkmenistan **95 H6** 39.14N 54.33E
Gümüshane Turkey **57 N4** 40.26N 39.26E
Guna India **96 F5** 24.39N 77.19E
Gunnbjørn Fjeld *mtn.* Greenland **63 P4** 68.54N 29.48W
Guntur India **97 G4** 16.20N 80.27E
Gurgueia *r.* Brazil **77 F4** 6.45S 43.35W
Gurupi *r.* Brazil **77 F4** 1.13S 46.06W
Gushgy Turkmenistan **95 J6** 35.14N 62.15E
Guwahati India **97 I6** 26.05N 91.55E
Guyana S. America **74 D7** 5.00N 59.00W
Gwadar Pakistan **96 C6** 25.09N 62.21E
Gwalior India **97 F6** 26.12N 78.09E
Gweebarra B. Rep. of Ire. **20 C4** 54.52N 8.30W
Gweru Zimbabwe **86 B3** 19.25S 29.50E
Gwynedd *d.* Wales **9 D3** 53.00N 4.00W
Gydanskiy Pen. Russian Fed. **58 J5** 70.00N 78.30E
Gyöngyös Hungary **54 F2** 47.47N 19.56E
Győr Hungary **54 E2** 47.41N 17.40E
Gypsumville Canada **62 I3** 51.47N 98.38W
Gyzylarbat Turkmenistan **95 I6** 39.00N 56.23E

H

Haapajärvi Finland **43 F3** 63.45N 25.20E
Haapsalu Estonia **43 E2** 58.58N 23.32E
Haarlem Neth. **42 D4** 52.22N 4.38E
Habaswein Kenya **87 B3** 1.06N 39.26E
Habban Yemen **95 G1** 14.21N 47.04E
Hachijo-jima *i.* Japan **106 C2** 33.00N 139.50E
Hachinohe Japan **106 D4** 40.30N 141.30E
Haddington Scotland **17 G3** 55.57N 2.47W
Haderslev Denmark **43 B1** 55.15N 9.30E
Hadhramaut *f.* Yemen **95 G2** 16.30N 49.30E
Hadleigh England **11 F3** 52.03N 0.58E
Halabja Iraq **95 G6** 35.11N 45.59E
Haeju N. Korea **103 N5** 38.04N 125.40E
Hagadera Kenya **87 C3** 0.01N 40.21E
Hagar Nish Plateau *f.* Eritrea **94 E2** 17.00N 38.00E
Hagen Germany **42 G3** 51.22N 7.27E
Hags Head Rep. of Ire. **20 B2** 52.56N 9.29W
Hai Tanzania **87 B2** 3.19S 37.08E
Haifa Israel **94 D5** 32.49N 34.59E
Haikou China **103 K1** 20.05N 110.25E
Ha'il Saudi Arabia **94 F4** 27.31N 41.45E
Hailar China **103 L7** 49.15N 119.41E
Hailsham England **11 F1** 50.52N 0.17E
Hainan *i.* China **103 J1** 18.30N 109.40E
Hainaut *d.* Belgium **42 C2** 50.30N 3.45E
Haines U.S.A. **62 E3** 59.11N 135.23W
Hai Phong Vietnam **104 D8** 20.58N 106.41E
Haiti C. America **71 J4** 19.00N 73.00W
Haiya Sudan **94 E2** 18.17N 36.21E
Hajmah Oman **95 I2** 19.55N 56.15E
Hakodate Japan **106 D4** 41.46N 140.44E
Halden Norway **43 B2** 59.08N 11.13E
Halesowen England **10 C3** 52.27N 2.02W
Halesworth England **11 G3** 52.21N 1.30E
Halifax Canada **63 L2** 44.38N 63.35W
Halifax England **15 F2** 53.43N 1.51W
Halkirk Scotland **19 F3** 58.30N 3.30W
Halladale *r.* Scotland **19 F3** 58.32N 3.53W
Hall Beach *town* Canada **63 J4** 68.40N 81.30W
Halle Belgium **42 D2** 50.45N 4.14E
Halle Germany **48 E4** 51.28N 11.58E
Hall Is. Fed. States of Micronesia **108 K7** 8.37N 152.00E
Hall's Creek *town* Australia **110 B4** 18.13S 127.39E
Halmahera *i.* Indonesia **105 H4** 0.45N 128.00E
Halmstad Sweden **43 C2** 56.41N 12.55E
Halstead England **11 F2** 51.57N 0.39E
Haltwhistle England **15 E3** 54.58N 2.27W
Ham France **42 C1** 49.45N 3.04E
Hamadan Iran **95 G5** 34.47N 48.33E
Ḥamāh Syria **94 E6** 35.09N 36.44E
Hamamatsu Japan **106 C2** 34.42N 137.42E
Hamar Norway **43 B3** 60.47N 10.55E
Hambleton Hills England **15 F3** 54.15N 1.11W
Hamburg Germany **48 D5** 53.33N 10.00E
Hämeenlinna Finland **43 F3** 61.00N 24.25E
Hamersley Range *mts.* Australia **110 A3** 22.00S 118.00E
Hamhung N. Korea **103 N5** 39.54N 127.35E
Hami China **102 G6** 42.40N 93.30E
Hamilton Bermuda **71 L7** 32.18N 64.48W
Hamilton Canada **65 K5** 43.15N 79.50W
Hamilton New Zealand **111 G2** 37.47S 175.17E
Hamilton Scotland **16 E3** 55.46N 4.02W
Hamim, Wadi al *r.* Libya **53 H3** 32.06N 23.58E
Hamina Finland **43 F3** 60.33N 27.15E
Hamm Germany **48 C4** 51.40N 7.49E
Hammamet, G. of Tunisia **52 F4** 36.05N 10.40E
Hammerdal Sweden **43 C3** 63.35N 15.20E
Hammerfest Norway **43 E5** 70.40N 23.44E
Hampshire *d.* England **9 E2** 51.10N 1.20W
Hampshire Downs *hills* England **10 D2** 51.18N 1.25W
Hamstreet England **11 F2** 51.03N 0.52E
Hamun-e Jaz Murian *l.* Iran **95 I4** 27.00N 59.20E
Hanamaki Japan **106 D3** 39.23N 141.07E
Handa I. Scotland **18 D3** 58.23N 5.12W
Handan China **103 K5** 36.37N 114.26E
Handeni Tanzania **87 B2** 5.26S 38.02E
Hanggin Houqi China **103 J6** 40.52N 107.04E
Hangzhou China **103 M4** 30.10N 120.07E
Hanmni Mashkel *l.* Pakistan **95 J4** 28.15N 63.00E
Hannibal U.S.A. **65 H4** 39.41N 91.25W
Hannover Germany **48 D5** 52.23N 9.44E
Hanoi Vietnam **104 D8** 21.01N 105.52E
Hantsavichy Belarus **55 J5** 52.49N 26.29E
Hanzhong China **103 J4** 33.08N 107.04E
Haparanda Sweden **43 E4** 65.50N 24.05E
Happy Valley-Goose Bay *town* Canada **63 L3** 53.16N 60.14W
Harare Zimbabwe **86 C3** 17.43S 31.05E
Harbin China **103 N7** 45.45N 126.41E
Hardangervidda *f.* Norway **43 A3** 60.20N 8.00E
Harderwijk Neth. **42 E4** 52.21N 5.37E
Haren Germany **42 G4** 52.48N 7.15E
Hargele Ethiopia **87 C4** 5.19N 42.04E
Hargeysa Somalia **85 I2** 9.31N 44.02E
Har Hu *l.* China **102 H5** 38.20N 97.40E
Hari *r.* Afghan. **95 J6** 35.42N 61.12E
Haria Canary Is. **46 Z2** 29.09N 13.30W
Harlech Wales **12 C4** 52.52N 4.08W
Harleston England **11 G3** 52.25N 1.18E
Harlingen Neth. **42 E5** 53.10N 5.25E
Harlow England **11 F2** 51.47N 0.08E
Harney Basin *f.* U.S.A. **64 C5** 43.20N 119.00W
Härnösand Sweden **43 D3** 62.37N 17.55E
Har Nuur *l.* Mongolia **102 G7** 48.10N 93.30E
Harpenden England **11 E2** 51.49N 0.22W
Harray, Loch of Scotland **19 F4** 59.03N 3.15W
Harricana *r.* Canada **63 K3** 51.10N 79.45W
Harris *i.* Scotland **18 C2** 57.50N 6.55W
Harris, Sd. of Scotland **18 B2** 57.43N 7.05W
Harrisburg U.S.A. **65 K5** 40.35N 76.59W
Harrison, C. Canada **63 M3** 55.00N 58.00W
Harrogate England **15 F2** 53.59N 1.32W
Hârsova Romania **57 H6** 44.41N 27.56E
Harstad Norway **43 D5** 68.48N 16.30E
Harteigan *mtn.* Norway **43 A3** 60.11N 7.05E
Harter Fell *mtn.* England **14 E3** 54.27N 2.51W
Hart Fell *mtn.* Scotland **17 F3** 55.25N 3.25W
Hartford U.S.A. **65 L5** 41.40N 72.51W
Hartland England **13 C2** 50.59N 4.29W
Hartland Pt. England **13 C3** 51.01N 4.32W
Hartlepool England **15 F3** 54.42N 1.11W
Hartlepool *d.* England **9 E3** 54.42N 1.11W
Har Us Nuur *l.* Mongolia **102 G7** 48.10N 92.10E
Harwich England **11 G2** 51.56N 1.18E
Haryana *d.* India **96 F6** 29.15N 76.00E
Haslemere England **10 E2** 51.05N 0.41W
Hasselt Belgium **42 E2** 50.56N 5.20E
Hassi Messaoud Algeria **84 E5** 31.43N 6.03E
Hässleholm Sweden **43 C2** 56.09N 13.45E
Hastings England **11 F1** 50.51N 0.36E
Hatfield England **15 F2** 53.36N 0.59W
Ha Tinh Vietnam **104 D7** 18.21N 105.55E
Hatteras, C. U.S.A. **65 K4** 35.14N 75.31W
Hattiesburg U.S.A. **65 I3** 31.25N 89.19W
Haud *f.* Ethiopia **85 I2** 8.00N 46.00E
Haugesund Norway **43 A2** 59.25N 5.16E
Haukivesi *l.* Finland **43 G3** 62.10N 28.30E
Haut Folin *mtn.* France **44 E5** 47.00N 4.00E
Hauts Plateaux Algeria **52 C3** 34.00N 0.10W
Havana Cuba **71 H5** 23.07N 82.25W
Havant England **10 E1** 50.51N 0.59W
Havel *r.* Germany **48 F5** 52.51N 11.57E
Haverfordwest Wales **12 C3** 51.48N 4.59W
Haverhill England **11 F3** 52.06N 0.27E
Havre U.S.A. **64 E6** 48.34N 109.45W
Havre-St.-Pierre Canada **63 L3** 50.15N 63.36W
Hawaii *i.* Hawaiian Is. **108 P8** 19.30N 155.30W
Hawaiian Is. Pacific Oc. **108 O9** 21.00N 160.00W
Hawarden Wales **12 D5** 53.11N 3.02W
Hawes England **15 E3** 54.18N 2.12W
Haweswater Resr. England **14 E3** 54.30N 2.45W
Hawick Scotland **17 G3** 55.25N 2.47W
Hawke B. New Zealand **111 G2** 39.18S 177.15E
Hawkhurst England **11 F2** 51.02N 0.31E
Hawthorne U.S.A. **64 C4** 38.13N 118.37W
Haxby England **15 F3** 54.02N 1.06W
Hay Australia **110 D2** 34.21S 144.31E
Hay *r.* Canada **62 G3** 60.49N 115.52W
Haydarabad Iran **94 G6** 37.09N 45.27E
Haydon Bridge England **15 E3** 54.58N 2.14W
Hayle England **13 B2** 50.12N 5.25W
Hay-on-Wye Wales **12 D4** 52.04N 3.09W
Hay River *town* Canada **62 G4** 60.51N 115.42W
Haywards Heath *town* England **11 E1** 51.00N 0.05W
Hazarajat *f.* Afghan. **95 K5** 33.00N 66.00E
Hazebrouck France **42 B2** 50.43N 2.32E
Heacham England **11 F3** 52.55N 0.30E
Headcorn England **11 F2** 51.11N 0.37E
Heanor England **15 F2** 53.01N 1.20W
Heathfield England **11 F1** 50.58N 0.18E
Hebei *d.* China **103 L5** 39.20N 117.15E
Hebron Jordan **94 E5** 31.32N 35.06E
Hecate Str. Canada **62 E3** 53.00N 131.00W
Hechi China **103 J2** 24.42N 108.02E
Heckington England **15 G1** 52.59N 0.18W
Hede Sweden **43 C3** 62.27N 13.30E
Heerenveen Neth. **42 E4** 52.57N 5.55E
Heerlen Neth. **42 E2** 50.53N 5.59E
Hefei China **103 L4** 31.55N 117.18E
Hegang China **103 O7** 47.36N 130.30E
Heidelberg Germany **48 D3** 49.25N 8.42E
Heighington England **15 G2** 53.12N 0.28W
Heilbronn Germany **48 D3** 49.08N 9.14E
Heilongjiang *d.* China **103 N7** 47.00N 126.00E
Heinola Finland **43 F3** 61.13N 26.05E
Hekla *mtn.* Iceland **43 Y2** 64.00N 19.45W
Helena U.S.A. **64 D6** 46.35N 112.00W
Helensburgh Scotland **16 E4** 56.01N 4.44W
Heligoland B. Germany **48 D6** 54.00N 8.15E
Hellín Spain **46 E3** 38.31N 1.43W
Helmand *r.* Asia **95 J5** 31.10N 61.20E
Helmond Neth. **42 E3** 51.28N 5.40E
Helmsdale Scotland **19 F3** 58.08N 3.40W
Helmsdale *r.* Scotland **19 F3** 58.06N 3.40W
Helmsley England **15 F3** 54.14N 1.04W
Helong China **106 A4** 42.38N 128.58E
Helsingborg Sweden **43 C2** 56.05N 12.45E
Helsingør Denmark **43 C2** 56.03N 12.38E
Helsinki Finland **43 F3** 60.08N 25.00E
Helston England **13 B2** 50.07N 5.17W
Helvellyn *mtn.* England **14 D3** 54.31N 3.00W
Hemel Hempstead England **11 E2** 51.46N 0.28W
Henan *d.* China **103 K4** 33.45N 113.00E
Henares *r.* Spain **46 D4** 40.26N 3.35W
Henderson I. Pacific Oc. **109 S4** 24.20S 128.20W
Hendon England **11 E2** 51.35N 0.14W
Henfield England **11 E1** 50.56N 0.17W
Hengelo Neth. **42 F4** 52.16N 6.46E
Hengoed Wales **12 D3** 51.39N 3.14W
Hengyang China **103 K3** 26.58N 112.31E
Heniches'k Ukraine **55 N2** 46.10N 34.49E
Henley-on-Thames England **10 E2** 51.32N 0.53W
Hennef Germany **42 G2** 50.47N 7.17E
Henrietta Maria, C. Canada **63 J3** 55.00N 82.15W
Henzada Myanmar **97 J4** 17.38N 95.35E
Herat Afghan. **95 J5** 34.21N 62.10E
Hereford England **10 C3** 52.04N 2.43W
Herefordshire *d.* England **9 D3** 52.04N 2.43W
Herm *i.* Channel Is. **13 Y9** 49.28N 2.27W
Herma Ness *c.* Scotland **19 Z9** 60.50N 0.54W
Hermosillo Mexico **70 B6** 29.15N 110.59W
Herne Germany **42 G3** 51.32N 7.12E
Herne Bay *town* England **11 G2** 51.23N 1.10E
Herning Denmark **43 B2** 56.08N 9.00E
Hertford England **11 E2** 51.48N 0.05W
Hertfordshire *d.* England **9 E2** 51.51N 0.05W
Heswall England **14 D2** 53.20N 3.06W
Hetton England **15 E3** 54.01N 2.05W
Hexham England **15 E3** 54.58N 2.06W
Heysham England **14 E3** 54.03N 2.53W
Heywood England **15 E2** 53.36N 2.13W
Hidaka-sammyaku *mts.* Japan **106 D4** 42.50N 143.00E
Hidalgo *d.* Mexico **70 E5** 20.50N 98.30W
Hidalgo del Parral Mexico **70 C6** 26.58N 105.40W
Higashi-suido *str.* Japan **106 A2** 34.00N 129.30E
Higham Ferrers England **11 E3** 52.18N 0.36W
High Atlas *mts.* Morocco **84 D5** 32.00N 5.50W
Highbridge England **13 E3** 51.13N 2.59W
Highclere England **10 D2** 51.22N 1.22W
Highland *d.* Scotland **8 C5** 57.42N 5.00W
High Peak *mtn.* England **15 F2** 53.22N 1.48W
High Seat *hill* England **15 E3** 54.23N 2.18W
Highworth England **10 D2** 51.38N 1.42W
High Wycombe England **10 E2** 51.38N 0.46W
Hiiumaa *i.* Estonia **43 E2** 58.50N 22.30E
Hijaz *f.* Saudi Arabia **94 E4** 26.00N 37.30E
Hildesheim Germany **48 D5** 52.09N 9.58E
Hillerød Denmark **43 C1** 55.56N 12.18E
Hillside Scotland **19 G1** 56.45N 2.29W
Hilpsford Pt. England **14 D3** 54.02N 3.10W
Hilversum Neth. **42 E4** 52.14N 5.12E
Himachal Pradesh *d.* India **96 F7** 31.45N 77.30E
Himalaya *mts.* Asia **97 G6** 29.00N 84.00E
Hinckley England **10 D3** 52.33N 1.21W
Hinderwell England **15 G3** 54.32N 0.46W
Hindhead England **10 E2** 51.06N 0.42W
Hindley England **14 E2** 53.32N 2.35W
Hindu Kush *mts.* Asia **95 K6** 36.40N 70.00E
Hinnøya *i.* Norway **43 C5** 68.30N 16.00E
Hiraman *r.* Kenya **87 B2** 1.05S 39.55E
Hirosaki Japan **106 D4** 40.34N 140.28E
Hiroshima Japan **106 B2** 34.30N 132.27E
Hirson France **42 D1** 49.56N 4.05E
Hirwaun Wales **12 D3** 51.43N 3.30W
Hispaniola *i.* C. America **71 J5** 20.00N 71.00W
Hitachi Japan **106 D3** 36.35N 140.40E
Hitchin England **11 E2** 51.57N 0.16W
Hitra *i.* Norway **43 B3** 63.30N 8.50E
Hiva Oa *i.* Marquesas Is. **109 R5** 9.45S 139.00W
Hjälmaren *l.* Sweden **43 C2** 59.10N 15.45E
Hjørring Denmark **43 B2** 57.28N 9.59E
Hlybokaye Belarus **55 J6** 55.07N 27.42E
Hobart Australia **110 D1** 42.54S 147.18E
Hobro Denmark **43 B2** 56.38N 9.48E
Hô Chi Minh Vietnam **104 D6** 10.46N 106.43E
Hoddesdon England **11 E2** 51.46N 0.01W
Hodeida Yemen **94 F1** 14.50N 42.58E
Hodnet England **10 C3** 52.51N 2.35W
Hoek van Holland Neth. **42 D3** 51.59N 4.08E
Hof Germany **48 E4** 50.19N 11.56E
Höfn Iceland **43 Z2** 64.16N 15.10W
Hofsjökull *mtn.* Iceland **43 Y2** 64.50N 19.00W
Hofuf Saudi Arabia **95 G4** 25.20N 49.34E
Hoggar *mts.* Algeria **84 E4** 24.00N 5.50E
Hohhot China **103 K6** 40.49N 111.37E
Hokkaido *i.* Japan **106 D4** 43.00N 144.00E
Holbæk Denmark **43 B1** 55.42N 11.41E
Holbeach England **11 F3** 52.48N 0.01E
Holbeach Marsh England **11 F3** 52.50N 0.05E
Holbrook U.S.A. **64 E3** 34.58N 110.00W
Holderness *f.* England **15 G2** 53.45N 0.05W
Holguín Cuba **71 I5** 20.54N 76.15W
Hollabrunn Austria **54 E3** 48.34N 16.05E
Holland Fen *f.* England **15 G2** 53.02N 0.12W
Hollesley B. England **11 G3** 52.02N 1.33E
Hollington England **11 F1** 50.51N 0.32E
Hollingworth England **15 F2** 53.28N 1.59W
Holme-on-Spalding-Moor England **15 G2** 53.50N 0.47W
Holmfirth England **15 F2** 53.34N 1.48W
Holon Israel **94 D5** 32.01N 34.46E
Holstebro Denmark **43 B2** 56.22N 8.38E
Holsworthy England **13 C2** 50.48N 4.21W
Holt England **11 G3** 52.55N 1.04E
Holyhead Wales **12 C5** 53.18N 4.38W
Holyhead B. Wales **12 C5** 53.22N 4.40W
Holy I. England **15 F4** 55.41N 1.47W
Holy I. Wales **12 C5** 53.15N 4.38W
Holywell Wales **12 D5** 53.17N 3.13W
Homa Bay *town* Kenya **87 A2** 0.32S 34.27E
Homayunshahr Iran **95 H5** 32.42N 51.28E
Homburg Germany **42 G1** 49.19N 7.20E
Home B. Canada **63 L4** 69.00N 66.00W
Homs Syria **94 E5** 34.44N 36.43E
Homyel Belarus **55 L5** 52.25N 31.00E
Hondo *r.* Mexico **70 G4** 18.33N 88.22W
Honduras C. America **70 G4** 15.00N 87.00W
Honduras, G. of Carib. Sea **60 K3** 16.20N 87.30W
Hønefoss Norway **43 B3** 60.10N 10.16E
Hong Kong China **103 K2** 22.30N 114.10E
Honiara Solomon Is. **111 E5** 9.27S 159.57E
Honiton England **13 D2** 50.48N 3.13W
Honley England **15 F2** 53.34N 1.46W
Honolulu Hawaiian Is. **108 P9** 21.19N 157.50W
Honshu *i.* Japan **106 C3** 36.00N 138.00E
Hood, Mt. U.S.A. **64 B6** 45.23N 121.41W
Hood Pt. Australia **110 A2** 34.23S 119.34E
Hoogeveen Neth. **42 F4** 52.44N 6.29E
Hook England **10 E2** 51.17N 0.55W
Hook Head Rep. of Ire. **20 E2** 52.07N 6.55W
Hooper Bay *town* U.S.A. **62 B4** 61.29N 166.10W
Hoorn Neth. **42 E4** 52.38N 5.03E
Hopedale Canada **63 L3** 55.30N 60.10W
Hope, Loch Scotland **19 E3** 58.27N 4.38W
Hope, Pt. U.S.A. **59 V4** 68.00N 167.00W
Horley England **11 E2** 51.11N 0.11W
Horlivka Ukraine **55 P3** 48.17N 38.05E
Hormuz, Str. of Asia **95 I4** 26.35N 56.20E
Horn *c.* Iceland **43 X2** 66.28N 22.27W
Horn, C. S. America **75 C1** 55.47S 67.00W
Hornavan *l.* Sweden **43 D4** 66.15N 17.40E
Horncastle England **15 G2** 53.13N 0.08W
Hornepayne Canada **65 J6** 49.14N 84.48W
Hornsea England **15 G2** 53.55N 0.10W
Horodnya Ukraine **55 L4** 51.54N 31.37E
Horodok Ukraine **55 H3** 49.48N 23.39E
Horrabridge England **13 C2** 50.30N 4.05W
Horsens Denmark **43 B1** 55.53N 9.53E
Horsham Australia **110 D2** 36.45S 142.15E
Horsham England **11 E2** 51.04N 0.20W
Horten Norway **43 B2** 59.25N 10.30E
Horwich England **14 E2** 53.37N 2.33W
Hospitalet de Llobregat Spain **46 G4** 41.20N 2.06E
Hotan China **102 E5** 37.07N 79.57E
Houffalize Belgium **42 E2** 50.08N 5.50E
Houghton-le-Spring England **15 F3** 54.51N 1.28W
Houghton Regis England **11 E2** 51.51N 0.30W
Hourn, Loch Scotland **18 D2** 57.05N 5.35W
Houston U.S.A. **65 G2** 29.45N 95.25W
Hovd Mongolia **102 G7** 48.00N 91.45E
Hove England **11 E1** 50.50N 0.10W
Hoveton England **11 G3** 52.45N 1.23E
Howden England **15 G2** 53.45N 0.52W
Howland I. Pacific Oc. **108 N7** 0.48N 176.38W
Hoy *i.* Scotland **19 F3** 58.51N 3.17W
Hoyanger Norway **43 A3** 61.13N 6.05E
Hoyerswerda Germany **48 G4** 51.26N 14.14E
Hövsgöl Nuur *l.* Mongolia **103 I8** 51.00N 100.30E
Hradec Králové Czech Rep. **54 D4** 50.13N 15.50E
Huacho Peru **76 C3** 11.05S 77.36W
Huaibei China **103 L4** 33.58N 116.50E
Huainan China **103 L4** 32.41N 117.06E
Huallaga *r.* Peru **76 C4** 5.05S 75.36W
Huambo Angola **86 A3** 12.47S 15.44E
Huancayo Peru **76 C3** 12.15S 75.12W
Huang He *r.* China **103 L5** 37.55N 118.46E
Huangshi China **103 L4** 30.13N 115.05E
Huascaran *mtn.* Peru **74 B6** 9.20S 77.36W
Hubei *d.* China **103 K4** 31.15N 112.15E
Hubli India **96 E4** 15.20N 75.14E
Hucknall England **15 F2** 53.03N 1.12W
Huddersfield England **15 F2** 53.38N 1.49W
Hudiksvall Sweden **43 D3** 61.45N 17.10E
Hudson *r.* U.S.A. **65 L5** 40.45N 74.00W
Hudson B. Canada **63 J3** 58.00N 86.00W
Hudson Str. Canada **63 K4** 62.00N 70.00W
Huê Vietnam **104 D7** 16.28N 107.35E
Huelva Spain **46 B2** 37.15N 6.56W
Huércal-Overa Spain **46 E2** 37.23N 1.56W
Huesca Spain **46 E5** 42.02N 0.25W
Huila *mtn.* Colombia **76 C5** 3.00N 75.59W
Huizhou China **103 K2** 23.05N 114.29E
Hulin China **106 B5** 45.44N 132.59E
Hull Canada **65 K6** 45.26N 75.45W
Hulun Nur *l.* China **103 L7** 49.00N 117.20E
Humber, Mouth of the England **15 G2** 53.40N 0.12W
Humphreys Peak *mtn.* U.S.A. **64 D4** 35.21N 111.41W
Húnaflói *b.* Iceland **43 X2** 65.45N 20.50W
Hunan *d.* China **103 K3** 27.30N 111.30E
Hunchun China **106 B4** 42.55N 130.28E
Hunchun *r.* China **106 B4** 42.42N 130.10E

Northamptonshire *d.* England **9 E3** 52.15N 1.00W
North Ayrshire *d.* Scotland **8 C4** 55.30N 5.00W
North Battleford Canada **62 H3** 52.47N 108.19W
North Bay *town* Canada **63 K2** 46.20N 79.28W
North Berwick Scotland **17 G4** 56.04N 2.43W
North C. New Zealand **111 G2** 34.28S 173.00E
North C. Norway **43 F5** 71.10N 25.45E
North Carolina *d.* U.S.A. **65 K4** 35.30N 79.00W
North Cave England **15 G2** 53.47N 0.39W
North Channel U.K. **16 D2** 55.00N 5.30W
North China Plain *f.* China **90 M6** 34.30N 117.00E
North Dakota *d.* U.S.A. **64 F6** 47.00N 100.00W
North Donets *r.* Ukraine/Russian Fed. **55 O3** 49.08N 37.28E
North Dorset Downs *hills* England **10 C1** 50.46N 2.25W
North Downs *hills* England **11 F2** 51.18N 0.40E
North Dvina *r.* Russian Fed. **58 G4** 64.40N 40.50E
North-Eastern *d.* Kenya **87 C3** 1.00N 40.00E
North East Lincolnshire *d.* England **9 E3** 53.33N 0.10W
Northern Ireland *d.* U.K. **16 C2** 54.40N 6.45W
Northern Mariana Is. Pacific Oc. **105 K7** 15.00N 145.00E
Northern Sporades *is.* Greece **56 F3** 39.00N 24.00E
Northern Territory *d.* Australia **110 C4** 20.00S 133.00E
North Esk *r.* Scotland **19 G1** 56.45N 2.25W
North European Plain *f.* Europe **34 F3** 56.00N 27.00E
North Foreland *c.* England **11 G2** 51.23N 1.26E
North Frisian Is. Germany **48 D6** 54.30N 8.00E
North Hykeham England **15 G2** 53.10N 0.36W
North I. New Zealand **111 G2** 39.00S 175.00E
North Korea Asia **103 N6** 40.00N 128.00E
North Lanarkshire *d.* Scotland **8 D4** 55.50N 3.50W
North Lincolnshire *d.* England **9 E3** 53.35N 0.40W
North Pacific Ocean **108 N10** 35.00N 170.00W
North Platte U.S.A. **64 F5** 41.09N 100.45W
North Platte *r.* U.S.A. **64 F5** 41.09N 100.55W
North Ronaldsay *i.* Scotland **19 G4** 59.23N 2.26W
North Ronaldsay Firth *est.* Scotland **19 G4** 59.20N 2.25W
North Sea Europe **34 D3** 56.00N 4.00E
North Shields England **15 F4** 55.01N 1.26W
North Somercotes England **15 H2** 53.28N 0.08W
North Somerset *d.* England **9 D2** 51.20N 2.45W
North Sunderland England **15 F4** 55.34N 1.39W
North Tidworth England **10 D2** 51.14N 1.40W
North Tyne *r.* England **15 E3** 54.59N 2.08W
North Ugie *r.* Scotland **19 H2** 57.31N 1.48W
North Uist *i.* Scotland **18 B2** 57.35N 7.20W
Northumberland *d.* England **8 D4** 55.12N 2.00W
North Walsham England **11 G3** 52.49N 1.22E
North West C. Australia **108 G4** 21.48S 114.10E
Northwest Territories *d.* Canada **62 I4** 66.00N 110.00W
Northwich England **15 E2** 53.16N 2.30W
North York Moors *hills* England **15 G3** 54.21N 0.50W
North Yorkshire *d.* England **9 E4** 54.14N 1.14W
Norton England **15 G3** 54.08N 0.47W
Norton Fitzwarren England **13 D3** 51.02N 3.09W
Norton Sound *b.* U.S.A. **62 B4** 63.50N 164.00W
Norway Europe **43 B3** 65.00N 13.00E
Norway House *town* Canada **62 I3** 53.59N 97.50W
Norwegian Sea Europe **34 D4** 66.00N 2.00E
Norwich England **11 G3** 52.38N 1.17E
Nos de Cachi *mtn.* Argentina **76 D2** 24.50S 66.25W
Noshiro Japan **106 D4** 40.13N 140.06E
Noss, Isle of Scotland **19 Y9** 60.08N 1.01W
Nottingham England **10 D3** 52.57N 1.10W
Nottingham *d.* England **9 E3** 52.57N 1.10W
Nottinghamshire *d.* England **9 E3** 53.10N 1.00W
Nouâdhibou Mauritania **84 C4** 20.54N 17.01W
Nouakchott Mauritania **84 C3** 18.09N 15.58W
Nouméa N. Cal. **111 F3** 22.16S 166.27E
Noup Head Scotland **19 F4** 59.20N 3.04W
Nova Friburgo Brazil **77 F2** 22.16S 42.32W
Nova Iguaçu Brazil **77 F2** 22.45S 43.27W
Nova Kakhovka Ukraine **55 M2** 46.51N 33.26E
Novara Italy **50 C6** 45.27N 8.37E
Nova Scotia *d.* Canada **63 L2** 45.00N 64.00W
Novaya Sibir' *i.* Russian Fed. **59 Q5** 75.20N 148.00E
Novaya Zemlya *i.* Russian Fed. **58 H5** 74.00N 56.00E
Nové Zámky Slovakia **54 F2** 47.59N 18.11E
Novgorod Russian Fed. **58 F3** 58.30N 31.20E
Novi Pazar Yugo. **56 E5** 43.08N 20.28E
Novi Sad Yugo. **56 D6** 45.16N 19.52E
Novodvinsk Russian Fed. **58 G4** 64.25N 40.42E
Novo Hamburgo Brazil **77 E2** 29.37S 51.07W
Novohrad-Volyns'kyy Ukraine **55 J4** 50.34N 27.32E
Novokuznetsk Russian Fed. **58 K3** 53.45N 87.12E
Novomoskovsk Russian Fed. **55 P6** 54.06N 38.15E
Novomoskovs'k Ukraine **55 N3** 48.38N 35.15E
Novorossiysk Russian Fed. **58 F2** 44.44N 37.46E
Novosibirsk Russian Fed. **58 K3** 55.04N 82.55E
Novyy Oskol Russian Fed. **55 O4** 50.46N 37.52E
Novyy Port Russian Fed. **58 J4** 67.38N 72.33E
Nowshera Pakistan **95 L5** 34.01N 71.59E
Nowy Sącz Poland **54 G3** 49.39N 20.40E
Noyabr'sk Russian Fed. **58 J4** 63.10N 75.40E
Noyon France **42 C1** 49.35N 3.00E
Nu'aym *f.* Oman **95 I3** 22.30N 56.30E
Nuba, L. Egypt **94 D3** 22.20N 31.40E
Nuba Mts. Sudan **94 D1** 12.00N 31.00E
Nubian Desert Sudan **85 H4** 21.00N 34.00E
Nuevo Laredo Mexico **70 E6** 27.30N 99.30W
Nuevo León *d.* Mexico **70 E6** 26.00N 99.00W
Nui *i.* Tuvalu **111 G5** 7.12S 177.10E
Nu Jiang *r. see* **Salween** *r.* China **102**
Nukufetau *i.* Tuvalu **111 G5** 8.00S 178.25E
Nuku Hiva *i.* Marquesas Is. **109 Q6** 8.56S 140.00W
Nukunono *i.* Pacific Oc. **108 N6** 9.10S 171.55W
Nukus Uzbekistan **58 H2** 42.28N 59.07E
Nullarbor Plain *f.* Australia **110 B2** 31.30S 128.00E
Numazu Japan **106 C3** 35.08N 138.50E
Nunavut *d.* Canada **63 I4** 67.00N 96.00W
Nuneaton England **10 D3** 52.32N 1.29W
Nunivak I. U.S.A. **62 B3** 60.00N 166.30W
Nuoro Italy **50 C4** 40.19N 9.20E
Nuqrah Saudi Arabia **94 F4** 25.35N 41.28E
Nurmes Finland **43 G3** 63.32N 29.10E
Nürnberg Germany **48 E3** 49.27N 11.05E
Nushki Pakistan **95 K4** 29.33N 66.01E
Nuuk Greenland **63 M4** 64.10N 51.40W
Nyahururu Kenya **87 B3** 0.02N 36.22E
Nyala Sudan **85 G3** 12.01N 24.50E
Nyambeni Hills Kenya **87 B3** 0.15N 38.00E
Nyanza *d.* Kenya **87 A2** 0.30S 34.20E
Nyasa, L. Africa **86 C3** 12.00S 34.30E
Nyborg Denmark **43 B1** 55.19N 10.49E
Nybro Sweden **43 C2** 56.44N 15.55E
Nyeri Kenya **87 B2** 0.25S 36.56E
Nyíregyháza Hungary **54 G2** 47.59N 21.43E
Nyiru, Mt. Kenya **87 B3** 2.09N 36.50E
Nykarleby Finland **43 E3** 63.22N 23.30E
Nykøbing Denmark **43 B1** 54.47N 11.53E
Nyköping Sweden **43 D2** 58.45N 17.03E
Nynäshamn Sweden **43 D2** 58.54N 17.55E
Nyurba Russian Fed. **59 N4** 63.18N 118.28E
Nzoia *r.* Kenya **87 A3** 0.03N 33.58E

O

Oadby England **10 D3** 52.37N 1.07W
Oahe, L. U.S.A. **64 F6** 45.45N 100.20W
Oahu *i.* Hawaiian Is. **108 P9** 21.30N 158.00W
Oakengates England **10 C3** 52.42N 2.29W
Oakham England **10 E3** 52.40N 0.43W
Oakland U.S.A. **64 B4** 37.50N 122.15W
Oates Land *f.* Antarctica **112** 70.00S 155.00E
Oaxaca Mexico **70 E4** 17.05N 96.41W
Oaxaca *d.* Mexico **70 E4** 17.30N 97.00W
Ob *r.* Russian Fed. **58 I4** 66.50N 69.00E
Ob, G. of Russian Fed. **58 J4** 68.30N 74.00E
Oban Scotland **16 D4** 56.26N 5.28W
Obi *i.* Indonesia **105 H3** 1.45S 127.30E
Obidos Brazil **77 E4** 1.55S 55.31W
Obihiro Japan **106 D4** 42.55N 143.00E
Obninsk Russian Fed. **55 O6** 55.15N 36.41E
Oboyan' Russian Fed. **55 O4** 51.13N 36.17E
Occidental, Cordillera Colombia **74 B7** 5.00N 76.15W
Occidental, Cordillera *mts.* Chile **76 D3** 20.00S 69.00W
Occidental, Cordillera *mts.* Peru **76 C3** 14.00S 74.00W
Ocean Falls *town* Canada **62 F3** 52.24N 127.42W
Ochakiv Ukraine **55 L2** 46.37N 31.33E
Ochil Hills Scotland **17 F4** 56.16N 3.25W
October Revolution *i.* Russian Fed. **59 L5** 79.30N 96.00E
Ódáðahraun *mts.* Iceland **43 Y2** 65.00N 17.30W
Odate Japan **106 D4** 40.16N 140.34E
Ödemiş Turkey **57 I3** 38.12N 28.00E
Odense Denmark **43 B1** 55.24N 10.25E
Oder *r.* Poland/Germany **54 D5** 53.30N 14.36E
Odessa Ukraine **55 L2** 46.30N 30.46E
Odessa U.S.A. **64 F3** 31.50N 102.23W
Odintsovo Russian Fed. **55 O6** 55.38N 37.18E
Odorheiu Secuiesc Romania **55 I2** 46.18N 25.18E
Ofanto *r.* Italy **50 G4** 41.22N 16.12E
Offaly *d.* Rep. of Ire. **20 D3** 53.15N 7.30W
Offenbach am Main Germany **48 D4** 50.06N 8.46E
Offenburg Germany **48 C3** 48.29N 7.57E
Ogaden *f.* Ethiopia **85 I2** 7.50N 45.40E
Ogaki Japan **106 C3** 35.25N 136.36E
Ogasawara-shoto *is.* Japan **108 J9** 27.00N 142.10E
Ogbomoso Nigeria **84 E2** 8.05N 4.11E
Ogden U.S.A. **64 D5** 41.14N 111.59W
Ogilvie *r.* Canada **62 E4** 66.10N 134.10W
Oglio *r.* Italy **50 D6** 45.02N 10.39E
Ogoki *r.* Canada **65 I7** 51.35N 86.00W
Ogooué *r.* Gabon **84 E1** 1.00S 9.05E
Ogulin Croatia **56 B6** 45.17N 15.14E
O'Higgins, L. Chile **75 B2** 48.53S 73.10W
Ohio U.S.A. **65 J5** 40.00N 83.00W
Ohio *r.* U.S.A. **65 I4** 37.07N 89.10W
Ohrid Macedonia **56 E4** 41.06N 20.48E
Ohrid, L. Albania/Macedonia **56 E4** 41.00N 20.43E
Oich, Loch Scotland **18 E2** 57.04N 4.46W
Oil City U.S.A. **65 K5** 41.26N 79.30W
Oise *r.* France **44 E6** 49.00N 2.10E
Oita Japan **106 B2** 33.15N 131.40E
Oiti *mtn.* Greece **56 F3** 38.48N 22.15E
Ojinaga Mexico **70 D6** 29.35N 104.26W
Ojos del Salado *mtn.* Chile/Argentina **76 D2** 27.05S 68.05W
Okanogan *r.* U.S.A. **64 B6** 47.45N 120.05W
Okavango Delta Botswana **86 B3** 19.30S 23.00E
Okaya Japan **106 C3** 36.03N 138.00E
Okayama Japan **106 B2** 34.40N 133.54E
Okeechobee, L. U.S.A. **65 J2** 27.00N 80.45W
Okefenokee Swamp *f.* U.S.A. **65 J3** 30.40N 82.40W
Okehampton England **13 C2** 50.44N 4.01W
Okha India **96 D5** 22.25N 69.00E
Okha Russian Fed. **59 Q3** 53.35N 142.50E
Okhotsk Russian Fed. **59 Q3** 59.20N 143.15E
Okhotsk, Sea of Russian Fed. **59 Q3** 55.00N 150.00E
Okhtyrka Ukraine **55 N4** 50.19N 34.54E
Okinawa *i.* Japan **103 N3** 26.30N 128.00E
Oki-shoto *is.* Japan **106 B3** 36.10N 133.10E
Oklahoma *d.* U.S.A. **64 G4** 35.00N 97.00W
Oklahoma City U.S.A. **64 G4** 35.28N 97.33W
Oksskolten *mtn.* Norway **43 C4** 66.00N 14.24E
Öland *i.* Sweden **43 D2** 56.50N 16.50E
Olbia Italy **50 C4** 40.55N 9.29E
Old Crow Canada **62 E4** 67.34N 139.43W
Oldenburg Germany **48 D5** 53.08N 8.13E
Oldenzaal Neth. **42 F4** 52.19N 6.55E
Oldham England **15 E2** 53.33N 2.08W
Old Head of Kinsale *c.* Rep. of Ire. **20 C1** 51.37N 8.33W
Old Leake England **15 H2** 53.02N 0.06E
Oldmeldrum Scotland **19 G2** 57.20N 2.20W
Olean U.S.A. **65 K5** 42.05N 78.26W
Olekminsk Russian Fed. **59 O4** 60.25N 120.00E
Olenek Russian Fed. **59 N4** 68.38N 112.15E
Olenek *r.* Russian Fed. **59 O5** 73.00N 120.00E
Oléron, Île d' *i.* France **44 C4** 45.55N 1.16W
Olevs'k Ukraine **55 J4** 51.12N 27.35E
Olinda Brazil **77 G4** 8.00S 34.51W
Oliva, Cordillera de *mts.* Chile/Argentina **76 D2** 29.30S 70.00W
Olney England **10 E3** 52.09N 0.42W
Olomouc Czech Rep. **54 E3** 49.36N 17.16E
Olongapo Phil. **104 G7** 14.52N 120.16E
Oloron France **44 C3** 43.12N 0.35W
Olsztyn Poland **54 G5** 53.48N 20.29E
Olteniţa Romania **56 H6** 44.05N 26.31E
Oltet *r.* Romania **56 G6** 44.13N 24.28E
Olym *r.* Russian Fed. **55 P5** 52.25N 38.05E
Olympus *mtn.* Cyprus **57 K1** 34.55N 32.52E
Olympus *mtn.* Greece **56 F4** 40.04N 22.20E
Omagh N. Ireland **16 B2** 54.35N 7.20W
Omaha U.S.A. **64 G5** 41.15N 96.00W
Oman Asia **95 I3** 22.30N 57.30E
Oman, G. of Asia **95 I4** 25.00N 58.00E
Ombersley England **10 C3** 52.17N 2.13W
Ombrone *r.* Italy **50 D5** 42.40N 11.00E
Omdurman Sudan **85 H3** 15.37N 32.59E
Ommen Neth. **42 F4** 52.32N 6.25E
Omolon *r.* Russian Fed. **59 R4** 68.50N 158.30E
Omo Nat. Park Ethiopia **87 B4** 6.00N 35.40E
Omono *r.* Japan **106 D3** 39.44N 140.05E
Omsk Russian Fed. **58 J3** 55.00N 73.22E
Omulew *r.* Poland **54 G5** 53.05N 21.32E
Onchan I.o.M. **14 C3** 54.11N 4.27W
Ondjiva Angola **86 A3** 17.03S 15.41E
Onega, L. Russian Fed. **58 F4** 62.00N 35.30E
Onesti Romania **55 J2** 46.14N 26.44E
Ongole India **97 G4** 15.31N 80.04E
Onitsha Nigeria **84 E2** 6.10N 6.47E
Ono-i-Lau *i.* Fiji **108 N4** 19.00S 178.30W
Ontario *d.* Canada **63 J3** 52.00N 86.00W
Ontario, L. N. America **65 K5** 43.40N 78.00W
Ontong Java Atoll Solomon Is. **111 E5** 5.20S 159.30E
Oostende Belgium **42 B3** 51.13N 2.55E
Oosterschelde *est.* Neth. **42 C3** 51.35N 3.57E
Oost-Vlaanderen *d.* Belgium **42 C3** 51.00N 3.45E
Opochka Russian Fed. **43 G2** 56.41N 28.42E
Opole Poland **54 E4** 50.40N 17.56E
Oporto Portugal **46 A4** 41.09N 8.37W
Oradea Romania **54 G2** 47.03N 21.55E
Oran Algeria **84 D5** 35.45N 0.38W
Orange France **44 F4** 44.08N 4.48E
Orange *r.* R.S.A. **86 A2** 28.43S 16.30E
Orange, Cabo *c.* Brazil **74 D7** 4.25N 51.32W
Orangeburg U.S.A. **65 J3** 33.28N 80.53W
Orchila *i.* Venezuela **71 K3** 11.52N 66.10W
Orchy *r.* Scotland **16 E4** 56.26N 5.00W
Ord, Mt. Australia **110 B4** 17.19S 125.30E
Ordu Turkey **57 M4** 41.00N 37.52E
Örebro Sweden **43 C2** 59.17N 15.13E
Oregon *d.* U.S.A. **64 B5** 44.00N 120.00W
Orel Russian Fed. **55 O5** 52.58N 36.04E
Ore Mts. Europe **48 F4** 50.30N 12.50E
Orenburg Russian Fed. **58 H3** 51.50N 55.00E
Orford Ness *c.* England **11 G3** 52.05N 1.36E
Orhei Moldova **55 K2** 47.24N 28.50E
Oriental, Cordillera *mts.* Colombia **74 B7** 5.00N 74.30W
Oriental, Cordillera *mts.* Peru/Bolivia **76 C3** 14.00S 70.00W
Orinoco *r.* Venezuela **74 C7** 9.00N 61.30W
Orinoco Delta *f.* Venezuela **74 C7** 9.00N 61.30W
Orissa *d.* India **97 G5** 20.15N 84.00E
Oristano Italy **50 C3** 39.53N 8.36E
Oristano, G. of Med. Sea **50 C3** 39.50N 8.30E
Orivesi *l.* Finland **43 G3** 62.20N 29.30E
Orizaba Mexico **70 E4** 18.51N 97.08W
Orkney *d.* Scotland **8 D6** 59.00N 3.00W
Orkney Is. Scotland **19 F4** 59.00N 3.00W
Orlando U.S.A. **65 J2** 28.33N 81.21W
Orléans France **44 D5** 47.54N 1.54E
Ormoc Phil. **105 G6** 11.01N 124.36E
Ormskirk England **14 E2** 53.35N 2.53W
Orne *r.* France **44 C6** 49.17N 0.10W
Örnsköldsvik Sweden **43 D3** 63.19N 18.45E
Oronsay *i.* Scotland **16 C4** 56.01N 6.14W
Orosei Italy **50 C4** 40.23N 9.40E
Orosei, G. of Med. Sea **50 C4** 40.15N 9.45E
Orrin *r.* Scotland **19 E2** 57.31N 4.28W
Orsha Belarus **55 L6** 54.30N 30.23E
Orsk Russian Fed. **58 H3** 51.13N 58.35E
Orşova Romania **56 F6** 44.42N 22.22E
Oruro Bolivia **76 D3** 18.05S 67.00W
Osaka Japan **106 C2** 34.40N 135.30E
Osa Pen. Costa Rica **71 H2** 8.20N 83.30W
Oshakati Namibia **86 A3** 17.47S 15.30E
Oshawa Canada **63 K2** 43.53N 78.51W
Osizweni R.S.A. **86 C2** 27.45S 30.11E
Ösjön *l.* Sweden **43 C3** 63.48N 15.40E
Oskarshamn Sweden **43 D2** 57.16N 16.25E
Oskil *r.* Ukraine **55 O3** 49.08N 37.10E
Oskol *r. see* **Oskil** *r.* Russian Fed. **55**
Oslo Norway **43 B2** 59.56N 10.45E
Osmancık Turkey **57 L4** 40.58N 34.50E
Osmaniye Turkey **57 M2** 37.04N 36.15E
Osnabrück Germany **48 D5** 52.17N 8.03E
Osorno Chile **75 B2** 40.35S 73.14W
Osorno Spain **46 C5** 42.24N 4.22W
Oss Neth. **42 E3** 51.46N 5.31E
Ossa *mtn.* Greece **56 F3** 39.47N 22.41E
Ossa, Mt. Australia **110 D1** 41.52S 146.04E
Österdal *r.* Sweden **43 C3** 61.03N 14.30E
Østerdalen *f.* Norway **43 B3** 62.00N 11.00E
Östersund Sweden **43 C3** 63.10N 14.40E
Ostrava Czech Rep. **54 F3** 49.50N 18.15E
Ostrogozhsk Russian Fed. **55 P4** 50.52N 39.03E
Ostrov Russian Fed. **43 G2** 57.22N 28.22E
Ostrów Mazowiecka Poland **54 G5** 52.50N 21.56E
Ostrzeszów Poland **54 E4** 51.25N 17.55E
Osŭm *r.* Bulgaria **56 G5** 43.41N 24.51E
Osumi-kaikyo *str.* Japan **106 B2** 31.30N 131.00E
Osuna Spain **46 C2** 37.14N 5.06W
Oswestry England **10 B3** 52.52N 3.03W
Otaru Japan **106 D4** 43.14N 140.59E
Otjiwarongo Namibia **86 A2** 20.30S 16.39E
Otley England **15 F2** 53.54N 1.41W
Otranto Italy **50 H4** 40.09N 18.30E
Otranto, Str. of Med. Sea **56 D4** 40.10N 19.00E
Otta Norway **43 B3** 61.46N 9.33E
Ottawa Canada **63 K2** 45.25N 75.43W
Ottawa *r.* Canada **63 K2** 45.23N 73.55W
Ottawa Is. Canada **63 J3** 59.50N 80.00W
Otter *r.* England **13 D2** 50.38N 3.19W
Otterburn *town* England **15 E4** 55.14N 2.10W
Ottery *r.* England **13 C2** 50.39N 4.20W
Ottignies Belgium **42 D2** 50.40N 4.34E
Oturkpo Nigeria **84 E2** 7.16N 8.16E
Ouachita *r.* U.S.A. **65 H3** 31.52N 91.48W
Ouachita Mts. U.S.A. **65 H3** 34.40N 94.30W
Ouagadougou Burkina **84 D3** 12.20N 1.40W
Ouargla Algeria **84 E5** 32.00N 5.16E
Ouarzazate Morocco **84 D5** 30.57N 6.50W
Oudenaarde Belgium **42 C2** 50.50N 3.37E
Ouésso Congo **86 A5** 1.38N 16.03E
Ouezzane Morocco **52 B3** 34.52N 5.35W
Oughter, Lough Rep. of Ire. **20 D4** 54.01N 7.28W
Ouistreham France **44 C6** 49.17N 0.15W
Oujda Morocco **84 D5** 34.41N 1.45W
Oulainen Finland **43 F4** 64.17N 24.50E
Oulton England **11 G3** 52.28N 1.45E
Oulu Finland **43 F4** 65.02N 25.27E
Oulujärvi *l.* Finland **43 F4** 64.30N 27.00E
Oundle England **11 E3** 52.29N 0.29W
Oupeye Belgium **42 E2** 50.42N 5.39E
Ourense Spain **46 B5** 42.20N 7.52W
Ouse *r.* E.Sussex England **11 F1** 50.46N 0.03E
Ouse *r.* E.Yorks. England **15 G2** 53.41N 0.42W
Outer Hebrides *is.* Scotland **18 B2** 58.00N 7.35W
Outokumpu Finland **43 G3** 62.43N 29.05E
Out Skerries *is.* Scotland **19 Z9** 60.20N 0.45W
Ovamboland *f.* Namibia **86 A3** 17.45S 17.00E
Overijssel *d.* Neth. **42 F4** 52.25N 6.30E
Overton Wales **12 E4** 52.58N 2.56W
Övertorneå Sweden **43 E4** 66.22N 23.40E
Oviedo Spain **46 C5** 43.21N 5.50W
Ovruch Ukraine **55 K4** 51.20N 28.50E
Owando Congo **86 A4** 0.30S 15.48E
Owen Falls Dam Uganda **87 A3** 0.27N 33.10E
Owensboro U.S.A. **65 I4** 37.46N 87.07W
Owen Sound *town* Canada **63 J2** 44.34N 80.56W
Owen Stanley Range *mts.* P.N.G. **110 D5** 9.30S 148.00E
Öxarfjördhur *est.* Iceland **43 Y2** 66.12N 16.30W
Oxelösund Sweden **43 D2** 58.40N 17.10E
Oxford England **10 D2** 51.45N 1.15W
Oxfordshire *d.* England **9 E2** 51.46N 1.20W
Oxnard U.S.A. **64 C3** 34.12N 119.11W
Oxted England **11 F2** 51.16N 0.01E
Oyama Japan **106 C3** 36.18N 139.48E
Oykel *r.* Scotland **19 E2** 57.52N 4.22W
Ozark Plateau U.S.A. **65 H4** 36.00N 93.35W
Ózd Hungary **54 G3** 48.14N 20.18E

P

Paamiut Greenland **63 N4** 62.05N 49.30W
Pabbay *i.* W.Isles Scotland **18 B1** 56.51N 7.35W
Pabbay *i.* W.Isles Scotland **18 B2** 57.46N 7.14W
Pachuca Mexico **70 E5** 20.10N 98.44W
Pacific Ocean **109**
Padang Indonesia **104 C3** 0.55S 100.21E
Padangpanjang Indonesia **104 C3** 0.30S 100.26E
Paderborn Germany **48 D4** 51.43N 8.44E
Padiham England **15 E2** 53.49N 2.19W
Padre I. U.S.A. **64 G2** 27.00N 97.20W
Padstow England **13 C2** 50.33N 4.57W
Padua Italy **50 D6** 45.27N 11.52E
Pag *i.* Croatia **56 B6** 44.28N 15.00E
Pagadian Phil. **105 G5** 7.50N 123.30E
Pagan *i.* N. Mariana Is. **105 L7** 18.08N 145.46E
Paget, Mt. South Georgia **75 F1** 54.23S 36.45W
Paignton England **13 D2** 50.26N 3.34W
Päijänne *l.* Finland **43 F3** 61.30N 25.30E
Painswick England **10 C2** 51.47N 2.11W
Paisley Scotland **16 E3** 55.50N 4.26W
Pakistan Asia **96 D6** 30.00N 70.00E
Pakokku Myanmar **97 J5** 21.20N 95.10E
Pakxé Laos **104 D7** 15.05N 105.50E
Palana Russian Fed. **59 R3** 59.05N 159.59E
Palau Pacific Oc. **105 I5** 7.00N 134.25E
Palawan *i.* Phil. **104 F5** 9.30N 118.30E
Palembang Indonesia **104 C3** 2.59S 104.50E
Palencia Spain **46 C5** 42.01N 4.34W
Palermo Italy **50 E3** 38.09N 13.22E
Pali India **96 E6** 25.46N 73.20E
Palk Str. India/Sri Lanka **97 F2** 10.00N 79.40E
Pallisa Uganda **87 A3** 1.08N 33.43E
Palma de Mallorca Spain **46 G3** 39.36N 2.39E
Palmas, C. Liberia **84 D2** 4.30N 7.55W
Palmer Land *f.* Antarctica **112** 74.00S 66.00W
Palmerston I. Cook Is. **108 O5** 18.04S 163.10W
Palmerston North New Zealand **111 G1** 40.21S 175.37E
Palmi Italy **50 F3** 38.22N 15.50E
Palmira Colombia **74 B7** 3.33N 76.17W
Palmyra Syria **94 E5** 34.36N 38.15E
Palmyra I. Pacific Oc. **108 O7** 5.52N 162.05W
Palopo Indonesia **104 G3** 3.01S 120.12E
Palos, Cabo de *c.* Spain **46 E2** 37.38N 0.41W
Palu Indonesia **104 F3** 0.54S 119.52E
Pamiers France **44 D3** 43.07N 1.36E
Pamirs *mts.* Tajikistan **102 C5** 37.50N 73.30E
Pampa U.S.A. **64 F4** 35.32N 100.58W
Pampas *f.* Argentina **75 C3** 35.00S 63.00W
Pamplona Spain **46 E5** 42.49N 1.39W
Panaji India **96 E4** 15.29N 73.50E
Panama C. America **71 H2** 9.00N 80.00W
Panama Canal Panama **71 I2** 9.21N 79.54W
Panama City Panama **71 I2** 8.57N 79.30W
Panama City U.S.A. **65 I3** 30.10N 85.41W
Panamá, G. of Panama **71 I2** 8.30N 79.00W
Panay *i.* Phil. **105 G6** 11.10N 122.30E
Panevėžys Lithuania **55 I6** 55.44N 24.24
Pangani Tanzania **87 B2** 5.26S 38.59E
Pangkalanbuun Indonesia **104 E3** 2.43S 111.38
Pangkalpinang Indonesia **104 D3** 2.05S 106.09
Pangnirtung Canada **63 L4** 66.05N 65.45
Panjgur Pakistan **95 J4** 26.58N 64.06
Pantelleria *i.* Italy **50 E2** 36.48N 12.00
Paola Italy **50 G3** 39.21N 16.03
Papa Stour *i.* Scotland **19 Y9** 60.20N 1.42
Papa Westray *i.* Scotland **19 G4** 59.22N 2.54
Papenburg Germany **42 G5** 53.05N 7.25
Paphos Cyprus **57 K1** 34.45N 32.25
Papua, G. of P.N.G. **110 D5** 8.50S 145.00
Papua New Guinea Austa. **110 D5** 6.00S 148.00
Par England **13 C2** 50.21N 4.43
Pará *d.* Brazil **77 E4** 4.00S 53.00
Paracel Is. S. China Sea **104 E7** 16.20N 112.00
Paragua *r.* Bolivia **77 D3** 13.28S 61.50
Paraguai *r. see* Paraguay *r.* Brazil **77**
Paraguay S. America **77 E2** 23.00S 58.00
Paraguay *r.* Argentina **77 E2** 27.30S 58.50
Paraíba *r.* Brazil **75 E4** 21.45S 41.10
Paraíba *d.* Brazil **77 G4** 7.30S 36.30
Parakow Benin **84 E2** 9.23N 2.40
Paramaribo Suriname **74 D7** 5.52N 55.14
Paraná Argentina **77 D1** 31.45S 60.30
Paraná *r.* Argentina **75 D3** 34.00S 58.30
Paranã Brazil **77 F3** 12.30S 48.10
Paraná *d.* Brazil **77 E2** 24.30S 52.00
Paranaguá Brazil **77 F2** 25.32S 48.36
Paranaíba *r.* Brazil **77 E3** 20.00S 51.00

ıdley England **10 D3** 52.16N 1.52W
ıpino Russian Fed. **55 P6** 54.53N 38.07E
ırry England **11 G2** 51.18N 1.07E
ırt Desert Australia **110 D3** 28.30S 141.12E
ıttgart Germany **48 D3** 48.47N 9.12E
ır *r.* Belarus/Ukraine **55 J5** 52.07N 26.35E
akin Sudan **85 H3** 19.04N 37.22E
botica Yugo. **56 D7** 46.04N 19.41E
ceava Romania **55 J2** 47.39N 26.19E
chan *r.* Russian Fed. **106 B4** 42.53N 132.56E
ck *r.* Rep. of Ire. **20 C3** 53.16N 8.03W
cre Bolivia **76 D3** 19.05S 65.15W
dak Ukraine **55 N1** 44.52N 34.57E
dan Africa **85 G3** 14.00N 30.00E
dbury Canada **63 J2** 46.30N 81.01W
dbury England **11 F3** 52.03N 0.45E
dd *f.* Sudan **85 H2** 7.50N 30.00E
deten Mts. Czech Rep./Poland **54 E4** 50.30N 16.30E
ez Egypt **94 D4** 29.59N 32.33E
ez Canal Egypt **94 D5** 30.40N 32.20E
ez, G. of Egypt **94 D4** 28.48N 33.00E
ffolk *d.* England **9 F3** 52.16N 1.00E
guta *r.* Kenya **87 B3** 0.36N 36.04E
guti B. Tanzania **87 A2** 1.44S 33.36E
ḥar Oman **95 I3** 24.23N 56.43E
hl Germany **48 E4** 50.37N 10.43E
ir *r.* Rep. of Ire. **20 D2** 52.17N 7.00W
izhou China **103 K4** 31.46N 113.22E
kabumi Indonesia **104 D2** 6.55S 106.50E
kadana Indonesia **104 E3** 1.15S 110.00E
khinichi Russian Fed. **55 N6** 54.07N 35.21E
kkur Pakistan **96 D6** 27.42N 68.54E
la *i.* Norway **43 A3** 61.10N 4.50E
laiman Ranges *mts.* Pakistan **90 I5** 30.00N 68.00E
la Is. Indonesia **105 H3** 1.50S 125.10E
lawesi *i.* Indonesia **104 G3** 2.00S 120.30E
lina Romania **55 K1** 45.08N 29.40E
llana Peru **76 B4** 4.52S 80.39W
lmona Italy **50 E5** 42.04N 13.57E
lu Archipelago Phil. **105 G5** 5.30N 121.00E
lu Sea Pacific Oc. **104 G5** 8.00N 120.00E
matra *i.* Indonesia **104 C3** 2.00S 102.00E
mba *i.* Indonesia **104 F2** 9.30S 119.55E
mbawa *i.* Indonesia **104 F2** 8.45S 117.50E
mburgh Scotland **19 Y8** 59.53N 1.16W
mburgh Head Scotland **19 Y8** 59.51N 1.16W
mmer Isles *is.* Scotland **18 D3** 58.01N 5.26W
mqayıt Azerbaijan **58 G2** 40.35N 49.38E
my Ukraine **55 N4** 50.55N 34.49E
nart, Loch Scotland **18 D1** 56.42N 5.45W
nda Str. Indonesia **104 C2** 6.00S 105.50E
nderland England **15 F3** 54.55N 1.22W
ndsvall Sweden **43 D3** 62.22N 17.20E
nga Tanzania **87 B2** 4.25S 38.04E
ngaipenuh Indonesia **104 C3** 2.00S 101.28E
ngurlu Turkey **57 L4** 40.10N 34.23E
olijärvet *l.* Finland **43 F4** 66.18N 28.00E
onenjoki Finland **43 F3** 62.40N 27.06E
perior U.S.A. **65 H6** 46.42N 92.05W
perior, L. N. America **65 I6** 48.00N 88.00W
q ash Shuyukh Iraq **95 G5** 30.53N 46.28E
r Oman **95 I3** 22.23N 59.32E
rab Pakistan **95 K4** 28.29N 66.16E
rabaya Indonesia **104 E2** 7.14S 112.45E
rakarta Indonesia **104 E2** 7.32S 110.50E
rat India **96 E5** 21.10N 72.54E
rendranagar India **96 E5** 22.42N 71.41E
rgut Russian Fed. **58 J4** 61.13N 73.20E
rigao Phil. **105 H5** 9.47N 125.29E
rin Thailand **104 C6** 14.53N 103.29E
riname S. America **74 D7** 4.00N 56.00W
rrey *d.* England **9 E2** 51.16N 0.30W
rtsey *i.* Iceland **43 X1** 63.18N 20.37W
sangerd Iran **95 G5** 31.40N 48.06E
tak Jammu & Kashmir **97 F7** 33.12N 77.28E
therland *f.* Scotland **19 E3** 58.20N 4.20W
tlej *r.* Pakistan **96 E6** 29.26N 71.09E
tterton England **11 E3** 52.54N 0.06W
tton England **11 F3** 52.23N 0.07E
tton Bridge England **11 F3** 52.46N 0.12E
tton Coldfield England **10 D3** 52.33N 1.50W
tton in Ashfield England **15 F2** 53.08N 1.16W
va Fiji **111 G4** 18.08S 178.25E
vorov I. Cook Is. **108 O5** 13.15S 163.05W
wałki Poland **54 H6** 54.07N 22.56E
zhou Anhui China **103 L4** 33.38N 117.02E
zhou Jiangsu China **103 M4** 31.21N 120.40E
zu Japan **106 C3** 37.20N 137.15E
zuka Japan **106 C2** 34.51N 136.35E
albard *is.* Norway **58 D5** 76.00N 15.00E
apa *r.* Russian Fed. **55 N4** 51.44N 34.56E
eg Sweden **43 C3** 62.02N 14.20E
endborg Denmark **43 B1** 55.04N 10.38E
etogorsk Russian Fed. **43 G3** 61.07N 28.50E
tavy Czech Rep. **54 E3** 49.45N 16.27E
tlovods'k Ukraine **55 M3** 49.04N 33.15E
obodnyy Russian Fed. **59 O3** 51.24N 128.05E
abian Alps *mts.* Germany **48 D3** 48.20N 9.30E
adlincote England **10 D3** 52.47N 1.34W
affham England **11 F3** 52.38N 0.42E
ains I. Samoa **108 N5** 11.03S 171.06W
akopmund Namibia **86 A2** 22.40S 14.34E
ale *r.* England **15 F3** 54.05N 1.20W
anage England **10 D1** 50.36N 1.59W
an Is. Honduras **71 H4** 17.25N 83.55W
anley England **11 F2** 51.24N 0.12E
ansea Wales **12 D3** 51.37N 3.57W
ansea *d.* Wales **9 D2** 51.35N 4.10W
ansea B. Wales **12 D3** 51.33N 3.50W
aziland Africa **86 C2** 26.30S 31.30E
eden Europe **43 C2** 63.00N 16.00E
eetwater U.S.A. **64 F3** 32.37N 100.25W
ift Current *town* Canada **62 H3** 50.17N 107.49W
illy, Lough Rep. of Ire. **20 D5** 55.10N 7.32W
indon England **10 D2** 51.33N 1.47W
indon *d.* England **9 E2** 51.33N 1.47W
ineshead England **11 E3** 52.57N 0.10W
inoujście Poland **54 D5** 53.55N 14.18E
itzerland Europe **44 G5** 47.00N 8.00E
ords Rep. of Ire. **20 E3** 53.28N 6.13W
oil Pt. Rep. of Ire. **20 A2** 52.10N 10.27W
dney Australia **110 E2** 33.55S 151.10E
dney Mines *town* Canada **63 L2** 46.10N 60.10W
ktyvkar Russian Fed. **58 H4** 61.42N 50.45E
larna *mtn.* Norway/Sweden **43 C3** 63.01N 12.13E
lt *i.* Germany **43 B1** 54.50N 8.20E
racuse U.S.A. **65 K5** 43.03N 76.10W
Syrdar'ya *r.* Asia **58 I2** 46.00N 61.12E
Syria Asia **94 E5** 35.00N 38.00E
Syrian Desert Asia **94 E5** 32.00N 39.00E
Syzran Russian Fed. **58 G3** 53.10N 48.29E
Szczecin Poland **54 D5** 53.25N 14.32E
Szczecinek Poland **54 E5** 53.42N 16.41E
Szczytno Poland **54 G5** 53.34N 21.00E
Szeged Hungary **54 G2** 46.16N 20.08E
Székesfehérvár Hungary **54 F2** 47.12N 18.25E
Szekszárd Hungary **54 F2** 46.22N 18.44E
Szombathely Hungary **54 E2** 47.12N 16.38E

T

Tabas Iran **95 I5** 33.36N 56.55E
Tabasco *d.* Mexico **70 F4** 18.30N 93.00W
Tabatinga, Serra da *mts.* Brazil **77 F3** 10.00S 44.00W
Tábor Czech Rep. **54 D3** 49.25N 14.41E
Tabora Tanzania **86 C4** 5.02S 32.50E
Tabrīz Iran **95 G6** 38.05N 46.18E
Tabuaeran *i.* Kiribati **108 P7** 3.52N 159.20W
Tabuk Saudi Arabia **94 E4** 28.25N 36.35E
Täby Sweden **43 D2** 59.29N 18.04E
Tacloban Phil. **105 G6** 11.15N 124.59E
Tacna Peru **76 C3** 18.01S 70.15W
Tacoma U.S.A. **64 B6** 47.16N 122.30W
Tacuarembó Uruguay **77 E1** 31.42S 56.00W
Tadcaster England **15 F2** 53.53N 1.16W
Taegu S. Korea **103 N5** 35.52N 128.36E
Taejon S. Korea **103 N5** 36.20N 127.26E
Taf *r.* Wales **12 C3** 51.45N 4.29W
Taganrog Russian Fed. **53 K6** 47.14N 38.55E
Taganrog, G. of Ukraine/Russian Fed. **53 K6** 47.00N 38.30E
Tagbilaran Phil. **105 G5** 9.38N 123.53E
Tagula I. P.N.G. **110 E4** 11.30S 153.30E
Tagus *r.* Portugal **46 A3** 39.00N 8.57W
Tahat, Mt. Algeria **84 E4** 23.20N 5.40E
Tahiti *i.* Îs. de la Société **109 Q5** 17.37S 149.27W
Taibei Taiwan **103 M2** 25.05N 121.32E
Taidong Taiwan **103 M2** 22.49N 121.10E
Tain Scotland **19 E2** 57.49N 4.02W
Tainan Taiwan **103 M2** 23.01N 120.14E
Taiping Malaysia **104 C4** 4.54N 100.42E
Taita Hills Kenya **87 B2** 3.20S 38.17E
Taivalkoski Finland **43 G4** 65.35N 28.20E
Taivaskero *mtn.* Finland **43 E5** 68.02N 24.00E
Taiwan Asia **103 M2** 23.30N 121.00E
Taiwan Str. China/Taiwan **103 M2** 25.00N 120.00E
Taiyuan China **103 K5** 37.50N 112.30E
Taizhong Taiwan **103 M2** 24.09N 120.40E
Ta'izz Yemen **94 F1** 13.35N 44.02E
Tajikistan Asia **102 C5** 39.00N 70.30E
Tak Thailand **104 B7** 16.47N 99.10E
Takabba Kenya **87 C3** 3.25N 40.11E
Takamatsu Japan **106 B2** 34.28N 134.05E
Takaoka Japan **106 C3** 36.47N 137.00E
Take-shima *i. see* **Tok-to** *i.* Japan **106 B3**
Taklimakan Shamo *des.* China **102 E5** 38.10N 82.00E
Talagang Pakistan **95 L5** 32.55N 72.25E
Talara Peru **76 B4** 4.38S 81.18W
Talaud Is. Indonesia **105 H4** 4.20N 126.50E
Talavera de la Reina Spain **46 C3** 39.58N 4.50W
Talca Chile **75 B3** 35.28S 71.40W
Talcahuano Chile **75 B3** 36.40S 73.10W
Taldykorgan Kazakstan **102 D6** 45.02N 78.23E
Talgarth Wales **12 D3** 51.59N 3.15W
Taliabu *i.* Indonesia **105 G3** 1.50S 124.55E
Tallahassee U.S.A. **65 J3** 30.28N 84.19W
Tallinn Estonia **43 F2** 59.22N 24.48E
Taloyoak Canada **63 I4** 69.30N 93.20W
Talsi Latvia **43 E2** 57.15N 22.36E
Taltson *r.* Canada **62 G4** 61.35N 112.12W
Tamale Ghana **84 D2** 9.26N 0.49W
Tamanrasset Algeria **84 E4** 22.50N 5.31E
Tamar *r.* England **13 C2** 50.28N 4.13W
Tamaulipas *d.* Mexico **70 E5** 24.00N 98.20W
Tama Wildlife Res. Ethiopia **87 B4** 6.00N 36.00E
Tambach Kenya **87 B3** 0.32N 35.32E
Tambacounda Senegal **84 C3** 13.45N 13.40W
Tambelan Is. Indonesia **104 D4** 0.59N 107.35E
Tambov Russian Fed. **58 G3** 52.44N 41.28E
Tambre *r.* Spain **46 A5** 42.50N 8.55W
Tâmega *r.* Portugal **46 A4** 41.04N 8.17W
Tamiahua Lagoon Mexico **70 E5** 21.30N 97.20W
Tamil Nadu *d.* India **97 F3** 11.15N 79.00E
Tampa-St. Petersburg U.S.A. **65 J2** 27.58N 82.38W
Tampere Finland **43 E3** 61.32N 23.45E
Tampico Mexico **70 E5** 22.18N 97.52W
Tamworth Australia **110 E2** 31.07S 150.57E
Tamworth England **10 D3** 52.38N 1.42W
Tana *r.* Kenya **87 C2** 2.32S 40.32E
Tana, L. Ethiopia **85 H3** 12.00N 37.20E
Tanafjorden *est.* Norway **43 G5** 70.40N 28.30E
Tanami Desert Australia **110 C4** 19.50S 130.50E
Tanana U.S.A. **62 C4** 65.11N 152.10W
Tanaro *r.* Italy **50 C6** 45.01N 8.46E
Tando Adam Pakistan **96 D6** 25.46N 68.40E
Tandragee N. Ireland **16 C1** 54.21N 6.26W
Tanega-shima *i.* Japan **106 B2** 30.32N 131.00E
Tanga Tanzania **87 B1** 5.07S 39.05E
Tanganyika, L. Africa **86 B4** 5.37S 29.30E
Tangier Morocco **84 D5** 35.48N 5.45W
Tangshan China **103 L5** 39.37N 118.05E
Tanimbar Is. Indonesia **105 I2** 7.50S 131.30E
Tanjay Phil. **105 G5** 9.31N 123.10E
Tanjona Bobaomby *c.* Madagascar **86 D3** 11.58S 49.14E
Tanjona Vohimena *c.* Madagascar **86 D2** 25.34S 45.10E
Tanjungkarang Telukbetung Indonesia **104 D2** 5.28S 105.16E
Tanjungpandan Indonesia **104 D3** 2.44S 107.36E
Tanjungredeb Indonesia **104 F4** 2.09N 117.29E
Tank Pakistan **95 L5** 32.13N 70.23E
Tanna *i.* Vanuatu **111 F4** 19.30S 169.20E
Tanta Egypt **94 D5** 30.48N 31.00E
Tanzania Africa **86 C4** 5.00S 35.00E
Tao'an China **103 M7** 45.25N 122.46E
Taourirt Morocco **52 C3** 34.25N 2.53W
Tapachula Mexico **70 F3** 14.54N 92.15W
Tapajós *r.* Brazil **77 E4** 2.40S 55.30W
Tapauá *r.* Brazil **76 D4** 5.40S 64.20W
Tapi *r.* India **96 E5** 21.05N 72.45E
Taquari *r.* Brazil **77 E3** 19.00S 57.27W
Tar *r.* Rep. of Ire. **20 D2** 52.15N 7.48W
Tara *r.* Yugo. **56 D5** 43.23N 18.47E
Tarakan Indonesia **104 F4** 3.20N 117.38E
Tarancón Spain **46 D4** 40.01N 3.01W
Tarangire Nat. Park Tanzania **87 B2** 4.00S 36.00E
Taranto Italy **50 G4** 40.28N 17.14E
Taranto, G. of Italy **50 G4** 40.00N 17.20E
Tarapoto Peru **76 C4** 6.31S 76.23W
Tarbat Ness *c.* Scotland **19 F2** 57.52N 3.46W
Tarbert A. and B. Scotland **16 D3** 55.57N 5.45W
Tarbert A. and B. Scotland **16 D3** 55.51N 5.25W
Tarbert W.Isles Scotland **18 C2** 57.55N 6.50W
Tarbes France **44 D3** 43.14N 0.05E
Târgu-Jiu Romania **56 F6** 45.03N 23.17E
Târgu Mureş Romania **55 I2** 46.33N 24.34E
Târgu Secuiesc Romania **55 J2** 46.00N 26.08E
Tari P.N.G. **105 K2** 5.52S 142.58E
Tarija Bolivia **76 D2** 21.33S 64.45W
Tarīm Yemen **95 G2** 16.03N 49.00E
Tarim Basin *f.* China **102 E5** 40.00N 82.00E
Tarime Tanzania **87 A2** 1.20S 34.20E
Tarleton England **14 E2** 53.41N 2.50W
Tarn *r.* France **44 D4** 44.15N 1.15E
Tarnica *mtn.* Poland **54 H3** 49.05N 22.44E
Tarnów Poland **54 G4** 50.01N 20.59E
Taroudannt Morocco **52 B3** 30.31N 8.55W
Tarragona Spain **46 F4** 41.07N 1.15E
Tarsus Turkey **57 L2** 36.52N 34.52E
Tartary, G. of Russian Fed. **59 Q2** 47.40N 141.00E
Tartu Estonia **43 F2** 58.20N 26.44E
Ţarţūs Syria **57 L1** 34.55N 35.52E
Tashkent Uzbekistan **102 B6** 41.16N 69.13E
Tasiilaq Greenland **63 O4** 65.40N 38.00W
Tasikmalaya Indonesia **104 D2** 7.20S 108.16E
Tasmania *d.* Australia **110 D1** 42.00S 147.00E
Tasman Sea Pacific Oc. **111 F2** 38.00S 160.00E
Tatarbunary Ukraine **55 K1** 45.49N 29.34E
Tatarsk Russian Fed. **58 J3** 55.14N 76.00E
Tatvan Turkey **94 F6** 38.31N 42.15E
Taubaté Brazil **77 F2** 23.00S 45.36W
Taung-gyi Myanmar **97 J5** 20.49N 97.01E
Taunton England **13 D3** 51.01N 3.07W
Taunus *mts.* Germany **48 D4** 50.07N 8.10E
Taupo, L. New Zealand **111 G2** 38.45S 175.30E
Taurus Mts. Turkey **57 K2** 37.15N 34.00E
Taverham England **11 G3** 52.40N 1.13E
Tavira Portugal **46 B2** 37.07N 7.39W
Tavistock England **13 C2** 50.33N 4.09W
Tavoy Myanmar **97 J3** 14.07N 98.18E
Tavy *r.* England **13 C2** 50.27N 4.10W
Taw *r.* England **13 C3** 51.05N 4.05W
Tawau Malaysia **104 F4** 4.16N 117.54E
Tawe *r.* Wales **12 D3** 51.38N 3.56W
Tawitawi *i.* Phil. **104 G5** 5.05N 120.00E
Tay *r.* Scotland **17 F4** 56.21N 3.18W
Tay, Loch Scotland **16 E4** 56.32N 4.08W
Tayma' Saudi Arabia **94 E4** 27.37N 38.30E
Taymyr, L. Russian Fed. **59 M5** 74.20N 101.00E
Taymyr Pen. Russian Fed. **59 L5** 75.30N 99.00E
Tayport Scotland **17 G4** 56.27N 2.53W
Taytay Phil. **104 F6** 10.47N 119.32E
Taz *r.* Russian Fed. **58 J4** 67.30N 78.50E
Taza Morocco **52 C3** 34.16N 4.01W
Te Anau, L. New Zealand **111 F1** 45.25S 167.43E
Tébessa Algeria **52 E4** 35.22N 8.08E
Tebingtinggi Indonesia **104 B4** 3.20N 99.08E
Tecuci Romania **55 J1** 45.49N 27.27E
Tedzhen Turkmenistan **95 J6** 37.26N 60.30E
Tees *r.* England **15 F3** 54.35N 1.11W
Tees B. England **15 F3** 54.40N 1.07W
Tefé *r.* Brazil **76 D4** 3.35S 64.47W
Tegucigalpa Honduras **70 G3** 14.05N 87.14W
Teguise Canary Is. **46 Z2** 29.03N 13.36W
Tehran Iran **95 H6** 35.40N 51.26E
Tehuantepec, G. of Mexico **70 F4** 16.00N 95.00W
Teide, Pico del *mtn.* Canary Is. **46 X2** 28.17N 16.39W
Teifi *r.* Wales **12 C4** 52.05N 4.41W
Teign *r.* England **13 D2** 50.32N 3.36W
Teignmouth England **13 D2** 50.33N 3.30W
Teith *r.* Scotland **17 E4** 56.09N 4.00W
Tekirdağ Turkey **56 H4** 40.59N 27.30E
Tel Aviv Yafo Israel **94 D5** 32.05N 34.46E
Teles Pires *r.* Brazil **77 E4** 7.20S 57.30W
Telford England **10 C3** 52.42N 2.30W
Telford and the Wrekin *d.* England **9 D3** 52.42N 2.30W
Teme *r.* England **10 C3** 52.10N 2.13W
Temirtau Kazakstan **102 C8** 50.05N 72.55E
Temple U.S.A. **64 G3** 31.06N 97.22W
Temple Ewell England **11 G2** 51.09N 1.16E
Templemore Rep. of Ire. **20 D2** 52.48N 7.51W
Temryuk Russian Fed. **57 M6** 45.16N 37.24E
Temuco Chile **75 B3** 38.45S 72.40W
Tena Ecuador **76 C4** 1.00S 77.48W
Tenasserim Myanmar **97 J3** 12.05N 99.00E
Tenbury Wells England **10 C3** 52.18N 2.35W
Tenby Wales **12 C3** 51.40N 4.42W
Ten Degree Channel Indian Oc. **97 I2** 10.00N 92.30E
Tendo Japan **106 D3** 38.22N 140.22E
Tenerife *i.* Canary Is. **46 X2** 28.10N 16.30W
Tengiz, L. Kazakstan **102 B8** 50.30N 69.00E
Tennessee *r.* U.S.A. **65 I4** 37.10N 88.25W
Tennessee *d.* U.S.A. **65 I4** 36.00N 86.00W
Tenryu *r.* Japan **106 C2** 34.42N 137.44E
Tenterden England **11 F2** 51.04N 0.42E
Teófilo Otôni Brazil **77 F3** 17.52S 41.31W
Tepic Mexico **70 D5** 21.30N 104.51W
Teplice Czech Rep. **54 C4** 50.40N 13.50E
Teraina *i.* Kiribati **108 O7** 4.30N 160.02W
Teramo Italy **50 E5** 42.40N 13.43E
Terebovlya Ukraine **55 I3** 49.18N 25.44E
Teresina Brazil **77 F4** 4.50S 42.50W
Tergnier France **42 C1** 49.39N 3.18E
Termez Uzbekistan **95 K6** 37.15N 67.15E
Terminillo, Monte *mtn.* Italy **50 E5** 42.29N 13.00E
Términos Lagoon Mexico **70 F4** 18.30N 91.30W
Termoli Italy **50 F4** 41.58N 14.59E
Tern *r.* England **10 C3** 52.40N 2.38W
Ternate Indonesia **105 H4** 0.48N 127.23E
Terneuzen Neth. **42 C3** 51.20N 3.50E
Terni Italy **50 E5** 42.34N 12.44E
Ternopil' Ukraine **55 I3** 49.35N 25.39E
Terrace Canada **62 F3** 54.31N 128.32W
Terrassa Spain **46 F4** 41.34N 2.00E
Terre Haute U.S.A. **65 I4** 39.27N 87.24W
Terrington Marsh England **11 F3** 52.47N 0.15E
Terschelling *i.* Neth. **42 E5** 53.25N 5.25E
Teseney Eritrea **94 E2** 15.05N 36.41E
Teslin Canada **62 E4** 60.10N 132.42W
Test *r.* England **10 D1** 50.55N 1.29W
Tetas, Punta *c.* Chile **76 C2** 23.32S 70.39W
Tetbury England **10 C2** 51.37N 2.09W
Tete Mozambique **86 C3** 16.10S 33.30E
Tetney England **15 G2** 53.30N 0.01W
Tétouan Morocco **84 D5** 35.34N 5.22W
Teviot *r.* Scotland **17 G3** 55.36N 2.26W
Teviothead Scotland **17 G3** 55.20N 2.56W
Tewkesbury England **10 C2** 51.59N 2.09W
Texarkana U.S.A. **65 H3** 33.28N 94.02W
Texas *d.* U.S.A. **64 G3** 32.00N 100.00W
Texel *i.* Neth. **42 D5** 53.05N 4.47E
Texoma, L. U.S.A. **64 G3** 34.00N 96.40W
Tezpur India **97 I6** 26.38N 92.49E
Thai Binh Vietnam **104 D8** 20.27N 106.20E
Thailand Asia **104 C7** 16.00N 101.00E
Thailand, G. of Asia **104 C6** 11.00N 101.00E
Thai Nguyên Vietnam **104 D8** 21.31N 105.55E
Thal Desert Pakistan **95 L5** 31.30N 71.40E
Thame England **10 E2** 51.44N 0.58W
Thame *r.* England **10 D2** 51.38N 1.10W
Thames *r.* England **11 F2** 51.30N 0.05E
Thanh Hoa Vietnam **104 D7** 19.50N 105.48E
Thar Desert India **96 E6** 28.00N 72.00E
Thasos *i.* Greece **56 G4** 40.40N 24.39E
Thatcham England **10 D2** 51.25N 1.15W
Thaton Myanmar **97 J4** 16.56N 97.20E
Thaxted England **11 F2** 51.57N 0.21E
The Bahamas C. America **71 I5** 23.30N 75.00W
The Calf *mtn.* England **14 E3** 54.21N 2.32W
The Cheviot *mtn.* England **15 E4** 55.29N 2.10W
The Everglades *f.* U.S.A. **65 J2** 26.00N 80.30W
The Gambia Africa **84 C3** 13.30N 15.00W
The Great Oasis Egypt **94 D3** 24.30N 30.40E
The Grenadines *is.* Windward Is. **71 L3** 12.35N 61.20W
The Gulf Asia **95 H4** 27.00N 50.00E
The Hague Neth. **42 D4** 52.05N 4.16E
Thelon *r.* Canada **62 I4** 64.23N 96.15W
The Marsh *f.* England **11 F3** 52.50N 0.10E
The Minch *str.* Scotland **18 D3** 58.10N 5.50W
The Mullet *pen.* Rep. of Ire. **20 A4** 54.10N 10.05W
The Mumbles Wales **12 C3** 51.34N 4.00W
The Naze *c.* England **11 G2** 51.53N 1.17E
The Needles *c.* England **10 D1** 50.39N 1.35W
The North Sd. Scotland **19 G4** 59.18N 2.45W
Theodore Roosevelt *r.* Brazil **77 D4** 7.33S 60.24W
The Old Man of Coniston *mtn.* England **14 D3** 54.22N 3.08W
The Pas Canada **62 H3** 53.50N 101.15W
The Pennines *hills* England **15 E3** 54.40N 2.20W
The Rhinns of Galloway *f.* Scotland **16 D2** 54.50N 5.02W
The Slot *str.* Solomon Is. **111 E5** 7.30S 157.00E
The Snares *is.* New Zealand **108 L2** 48.00S 166.30E
The Solent *str.* England **10 D1** 50.45N 1.20W
The Sound England **13 C2** 50.20N 4.10W
Thessaloniki Greece **56 F4** 40.38N 22.56E
Thessaloniki, G. of Med. Sea **56 F4** 40.10N 23.00E
The Storr *mtn.* Scotland **18 C2** 57.30N 6.11W
Thet *r.* England **11 F3** 52.25N 0.44E
Thetford England **11 F3** 52.25N 0.44E
Thetford Mines Canada **65 L6** 46.05N 71.18W
The Trossachs *f.* Scotland **16 E4** 56.15N 4.25W
The Wash *b.* England **11 F3** 52.55N 0.15E
The Weald *f.* England **11 F2** 51.05N 0.20E
Thiers France **44 E4** 45.51N 3.33E
Thiès Senegal **84 A3** 14.48N 16.56W
Thika Kenya **87 B2** 1.04S 37.04E
Thimbu Bhutan **97 H6** 27.29N 89.40E
Thionville France **44 G6** 49.22N 6.11E
Thira *i.* Greece **56 G2** 36.24N 25.27E
Thirlmere *l.* England **14 D3** 54.32N 3.04W
Thirsk England **15 F3** 54.15N 1.20W
Thisted Denmark **43 B2** 56.57N 8.42E
Thomastown Rep. of Ire. **20 D2** 52.31N 7.08W
Thompson Canada **62 I3** 55.45N 97.54W
Thornaby-on-Tees England **15 F3** 54.34N 1.18W
Thornbury England **10 C2** 51.36N 2.31W
Thorne England **15 G2** 53.36N 0.56W
Thornhill Scotland **17 F3** 55.15N 3.46W
Thornton England **14 E2** 53.53N 3.00W
Thrapston England **11 E3** 52.24N 0.32W
Thuin Belgium **42 D2** 50.21N 4.20E
Thule *see* **Qaanaaq** Greenland **63**
Thun Switz. **44 G5** 46.46N 7.38E
Thunder Bay *town* Canada **63 J2** 48.25N 89.14W
Thüringian Forest *mts.* Germany **48 E4** 50.40N 10.50E
Thurles Rep. of Ire. **20 D2** 52.41N 7.50W
Thursby England **14 D3** 54.51N 3.03W
Thurso Scotland **19 F3** 58.35N 3.32W
Thurso *r.* Scotland **19 F3** 58.35N 3.32W
Thurso B. Scotland **19 F3** 58.35N 3.32W
Tianjin China **103 L5** 39.08N 117.12E
Tianshui China **103 J4** 34.25N 105.58E
Tiaret Algeria **52 D4** 35.28N 1.21E
Tibaji *r.* Brazil **77 E2** 22.45S 51.01W
Tibati Cameroon **84 F2** 6.25N 12.33E
Tiber *r.* Italy **50 E4** 41.45N 12.16E
Tiberias, L. Israel **94 E5** 32.49N 35.36E
Tibesti *mts.* Chad **85 F4** 21.00N 17.30E
Tibet *d.* China **102 F4** 32.20N 86.00E
Tibetan Plateau *f.* China **102 F4** 34.00N 86.15E
Tiburón *i.* Mexico **70 B6** 29.00N 112.25W
Ticehurst England **11 F2** 51.02N 0.23E
Tidjikja Mauritania **84 C3** 18.29N 11.31W
Tiel Neth. **42 E3** 51.53N 5.26E
Tielt Belgium **42 C3** 51.00N 3.20E
Tienen Belgium **42 D2** 50.49N 4.56E
Tien Shan *mts.* Asia **102 D6** 42.00N 80.30E
Tierra del Fuego *i.* S. America **75 C1** 54.00S 68.30W
Tiétar *r.* Spain **46 C3** 39.50N 6.00W
Tiflis Georgia **58 G2** 41.43N 44.48E
Tighina Moldova **55 K2** 46.50N 29.29E
Tigre *r.* Peru **76 C4** 4.30S 74.05W
Tigre *r.* Venezuela **71 L2** 9.20N 62.30W
Tigris *r.* Asia **95 G5** 31.00N 47.27E
Tihamah *f.* Saudi Arabia **94 F2** 20.00N 40.30E
Tijuana Mexico **70 A7** 32.29N 117.10W
Tikhoretsk Russian Fed. **53 L6** 45.52N 40.07E
Tikrīt Iraq **94 F5** 34.36N 43.42E
Tiksi Russian Fed. **59 O5** 71.40N 128.45E
Tilburg Neth. **42 E3** 51.34N 5.05E
Tilbury England **11 F2** 51.28N 0.23E
Tilehurst England **10 D2** 51.27N 1.02W
Till *r.* England **15 E4** 55.41N 2.12W
Tillabéri Niger **84 E3** 14.28N 1.27E

W

References

Social Trends 25 1995 edition HMSO
Regional Trends 30 1995 edition HMSO
FAO Yearbook Production 1994
World Health Statistics Annual 1994
UN Monthly Bulletin of Statistics
UN World Population Chart 1994
World Bank Atlas 1995
World Resources 1994-1995

Photo credits

Satellite images : Science Photo Library
Cover : Images Colour Library

Acknowledgements

General Bathymetric Chart of the Oceans (GEBCO)
International Hydrographic Organisation, Monaco
National Atlas and Thematic Mapping Organisation, Calcutta, India
Ministry of Planning and National Development, Nairobi, Kenya
Instituto Geográfico e Cartográfico, São Paulo, Brazil
Rotterdam Municipal Port Management, Rotterdam, Netherlands